Language Policies in Education

Critical Issues

Language Policies in Education

Critical Issues

Edited by

James W. Tollefson
Department of English
University of Washington

 LAWRENCE ERLBAUM ASSOCIATES, PUBLISHERS
2002   Mahwah, New Jersey   London

President/CEO: Lawrence Erlbaum
Executive Vice-President, Marketing: Joseph Petrowski
Senior Vice-President, Book Production: Art Lizza
Director, Editorial: Lane Akers
Director, Sales and Marketing: Robert Sidor
Director, Customer Relations: Nancy Seitz
Senior Acquisitions Editor: Naomi Silverman
Assistant Editor: Lori Hawver
Cover Design: Kathryn Houghtaling Lacey
Textbook Production Manager: Paul Smolenski
Full-Service Compositor: TechBooks
Text and Cover Printer: Sheridan Books, Inc.

This book was typeset in 10/12 pt. Times Roman, Bold, and Italic.
The heads were typeset in Americana and Americana Bold.

Lawrence Erlbaum Associates, Inc., Publishers
10 Industrial Avenue
Mahwah, NJ 07430

Library of Congress Cataloging-in-Publication Data

Language policies in education : critical issues / edited by James W. Tollefson.
       p.   cm.
    Includes bibliographical references and index.
    Contents: Critical issues in educational language policy / James W.
Tollefson—Evolving influences on educational language policies / Mary
McGroarty—Accessing language rights in education : a brief history of the U.S.
context / Terrence G. Wiley—Reflections on language policy in Canada / Barbara
Burnaby—Language policy and docile bodies : Hong Kong and governmentality /
Alastair Pennycook—Who will guard the guardians themselves? : national interest
versus factional corruption in policy making for ESL in Australia / Helen
Moore—Language planning and the perils of ideological solipsism / Thomas S.
Donahue—Minority language politics in north India / Selma K. Sonntag—Language
rights and the destruction of Yugoslavia / James W. Tollefson—Language policy in
modern Japanese education / Florian Coulmas—Language education and foreign
relations in Vietnam / Sue Wright—Language planning in Korea / Sook Kyung Jung
and Bonny Norton—The English language in African education / Alamin M.
Mazrui—Between possibility and constraint : indigenous language education,
planning, and policy in the United States / Teresa L. McCarty—The critical villager :
transforming language and education in Solomon Islands / David Welchman Gegeo
and Karen Ann Watson-Gegeo—Looking outward / James W. Tollefson.
    ISBN 0-8058-3600-4 (alk. paper)—ISBN 0-8058-3601-2 (pbk. : alk. paper)
    1. Language and education.   2. Language policy.   3. Language planning.
I. Tollefson, James W.

P40.8 .L369   2002
306.44'9—dc21

                                                                     2001023197

Contents

Preface

Research on language policy as a distinct field of study can be traced to the 1960s, when Joshua Fishman, Charles A. Ferguson, and other pioneers saw the need for intensive research on the central importance of language in the processes of national development. Their work led the way in linking language policies with fundamental social, political, and economic issues. That first generation of research, which lasted through most of the 1970s, was followed by a period of quiescence during the 1980s, when language policy specialists questioned many of the fundamental assumptions of the field. Indeed, this period of reflection was for many researchers a time of disillusionment with language policy studies. In the past decade, however, we have witnessed the rapid growth of a second generation of published research on language policy. This new wave of research has broadened the field from the earlier focus on language and development, to include other concerns such as the role of language policies in establishing and maintaining socioeconomic inequality. This volume aims to explore one key area that has received attention in this new period of research: language policies in education. The collection is intended for scholars and other specialists in language policy, education, applied linguistics, critical linguistics, and language teaching. It is designed to be adopted in graduate and advanced undergraduate courses on language policy and language education.

Though the topic of language policies in education is a vast one, researchers in the area share a belief in the central role of language learning and language use in educational institutions. Indeed, much of education involves complex linguistic interactions between students and teachers and among students. These interactions both reflect and shape the linguistic hierarchies that are essential components in broad social, political, and economic systems of equality and inequality. Due to the central importance of educational institutions in determining political power and economic opportunity, language policies in education are thus seen as having a key role in organizing social and political systems.

A single volume on language policies in education of necessity must be selective. As editor, I have been guided by the belief that language policies in education must be understood in connection with broad social, political, and economic forces that shape not only education, but social life generally. Therefore, I have sought articles for this collection that move outward from educational concerns of the classroom toward broader social, political, and economic issues. The authors of this collection share the belief that language policies in education are not merely about choice of language as medium of instruction, but instead are often central to a host of social processes.

The articles are divided into six sections. The first section, "Overviews," begins with the editor's introduction to the collection, including a survey of critical issues in language policy in education and a preview of the articles in this book. In Chapter 2, Mary McGroarty summarizes some of the important limitations in popular approaches to analyzing language policy in education, and then examines key social theories that offer new opportunities for understanding educational language policy.

In Part II, "Competing Agendas," Terrence G. Wiley and Barbara Burnaby examine educational language policies in the United States and Canada. Wiley focuses on the history of language rights affecting access to education in the U.S., while Burnaby offers detailed analysis of three key examples of language policymaking in Canada: federal official language policies designed to manage French-English group relations, Ontario's programs for managing access to English language training for immigrants, and educational programs on the east coast of St. James Bay that use the Cree language as medium of instruction.

Part III, "Language Policy and Governance," includes three articles that examine the role of language policy in cultural and political governance. Tracing the development of language policies in education in colonial Hong Kong, Alastair Pennycook shows how language policy was both linked to the discursive construction of Hong Kong Chinese as politically passive ("docile political bodies"), and part of an attempt to bring about such docility through conservative educational curricula and instruction (thereby creating "docile bodies"). While Pennycook's focus is on cultural governance, Helen Moore and Thomas S. Donahue examine political processes of governance. Moore traces profound changes in language policies in Australia during the 1990s, demonstrating that these changes were linked to a broad conservative attempt to roll back progressive policies and programs developed during the 1980s. Donahue uses the debate over the

Official English movement in Arizona to illustrate fundamental characteristics of the electoral process in the United States; concerned with normlessness and political manipulation in U.S. politics, Donahue presents his
case for critical language education.

Part IV, "Managing Language Conflict," continues the analysis of the
politics of educational language policy by examining two countries in
which language policies in education have been central to state efforts
to manage sociopolitical conflict. Selma K. Sonntag looks at two important
cases of minority language politics in North India, while James W. Tollefson
examines the important role that debates over educational language policies played in the breakup of Yugoslavia.

Part V, "Language and Global Relations," includes four chapters that
link educational language policies with processes of globalization. Florian
Coulmas traces language policy in Japanese education from the Meiji era
(1868–1911) until the end of the 20th century, focusing in particular on the
link between language and Japanese nationhood and on the impact of increasing linguistic diversity in Japan upon language policies in the schools.
Sue Wright describes recent changes in language policies in Vietnam that
have been motivated by the government's efforts to establish and develop
economic and political relations with the capitalist West. Sook Kyung Jung
and Bonny Norton examine Korea's new national elementary English program, initiated in 1997 after the Presidential Committee for Globalization
Policy recommended reform of Korean language education policy as part
of the government's campaign to achieve rapid economic growth and internationalization of the economy. In the final chapter in this section, Alamin
M. Mazrui explores the profound cultural consequences of the choice of
English as a medium of instruction in Anglophone Africa. After showing
how African intellectual and scientific dependency on the West is inextricably linked with linguistic dependency, Mazrui explores social and educational processes of decolonization that offer hope for breaking the chains
of dependency.

Part VI, "Critical Pedagogy and Social Change," focuses on educational
programs in which learners successfully engage in constructing indigenous identities in the indigenous language. Drawing upon critical theories of language and education and her 20 years of experience working
with indigenous educators, Teresa L. McCarty examines three key cases
of indigenous community schools: the Rough Rock Navajo and Peach
Springs Hualapai Bilingual/Bicultural Programs in the U.S. Southwest,
and the Hawaiian Immersion Schools. David Welchman Gegeo and Karen
Ann Watson-Gegeo explore innovative rural classrooms and village-based
educational projects in the Solomon Islands. Both McCarty and Gegeo/
Watson-Gegeo present paradigms for education based upon links between

school and community and indigenous knowledge and practice. Finally, James W. Tollefson offers an integrative summary of the central themes of this book and explores the crucial importance of educational language policies worldwide.

A volume such as this is always a collaborative project. As editor, I am grateful first of all to the authors of these articles, who have worked hard to link their analysis of language policies in education with some of the fundamental social issues of our time. Rebecca Sherry brought her considerable skills, experience, and talents to her work as research assistant for this project. Generous financial support was made available from the University of Washington, in particular the Dean's Office of the College of Arts and Sciences and Shawn Wong, Chair of the Department of English. Above all, I am grateful to our publisher, Lawrence Erlbaum Associates, and particularly to Naomi Silverman, editor for this project, for their commitment to publishing challenging and critical research in sociolinguistics, language education, and applied linguistics.

List of Contributors

Barbara Burnaby, Memorial University of Newfoundland

Florian Coulmas, Gerhard Mercator University, Duisburg

Thomas S. Donahue, San Diego State University

David Welchman Gegeo, California State University, Monterey Bay

Sook Kyung Jung, University of British Columbia

Alamin M. Mazrui, Ohio State University

Teresa L. McCarty, University of Arizona

Mary McGroarty, Northern Arizona University

Helen Moore, Ontario Institute for Studies in Education, University of Toronto

Bonny Norton, University of British Columbia

Alastair Pennycook, University of Technology, Sydney

Selma K. Sonntag, Humboldt State University

James W. Tollefson, University of Washington

Karen Ann Watson-Gegeo, University of California, Davis

Terrence G. Wiley, Arizona State University

Sue Wright, Aston University

I

Overviews

The two chapters in this section examine the following critical issue: What are the major forces affecting language policies in education and how do these forces constrain policies and public discussion of policy alternatives? In Chapter 1, the introduction to this book, James W. Tollefson explains the purpose of this book and describes four key ideas that recur throughout the chapters. The introduction summarizes each chapter and ends with a list of six critical issues explored in this collection.

In Chapter 2, Mary McGroarty seeks to broaden the scope of language policy studies by summarizing relevant theoretical work in related areas of social theory. Arguing that a narrow focus on choice of language of instruction and decisions about curriculum and teaching practice limits the ability of the field to develop adequate theoretical models of language policy in education, McGroarty links language policy with theoretical work in other areas. Specifically, McGroarty explores the value for language policy studies of research on "core values" of individuals and groups, competing notions of the purpose(s) of education, differing conceptions of citizenship, and the processes of educational policy making. All of these areas offer rich opportunities for theorizing language policy in education.

1

Introduction: Critical Issues in Educational Language Policy

James W. Tollefson
University of Washington

In recent years, the field of applied linguistics has experienced rapidly growing interest in two areas. The first is critical linguistics, which focuses on the study of language within its social, political, and historical context, with a primary concern for (in)equality, linguistic discrimination, and language rights (e.g., see Fairclough, 1989; Hodge & Kress, 1996; Joseph & Taylor, 1990; Pennycook, 1994, 1998; Phillipson, 1992, 2000; Skutnabb-Kangas, 2000). A second area of growing interest is language policy, which examines the role of governments and other powerful institutions in shaping language use and language acquisition (e.g., see Cooper, 1989; Corson, 1990, 1999; Herriman & Burnaby, 1996; Kaplan & Baldauf, 1997; Ricento & Burnaby, 1998; Tollefson, 1991, 1995). The rapid development of critical linguistics has led to graduate and undergraduate courses, numerous books and journal articles, and a lively interchange among language specialists working in the field. Simultaneously, courses in language policy have now become commonplace in graduate programs in education, linguistics, applied linguistics, and language teaching.

Critical linguistics and language policy come together in the study of language policies in education. How do language policies in schools create inequalities among learners? How do policies marginalize some students while granting privilege to others? How do language policies in education

3

serve the interests of dominant groups within societies? How can linguistic minorities further their interests through attempts to change language policies in schools? These questions are at the heart of fundamental debates about the role of schools in society, the links between education and employment, and conflicts between linguistic minorities and "mainstream" populations.

Language Policies in Education: Critical Issues is a collection of articles that exemplify major theories and research methods used in the study of language policy in education worldwide. The authors examine *critical* issues—those we believe to be of central importance to understanding the profound societal impact of educational language policies. In addition, the articles highlight three other meanings of *critical*. First, "critical" refers to the field of critical linguistics. Though a wide range of methods, theories, and issues are subsumed under the term, critical linguistics generally refers to work that is influenced by critical theory (e.g., Forester, 1985) and emphasizes the relationships among language, power, and inequality, which are held to be central concepts for understanding language and society. Critical linguistics entails social activism: linguists are seen as responsible not only for understanding how dominant social groups use language for establishing and maintaining social hierarchies, but also for investigating ways to alter those hierarchies. Thus within the field of critical linguistics, research and practice are inextricably linked through this important social and political role for linguists and their work.

A second meaning of the term "critical" is that scholars and students in language policy studies should develop their ability to critically "read" language policies, that is, to understand the social and political implications of particular policies adopted in specific historical contexts. In order to do so, we must distinguish between the discourse of policy debate and the consequences of policies. Too often, policy documents and the rationales offered for them by policymakers and state authorities are taken at face value. A critical perspective toward language policy emphasizes the importance of understanding how public debates about policies often have the effect of precluding alternatives, making state policies seem to be the natural condition of social systems (see Fairclough, 1989). Moreover, a critical perspective aggressively investigates how language policies affect the lives of individuals and groups who often have little influence over the policymaking process.

Third, this book includes articles that are critical of traditional analyses, which often fail to capture the complex social and political context of language policies, and too often accept uncritically the claims of state authorities. The traditional perspective remains dominant in much of language policy research, exemplified by the widely held assumption that policies are usually adopted in order to enhance communication, to encourage feelings of national unity and group cooperation, and to bring about greater social and economic equality (cf. Eastman, 1983). In contrast, a critical perspective explores the links between language policies and inequalities of class, region, and ethnicity/nationality.

Though the articles in this collection are varied in the contexts they examine, the underlying theories and methods of analysis, and the issues that are important in each context, it nevertheless is possible to identify four key ideas that recur throughout these contributions. First, multilingualism is commonplace in contemporary states (cf. Schmidt, 1998). Despite the widely held belief that monolingual states are more efficient than multilingual ones (Sonntag & Pool, 1987), in fact all large political units throughout the world are multilingual. Indeed, the migration of labor that is associated with globalization is likely to increase the presence of linguistic minorities in many contexts, particularly in regions and countries that are relatively well developed economically. Thus policies that seek to reduce language diversity are in most cases highly unrealistic. In perhaps the strongest statement about the pervasiveness of language diversity, Lippi-Green (1997) argues that policies attempting to ensure that everyone speaks the same language variety are no more realistic than policies requiring everyone to be the same height. The articles in this collection examine a wide range of policy responses to language diversity in different contexts worldwide.

Second, language policies in education are an important mechanism by which states manage social and political conflict. A central concern of language policy analysis is the role of particular policies in mobilizing public opinion, channeling political energy, and allocating economic resources. Policies can be used to create, sustain, or resolve conflict. It is important to keep in mind that state authorities or particular ethnolinguistic groups in some settings may view language policy conflict as advantageous for their own political aims (e.g., Yugoslavia). In other settings, a major goal of policymakers may be the use of educational language policies to reduce the potential for social and political conflict (e.g., colonial Hong Kong, where a politically weakened local population served British colonial interests).

Third, conflicts about language policy usually have their source in group conflicts in which language symbolizes some aspect of a struggle over political power and economic resources. Therefore in order to understand language policy debates and the role of language policy in contemporary states, we must examine the underlying social, economic, and political struggles that language can symbolize. The symbolic value of language can have profound consequences, not only for language minorities seeking to negotiate complex and changing identities, but also for dominant groups seeking to retain various forms of political and economic power.

When language is perceived as a marker of group identity and a determiner of access to political power and economic resources, then the probability of language conflict increases, and ethnolinguistic groups may be mobilized around issues of language. Thus the local dynamics of sociopolitical relations among competing ethnolinguistic groups must be carefully analyzed if the relationship between language and power is to be understood in a particular setting.

A fourth recurring idea in the articles in this book is the close and complex relationship between language policy and ideology. Although the term "ideology" has varying meanings, it is possible to identify key components of a conception of ideology that shapes research in educational language policy: (1) Individuals in social situations construct realities through discursive processes. These realities are designed in part to influence the actions of others (see Fairclough, 1989; Hodge & Kress, 1996). In this sense, language is central to social control. As Hodge and Kress point out, "language is an instrument of control as well as of communication" (1996, p. 6). The perspective of language as ideology highlights the role of language in manipulation. Indeed, language is ideological in the sense that it is fundamentally involved in "systematic distortion" (Hodge and Kress, 1996, p. 6) in the service of particular class or ethnolinguistic interests. An important issue in language policy research is the study of how policies are shaped by ideologies, and how discursive processes naturalize policies that are adopted in the interests of dominant ethnolinguistic groups. (2) Language is not only socially and historically situated, it is also contested. This means that language policy can be an arena for the interplay of contested ideologies. In providing a rationale for policies, state authorities often understand that the most effective ideology is one which comes to be seen as common sense, and thus is largely outside the realm of explicit debate (Fairclough, 1989; Tollefson, 1991). In this sense, the study of ideology helps us understand how the language policymaking process is "grounded in culture" (Lippi-Green, 1997, p. 64). A central concern for linguistic minorities in many contexts is the struggle to resist policies promulgated by more powerful ethnolinguistic groups; resistance entails not only policy debate, but also the contest of alternative ideologies.

PREVIEW OF THE CHAPTERS

The articles in this collection confront a range of important issues in a variety of contexts worldwide. In "Evolving Influences on Educational Language Policies," Mary McGroarty examines some of the important contemporary influences on language policies in education. In particular, she surveys social theories that she considers most relevant to understanding language policies in education. These theories explore four key questions: How are language policies in education shaped by "core values"? How do public debates about the purposes of education have impact on educational language policies? What is the relationship between educational language policies and competing conceptions of citizenship, particularly in the area of language rights? What are the central mechanisms for educational decision making and how do those mechanisms constrain pluralist language policies? McGroarty uses her discussion of these issues in order to analyze the possibilities for gaining support for bilingual education policies in the United States. Her overview of influences on language education policies is a call for language policy researchers to develop theoretical frameworks that are linked to social theory; in McGroarty's view, this development is necessary if language policy theory is to account for practical decisions regarding language policies in education.

In the United States, much of the literature on language rights generally and on language rights in education specifically has focused on formal and official language policies. In "Accessing Language Rights in Education: A Brief History of the U.S. Context," Terrence G. Wiley provides a history of the extent to which language minorities in the United States have had *access* to language rights in educational contexts at national, local, and institutional levels. More specifically, the chapter addresses the following historical questions: (1) To what extent have language policies in schools been grounded in societal antagonisms toward language minority groups? (2) How have minority groups responded to these policies? (3) To what extent have legal rights been recognized and enforced by the government and school authorities, and particularly what has been the impact of key court cases about language rights and access to education? (4) What are the long term effects of these policies on language minority groups? Wiley's chapter emphasizes the need for a greater understanding of how access to language rights is central to language policies in education and also how it impacts other human rights.

Like other countries, Canada is influenced by the rapid increase in language contact brought about by migration, technological changes in transportation and communication, and globalization. These changes have consequences for language policies at the federal and provincial levels, where language policies affect three categories of languages: the two major official languages (English and French), the languages of immigrants, and a variety of indigenous minority languages. Policies for these three categories of languages confront quite different questions. A major concern of policymakers at the federal level is the social, economic, and political relations between the French- and English-speaking communities.

Accordingly, detailed languages policies have been adopted in this area. Secondly, Canada has a large population of immigrants, for whom language education plays an important role in economic and social integration. Policymakers must determine the kinds of language training provided through public funds and the role of public educational institutions and non-governmental agencies in providing this education. A third issue concerns the teaching of minority "heritage" languages in schools. What should be the government's role in maintaining these languages? What should be the response of the educational system to linguistic minority communities that often face serious economic and social problems? In her discussion of educational language policy in Canada, titled "Reflections on Language Policy in Canada: Three Examples," Barbara Burnaby examines one example of policy for each of these three categories of language. First, she explores the limited impact on language use of federal language policies aimed at managing French-English relations. Second, she explores programs of the provincial government of Ontario for immigrants who do not speak English or French. Third, she describes innovative educational programs using the Cree language as a medium of instruction on the east coast of St. James Bay.

In his continuing efforts to explore language policies within a discourse analytic framework, Alastair Pennycook views language policy as a crucial tool for cultural governance. In "Language Policy and Docile Bodies: Hong Kong and Governmentality," Pennycook examines colonial language policy in Hong Kong (though also with reference to other colonial contexts). Using Foucault's (1991) notion of governmentality as a central analytical tool, Pennycook demonstrates that colonial language policy was both linked to the discursive construct of Hong Kong Chinese as politically passive (i.e., as "docile political bodies"), and simultaneously part of an attempt to bring about such docility through conservative educational curricula (i.e., Hong Kong Chinese as "docile cultural bodies"). He argues persuasively that language policy in education is not merely about choosing the medium of instruction in schools, but rather a cornerstone of cultural governance, in part through its crucial role in producing and reflecting constructions of the Other. This understanding of language policy as cultural governance has significant implications not just for Hong Kong but also for all contexts of language policy.

Helen Moore also uses Foucault's notion of "governmentality," as well as Hindess' (1997) notion of "factions" to understand the profound changes that took place in language policy in Australia during the 1990s. Based upon interviews with key policymakers as well as her own involvement in the policy debates, Moore examines the struggles that took place between shifting alliances that frequently blurred the boundaries between educational, bureaucratic, and political interests. In her provocatively titled chapter, "Who Will Guard the Guardians Themselves? National Interest versus Factional Corruption in Policymaking for ESL in Australia," Moore seeks to understand the processes by which the views of language minorities and professional English teachers came to be defined as "factional" concerns and therefore marginal to policies promulgated by those who purported to work in the "national" interest.

In earlier work, Thomas S. Donahue (1995) argued that the heavily politicized English as an Official Language movement shows a characteristic of "compensatory opinion." Rather than promoting a well thought-out and socially responsible cause, proponents of the movement have indulged in a variety of low-level political tactics and quarrels which have served to divide opinion in the voting public on issues of bilingual education and planned official language varieties. As a result, although certain individuals have gained political influence, the Official English debate ultimately has served as a distraction from serious social problems involving growing inequities in power and wealth within the United States. In his follow up research reported here, Donahue examines the most recent phase of the Official English movement in the state of Arizona, where the political energy became so extreme that proponents themselves fell victim to the distractions in the issue, resulting in the decision by the United States Supreme Court that Arizonans for Official English had neither appropriate standing in the key lawsuit about Official English nor a direct stake in its outcome. Donahue argues that Official English proponents in Arizona failed in this crucial judicial test of their movement because of their flawed planning sequence: they articulated first a point of view, and only then constructed mismatched and inconsistent arguments as a rationale to support those views. Donahue does not see the narrow and unsatisfactory debate over Official English in Arizona as an isolated case, but rather argues that it exemplifies important trends in the political process in the United States, particularly at times of elections. As suggested by his title, "Language Planning and the Perils of Ideological Solipsism," Donahue uses the Official English controversy in Arizona to explain broad links between language and American politics, and argue that a critical approach to education offers an alternative to the fractured and disrupted political debate that too often characterizes language policy in the U.S.

In her continuing research on language policies in India, Selma K. Sonntag is interested in the role of educational language policies in political struggles in that country. In "Minority Language Politics in North India," she examines the relationship between the symbolic politics of language and the practical pedagogical value of minority language use in education in North India. She compares and contrasts two cases of minority language demands: those of Nepali speakers in West Bengal and those of Urdu speakers in Uttar Pradesh. In both cases, the symbolic politics of seeking official recognition has taken precedence over pedagogical concerns of minority language use in education. But the particular demands and state accommodation of those demands have differed, with Nepali receiving state level recognition decades before receiving federal (Union level) recognition, and Urdu following the sequence in reverse, with federal recognition preceding state recognition. Sonntag shows that these two North Indian cases reveal much about the political context of language policy in federal liberal democracies. The administrative system responsible for language policy (federalism), the ideological context in which policy is justified (liberalism), and the process through which the policy is formulated (democratic) all temper the strategies adopted by linguistic minorities in India to safeguard their interests.

Language policy in education played an important role in the events leading to the destruction of Yugoslavia and in the efforts of newly independent states in the region to gain acceptance by Western European powers. In "Language Rights and the Destruction of Yugoslavia," James W. Tollefson shows that language in education policy was until the 1980s a central component in state efforts to maintain a united Yugoslavia; and that during the 1980s it became an important mechanism with which Serb authorities in Belgrade drove Slovenia, Croatia, and Bosnia toward independence. Language rights until the 1980s were essential to a federal strategy to satisfy the national aspirations of groups having major economic and political power (Serbs, Croats, and Slovenes), as well as to accommodate the continuing demands for autonomy from Albanians, Hungarians, Bosnians, and other nationalities. Thus the Serb effort in the 1980s and 1990s to gain control of the educational curriculum and rescind the system of language rights had the predictable consequence of pushing other nationalities towards secession. The chapter also summarizes recent efforts by the newly independent state of Slovenia to forge a new language policy that simultaneously preserves the system of language rights developed in pre-independence Yugoslavia, while also moving the country toward greater integration with a united Europe. The chapter concludes that Slovene efforts to spell out language rights have important implications for managing language conflict in other contexts.

Although Japan has a relatively high degree of ethnolinguistic homogeneity, the idea that the people inhabiting the Japanese archipelago should all speak one language is of recent origin. Prior to the opening of Japan to foreign trade at gun point by the Americans in the middle of the 19th century, the linguistic situation was marked by a much higher degree of regional and social fragmentation than is the case today. The actual sociolinguistic changes that have occurred in Japan over the past 130 years have been accompanied and, to some extent, promoted by changing ideological views about language. In "Language Policy in Modern Japanese Education," Florian Coulmas reviews the major ideological positions articulated by the Japanese government and intellectual opinion leaders about Japanese and other languages from the Meiji period (1868–1911) until the present. Coulmas pays particular attention to the notion of a "national language," which served as an important tool for unifying the nation in its attempt to catch up with the more developed nations of the West. Once the Japanese started to build their own empire, the national language was charged with new tasks dictated by a policy of assimilation. Although the language policy goals of empire were abandoned after Japan's defeat in World War II, linguistic nationalism has not disappeared entirely from the ideological spectrum. Against the backdrop of the processes of globalization and immigration, and a discourse on internationalization and cross-cultural understanding, the purported need to defend Japanese and secure its place in the world continues to be an undercurrent of discussions about language policy in Japan.

As its former command economy opens up to the capitalist market, Vietnam finds itself in a difficult position linguistically, without adequate numbers of speakers of English, French, and other languages necessary for facilitating new political and economic relationships with the West. In "Language Education and Foreign Relations in Vietnam," Sue Wright examines the complex historical reasons for this situation, which is rooted in Vietnam's contentious relations with other countries. Wright looks at the patterns of exchange and commerce in which Vietnam has recently become involved, and assesses some of the communication needs of Vietnam as it opens up to regionalization and globalization. The chapter also discusses the difficulties and constraints, both material and political, that affect Vietnamese attempts to train significant numbers of its population to provide a linguistic bridge to other countries, and particularly the capitalist world.

In 1997, the Korean government launched a new nationwide English program for elementary school students, focusing mainly on spoken English. The decision to create a national English program, supported by heavy funding for teacher training, materials, and educational technology, was the result of recommendations made by the Presidential Committee for Globalization Policy, which concluded that expansion of English language teaching into lower elementary levels and reversal of the long-standing emphasis on grammar and translation are crucial to the government's goals of rapid economic expansion and full integration of Korea in the global capitalist economy. In "Language Planning in Korea: The New

Elementary English Program," Sook Kyung Jung and Bonny Norton investigate the impact of this policy on classroom practice, through case studies of three elementary schools in the Seoul area. They report that teachers' resistance to the new policy in part expresses widely held concern about the relative emphasis given to English and Korean in the educational system, and in part must be understood in the light of the concrete and particular teaching circumstances facing individual teachers in different schools.

In much of Anglophone Africa, there has been increasing demand for "more" and "better" English as a way of improving educational standards in other subjects. Meanwhile, in Francophone Africa, the spread of English is increasingly threatening the position of French—sometimes as a matter of deliberate policy, as in Rwanda, and sometimes due to pressures beyond policy control, as in Zaire. Behind these developments are the forces of globalization in the aftermath of the Cold War, including conditions imposed on African economies by the World Bank and the International Monetary Fund and the triumph of market ideologies. In his examination of English in higher education in Anglophone Africa, titled "The English Language in African Education: Dependency and Decolonization," Alamin M. Mazrui examines the impact of language in education policies upon the continent's search for decolonization and its relationship with the West. Concerned particularly with the potential for African countries to determine their own destinies in education, Mazrui proposes five processes to bring about the decolonization of African education.

"What if the children forget the native language?" In "Between Possibility and Constraint: Indigenous Language Education, Planning, and Policy in the United States," Teresa L. McCarty cites this question by an elder from the Navajo community of Rough Rock, Arizona, in order to capture the enormity of the crisis of language loss in Native American communities today. Of 175 languages indigenous to what is now the U.S., only twenty have child speakers. Without some immediate and effective intervention, all these languages will disappear in the next 30 to 40 years. Using oral testimony from speakers, case studies of language reclamation work underway, and her long involvement in indigenous language education in the U.S. Southwest, McCarty explores three specific struggles to revive indigenous languages: Rough Rock Navajo and Peach Springs Hualapai Bilingual/Bicultural Programs in the U.S. Southwest, and the Hawaiian Immersion Schools. McCarty's chapter highlights the personal and social stakes of minority language programs and the contested ground of schools as sites of language renewal. Finally, McCarty explores the possibilities and constraints of a critical pedagogy for language revival in light of a theoretical and practical framework for indigenous language in education policy.

In their latest report on their ongoing research in the Solomon Islands, "The Critical Villager: Transforming Language and Education in Solomon

Islands," David Welchman Gegeo and Karen Ann Watson-Gegeo examine education in rural villages on Malaita, where members of Solomon Islands' largest linguistic and ethnic minority group (no ethnic group is in the majority) are beginning to rethink language, education, and development, and to pursue intellectual and practical projects that (re)construct knowledge for local empowerment. For the first decade after Solomon Islands achieved independence in 1978, rural villagers held out hope that the postcolonial government would take leadership in rural development. Villagers also continued to believe that schools were the primary source of knowledge and the key to economic success for their children. In the past 10 years, however, the failure of national and provincial institutions to bring about meaningful rural development, and the implementation of national ethnic policies that discriminate against Malaita schools and children, are being answered by an emerging critical perspective among a growing number of local villagers. Against the backdrop of their many years of ethnographic research in the Solomon Islands, Gegeo and Watson-Gegeo examine two directions of this emerging critical perspective: (1) *counterhegemonic teaching* in rural classrooms, which they illustrate with the pedagogical practices of two teachers in a rural primary school who are using indigenous language and cultural practices in the classroom in ways that transform children's experience of schooling and challenge neocolonial practices; (2) *dehegemonic village-based projects* that make effective and creative use of people's literacy skills, indigenous knowledge, and previous off-island experiences. Of particular importance is a research project on Kwara'ae language and culture entirely conceived and carried out by villagers with no expectation of material gain, but with the dual goals of creating knowledge about their own language and culture, while increasing their own critical thinking and literacy skills. Gegeo and Watson-Gegeo use these examples to explore the possibilities of a new paradigm for rural education in the Solomon Islands, based on indigenous knowledge and practices, local control of education, and incorporating an expanded conception of literacy.

Finally, the last chapter, "Conclusion: Looking Outward," summarizes the key findings of the research in this collection, and suggests important implications for continuing research on language policies in education.

SIX CRITICAL ISSUES

Although the chapters in this collection analyze a wide range of different contexts for educational language policy, taken together the articles examine six critical issues in the field: (1) What are the major forces affecting language policies in education and how do these forces constrain policies and the public discussion of policy alternatives? (2) How do state authorities use educational language policies to manage access to language rights and language education, and what are the consequences of specific programs and policies for language minority communities? (3) How do state authorities use language policy for the purposes of political and cultural governance? (4) How do language policies in education help to create, sustain, or reduce political conflict among different ethnolinguistic groups? (5) How are local policies and programs in language education affected by global processes such as colonialism, decolonization, the spread of English, and the growth of the integrated capitalist economy? (6) How can indigenous peoples and other language minorities develop educational policies and programs that serve their social and linguistic needs, in the face of significant pressures exerted by more powerful social and ethnolinguistic groups?

These critical issues are of profound importance for minority language communities, policymakers, language teachers, and scholars alike.

REFERENCES

Cooper, R. L. (1989). *Language planning and social change.* Cambridge: Cambridge University Press.

Corson, D. (1990). *Language policy across the curriculum.* Clevedon: Multilingual Matters.

Corson, D. (1999). *Language policy in schools.* Mahway, NJ: Lawrence Erlbaum Associates.

Donahue, T. L. (1995). American language policy and compensatory opinion. In J. W. Tollefson (Ed.), *Power and inequality in language education* (pp. 112–141). Cambridge: Cambridge University Press.

Eastman, C. M. (1983). *Language planning: An introduction.* San Francisco: Chandler & Sharp.

Fairclough, N. (1989). *Language and power.* London: Longman.

Forester, J. (Ed.). (1985). *Critical theory and public life.* Cambridge, MA: MIT Press.

Foucault, M. (1991). Governmentality. In G. Burchell, C. Gordon, & P. Miller (Eds.). *The Foucault effect: Studies in governmentality* (pp. 87–104). Hemel Hempstead: Harvester Wheatsheaf.

Herriman, M. & Burnaby, B. (Eds.). (1996). *Language policies in English-dominant countries.* Clevedon: Multilingual Matters.

Hindess, B. (1997). Politics and governmentality. *Economy and Society, 26,* 257–272.

Hodge, R. & Kress, G. (1996). *Language as ideology.* London: Routledge.

Joseph, J. E. & Taylor, T. J. (Eds.). (1990). *Ideologies of language.* London: Routledge.

Kaplan, R. B. & Baldauf, R. B. (1997). *Language planning: From practice to theory.* Clevedon: Multilingual Matters.

Lippi-Green, R. (1997). *English with an accent: Language, ideology, and discrimination in the United States.* London: Routledge.

Pennycook, A. (1994). *The cultural politics of English as an international language.* London: Longman.

Pennycook, A. (1998). *English and the discourses of colonialism.* London: Routledge.

Phillipson, R. (1992). *Linguistic imperialism.* Oxford: Oxford University Press.

Phillipson, R. (Ed.). (2000). *Rights to language: Equity, power, and education.* Mahway, NJ: Lawrence Erlbaum Associates.

Ricento, T. & Burnaby, B. (Eds.). (1998). *Language and politics in the United States and Canada: Myths and realities.* Mahway, NJ: Lawrence Erlbaum Associates.

Schmidt, R. (1998). The politics of language in Canada and the United States: Explaining the differences. In T. Ricento & B. Burnaby, *Language and politics in the United States and Canada: Myths and realities* (pp. 37–70). Mahway, NJ: Lawrence Erlbaum Associates.

Skutnabb-Kangas, T. (2000). *Linguistic genocide in education—or worldwide diversity and human rights?* Mahway, NJ: Lawrence Erlbaum Associates.

Sonntag, S. K. & Pool, J. (1987). Linguistic denial and linguistic self-denial: American ideologies of language. *Language Problems and Language Planning, 11,* 46–65.

Tollefson, J. W. (1991). *Planning language, planning inequality: Language policy in the community.* London: Longman.

Tollefson, J. W. (Ed.). (1995). *Power and inequality in language education.* Cambridge: Cambridge University Press.

2

Evolving Influences on Educational Language Policies

Mary McGroarty
Northern Arizona University

Language policies in education represent a critical arena in which a society's expectations for the success of its future members are simultaneously expressed, enabled, and constrained. At times, choices about matters such as the language of instruction become controversial, as in the case of bilingual education in the contemporary United States, when such choices appear to contradict commonsense assumptions. More often, though, the social values and mores shaping the curriculum, materials, methodologies, and even the language of instruction are implicit, part of the "hidden curriculum" by which schools function. Furthermore, all social policies, including those related to language and education, operate in a dynamic social environment where other currents of social, political, economic, and psychological changes carry their own momentum and interact with official decisions and the day-to-day activities of schools and classrooms.

In this chapter, I examine some of the social theories most relevant to educational policy in order to set consideration of educational language policy in the broad intellectual context it warrants. The many complex questions related to the roles of language in education, matters of language choice for instruction and evaluation, and the language abilities expected of students and teachers, among others, cannot be analyzed apart from some of the basic questions that motivate social and political theory. It is crucial to identify these underlying but neglected areas that bear on the formulation of language policies, for they facilitate clearer understanding of related conceptual issues and a more systematic and particularized approach to specific pedagogical dilemmas. To illuminate matters related to educational language policy, I first note some of the limitations of approaches used in language-related fields and then turn to the work of contemporary scholars in political science, philosophy, and law in order to demonstrate that language policies are determined by a set of complicated interrelationships among historical traditions, the local and national governance structures affecting education, and the ever more international and diverse groups of students entering schools (especially in most of the principal English-speaking countries). After reviewing some of the main thrusts of theoretical developments affecting education and language education, I show how these developments have or could improve the understanding of bilingual education in the United States particularly.

LIMITATIONS OF CURRENT APPROACHES

In recent years, the academic world has begun to theorize the area of language ideology as a distinctive topic (e.g., Blommaert, 1999; Schieffelin, Woolard, & Kroskrity, 1998). Discussions of language ideology, while certainly pertinent to consideration of language education generally and bilingual education specifically, are often more descriptive of the perceptions of majority group members whose opinions are expressed in mass media (e.g., see Silverstein, 1996) than of the processes of educational decision making that affect language education programs. Certainly public perceptions affect educational decision making, but so do several other factors such as cultural shifts, structural factors, and local sociopolitical climates that have been less widely applied to discussions of language education despite their pertinence.

Empirical work focused directly on bilingual programs also has its limitations. Cummins (1999) has called attention to the relative limitations of reliance on experimental and quasi-experimental empirical studies in evaluating bilingual programs, noting that such work is an essential, though only partial, aspect of judging educational success. Equally vital and usually overlooked, in his view, is the construction of a coherent theoretical framework that would allow educational programs and outcomes to be assessed according to their consistency with a theoretically sound approach. I concur that comparative empirical studies are essential but can only tell part of the story, and I extend Cummins' call for a coherent theory to those wishing to elaborate a theoretical basis for the understanding of all educational language policies. It is particularly important to raise basic questions about the nature and purpose of education and the degree to which it is reasonable or appropriate to speak of rights to education generally and rights to education in a particular language specifically. Thus consideration of the evolving influences on educational language policy must connect with current discourse on the question of social rights and claims, an area marked by lack of consensus on the theoretical as well as political plane.

A final limitation in many approaches to identification of language policy influences is the tacit acceptance of oversimplified models of international and intranational relations. Many current discussions of language policy connect, appropriately, with issues of globalization and effects on language learning (Phillipson & Skutnabb-Kangas, 1999) and the definition of language rights as expressions of human rights (e.g., see Phillipson, 2000; Skutnabb-Kangas & Phillipson, 1994). Yet definitions of human rights are not static. Despite the universalizing impulse noted during the mid-twentieth century, instantiated in such documents as the UNESCO Declaration of Human Rights, definitions of rights are recognized as expressive of particular national and cultural dimensions that are not necessarily equivalent and do not necessarily translate automatically from one social setting to another. Social theorists argue that global, national, and local actions are embedded in complex ways, and that the physical location in which any activity takes place is only one of the features dictating the sphere of action to which it refers (Sassen, 1999, 1998). These national and cultural dimensions of rights and claims manifest themselves in the historical traditions, political developments, and legal codes that surround education, including language education, and recent scholarship provides some provocative avenues for identification of underlying issues. I organize this discussion of these issues around some of the key questions related to educational language policy, using as points of departure the concepts of core values, the role of education, the nature of citizenship, and the mechanisms for educational decision making.

HOW DOES LANGUAGE EDUCATION EXPRESS CORE VALUES?

The educational language policies of any country reflect social judgments not only about language but a host of factors that, at first glance, bear no overt relationship to language. Thus, in examining influences that affect language policy, it is worthwhile to ask about the particular constellations of values that pervade public discourse. In the last two decades, scholars

have raised awareness of the value dimensions affecting language education. Sonntag and Pool (1987) showed that most Americans (whether or not
they support special services for linguistic minorities) share many assumptions about language, including, for example, the validity of competence
in English as an indicator of national loyalty, the presumed neutrality of
standard English, and the sufficiency of willpower for its mastery. Ricento
(1998, pp. 89–91) remarks that, in the United States, provision of bilingual education challenges some deeply held values, such as the belief in
a common historical experience, the belief that cultural integrity requires
linguistic unity, the belief that language use is a private matter better left
to families to decide, and the belief that ethnolinguistic groups deserve no
special protection of their intangible cultural resources such as language.
Smolicz (1980, 1991) has applied the related notion of core value specifically to language in discussing multilingualism, noting that "some ethnic
groups are more language-centered than others, and that for some nations
other cultural factors, such as a specific religion, social structure, or racial
affiliation may prove of greater core significance than language" (1991,
p. 38). Discussions of language issues are nested in additional ideological currents; Tollefson remarks that "in most countries, including the U.S.,
debates about language are conditioned by two powerful discourses of
equality and national unity" (2000, p. 17). The force of these discourses
and the concurrent complementary and competing discourses that shape
language policy will be further explicated below.

Value orientations are not static, but respond to alterations in social conditions at various rates and in various ways. Hence, in order to get a sense
of the values affecting U.S. language policy, we must identify core values
and frontiers for changes in such values. Based on results of public opinion polls since World War II, Yankelovich (1994) identifies eleven values
on which most Americans agree (freedom, equality before the law, equality of opportunity, fairness, achievement, patriotism, democracy, caring
beyond the self, religion, luck, and American exceptionalism; pp. 23–24)
and sixteen areas in which values have changed over the last fifty years,
in large part, he holds, because of relative affluence. Most important for
considerations of language policy are two domains of change: greater acceptance of pluralism and greater emphasis on choice and individualism as
expressive of an individual's uniqueness (1994, p. 22). Yet greater emphasis
on pluralism does not necessarily translate into social harmony, because
"greater pluralism requires more skilled management" and the institutions that structure social relations, "especially the schools and the justice
system, do not work well" (1994, p. 31). Moreover, as Mansbridge (1997,
pp. 133–44) remarks, expectations of governmental performance in the
United States have risen over the last thirty years, although willingness to

sustain a level of taxation adequate to meet higher expectations has not, thus adding economic pressures to situations already affected by value conflicts.

Other scholars have noted similar shifts in advanced industrial societies (including those of Europe, North America, and Japan) moving from a materialist to a postmaterialist perspective. Inglehart (1990) documents shifts away from state authority towards greater individual autonomy in the political cultures of the sixteen countries for which he examined data from different generations. Such a shift contributes to emergence of modern mass democracy, predicated on mass participation in politics and mass support for democratic institutions. In such societies, education exerts a perceptible effect, second only to religiosity, on subjective sense of well-being: "Education is probably the most important single factor shaping one's life in advanced industrial society" because "educational level sets the limits to the type of career one enters, how much money one earns, and how much social prestige one possesses and influences the communication networks one is exposed to throughout life" (1990, pp. 227–228). Hence access to education remains an important avenue of personal progress. Related cross-national research comparing the United States, Canada, and Mexico substantiates a shift from materialist to postmaterialist positions and points to three trends with potential to affect education and, consequently, the choices about language embedded within educational systems: (a) less confidence in governmental institutions and in other traditionally authoritative institutions such as churches, schools, and the legal system; (b) less willingness to accept elite authority; and (c) an increasing likelihood to participate in political processes, and most often to take specific actions related to particular decisions rather than to endorse positions of a political party (Inglehart, Nevitte, & Basañez, 1996, p. 168). While not all analysts agree that postmodern, postmaterialist developments will lead to increased well-being, even when incomes rise (see Lane, 2000, for counterarguments), even those who posit a causal link between education and personal happiness recognize the major role of education in affecting access to jobs, one component of contemporary life satisfaction.

WHAT IS THE PURPOSE OF EDUCATION?

Is the purpose of education (and thus of formal language education programs) only or principally to get a job? This is an area of contention in theory and in practice. Every society provides for the education of its younger members to ensure continuity. In the words of social philosopher Michael Walzer, education is "a program for social survival" which is "always relative to the society for which it is designed" (1983, p. 197). Yet, in any democratic society, education is not and ought not be merely reproductive of the social structure as it exists; it is also meant, in Walzer's conception and that of many other commentators concerned about just societies, to identify and nurture the particular talents and abilities of individual students. In societies dedicated to "simple equality," in Walzer's terms, all students learn the same things; in contrast, in societies with some commitment to active pluralism (Walzer's "complex equality"), students are encouraged and directed to go beyond the common store of knowledge, once it is mastered, to pursue additional goals in line with individual interests and capacities. Note that in this discussion, as in the language policy framework critiqued by Tollefson (2000), the notion of equality figures prominently. There is a tension in education between what Walzer terms the "direct reproduction" of social and cultural knowledge and practices and the "mediated education" in which students are engaged in dialog and taught to raise questions and think for themselves. Mediated education, formerly a privilege granted to the few children of elite families who could seek out such education and pay for it, should (in just societies) be available to all who can profit from it, all who will eventually exercise the role of citizen.

Such education for citizenship raises questions and produces skeptics. Hence, in seeking to build and support a degree of personal autonomy and ability to engage in consensus building, it invokes instructional processes that do not always have clear answers or lead to similar conclusions. Thus such education makes many uneasy because of its potential to lead students to challenge the *status quo*. Yet education for citizenship conceived in this light reflects the tensions and dynamism of a large and complex democratic country. Another citizenship theorist, philosopher Bernard Dauenhauer, remarks that the "educational practices of many democratic states . . . display a tension among competing pressures," namely "pressure to provide an education that preserves society's unity" and "pressures to make available an education that respects and supports its diversity" (1996, p. 147). One of the principal tasks of education, in his view, is not to abolish or ignore this tension, but to maintain it, for education is one of the social institutions that affects a large proportion of the population. Its ability to "preserve the tension between these two general pressures" is one of the ways it promotes social continuity while simultaneously preventing both social disintegration and reduction to homogeneity (1996, p. 147). At the same time, he notes that such an education cannot pretend to ignore moral judgments and value implications: "an appropriate democratic education neither can nor should be one that is wholly neutral concerning which sorts of lives are good lives to lead" (1996, p. 149). While public education cannot proffer a particular religious doctrine, it nonetheless reflects a range of culturally sanctioned choices regarding moral values. The extent to which education should encourage skeptical, critical attitudes is controversial, though; traditionalists are concerned that too progressive an education could lead children to question parental and other traditional authorities (Kymlicka & Norman, 1995, pp. 299–300). Again we come to the role of values in education; education for adult citizenship, as theorized by many social scientists, requires that students and teachers identify, confront, and defend their reasons for taking particular actions.

This view is related to observed instructional practice. Walzer's vision of mediated education—education in which students are active in asking questions and interrogating their circumstances—finds a parallel in many calls for educational reform in all classrooms at all levels. After observing classes in thirty-eight American high schools, Goodlad (1984) found that instruction in the great majority of classrooms in nearly all subjects reflected a direct transmission model, in which teachers lectured on material in the textbook and students were then tested on the same. There was very little active engagement of students and teachers going beyond textbook material through participatory activities or probing discussion. The transmission model of education, rather than a more engaged and participatory approach, also characterized the great majority of classrooms observed during the most recent large-scale, systematic study of bilingual and English as a second language (ESL) programs at the elementary level (Ramírez, 1992). As Cummins (1999) has noted, for bilingual programs to represent good quality education, it is not enough that they be delivered in two languages (that is, that they be genuinely bilingual); they must also represent effective and challenging instruction. Thus, in bilingual programs, the issue of program quality includes but is not limited to considerations of the language of academic instruction; areas such as the quality of the curriculum, the materials and instructional methods and activities used to support it, and the range and authenticity of assessments used, all items to be discussed more specifically below, contribute to educational quality (Brisk, 1998).

HOW DO EDUCATIONAL LANGUAGE POLICIES RELATE TO CITIZENSHIP?

Contemporary philosophers thus envision education as the preparation of citizens. For those who are not full adult citizens, either children or newcomers, such theories of citizenship have important ramifications for the nature and quality of educational opportunities offered (or not offered). In posing the question of how educational language policies relate to citizenship, I want to implicate not only the formal requirements for becoming a citizen (which, in many English-speaking countries, include some evidence of ability to understand basic conversational English), but also the implicit expectations related to citizenship as the only social role common to all adults. Some of the most important, and most neglected, areas of social theory that bear on language policy have to do with evolving definitions of citizenship. Legal definitions of citizenship invoke notions of boundary closure and membership status that is, to one degree or another, confirmed by a known national authority, yielding a simple yes/no answer to the question of whether a person is a citizen of a particular country. However, fluid and multiple identities are characteristic of many individuals today (Benhabib, 1997), including second language learners and users, although the professional discourse of language teachers also too often presents a simple dichotomy (Harklau, 2000). Increasing international movements of peoples in this time of globalization have made the nature and associated claims of rights related to citizenship status an area of contention; scholars have even ventured to suggest that provisions for dual or multiple citizenship be reformed (Schuck, 1998, Kymlicka, 1995, 1996). Sociologists (e.g., Portes, 1997) have noted that, in the United States, the newest immigrants have entered a milieu characterized sometimes by isolation, sometimes by a creative, "transnational" solution to economic survival. Political philosopher Seyla Benhabib observes: "Globalization . . . has brought to a head conflicts between human rights and the claim to self-determination of sovereign collectivities" (1999, p. 710). She further notes that "citizenship and naturalization claims of foreigners, denizens, and residents within the borders of a polity, as well as the laws, norms, and rules governing such procedures are pivotal social practices through which the normative perplexities of human rights and sovereignty can be most acutely observed" (p. 711). Thus the question of whether education, and, as a corollary, education in a particular language, can be considered a right of all citizens must be answered by examination of the concrete practices related to delivery of education. Examination of related practices reveals that, in the United States, the issue of who qualifies for education has been interpreted to mean all children present in a geographical area. With respect to education, U.S. courts have, in effect, affirmed that all children who are resident in the country qualify for public education, thus establishing (through legal challenge to initial exclusion) any child's access to public educational services offered. The related Supreme Court decision, *Plyler v. Doe*, argued in 1982, bypassed international law as the basis for judgment (although plaintiffs in a related case had held that the right to a free public education had been codified in the Universal Declaration of Human Rights) and instead referenced the equal protection clause of the

Constitution, thus connecting educational access to a legal basis more widely accepted in the United States (Jacobson, 1996, p. 101). It is no surprise that connecting education to the Constitution proved a way to justify provision of services in the relatively conservative social environment of the early 1980s. (In contrast, other forms of social rights, such as welfare rights, have never enjoyed broad acceptance in the United States, or been extended routinely to newcomers unless they represented specific affected groups such as Cuban or Vietnamese refugees, each of whom qualified for special status through related Congressional actions; see McGroarty, 1996).

The nature and extent of individual or group rights to any kind of services reflect, in part, particular political approaches to the rights of citizens. These differ substantially according to the political regime within which they are elaborated (Aleinikoff & Klusmeyer, 2000). In an extensive treatment of the meaning of citizenship, Janoski (1998) identifies four general types of citizenship rights: legal rights (e.g., rights to equal treatment, expressive rights such as freedom of speech, right to own property); political rights (right to vote, right to hold office, right to form or join a political party); social rights ("enabling" rights such as access to health care, "opportunity rights" such as access to education); and participation rights (rights to job security, collective bargaining) (pp. 31 ff). These classes of rights developed at different times and differ across the world's advanced industrialized countries according to both historical factors and type of regime, whether traditional (e.g., Germany, France, Belgium), liberal (Australia, Canada, Japan, the United States), or social democratic (Sweden, Norway, Denmark). While noting that it is difficult to do precise cross-national comparisons of citizenship rights because "they are not in the same units," (p. 206), Janoski argues that comparisons can still be accomplished by ranking countries on the relative types of rights, and then comparing their relative ranking of various types of rights. Following this methodology, he provides data to support the hypothesis that liberal countries such as the United States developed political democracy relatively quickly, with greater elaboration and codification of legal and political rights and relatively less emphasis on social and participation rights, while traditional regimes elaborated social and participation rights more than individual legal and political rights. Social democratic countries show relatively high levels in all four classes of rights. It is not amiss to view this typology of citizenship rights together with approaches to language policies that emphasize relationship to deep or core values of a country (e.g., see Ricento, 1998, and McGroarty, 1997, on the United States) in developing a systematic approach to analysis of educational language policies.

CAN DEMOCRACIES MANIFEST PLURALISM IN EDUCATION?

One of the liveliest debates in contemporary social theory addresses the degree to which liberal democracies that depend on majority rule can accommodate pluralism in policy and action (Galston, 1999). It is worthwhile to explicate some dimensions of this debate, particularly conceptualizations of negative and positive liberty, because of their relevance to educational policies. In many situations, educational alternatives reflect what Galston notes are the most difficult political quandaries: "not between good and bad but between good and good" (1999, p. 771), with differing definitions of what is good accounting for the alternatives. Liberal societies, in Galston's view, accord extremely high importance to negative liberty—the ability of individuals to make choices about competing visions of goods and values unconstrained by governmental or other institutional strictures and to live according to the choices made. Negative liberty is, then, the right to make choices that others cannot interfere with. Positive liberty, on the other hand, represents the duties of communities to those who need services; it is an affirmative responsibility to provide something to a person or group. Within the realm of social theory and the law, discussions of negative and positive liberty have developed a substantial body of theory and legal precedent relevant to the elaboration of rights and responsibilities. Because of the current emphases on rights to language and rights to education, it is instructive to refer to this literature when endeavoring to develop an adequate formulation for both theory and practical decisions.

The topic of rights and responsibilities is vast, but some recent treatments illuminate the complexity of the many related issues and also usefully apply considerations to contemporary language controversies. Legal scholar Richard Primus (1999) reviews the Anglo-American usage of the term "rights" and shows that, since Hohfeld's classic formulation published in 1919, it has been used to refer to four distinct phenomena, each of which has different entailments, may be conceptualized and defended differently within the disciplines of sociology, moral philosophy, and the law, and has undergone change and expansion in subsequent discussions. Most central to issues of education and language policy are the rights *to* something, or claim rights, and rights to *do* something free of interference, or liberty rights. Applying these concepts to language education, we can then ask: is there a right to education? If so, is there a right to education in a specific language? Answers based on contemporary theories of pluralism provide some helpful direction here, but they do not (and, from the perspective of liberal political theory that privileges individual choice, cannot) offer universally applicable answers (Galston, 1999). Rather, answers to these two key questions must be posed and answered within the moral, legal, and political framework that governs education in any country. Will Kymlicka, the Canadian legal theorist who has articulated the most extensive justification for minority rights, supports explicit recognition of minority language use in education (and in other public domains such as government services) if such use can be shown to correct historic disadvantage, but also notes that "the legitimate scope of such rights will vary with the circumstances" (1995a, p. 110).[1] Michael Hartney (1995), another Canadian legal philosopher, notes that language discussions in Quebec have featured three different and at times incompatible definitions of "collective rights" with respect to promotion of French and restrictions on English; such incompatibility has complicated analysis of underlying legal issues (1995, pp. 221–222). But theoretical inconsistencies do not obviate the need for a common means of communication. Many theorists who espouse a pluralist, liberal view of social relations hold that groups come to develop the ability to get along in relative harmony through the "practical rationality" that can only be achieved through dialog; meaningful dialog thus demands ability to communicate with each other. Choice of language to be used in public domains such as education is thus "the most difficult question that a multicultural and multiethnic society has to address (Addis, 1997, p. 138) because "language is not a mere medium of reality. It is partly constitutive of that reality" (1997, p. 138). Educational practices, too, partly constitute reality, thus manifesting the nature of language policy in education through the pedagogical approaches chosen. Even in countries historically committed to a liberal political tradition that honors unconstrained individual choice, "the right to free speech does not tell us what an appropriate language policy is" (Kymlicka, 1995b, p. 18) in education or in any other domain. To formulate and defend appropriate language policies for education in democratic societies, advocates of pluralism must identify and engage with relevant national and local patterns of educational decision making. These patterns have their own dimensions of complexity and specificity, as the following section, which concentrates on the United States, indicates.

---

[1]Kymlicka's presentations (1995a, 1996) usefully distinguish the potential language claims of voluntary immigrant minorities and what he calls "national minorities"—generally equivalent to Ogbu's involuntary minorities (Ogbu, 1978; Gibson & Ogbu, 1991)—such as native indigenous groups. For reasons of space, I do not discuss these differences and their potential consequences for the determination of appropriate language policy in this chapter, but it should be noted that the often contrasting histories and contemporary situations of each different type of minority group would justify potentially different language in education policies.

HOW ARE EDUCATIONAL DECISIONS MADE?

In provision of educational services, decision points and scope of decisions vary according to national, provincial, and local governance structures. The degree to which educational decisions are local decisions varies dramatically. In the United States, local control of education, with local control defined as control by elected school boards, is considerable (McGroarty, 1997), relatively greater than that found in other large English-speaking countries such as Canada or Australia, where provincial and sometimes national agencies have relatively greater responsibility for curricular decisions. Furthermore, because education is, in the U.S. Constitution, one of the areas of responsibilities reserved to each of the fifty states, the particular political culture of each state is a factor in identifying the profile of educational values most relevant to support for particular language education programs, including bilingual instruction.

Like national values, the sociopolitical values of each state also change; again, like national values, they change in different areas and at different rates. However, despite alterations in opinion shaped by population mobility, economic change, and the passage of time, there is probably enough stability in the "assumptive worlds" of educational policymakers identified in the 1980s by Marshall, Mitchell, and Wirt (1989) to merit their use in examining the underpinnings of current attitudes toward provision of bilingual education in some U.S. states. Drawing on prior scholarship investigating the value orientations of policy elites, these political scientists defined three distinct orientations to the role of government in social life: *individualistic*, in which government is defined as a mechanism to facilitate the efficient operation of the marketplace (represented in their sampling by Illinois and Pennsylvania); *moralistic*, in which government is defined as a means to achieve coordinated action for the common good (Wisconsin, California); and *traditionalistic*, in which government is defined as a means to maintain the existing order (Arizona, West Virginia) (1989, pp. 110 ff.). They then investigated the response of 112 members of educational policy elites (who differed in roles, identity, and influence) toward a set of questions designed to elicit opinions about the four major values driving educational decisions in the mid-1980s: equity, efficiency, quality, and choice. Their findings indicated that all shapers of educational policies could readily articulate the differences in their state's perspective and consequent approach to the four major and often competing values then affecting educational policy. In many cases, the researchers found, these local authorities recognized that federal drives toward greater equity in educational services, renewed by the Great Society programs of the 1960s, had been mitigated by subsequent emphases on quality and efficiency.

Nevertheless, policymakers' opinions regarding the relative importance of these four values were consistent with each state's particular historical and political development. Policy elites understood that, operating in a real world with several constraints, "not all values could be given sufficient resources at a given time" and that "varying pressures [caused] them to alter policy thrusts" (p. 171). In directing educational policy, these decision makers went about balancing the two fundamental thrusts of meritocratic versus democratic demands on the educational systems through actions consonant with each state's political culture (p. 166).

In judging the practical import of such research in understanding support for (or resistance to) bilingual education, it is worth noting that two of the states in the Marshall, Mitchell, and Wirt sample, California and Illinois, are those with the largest numbers of language minority students, while a third, Arizona, is among the eight top states having Hispanic student enrollments greater than 100,000 in its school-age population (Trueba, 1998, p. 256). Although the sociopolitical climate in all states has changed since the mid-1980s, this analysis of state-level political cultures suggests that advocacy for innovative language education programs must take somewhat different forms in different localities. Recent research on U.S. public opinion related to the perceived efficacy of different levels of government in improving education magnifies the importance of grasping each individual state's decision context: despite a general decline in trust towards governmental institutions over the last thirty years, Americans have relatively greater confidence in the ability of states rather than the federal government to improve education by a very substantial margin, 72% to 22% (Blendon et al., 1997, p. 212). Hence, school systems in which advocates for bilingual education (or any other specially targeted services for particular populations) have built and maintained credibility with local school board members and communities of parents and students have the potential for establishing and maintaining innovations such as bilingual programs.

Marshall, Mitchell, and Wirt's analysis was done before the recent initiative campaigns aimed at limiting access to bilingual education. Dicker (2000) traces the history of some of the state-level efforts to limit bilingual education through English-only legislation and ballot initiatives like California's Proposition 227, sponsored by software developer Ron Unz. Another Unz-originated initiative (Proposition 203) on the Arizona ballot in November, 2000, was more stringent than California's, and closed some of the "loopholes," such as relatively quick access to parental waivers to allow children to participate in bilingual programs despite the initiative emphasizing a one-year transition to English (Crawford, 2000). The impact of ballot initiatives has been criticized by many, including political journalist David Broder (2000), because wealthy individuals or groups can achieve their goals by purchasing the number of signatures necessary to get a measure on the ballot and then selectively publicizing the measure so that voters may not realize the implications of a simple "yes" or "no" vote. From the perspective of political strategy, then, research on the sociopolitical climate of each state also suggests that support for bilingual education (which may be operationalized as opposition to English-only legislation and ballot initiatives) should be developed and maintained through channels of policy influence that may differ across state contexts.[2] For example, in Arizona, opponents of Proposition 203 (that is, supporters of bilingual education) emphasized that the Arizona version of the Unz initiative deprived school systems of local control over program choice for one group of students. Because local control is both a national value and a deeply held orientation in Arizona, it was hoped that such an approach would generate relatively more support than one that appealed, for example, to the technical expertise of teachers and administrators as a basis for bilingual program support, even though the latter is absolutely essential to the delivery of good quality programs.[3] The expertise of teachers and administrators is not highly esteemed in public discourse.

Yet turning to local control (in the case of a traditional U.S. state like Arizona) or other values that appeal to state as against national constituencies will not and cannot address inequities in services to language minority students in the absence of a national climate of commitment to pluralism, effective leadership, and an adequate resource base. (Indeed, that is one of the reasons Kymlicka [1995a, Ch. 6] justifiably rejects reliance on purely local approaches, which he sees as too often the remedy of choice in U.S. politics and political discourse; it elides the question of which political subunits are most relevant to certain decisions and ignores practices such as

---

[2]Support for English-only legislation also shows some variation by region, in part because of differential salience of ethnic group loyalty and language ability, each of which exerts an independent influence on related attitudes; see Schatz, Sullivan, Flanigan, & Black, in press.

[3]Although Proposition 203, the Unz-sponsored measure requiring English immersion rather than bilingual education, passed by a vote of 63% to 37% in the state of Arizona as a whole, support was not uniform in all jurisdictions (see Arizona Secretary of State's Office, State of Arizona Official Canvass, http://www.sosaz.com/election/2000/General/Canvass2000GE.pdf, November 27, 2000). This proposition was, in fact, defeated in three counties, Apache, Coconino, and Navajo, that include portions of the Navajo and Hopi Reservations and have high proportions of native American voters amidst a relatively smaller total population than that found in the much larger urban areas of Phoenix and Tucson. These results, unremarked in both state and national media, show that opposition to the mandatory 'English immersion' required by Proposition 203 was considerable in areas where some portion of the voting public had had first-hand experience with language restriction in education.

gerrymandering that have distorted group representation.) Leaders elected through the conventional political processes, whether governors, state superintendents of education, or school board members, are attentive to voter desires; in much of the United States, language-minority communities are in situations similar to Latinos in Phoenix (Ortiz, 2000) and Los Angeles, whose electoral impact "lags far behind their numbers" (Lopez, 1996, p. 147). As Moran (2000) points out, the "new federalism" much touted in the 1980s in many areas, including education, worked against the expansion and improvement of bilingual programs in many ways by relaxing federal oversight and reducing actual federal appropriations at a time when rising numbers of immigrants entered the country, thus contributing to a decline in ideological commitment to pluralism, a lessened emphasis on the professional expertise available to guide practice, and fewer resources even as potential need for services increased.[4]

WHAT ARE THE POINTS OF LEVERAGE WITHIN THE U.S. EDUCATIONAL SYSTEM?

To promote support for pedagogical language policies that include bilingual education in the United States, then, at least three related but distinct political developments are crucial. First, language minority communities must develop a strong electoral presence. Second, voters from such communities must mobilize around language-in-education issues. This may well depend on each group's perspective on language as a core value (Smolicz, 1980, 1991). Such mobilization is more likely in some parts of the country than others (for related discussions, see Glazer, 2000; Portes & Stepick, 1993; and Schatz, Sullivan, Flanigan, & Black, in press). Attaining and holding some measure of political power increases the likelihood that members of language minority groups can influence language policies in education, though it does not guarantee any particular outcome.

A third point of possible leverage depends on the ability of the professional educators, researchers, and policymakers who advocate bilingual instruction to articulate its goals and accomplishments accurately and persuasively for fellow educators and for various public constituencies. In the

---

[4]When local control is vested in a single powerful individual such as a school superintendent, pro-bilingual community sentiment can be overridden. Soto's (1997) account of the dismantling of a relatively well accepted bilingual program attests to the power of district superintendents. In the United States, such officials are generally not elected directly (important local exceptions exist) but hired by school board members who are usually elected. Thus superintendents cannot operate without at least the tacit, and usually explicit, assent of the local school board.

last ten years, language researchers have begun to generate more nuanced views of the relationship between formal language learning and teaching and the many contextual factors that affect it. Detailed descriptions of the instructional processes observed in schools and programs help to provide the basis for accurate understanding and clearer expectations regarding what bilingual programs in schools can and cannot do. For educational researchers, then, there is ongoing and urgent reason to provide in-depth longitudinal case studies (e.g. Cahnmann, 1998; Freeman, 1998) as well as cross-sectional observations (Dentler & Hafner, 1997) documenting features of relatively more and less successful bilingual schools, programs, and classrooms. Ideally, such studies of educational institutions and programs should be complemented by ethnographic work that captures some of the subjective and individual complexities of bilingual language learning and use over time (e.g., Zentella, 1997). Language education professionals have started to move beyond the rhetoric of a single best program model, considered exclusive of context, to pose more difficult questions regarding the fit between the goals of a language education program, the wider social, linguistic, and cultural patterns, and the resources (tangible and intangible) available to provide good second language instruction that contributes to bilingualism (Genesee, 1999; McKay, 2000). Criticisms of bilingual education (for example, the claim that it has led to needlessly large bureaucracies; see Gonzalez, 2000, pp. 225–227) must be addressed with specific data relevant to the range of similar programs observed in comparable settings. Supporters of bilingual instruction have upheld its value on the basis of growing internationalization in the economic sphere (a position deserving some measure of scrutiny in the United States, as in Australia; see Clyne, 2000). Advocates have also linked considerations of optimal bilingual program features with concerns related to quality of education (e.g., Brisk, 1998), a connection that makes substantive as well as strategic sense. Like other practical actions taken to implement respect for diversity in liberal democracies, such efforts are perforce shaped by the particular circumstances of different bilingual communities and educational programs. In the realm of public discussion, it is important to find a variety of ways to report, repeat, and represent the achievements of sound bilingual education programs and other programs serving language minority students. Their accomplishments must be described accurately and include some notion of both standard academic achievement indices and the non-academic (but strongly educational) outcomes related to personal and interpersonal growth, development, and harmony. As Cummins (1999) suggests, the accumulating evidence should be examined for patterns of consistency with appropriate theory as well as nature of empirical results.

CONCLUSION

The multiple influences on contemporary language education policies include not only the climate of opinion related specifically to linguistic differences but also other developments in theoretical conceptions of citizenship, identity, education, equality, and the connections between them. Cultural shifts in the United States and elsewhere promote differing interpretations of these concepts. Intellectual efforts to work out the meaning of "complex equality" (Walzer, 1983) and complex or differentiated citizenship (Aleinikoff & Klusmeger, 2000; Dauenhauer, 1996; Kymlicka, 1995a, 1996) within diverse societies specify provision of universal education, but the crucial pedagogical decisions such as language choice are under-theorized and contested in many liberal democracies. At the same time, practical decisions regarding language in education are made by the various groups wielding power within educational governance structures enmeshed in distinctive national and local sociopolitical settings, all of which are variously permeable to innovations depending on a host of local, regional, and national values and circumstances. Advocates of bilingual instruction in particular societies will succeed to the extent that they can identify, achieve, and enable correspondences between the language education programs they endorse and the wider social goals of education.

ACKNOWLEDGMENT

I am indebted to Christopher Griffin of the Philosophy Department at Northern Arizona University for a very helpful exposition of the varieties of liberal political theory and to the editor of this volume for his patience and assistance in shaping the discussion in this chapter.

REFERENCES

Addis, A. (1997). On human diversity and the limits of toleration. In I. Shapiro & W. Kymlicka (Eds.), *Ethnicity and group rights (NOMOS XXXIX)* (Yearbook of the American Society for Political and Legal Philosophy) (pp. 112–153). New York: New York University Press.

Aleinikoff, A., & Klusmeger, D. (Eds.) (2000). *From migrants to citizens: Membership in a changing world.* Washington, DC: Carnegie Endorment for International Peace.

Arizona Secretary of State's Office. (November 27, 2000). State of Arizona Official Canvass. http://www.sosaz.com/election/2000/General/Canvass2000GE.pdf (accessed January 19, 2001).

Benhabib, S. (1997). Strange multiplicities: The politics of identity and difference in a global context. In A. Samatar (Ed.), *The divided self: Identity and globalization* (pp. 27–56). (*Macalester International*, Vol. 4). St. Paul, MN: Macalester College.

Benhabib, S. (1999). Citizens, residents, and aliens in a changing world: Political membership in the global era. *Social Research, 66,* 709–744.

Blendon, R., Benson, J., Morin, R., Altman, D., Brodie, M., Brossard, M., & James, M. (1997). Changing attitudes in America. In J. Nye, Jr., P. Zelikow, & D. King (Eds.), *Why people don't trust government* (pp. 205–216). Cambridge, MA: Harvard University Press.

Blommaert, J. (Ed.) (1999). *Language ideological debates.* Berlin: Mouton de Gruyter.

Brisk, M. E. (1998). *Bilingual education: From compensatory to quality schooling.* Mahwah, NJ: Lawrence Erlbaum Associates.

Broder, D. S. (2000). *Democracy derailed: Initiative campaigns and the power of money.* New York: Harcourt.

Cahnmann, M. (1998). Over thirty years of language-in-education policy and planning: Potter Thomas Bilingual School in Philadelphia. *Bilingual Research Journal, 22,* 65–81.

Clyne, M. (2000). Promoting multilingualism and linguistic human rights in the era of economic rationalism and globalization. In R. Phillipson (Ed.), *Rights to language* (pp. 160–163). Mahwah, NJ: Lawrence Erlbaum Associates.

Crawford, J. (2000, June 23). Revitalizing languages in an English-Only climate. Featured presentation at Learn in Beauty Conference, Northern Arizona University, Flagstaff.

Cummins, J. (1999). Alternative paradigms in bilingual education research: Does theory have a place? *Educational Researcher, 28,* 7, 26–32, 41.

Dauenhauer, B. (1996). *Citizenship in a fragile world.* Lanham, MD: Rowman & Littlefield.

Dentler, R., & Hafner, A. (1997). *Hosting newcomers: Structuring educational opportunities for immigrant children.* New York: Teachers College Press.

Dicker, S. (2000). Official English and bilingual education: The controversy over language pluralism in U.S. society. In J. K. Hall & W. Eggington (Eds.), *The sociopolitics of English language teaching* (pp. 45–66). Clevedon: Multilingual Matters.

Freeman, R. (1998). *Bilingual education and social change.* Clevedon: Multilingual Matters.

Galston, W. A. (1999). Value pluralism and liberal political theory. *American Political Science Review, 93,* 769–778.

Genesee, F. (Ed.) (1999). *Program alternatives for linguistically diverse students.* (Educational practice rep. no. 1). Santa Cruz, CA: Center for Research on Education, Diversity, and Excellence (CREDE).

Gibson, M. & Ogbu, J. (Eds.). (1991). *Minority status and schooling.* New York: Garland.

Glazer, N. (2000). On *Beyond the melting pot,* 35 years after. *International Migration Review, 34,* 270–279.

Gonzalez, J. (2000). *Harvest of empire: A history of Latinos in America.* New York: Viking Penguin.

Goodlad, J. (1984). *A place called school: Prospects for the future.* New York: McGraw-Hill.

Harklau, L. (2000). From the "good kids" to the "worst": Representations of English language learners across educational settings. *TESOL Quarterly, 34,* 35–67.

Hartney, M. (1995). Some confusions concerning collective rights. In W. Kymlicka (Ed.), *The rights of minority cultures* (pp. 202–227). Oxford: Oxford University Press.

Inglehart, R. (1990). *Culture shift in advanced industrial society.* Princeton: Princeton University Press.

Inglehart, R., Nevitte, N., & Basañez, M. (1996). *The North American trajectory: Cultural, economic, and political ties among the United States, Canada, and Mexico.* New York: Aldine de Gruyter.

Jacobson, D. (1996). *Rights across borders: Immigration and the decline of citizenship.* Baltimore: The Johns Hopkins Press.

Janoski, T. (1998) *Citizenship and civil society: A framework of rights and obligations in liberal, traditional, and social democratic regimes.* Cambridge: Cambridge University Press.

Kymlicka, W. (1995a). *Multicultural citizenship.* Oxford: Oxford University Press.

Kymlicka, W. (1995b). Introduction. In W. Kymlicka (Ed.), *The rights of minority cultures* (pp. 1–27). Oxford: Oxford University Press.

Kymlicka, W. (1996). Three forms of group-differentiated citizenship in Canada. In S. Benhabib (Ed.), *Democracy and difference: Contesting the boundaries of the political* (pp. 153–170). Princeton: Princeton University Press.

Kymlicka, W., & Norman, W. (1995). Return of the citizen: A survey of recent work on citizenship theory. In R. Beiner (Ed.), *Theorizing citizenship* (pp. 283–322). Albany: State University of New York Press.

Lane, R. E. (2000). *The loss of happiness in market democracies.* New Haven: Yale University Press.

Lopez, D. E. (1996). Language: Diversity and assimilation. In R. Waldinger & M. Bozorgmehr (Eds.), *Ethnic Los Angeles* (pp. 139–163). New York: Russell Sage Foundation.

Mansbridge, J. (1997). Social and cultural causes of dissatisfaction with U.S. government. In J. Nye, Jr., P. Zelikow, & D. King (Eds.), *Why people don't trust government* (pp. 133–153). Cambridge, MA: Harvard University Press.

Marshall, C., Mitchell, D., & Wirt, F. (1989). *Culture and education policy in the American states.* Bristol, PA: Falmer Press.

McGroarty, M. (1996). Language contact in social service institutions. In H. Goebl, P. Nelde, Z. Starý, & W. Wölck (Eds.), *Handbook of Contact Linguistics, Vol. 1*, Ch. 106 (pp. 865–871). Berlin: Walter de Gruyter.

McGroarty, M. (1997). Language policy in the USA: National values, local loyalties, pragmatic pressures. In W. Eggington & H. Wren (Eds.), *Language policy: Dominant English, pluralist challenges* (pp. 67–90). Amsterdam: John Benjamins.

McKay, S. L. (2000). English language learners and educational investments. In S. McKay & S.-L. Wong (Eds.), *New immigrants in the United States* (pp. 395–420). Cambridge: Cambridge University Press.

Moran, R. (2000). Legal investment in multilingualism. In S. McKay & S.-L. Wong (Eds.), *New immigrants in the United States* (pp. 421–442). Cambridge: Cambridge University Press.

Ogbu, J. (1978). *Minority education and caste.* New York: Academic Press.

Ortiz, P. (2000, March 13). Program prepares Latino leaders: Clout lags despite growing population. *The Arizona Republic*, pp. B1, B10.

Phillipson, R. (Ed.). (2000). *Rights to language: Equity, power, and education.* Mahwah, NJ: Lawrence Erlbaum Associates.

Phillipson, R., & Skutnabb-Kangas, T. (1999). Englishisation: One dimension of globalisation/L'anglicisation: Un aspect de la mondialisation. *AILA Review, 13*, 19–36.

Portes, A. (1997). Divergent destinies: Immigration, the second generation, and the rise of transnational communities. In P. Schuck & R. Münz (Eds.), *Paths to inclusion* (pp. 33–57). New York: Berghahn Books.

Portes, A., & Stepick, A. (1993). *City on the edge: The transformation of Miami.* Berkeley: University of California Press.

Primus, R. (1999). *The American language of rights.* Cambridge: Cambridge University Press.

Ramírez, J. D. (1992). Executive summary of Vols. I and II of *Final report: Longitudinal study of structured English immersion strategy, early-exit and late-exit transitional bilingual education programs for language minority students. Bilingual Research Journal, 16* (1/2), 1–62.

Ricento, T. (1998). National language policy in the United States. In T. Ricento & B. Burnaby (Eds.), *Language and politics in the United States and Canada: Myths and realities* (pp. 85–112). Mahwah, NJ: Lawrence Erlbaum Associates.

Sassen, S. (1998). *Globalization and its discontents*. New York: New Press.

Sassen, S. (1999). Embedding the global in the national: Implications for the role of the state. In A. Samatar (Ed.), *Globalization and economic space* (pp.31–44). (*Macalester International*, Vol. 7). St. Paul, MN: Macalester College.

Schatz, R., Sullivan, N., Flanigan, B., & Black, A. (In press.) Attitudes toward English language legislation: Predictors and rationales. *Intercultural Communication Studies*.

Schieffelin, B., Woolard, K., & Kroskrity, P. (Eds.) (1998). *Language ideologies: Practice and theory*. Oxford: Oxford University Press.

Schuck, P. (1998). Plural citizenships. In N. Pickus (Ed.), *Immigration and citizenship in the twenty-first century* (pp. 149–191). Lanham, MD: Rowman & Littlefield.

Silverstein, M. (1996). Monoglot "standard" in America: Standardization and metaphors of linguistic hegemony. In D. Brenneis & R. MacCaulay (Eds.). *The matrix of language* (pp. 284–306). Boulder, CO: Westview Press.

Skutnabb-Kangas, T., & Phillipson, R. (Eds.) (1994). *Linguistic human rights: Overcoming linguistic discrimination*. Berlin: Mouton de Gruyter.

Smolicz, J. J. (1980). Language as a core value of culture. *RELC Journal, 11*, 1, 1–13.

Smolicz, J. J. (1991). Language core values in a multicultural setting: An Australian experience. *International Review of Education, 37*, 33–52.

Sonntag, S., & Pool, J. (1987). Linguistic denial and linguistic self-denial: American ideologies of language. *Language Problems and Language Planning, 11*, 46–65.

Soto, L. D. (1997). *Language, culture, and power: Bilingual families and the struggle for quality education*. Albany: State University of New York Press.

Tollefson, J. (2000). Policy and ideology in the spread of English. In J. K. Hall & W. Eggington (Eds.), *The sociopolitics of English language teaching* (pp. 7–21). Clevedon: Multilingual Matters.

Trueba, E. T. (1998). The education of Mexican immigrant children. In M. Suárez-Orozco (Ed.), *Crossings: Mexican immigration in interdisciplinary perspectives* (pp. 251–275). Cambridge, MA: Harvard University Press.

Walzer, M. (1983). *Spheres of justice: A defense of pluralism and equality*. New York: Basic Books.

Yankelovich, D. (1994). How changes in the economy are reshaping American values. In H. J. Aaron, T. Mann, & T. Taylor (Eds.), *Values and public policy* (pp.16–53). Washington, D.C.: The Brookings Institution.

Zentella, A. C. (1997). *Growing up bilingual*. Malden, MA: Blackwell Publishers.

II

Competing Agendas

The chapters in Part II examine the following critical issue: How do state authorities use educational language policies to manage access to language rights and language education, and what are the consequences of specific programs and policies for language minority communities?

Analyses of language policies in education often focus on two particular areas: language rights in education, particularly the legislative and judicial basis for language rights; and educational program design and effectiveness, as measured by language assessments, employability, or other measures. Both of these concerns deserve careful historical analysis in order to understand how they derive from competing agendas of dominant and minority ethnolinguistic groups. In the two chapters in this section, Terrence G. Wiley and Barbara Burnaby examine the historical context of educational language policies in the United States and Canada, respectively. In Chapter 3, Wiley is particularly interested in the history of the selective distribution of language rights and educational programs, and their effect upon linguistic minority students in the United States. He provides a detailed historical overview of policies and events affecting the educational treatment and language rights of linguistic minorities in the United States and compares educational policies for the major indigenous and immigrant minorities. His historical analysis uses a typology of policy orientations: promotion-oriented, tolerance-oriented, restrictive-oriented, and repression-oriented. Wiley's study of the shifting orientations of language policies throughout U.S. history culminates in his analysis of the prospects for bilingual education and minority language revival and maintenance. Wiley's historical analysis concludes that although the right of language minority children to maintain their home languages remains protected in principle, language restriction movements in the United States have severely narrowed the ability of federal policies to support minority languages and programs.

In Chapter 4, Burnaby's analysis of federal policies affecting the official languages (French and English), provincial Ontario policies for immigrants, and Cree-language schools on the east coast of St. James Bay shows that federal policies often have limited impact on language behavior, that language is often a symbol in struggles over other issues, and that local control (as in the Cree medium programs) may be crucial for program success. Like Wiley, Burnaby is interested in the ongoing historical struggle over language policies in education. What are the major stakeholders in policy debates? How does the competition among stakeholders shape policy outcomes? Given the political struggle over policies in education, what are the prospects for success for minority language education? Together, Burnaby and Wiley show that language policy in education in Canada and the United States is intimately linked with larger struggles for political power and economic resources, and that the success of educational programs for speakers of minority languages fundamentally depends upon effective participation of minority groups and others in this struggle.

3

Accessing Language Rights in Education: A Brief History of the U.S. Context

Terrence G. Wiley
Arizona State University

This chapter addresses the question of the extent to which language minorities in the United States have been able to access language rights in education. In dealing with this issue, it is necessary to distinguish between the *right to access* an education that allows for social, economic, and political participation, and the *right* to an education *mediated* in one's mother tongue(s). For language minority students, both rights are essential if they are to participate in the broader society and maintain continuity with their home/community language.

Many children in the United States and a majority of children around the world enter schools where the language of instruction is different from the language spoken in their homes. Given the prevalence of language diversity in the United States and around the world, the fragile condition of language rights in education is lamentable. A small but persistent group of scholars has begun to address the issue (see for example, Kontra, Phillipson, Skutnabb-Kangas, & Varády, 1999a, 1999b).

A fundamental question underlying any discussion of educational language rights is the need to probe the assumptions about language rights more broadly. In this regard, Macías (1979) distinguishes between two types of rights. The first is "the right to freedom *from* discrimination on the basis of language" (p. 41). This in essence is a right to protection. The second is "the right to use one's language in the activities of communal life" (p. 41). This is essentially the right to expression. Macías concludes that "There is no right to choice of language ... except as it flows from these two rights above in combination with other rights, such as due process, equal enforcement of the laws, and so on" (pp. 41–42). However, in order for language rights to be asserted, the "identifiable and legal standing of a class based on language" must be recognized (p. 42). This latter point is particularly significant for understanding language minority rights in the United States and other Western countries, because of their emphasis on locating rights in the individual rather than in the group (Macías, 1979; Wiley, 1996a). In international law, "all of the existing rights ... are individual rights and freedoms, although their manifestations may involve more than one individual" (de Varenenes, 1999, p. 118). In the United States, the salience of language rights is largely derived from their association with other constitutional protections dealing with race, religion, and national origin.

Historically, rights and privileges have been distributed *selectively* based on the recognition of legal status. The significance of such status was dramatically illustrated in the 1994 California election in which Proposition 187 was designed to restrict health and educational rights of immigrants and their children who lacked the status of legal residents. The proposition was approved by a majority of those who voted; those targeted by 187 were unable to vote. In public debates over 187, the major arguments were between those who contended that rights to health and education should be restricted to *citizens* and *legal residents*. Opponents of 187 maintained that these entitlements were *human* rights and that children's human rights should not be surrendered merely because of the legal status of their parents. Subsequently, most provisions of 187 have been struck down in court, yet the controversy over immigrant rights and entitlements echoed around the country. A formal assault (Proposition 227) followed in 1998 on the right of language minority children to be educated bilingually and the right of their parents to make that choice for them.

For many in the United States, the idea that a child who speaks a minority language or vernacular dialect should have a *right* to instruction in his or her language is a peculiar idea—one that is weighed against the argument that the need for a common language is greater than any claims of language rights by minorities. However, the idea of language rights is not new. In 1953, a UNESCO resolution held that every child should have a right to attain literacy in his or her mother tongue. More recently, Skuttnab-Kangas (1995) has put forward her own proposal for a declaration of children's linguistic human rights based on the following three premises: "(1) Every child should have the right to identify positively with her original mother tongue(s) and have her identification accepted and respected by others. (2) Every child should have the right to learn the mother tongue(s) fully. (3) Every child should have the right to choose when she wants to use the mother tongue(s) in all official situations" (Skutnabb-Kangas, 1995, p. 45).

On its face, the first premise has been supported by most learning theorists and to some extent by U.S. courts in recent decades. The need for children to identify positively with their mother tongues(s) has provided part of the rationale for federal bilingual education programs that were implemented in the late 1960s. Nevertheless, gaining support for children's linguistic human rights and translating it into school policy is a major challenge. For instance, schools, policymakers, and pundits have generally not accepted as legitimate "non-standard" varieties of language such as Ebonics, Appalachian English, and Hawai'i Creole English, despite the authority of linguistic evidence that deems them to be legitimate (Rickford, 1999; Wolfram, Adger & Christian, 1999).

The second premise of the declaration implies that every child should have the right to become literate in his or her mother tongue. Creating educational policies for this part of the declaration is complicated by the fact that the majority of the world's estimated 6,000 to 7,000 languages are not used in schools and that many are not used as languages of literacy. In the U.S., even among the major languages taught, there has been a chronic undersupply of certified bilingual teachers for several decades.

The third premise extends the scope of language rights beyond the domain of education to "all official situations." It implies that the government should provide sufficient resources to accommodate language minorities. In the United States, the right to some accommodation has been made in cases dealing with educational, legal, economic and political access, but language rights remain on a very tenuous legal foundation (Piatt, 1992). Around the world, language rights frequently are ignored in the formulation of educational policies. Unfortunately, even if organizations such as the United Nations support language rights, member nations, including the United States, do not act on them because resolutions are not binding (Skutnabb-Kangas, 1999).

THE HISTORICAL CONTEXT OF LANGUAGE DIVERSITY IN THE UNITED STATES

Prior to European conquest and colonization, North America had a rich array of indigenous languages. In that portion of the continent that was to become the United States, the linguistic dominance of English, or what

Heath (1976) referred to as the "language status achievement" of the language, had occurred long before the first U.S. Census in 1790. Until the mid-19th century, a majority of immigrants were from predominantly English-dominant areas. Into the early 20th century, native language instruction and bilingual education were not uncommon in areas where language minority groups comprised a major portion of the local population (Kloss, 1977/1998).

In international discussions of language diversity, a distinction is made between *indigenous* language minorities and *national* language minorities (Skutnabb-Kangas, 1999). National language minorities are the language minority in a country other than where they are currently residing. In the United States, much of the discussion about language diversity and schooling has centered on immigrant language minorities. From an historical perspective, immigration has been an important source of language diversity. However, other sources are also important (see Table 3.1). Among the three major groupings of historical language minorities are (1) *immigrants* (including refugees), (2) *enslaved peoples* who were brought to the United States against their will, and (3) *indigenous peoples*. Macías (1999) expands the notion of indigenous peoples to include (a) those who inhabited an area that later became part of the United States prior to its national expansion into the region they occupied, and (b) groups that have an historical or cultural bond to the Americas before European colonization. In 1790, it is estimated that 23,000 Spanish-speaking people inhabited areas that would later became part of the southwestern United States (Leibowitz, 1971). For many, language shift to English resulted not from choice, but as a consequence of involuntary immigration and enslavement, or annexation and conquest.

Territorial expansion and forced incorporation notwithstanding, immigration was the major source of language diversity in the 19th and 20th centuries. Contrary to popular beliefs about immigration, the percentage of recent immigrants in the late 20th century, as a percentage of the total population, was *less* than it was during the early 20th century (Wiley, 1996b).

EDUCATIONAL LANGUAGE POLICIES AND THE BROADER SOCIETAL CONTEXT

A number of scholars contend that educational language policies are best understood in their relationship to broader societal policies, dominant beliefs, and power relationships among groups. Leibowitz (1969, 1971, 1974, 1982), for example, concluded that language policies have been used

TABLE 3.1

Historical Overview of Policies and Events Affecting The Educational
Treatment and Language Rights of Language Minorities

Time Period	Policy Orientations and Key Events	Implications for Educational Language Rights
1740–1845	Compulsory ignorance laws imposed under colonial rule and retained in slave codes of southern states.	Enslaved African Americans were barred from becoming literate until 1865. In some states, Whites could also be fined or punished for teaching African Americans to read.
	Treaty of Paris in 1783; Louisiana Purchase in 1803; Florida and adjacent areas annexed (1820).	Peoples in the Northwest Territories, and, subsequently, those in the Mississippi and Missouri river valleys were incorporated under U.S. territorial and later state laws.
	In 1819 the Civilization Fund Act enacted to promote English education and practical skills among Native American peoples.	Mission schools were established among some Native American peoples with less than spectacular results in promoting English and Anglo values.
	A Cherokee writing system developed (in 1822) by Sequoia.	Cherokee schools succeeded in promoting Cherokee literacy and biliteracy in English. By 1852 Choctaws, Creeks and Seminoles also operated their own school.
	German Bilingual Schools thrive, even amidst the Know Nothing Movement (1840–1850s).	German language instruction flourished through private and sectarian efforts in the Midwest. In 1837, Pennsylvania passed a law allowing for public schooling in German. In 1840, Ohio passed a law allowing for German-English public schooling.
1845–1905	Texas annexed 1845, followed by Oregon, Washington & Idaho by 1846; Treaty of Guadalupe Hidalgo & Mexican Cession (1848); Gadsden Purchase (1853); Alaska purchased in 1967; Hawaii, 1898; and Puerto Rico, 1901.	Peoples residing in Mexican territory were conquered and brought under U.S. territorial or state authority; indigenous/resident populations were incorporated and were subject to U.S. territorial and later state laws.

(Continued)

TABLE 3.1

(Continued)

Time Period	Policy Orientations and Key Events	Implications for Educational Language Rights
	The "treaty period" ended (1871). The first "off reservation" English-only boarding school established (1889).	Native American lost autonomy and governance of their schools. Among the Cherokee a gradual decline in literacy resulted as the policy of compulsory Americanization and English-only instruction persisted into the 1930s.
	German immigration peaked in the 1880s.	School-related English-only laws aimed at German Catholics were passed (1889), and subsequently repealed, Illinois and Wisconsin.
	Plessy v. Ferguson (1896)	The Supreme Court upheld the doctrine of "separate but equal" racial segregation.
1905–1923	Eastern and Southern European immigration increases (to WWI). Immigration restricted on the basis of national origin.	German instruction was gradually declining in the schools (public and private), but was nevertheless still prevalent until WWI. During WWI, German instruction was banned or dropped in most states. A majority of states passed laws officially designating English as the language of instruction and restricting the use of "foreign" languages.
1923–1950	*Meyer v. Nebraska* (1923) *Farrington v. Tokushige* (1927)	In 1923, the Supreme Court overturned a 1919 Nebraska law banning instruction in German. Several similar cases were decided during the 1920s, including one in Hawaii dealing with private schooling in Japanese.
	Tribal Restoration (1930s)	Deculturation policies aimed at Native Americans were relaxed from the 1930s to the 1950s.
	Guam added as a Territory (1945) Philippines granted independence.	Pacific Island peoples were incorporated.

(Continued)

TABLE 3.1

(Continued)

Time Period	Policy Orientations and Key Events	Implications for Educational Language Rights
1950–1960	Native American Termination Policies.	Renewed restrictions on Native Americans.
	Brown v. Board of Education (1954)	Termination of legal segregation (reversal of *Plessy v. Ferguson*).
1960–1980	1964 Civil Rights Act 1965 Immigration Act The 1968 Bilingual Education Act Tribal restoration (Phase II).	Civil rights and immigration reform provided legal protections from discrimination. The U.S. government broke new ground in allowing for expediency-oriented educational language policies. Restrictive policies toward Native Americans were again relaxed.
	Lau v. Nichols (1974) *Serna v. Portales* (1974) *Rios v. Read* (1978) *U.S. v. Texas* (1981)	The Supreme Court affirmed that school District must accommodate language minority children. Additional federal cases prescribed bilingual education in local contexts.
	M. L. King Jr. Elementary vs. Ann Arbor School District (1979)	A federal court ruled that the Ann Arbor School District must accommodate speakers of African American English
	Casteñeda v. Pickard (1981)	Criteria for acceptable program remedies were established.
1980–2000	English Only Movement 1981 to present.	There was a return to official designations of English as the official language coupled with restrictionism during a period of increased anti-immigrant sentiment.
	Reagan Administration (1980–88) backs away from enforcement of *Lau* Remedies.	The federal government de-emphasized bilingual education as a remedy.
	Native American Languages Preservation Act (1990).	Tolerance of Native American languages was expressed by the Federal government, which was largely symbolic.

(Continued)

TABLE 3.1

(Continued)

Time Period	Policy Orientations and Key Events	Implications for Educational Language Rights
	California's Propositions 63 (1986); 187 (1991); 209 (1996), and 227 (1998); Arizona's proposition 203.	A series of initiatives were proposed/passed in California and other states to restrict immigrant rights in education; and to restrict bilingual education.

Sources: Crawford, 1992, 1995; Hernández-Chávez, 1994; Kloss, 1977/1998; Leibowitz, 1969, 1971; Lyons, 1995; Macías, 1999; Wiley, 1998a, 1998b, 1999a; 2000; and Wiley & Lukes, 1996.

as instruments of *social control* (see Tollefson, 1991, and 1995, for related discussions of language planning as an instrument of *discourse, state,* and *ideological power*). Leibowitz's thesis was developed by analyzing the impact of official English policies and restrictive language policies across political, economic, and educational domains. He argued:

> The significant point to be noted is that language designation in all three areas followed a marked, similar pattern so that it is reasonably clear that one was responding not to the problems specifically related to that area (i.e., educational issues or job requirements in the economic sphere) but to broader problems in the society to which language was but one response. (1974, p. 6)

Leibowitz concluded that

> as English became officially designated for specific purposes, for example, as the language of instruction, or for voting, it was almost always coupled with restrictions on the use of other languages in addition to discriminatory legislation and practices in other fields against the minorities who spoke the language, including private indignities ... which made it clear that the issue was a broader one. (1974, p. 6)

Leibowitz (1971) also compared the restrictive impact of English-only policies imposed on German, Japanese, and Chinese immigrants as well as on Native Americans, Mexican Americans, and Puerto Rican Americans. He concluded that the motivations to impose official English language and to restrict native languages in schools corresponded to the general level of *hostility* of the dominant group toward various language minority groups.

A synopsis of the historical effects of educational policies and language polices on linguistic minority students is represented in Table 3.2, which

TABLE 3.2

Historical Comparison of Selected U.S. Linguistic Minority Groups' Initial Modes of Incorporation and Subsequent Educational Treatments

Ethnolinguistic Group	Initial Mode of Incorporation	English Compelled	Compulsory Ignorance Laws	Legally Segregated	Excluded from Schools	Quotas In Higher Education
African Americans	Enslaved	Yes	Yes	Yes	Yes	Yes
American Indians	Conquered	Yes	No	Yes	Yes	Yes
Mexican Americans	Conquered	Yes	No	Yes	No	Yes
Puerto Rican	Conquered	Yes	No	No	No	No
Pacific Peoples						
Filipinos	Conquered	Yes	No	No	No	No
Micronesians	Conquered	Yes	No	No	No	No
Polynesians	Conquered	Yes	No	No	No	No
Asian Americans						
Japanese	Immigrant	Yes	No	Yes	No	No
Korean	Immigrant	Yes	No	Yes	No	No
Chinese	Immigrant	Yes	No	Yes	Yes	No
Hong Kong Chinese	Immigrant	Yes	No	No	No	No
Taiwanese Chinese	Immigrant	Yes	No	No	No	No
Asian Indians	Immigrant	Yes	No	No	No	No
Cambodians	Refugee	Yes	No	No	No	No
Laotians & Hmong	Refugee	Yes	No	No	No	No
Vietnamese	Refugee	Yes	No	No	No	No

Adapted with permission from Weinberg (1997, p. 314)

TABLE 3.3

Policy Orientations with Implications for Educational Language Rights

Governmental/State/Agency Policy Orientation toward Language Rights	Policy Characteristics	Implications for Language Minority Educational Rights
Promotion-Oriented Policies	The government/state/agency allocates resources to support the official use of minority languages.	Examples outside the U.S. include the promotion of community languages, e.g., Welsh in the UK.
*Expediency-Oriented Laws	A weaker version of promotion laws not intended to expand the use of minority language, but typically used only for short-term accommodations.	E.g., Title VII bilingual education programs to accommodate perceived English deficiencies of speakers of languages other than English.
Tolerance-Oriented Policies	Characterized by the noticeable absence of state *intervention* in the linguistic life of the language minority community.	E.g., language schools; private/religious schools in which heritage/community languages are maintained by private resources.
Restrictive-Oriented Policies	Legal prohibitions or curtailments on the use of minority languages; age requirements dictating when a child may study a minority/foreign language.	E.g., Federal restriction on Native American languages in boarding schools; WWI era restrictions on foreign language instruction; Proposition 227 and similar measures, such as Arizona's Proposition 203.

TABLE 3.3
(Continued)

Null Policies	The significant absence of policy recognizing minority languages or language varieties.	Failure to consider the implications of language differences in instruction mediated only in English.
Repression-oriented Policies	Active efforts to eradicate minority languages.	E.g., outside the U.S., include equating the use/instruction in a minority language as a political crime (see Skutnabb-Kangas & Bucak, 1994).

This table draws from and expands Kloss' schema (1977/1998; see also Macías & Wiley, 1998). The "Null" and "Repression-Oriented" categories did not appear in Kloss' schema. Kloss also limited these categories to formal governmental/state policies. The contention here is that this schema can also be applied to institutional agencies and institutional contexts as well as to implicit/covert policies/practices.

*Expediency-oriented policies are a subcatagory of promotion-oriented policies.

specifies the initial mode of amalgamation and the subsequent policy management of each group. Although English was universally imposed, the experience of each group differed. Some groups were more restricted and segregated than others. Historically, only African Americans experienced the full gamut of inhumanities, including "compulsory ignorance" laws prior to 1865 (Weinberg, 1995).

The belief that *all* children deserve the right to educational opportunity in publicly supported education—let alone an equal opportunity to learn—received broad support gradually. It was not a widely held notion at the founding of the nation. During the 19th century, the idea that children should have a right to publicly supported education gained favor. However, even as it did, the right to equal educational opportunity was selectively withheld from many children of color, many of whom were also language minorities (Spring, 1994; Weinberg, 1995, 1997). Adding the force of law, the Supreme Court, in *Plessy v. Ferguson*, affirmed the dogma of segregated, *separate but equal* education, which stood from 1896 to 1954. It was not until the landmark *Brown v. Board of Education* (1954) decision that the court reasoned "it is doubtful that any child may reasonably be expected to succeed in life if he is denied the opportunity of an education" (cited from Leibowitz, 1982, p. 162). In the *Brown* decision, race had been the singular focus. Skuttnab-Kangas (1995) has recently made a similar case for linguistic access:

> If you want to have your fair share of the power and the resources (both material and non-material) of your native country, you have to be able to take part in the democratic processes in your country. You have to be able to negotiate, try to influence, to have a voice. The main instrument for doing that is language.... In a democratic country, it should be the duty of the school system to give every child, regardless of linguistic background the same chance to participate in the democratic process. If this requires that (at least) some of children (i.e., the linguistic minority children) become bilingual or multilingual, then it should be the duty of the educational system to make them bilingual/multilingual. (p. 42)

Implications of Policy Orientations for Language Minority Educational Rights

In assessing various policies toward language diversity and their implications for educational language rights, it is helpful to locate them in a language policy framework. Table 3.3 provides an overview of policy orientations of the federal government, states, and other agencies with the power to impose policies or practices that have the force of policy.

Table 3 builds from Kloss (1977/1998), who limited his analyses to formal policies imposed by law. However, in the United States, language behavior and language rights more commonly have been shaped by *implicit/covert* policies and by *informal* practices that can have the same, or even greater force than official policies (see Schiffman, 1996; Wiley, 1999a). Thus, it is useful to apply Table 3.3 to both formal and informal policies and practices. *Implicit policies* include those that may not start out to be language policies but have the effect of policy. *Covert policies,* as the word implies, are more ominous. They are policies that seek to use language or literacy requirements as a means of barring someone from social, political, educational, or economic participation (Wiley, in press). Historical examples include literacy requirements for voting and English literacy requirements for entry to the United States that have been used as gate-keeping mechanisms to exclude immigrants on the basis of their race or ethnicity (Leibowitz, 1969).

Promotion-oriented policies require governmental support. Historically, among language minority communities, there has never been any controversy over the need to promote English. By the 1920s, English had been designated as the official language of schooling in nearly all states. As a result, language promotion resources have flowed primarily into English instruction. At the institutional level, many colleges and universities have long had foreign/second language requirements, but college-level entry requirements for proficiency in English have helped to drive most language-related curricular policies since the late 19th century (Wright, 1980).

Although advocates of restrictive English-Only policies frequently depict contemporary advocates of bilingual education as being against the promotion of English, there is no evidence to support this. Most advocates of bilingual education and of linguistic human rights support the notion of "English Plus;" that is, they support the promotion of English *and* another language (Combs, 1992). Federally supported transitional bilingual education falls under the subcategory *expediency-oriented laws* (a subcategory of *promotion-oriented* policies in Table 3.3). *Expediency-oriented accommodations* are used to bridge contact between a minority population and the government, such as when the government/state sees a reason to try to improve communication with speakers of minority languages in order to facilitate assimilation (Kloss, 1977/1998; Wiley, 1999a).

A *tolerance-orientated* policy prevailed toward speakers of European languages up to the World War I era. During the colonial period and the early history of the republic, education among European-origin peoples was supported through private and sectarian means. In a climate of relative tolerance, German Americans provided support for schooling taught either in German or bilingually in German and English (Toth, 1990; Wiley, 1998a). Some states with large German-origin populations for a time even allowed for public supported education in German and German/English (Ohio and Pennsylvania), but, for the most part, it was incumbent on local and private stakeholders to foster education in community languages. African-origin peoples had a markedly different experience. *Restrictive* literacy policies appeared in slave codes in the 1740s. Slaveholders saw literacy as a direct threat to their ability to control the enslaved. *Compulsory illiteracy* laws remained on the books until 1865 (Weinberg, 1995). Kontra et al. note:

> The state/government can *restrict* minority languages in three ways. It can (1)...
> restrict the age-groups and the range of school subjects for which minority-
> medium education is provided... (2) [restrict] the number of languages through
> which education is made available... [and/or] (3) reduce the number of people
> entitled to minority medium education by obfuscation of who the rightholders/
> beneficiaries are. (p. 10)

During World War I, speakers of German, who were the second most populous linguistic group at that time, suddenly found themselves stigmatized and forced to use English (Wiley, 1998a). During the 1920s and 1930s, Chinese and Japanese community-based schools operated, often meeting resistance from territorial authorities in Hawaii and state authorities in California.

The *null* policy category (in Table 3.3) indicates the significant absence of policy. When educational policies have prescribed a one-size-fits-all approach, they have often disadvantaged language minority students by failing to address their special needs, histories, and circumstances (see Quezada, Wiley, & Ramírez, 1999/2000). Unless policy prescribes a special program of study of the language of instruction, language minorities are excluded, or at best, systematically disadvantaged in learning academic subjects.

School-based language requirements and standards can covertly be used as surrogates for more overtly racist policies. For example, in 1924, English Standard Schools were implemented in Hawaii. Placement was based on tests of standard English that were used to sort children into "standard," "nonstandard," and "feebleminded" educational tracks. Without resorting to overt racially based segregation, a system of racially segregated schooling was established largely on the basis of language proficiency. In his analysis of historical and contemporary school and university policies and practices in Hawaii, Haas (1992) concluded that many promote institutional racism. Among the examples he identified were failing to offer instruction in languages commonly spoken in linguistically diverse communities even when the communities have requested them; misassigning students to educational tracks based on their performance on tests of standard English which have been normed on national, rather than local populations (e.g., although about half of Hawaii's population is comprised of native speakers of Hawaii Creole English [HCE/"pidgin"], the SAT continues to be used as an entry requirement for admission to the state-supported university system); insufficient use of immigrant languages to communicate with parents; inadequately trained staff responsible for the education of language minority students; and underidentifying and under-serving language minority students due to the failure to recognize them as language minorities. Romaine (1994) concluded:

> Speakers of HCE have been discriminated against through education in a school system which originally was set up to keep out those who could not pass an English test. In this way it was hoped to restrict the admission of non-white children into the English Standard schools set up in 1924, which were attended mainly by Caucasian children. By institutionalizing what was essentially racial discrimination along linguistic lines, the schools managed to keep creole speakers in their place, maintaining distance between them and English speakers until after World War II. (p. 531; cf. Agbayani & Takeuchi, 1986; Benham & Heck, 1998; Kawamoto, 1993)

As in the case of speakers of other "non-standard" varieties of language, the failure of educators in Hawaii to recognize (through *null* policy) the language minority status of HCE as a distinct language variety positions its speakers as merely "substandard" articulators of English. Thus "deficiency" is located in the students, but not in the educational system responsible for educating them.

COURT DECISIONS ON LANGUAGE RIGHTS
AND EDUCATIONAL ACCESS

This section examines important U.S. court cases focused on language rights and educational access.

Meyer v. Nebraska, 262 U.S. 390 (1923). Following the xenophobia of World War I, Nebraska and other states passed laws prohibiting foreign language instruction. In many states, children were not allowed to study a foreign language until Grade 6, in others, not until Grade 8. The intent was to make foreign languages inaccessible during those ages when children would have the best opportunity for learning or retaining them. By 1923, several appeals challenging these restrictions had been filed to the Supreme Court (Piatt, 1992). The decisive case was *Meyer v. Nebraska* (1923). Meyer, a parochial school teacher, was convicted and fined for breaking a Nebraska law prohibiting foreign language teaching. Meyer appealed to the Nebraska Supreme Court and lost. The Nebraska court reasoned that teaching German to children of immigrants was unfavorable to national safety and self-interest. In 1923, the Supreme Court overturned the Nebraska court, arguing that in peacetime, no threat to national security could justify the restriction on teachers of foreign languages nor the limitation imposed on the parents who wished their children to learn them. By a 7-2 vote, the Nebraska law was held to be an infringement of the Due Process Clause of the Fourteenth Amendment (Edwards, 1923; Murphy, 1992; Piatt, 1992; Wiley, 1998a).

Although the *Meyer* ruling determined that unduly restrictive educational language policies were unconstitutional, it established a weak precedent for educational rights. The court accepted the hegemonic view that all citizens of the United States should be required to speak a common tongue (Murphy, 1992) and affirmed the "power of the state to compel attendance at some school and to make reasonable regulations for all schools, including a requirement that they shall give instructions in English" (cited in Norgren & Nanda, 1988, p. 188). The Supreme Court's decision affirmed the official status of English-language instruction. Even after *Meyer*, German-language instruction never recovered its pre-war levels (Wiley, 1998a).

Farrington v. Tokushige 273 U.S. 284, 298 (1927).

In a related decision, *Farrington v. Tokushige*, the Supreme Court, based on Meyer, ruled that the attempt by the territorial governor of Hawaii to impose restrictions on private or community-based Japanese, Korean, and Chinese foreign language schools was unconstitutional. *Farrington* was not without significance, because a large number of such schools had been established in Hawaii (Leibowitz, 1971) and California (Bell, 1935/1974), and many thrived during the 1920s and 1930s, just as similar schools do today. These heritage language schools provided supplemental instruction in native languages to the English-only instruction provided in public schools. During World War II, however, the right to Japanese instruction was prohibited in the federal internment camps in which Japanese Americans were imprisoned (U.S. Senate, 1943/1974).

Lau v. Nichols 414 U.S. 563, 565 (1974) and Related Cases.

The most significant legal case since *Meyer* with implications for language minority students' educational rights was *Lau v. Nichols* (1974). As historical background to the case, several facts are worth noting. The case was filled in San Francisco. California, like many other states, had a prior history of discriminating against racial and ethnolinguistic minorities. In California, discrimination on the basis of race, at one time, had a legal basis in state law. Anti-Chinese groups even succeeded in lobbying the U.S. government to pass the Chinese Exclusion Act of 1882, which restricted Chinese immigration for ten years. In addition, segregation of Asian-origin students was legal in California from the late 19th century to the mid-20th century. As late as 1943, the California Constitution had affirmed legal segregation of school children of Indian, Chinese, Japanese, or "Mongolian" parentage. This provision was not overturned until 1947. In 1905, the San Francisco School Board passed a resolution calling for the segregation of Japanese and Chinese students, arguing that its intent was

> not only for the purpose of relieving the congestion at the present prevailing in our schools, but also for the higher end that *our* children should not be placed in any position where their youthful impressions may be affected by association with pupils of the Mongolian race. (Resolution, 1905/1974; emphasis added)

As in many educational discrimination cases, litigation resulting in *Lau* was born out of the frustration of failed efforts on the part of parents and community activists to receive appropriate educational programs for language minority children. According to Li-Ching Wang, a community leader involved in the four-year litigation, the Chinese-American community held meetings with the San Francisco school administrators over a three-year period. They had "conducted numerous studies that demonstrated the needs of non-English speaking children, proposed different approaches to solve the problem," and staged demonstrations in protest of district inaction (De Avila, Steinman, & Wang, 1994, p. 13). As a last resort, Chinese American parents and community leaders filed a lawsuit in 1970, based on the following facts:

1. 2,856 Chinese speaking students in San Francisco Unified School District (SFUSD) needed special instruction in English.
2. 1,790 [Chinese speaking students] received no help or special instruction at all, not even the 40 minutes of ESL [provided to some students].
3. Of the remaining 1,066 Chinese speaking students who did receive some help, 623 received such help on a part-time basis and 433 on a full-time basis.
4. Only 260 of the 1,066 Chinese students receiving special instruction in English were taught by bilingual Chinese speaking teachers. (De Avila, Steinman, & Wang, 1994, p. 14)

The lower courts rejected the arguments of the plaintiffs. In 1973, the Ninth Circuit Court of Appeals sided with the school district, concluding:

> *The discrimination suffered by these children* is not the result of laws passed by the state of California, presently or historically, but *is the result of deficiencies created by the children themselves* in failing to know and learn the English language. (cited in De Avila, Steinman, & Wang, 1994, p. 16; emphases added)

Twenty years after the *Lau* decision, Edward Steinman, the attorney who had represented Kinney Lau, lamented that the attitude which had led to the struggle for *Lau* "cannot be changed by a court decision.... This statement [above] says that the child is inherently sinful for having the audacity not to know English when he or she enters the classroom" (De Avila, Steinman, & Wang, 1994, p. 17). What is even more remarkable is the similarity of the 1973 reasoning of the Ninth Circuit Court to the editorial remarks in the *San Francisco Chronicle*, printed 66 years earlier, in support of the segregation of Japanese children:

> The most prominent objection to the presence of Japanese in our public schools is their habit of sending young men to primary grades, where they sit side by side with very young [white] children, because in those grades only are the beginnings of English taught. That creates situations which often become painfully embarrassing. They are, in fact, unendurable.

> There is also objection to taking the time of the teachers to teach the English language to pupils, old or young, who do not understand it. It is a reasonable requirement that all pupils entering the schools shall be familiar with the language in which instruction is conducted. *We deny either the legal or moral obligation to teach any foreigner to read or speak the English language. And if we choose to do that for one nationality, this is our privilege.* (U.S. Senate, 1906/1974, p. 2972; emphasis added)

In delivering the 1974 opinion of the Supreme Court, Justice William O. Douglas focused on the connections between language and race, ethnicity, and national origin:

> The failure of the San Francisco school system to provide English language instruction to approximately 1,800 students of Chinese ancestry who do not speak English, or to provide them with other adequate instructional procedures, denies them a meaningful opportunity to participate in the public educational program and thus violates §601 of the Civil Rights Act of 1964, which bans discrimination based on "the ground of race, color, or national origin," in "any program or activity receiving financial assistance." (*Lau et al v. Nichols et al.*, 414 U.S. No. 72-6520; Reprinted in ARC, 1994, p. 6)

And, contradicting the entrenched notion that schools are not "legally or morally obligated to teach English," Douglas concluded,

> Basic English skills are at the very core of what these public schools teach. Imposition of a requirement that, *before a child can effectively participate in the educational program, he must already have acquired those basic skills is to make a mockery of public education.* We know that those who do not understand English are certain to find their classroom experiences wholly incomprehensible and in no way meaningful. (*Lau et al v. Nichols et al.*, 414 U.S. No. 72-6520; Reprinted in ARC, 1994, p. 8; emphasis added)

Contrary to a common misunderstanding, *Lau* did not mandate bilingual education. The plaintiffs had not requested a specific remedy, and Douglas left the prescription of possible remedies open, stating: "Teaching English to the students of Chinese ancestry is one choice. Giving instructions to this group in Chinese is another" (cited in ARC, p. 7). Soon after, federal authorities took the next step with the so-called *Lau* Remedies (see Crawford, 1992). The Lau Remedies attempted to spell out appropriate expediency-oriented policies that could be implemented in schools. However, these were subsequently withdrawn under the Reagan administration (see Crawford, 1995). Nevertheless, using *transitional* bilingual education (see Table 3.4) as a remedy was prescribed in several district court cases. The first was *Serna v. Portales Municipal Schools* in 1974 (*Serna* was also affirmed by the 10th U.S. Circuit Court of Appeals). Other important district court cases prescribing the remedy of transitional bilingual education include *U.S. v. Texas* (1981) and *Rios v. Read* (1978; see Leibowitz, 1982). However, in neither *Lau* nor related cases such as *Serna* did the courts address the constitutional issue of equal protection under the 14th Amendment. Rather, rulings were based on legislative protections against discrimination under the 1964 Civil Rights Act (Piatt, 1992).

The issue of determining whether or not the school districts have complied with *Lau* was left to federal courts to resolve (Jiménez, 1992). The definitive case to date is *Casteñeda v. Pickard* (1981). As Jiménez notes, the significance of *Casteñeda* is that it laid out an analytical framework or three-part test by which "appropriate actions" by school districts "to overcome language barriers" could be assessed (p. 248). The criteria were that any prescribed remedy must (a) be based on sound educational theory; (b) have a reasonable plan for implementation, including the hiring of appropriate personnel; and (c) produce positive educational results.

Martin Luther King Jr. Elementary School Children v. Ann Arbor School District Board (1979).

Children who speak non-standard language varieties, such as Hawaii Creole English, Appalachian English, and Ebonics, have often been ignored in discussions of language minority educational rights. The most important legal case in this area is *Martin Luther King Jr. Elementary School Children v. Ann Arbor School District Board*. Initially, this was brought as a racial discrimination suit in which race, class, and language were linked. Smitherman (1981), an expert witness for the defense, after the trial noted:

> The fate of black children as victims of miseducation continues to be the bottom line in the case. King began with a claim against the institutional mismanagement of the children ... It ended with a claim against the institutional

TABLE 3.4

A Typology of Bilingual Education

Type of Program	Typical Child	Language of the Classroom	Societal and Educational Aim	Language and/or Literacy Aim
Weak Forms of Education for Promoting Bilingualism and/or Biliteracy				
SUBMERSION (a.k.a. Structured Immersion)	Language Minority	Majority Language	Assimilation	Monolingualism
SUBMERSION (+ Withdrawal ESL)	Language Minority	Majority Language	Assimilation	Monolingualism
SEGREGATIONIST	Language Minority	Minority Language (forced, no choice)	Apartheid	Monolingualism
TRANSITIONAL	Language Minority	From Minority to Majority Language.	Assimilation	Relative Monolingualism
MAJORITY Lang. + Foreign Language	Language Minority	Majority Language with L2/FL Lessons	Limited enrichment	Limited Bilingualism
SEPARATIST	Language Minority	Minority Language (out of choice)	Detachment/autonomy	Limited Bilingualism
Strong Forms of Education for Promoting Bilingualism and/or Biliteracy				
Immersion	Language Majority	Bilingual, Initial Emphasis on L2	Pluralism and Enrichment	Bilingualiam and Biliteracy
Maintenance/ Heritage Language	Language Minority	Bilingual with Emphasis on L1	Maintenance/ Pluralism/Enrichment	Bilingualism and Biliteracy
Two-way/Dual Language	Mixed Language Minority & Majority	Minority and Majority Languages	Maintenance/ Pluralism/Enrichment	Bilingualism and Biliteracy
Mainstream Bilingual	Language Majority	Two Majority Languages	Maintenance/ Pluralism/Enrichment	Bilingualism and Biliteracy

This table is adapted with permission from Baker (1996, p. 172). Notes: (1) L2 = Second Language; L1 = First Language; FL = Foreign Language. (2) See pp. 172–197 for elaboration.

mismanagement of the language of the children ... Our argument and Judge
Joiner's ruling was that it is the obligation of educational institutions to accept
it as legitimate. (p. 20)

Although the judge's ruling affirmed the status of Ebonics/African
American English, his strategy in limiting the case to the single issue of
language demonstrates how language is used as a substitute for issues involving race and class (Wiley, 1999b). The judge in the King case avoided
race and class by focusing on the issue of language deficiency.

Several misunderstandings have developed regarding this case. One is
that the judge ordered Ebonics/Black English to be taught or *promoted* in
place of standard English. To the contrary, he was only trying to
accommodate the children's language differences. Another misperception
is that this case had the same force as *Lau* (see Baugh, 1995; Schiffman,
1996). However, unlike *Lau*, which reached the Supreme Court, *Ann Arbor*
was decided only at the federal district court-level. The school district,
which lost the decision, chose not to appeal it; thus, its impact was only
relevant in the Ann Arbor District (Baugh, 1995). Nevertheless, the decision
demonstrates the potential of *expediency* policies for removing the sole burden for acquiring standard English from students who do not enter school
speaking it (Wiley, 1999b).

In 1996, the Oakland School Board decided to use Ebonics as a bridge to
school English. Its decision was widely ridiculed by the press and popular media, and more viciously attacked by hate-oriented Internet websites.
What the press and media failed to focus on was the fact that the overwhelming majority of language minority children, including speakers of
Ebonics, are being educated in standard English by many teachers who
equate their students' language differences with language deficiencies (see
Ramírez et al., 1999).

LANGUAGE MINORITY EDUCATIONAL RIGHTS IN INSTITUTIONAL AND PROGRAMMATIC CONTEXTS

In order to evaluate access to educational language rights, it is useful to
analyze the various types of program models prescribed by legislation,
or otherwise available, and to consider their particular goals for language
minority students vis-à-vis the dominant society and in terms of their aims
for language and literacy development as well (see Table 3.4).

The political debate over bilingual education in the United States has
focused more on the phrase "bilingual education" rather than on program-
matic substance. As Lyons (1990/1995) has noted, the intent of one of the

initial sponsors of federal bilingual programs, Senator Yarbrough, was to address the needs of Spanish-speaking children. Initially, the proposal for bilingual education had strong bipartisan support, with some three-dozen bills being put forth. In a compromise move to expedite passage of the legislation, the designated target population was redefined as being "children of limited English-speaking ability." This shift in terminology away from "Spanish-speakers" had the appearance of being more inclusive. However, it also positioned the target population as members of a "remedial" group, defined by the lack of proficiency in English. Amendments to the Bilingual Education Act of 1978 relabeled the target population as being "limited English proficient" to underscore the emphasis on reading, writing, comprehension and cognitive skills in English. Yet "the new definition, while arguably clearer and more comprehensive, reinforced the deficit approach to educating language minority students" (Lyons, 1990/1995, p. 3).

Under the Bilingual Education Act and its reauthorized versions, the majority of programs offered under the "bilingual" label have been short-term *transitional* programs and programs in English as a second language. In Table 3.4, these models fall under the "weak" category because they fail to promote or maintain native languages. Also the societal and educational aims of these programs as well as their language/literacy aims promote "assimilation" and "monolingualism" (in English) respectively. Many so-called educational "reform" measures, such as Proposition 227 ("English for the Children") and Arizona's Proposition 203, have sought to restrict even "weak" *transitional* models of bilingual education.

CONCLUSION

The history of access to educational language rights in minority languages, from the colonial period to the present, indicates a mixed bag of official and unofficial policies. As English achieved highest status, colonial and early national policies and practices toward minority languages ranged from relative tolerance or indifference toward education in European languages and bilingual education, to the suppression of African tongues accompanied by compulsory ignorance laws imposed on enslaved African Americans. Policy differences toward each group suggest the extent to which language policies represented efforts to exert social control over various language minority groups based on their relative status vis-à-vis the English-speaking majority. From the early national period to the mid-19th century, policies toward Native Americans encouraged the acquisition of English over maintenance native languages. However, after the Civil War, policies toward American Indians shifted to *coercive assimilation* of English, accompanied by restrictions on the maintenance of native languages until the 1930s. From the late 1880s to the 1920s, restrictive policies (peaking during World War I) were also adopted toward European languages, most notably toward German, with the effect of reduced maintenance and a de-emphasis on German education in the schools. In the 1920s, the Supreme Court struck down the most restrictive prohibitions on "foreign" language instruction. Nevertheless, it affirmed the goal of a monolingual English speaking society and the imposition of English as the medium of instruction. In the 1960s, during a climate of heightened concern for civil rights, greater educational opportunity for all, and "remediation," bilingual education—with assimilation into English mediated education as its goal—was adopted as an *expediency* measure to promote greater educational access. During the anti-bilingual education movement of the 1990s, even weak forms of publicly supported bilingual education were subject to attack. California's Proposition 227 and Arizona's Proposition 203 were designed to strictly limit access to bilingual education and similar measures were introduced in a number of other states.

From the perspective of educational language rights, the 21st century begins with echoes of early 20th century restrictionism (cf. Tatalovich, 1995). At present, support for the right of language minority children in the United States to maintain their languages remains protected in principle. Unfortunately, the prospects for attaining such a goal survive largely outside the domain of federal education policy through the efforts of charter school *two-way immersion* programs (see Table 3.4) and freelance community-based organizations and private efforts. Thus, the struggle for educational language rights and linguistic human rights in the United States continues.

REFERENCES

Agbayani, A., & Takeuchi, D. (1986). English standard schools: A policy analysis. In N. Tsuchida (Ed.), *Issues in Asian and Pacific American education*, (p. 30–45). Minneapolis, MN: Asian/Pacific American Learning Resource Center, University of Minnesota.

Art, Research & Curriculum Associates (ARC), *Revisiting the Lau Decision: 20 years after*. Symposium Proceedings (November 3–4, 1994) (pp. 6–12). San Francisco, CA: ARC.

Baker, C. (1996). *Foundations of bilingual education and bilingualism*, 2nd Edition. Philadelphia, PA: Multilingual Matters.

Baugh, J. (1995). The law, linguistics and education: Educational reform for African American language minority students. *Linguistics and Education, 7*, 87–105.

Bell, R. (1935/1974). Japanese language schools in California. Public school education of second generation Japanese in California. Reprinted from S. Cohen (Ed.), *Education in the United States: A documentary history, Vol. 2*, (p. 2974–76). New York: McGraw-Hill. In *Educational-Psychology*, Vol. 1 (pp. 20–23). Stanford University Publications.

Benham, M. K. P., & Heck, R. H. (1998). *Culture and education in Hawaii: The silencing of native voices*. Mahwah, PA: Lawrence Erlbaum.

Combs, M. C. (1992). English Plus: Responding to English Only. In J. Crawford (Ed.), *Language loyalties: A source book on the official English controversy* (pp. 216–224). Chicago: University of Chicago Press.

Crawford, J. (1992). The question of minority language rights. In J. Crawford (Ed.), *Language loyalties: A source book on the official English controversy* (pp. 225–228). Chicago, IL: University of Chicago Press.

Crawford, J. (1995). *Bilingual education: History, politics, theory, and practice* (3rd Ed). Los Angeles, CA: Bilingual Education Services.

de Avila, E. A., Steinman, E., & Wang, L. C. (1994). Historical overview. In Art, Research & Curriculum Associates (ARC), *Revisiting the Lau Decision: 20 years after*. Symposium Proceedings (November 3–4, 1994) (pp. 13–21). San Francisco, CA: ARC.

de Varennes, F. (1999). *Language: A right and a resource approach to linguistic human rights* (pp. 117–146). Budapest: Central European University Press.

Edwards, I. N. (December, 1923). The legal status of foreign languages in the schools. *Elementary School Journal, 24*, pp. 270–278.

Haas, M. (1992). *Institutional racism: The case of Hawaii*. Westport, CN: Praeger.

Heath, S. B. (1976). Colonial language status achievement: Mexico, Peru, and the United States. In A. Verdoodt and R. Kjolseth (Eds.), *Language and sociology*. Louvain: Peeters.

Hernández-Chávez, E. (1994). Language policy in the United States: A history of cultural genocide. In T. Skutnabb-Kangas & R. Phillipson (Eds.), *Linguistic human rights: Overcoming linguistic discrimination* (pp. 141–158). Berlin: Mouton de Gruyter.

Jiménez, M. (1992). The educational rights of language minority children. In J. Crawford (Ed.), *Language loyalties: A source book on the official English controversy* (pp. 243–251). Chicago: University of Chicago Press.

Kawamoto, K. Y. (1993). Hegemony and language politics in Hawaii. *World Englishes, 12,* 193–207.

Kloss, H. (1977/1998). *The American bilingual tradition*. Center for Applied Linguistics and Delta Systems: Washington, DC and McHenry, IL. Original work published 1977.

Kontra, M., Phillipson, R., Skutnabb-Kangas, T, & Varády, T. (1999a). Conceptualizing and implementing linguistic human rights. In Author (Eds.), *Language: A right and a resource approaches to linguistic human rights* (pp. 1–21). Budapest: Central European University Press.

Kontra, M., Phillipson, R., Skutnabb-Kangas, T, & Varády, T. (Eds.). (1999b). *Language: A right and a resource approaches to linguistic human rights*. Budapest: Central European University Press.

Lau et al. v. Nichols et al. (U.S., 563-572, No. 72-6520). Reprinted in Art, Research & Curriculum Associates (ARC), *Revisiting the Lau Decision: 20 years after*. Symposium Proceedings (November 3–4, 1994) (pp. 6–12). San Francisco, CA: ARC.

Leibowitz, A. H. (1969). English literacy: Legal sanction for discrimination. *Notre Dame Lawyer, 25* (1), 7–66.

Leibowitz, A. H. (1971). *Educational policy and political acceptance: The imposition of English as the language of instruction in American schools*. Eric Document Reproduction Service No. ED 047 321.

Leibowitz, A. H. (1974, August). Language as a means of social control. Paper presented at the VIII World Congress of Sociology, University of Toronto, Toronto, Canada.

Leibowitz, A. H. (1982). *Federal recognition of the rights of minority language groups*. Rosslyn, VA: National Clearinghouse on Bilingual Education.

Lyons, J. (1990/1995). The past and future directions of federal bilingual-education policy. In

O. García & C. Baker (Eds.), *Policy and practice in bilingual education: Extending the foundations* (pp. 1–15). Clevedon, UK: Multilingual Matters. Reprinted from *Annals of the American Academy of Political and Social Sciences 508*, 66–80, 1990.

Macías, R. F. (1979). Choice of language as a human right–Public policy implications in the United States. In R. V. Padilla (Ed.), *Bilingual education and pubic policy in the United States* (pp. 39–75). Ypsilanti, MI: Eastern Michigan University.

Macías, R. F. (1999). Language policies and the sociolinguistics historiography of Spanish in the United States. In J. K. Peyton, P. Griffin, & R. Fasold (Eds.), *Language in action* (pp. 52–83). Creskill, NJ: Hampton Press.

Macías, R. F. & Wiley, T. G. (1998). Introduction. In H. Kloss, *The American bilingual tradition* (pp. vii–xiv). Washington, DC and McHenry, IL: Center for Applied Linguistics and Delta System.

Murphy, P. L. (1992). *Meyer v. Nebraska*. In K. L. Hall (Ed.), *The Oxford companion to the Supreme Court of the United States* (pp. 543–544). New York: Oxford University Press.

Norgren, J., & Nanda, S. (1988). *American cultural pluralism and the law*. New York: Praeger.

Piatt, B. (1992). The confusing state of minority language rights. In J. Crawford (Ed.), *Language loyalties: A source book on the official English controversy* (pp. 229–234). Chicago: University of Chicago Press.

Quezada, M. S., Wiley, T. G., & Ramírez, J. D. (1999/2000). How the reform agenda short-changes English learners. *Educational Leadership, 57*(4), 57–61.

Ramírez, J. D., Wiley, T. G., DeKlerk, G., & Le, E. (Eds.), (1999). *Ebonics in the urban debate*. Long Beach, CA: Center for Language Minority Education and Research (CLMER) California State University, Long Beach.

Romaine, S. (1994). Hawaii Creole English as a literacy language. *Language in Society, 23*(4), 527–554.

Resolution (1905/1974). Resolution of the San Francisco School Board. Reprinted in S. Cohen (Ed.), *Education in the United States: A documentary history, Vol. 2*, (p. 2971). New York: McGraw-Hill.

Rickford, J. R. (1999). Using the vernacular to teach the standard. In J. D. Ramírez, T. G. Wiley, H. DeKlerk, & E. Lee (Eds.), *Ebonics in the urban debate* (pp. 23–41). Long Beach, CA: Center for Language Minority Education and Research (CLMER) California State University, Long Beach.

Schiffman, H. F. 1996. *Linguistic culture and language policy*. London: Routledge.

Skutnabb-Kangas, T., & Bucak, S. (1994). In T. Skutnabb-Kangas & R. Phillipson (Eds.), *Linguistic human rights: Overcoming linguistic discrimination* (pp. 347–370). Berlin: Mouton de Gruyter.

Skutnabb-Kangas, T. (1995). Multilingualism and the education of minority children. In O. García & C. Baker (Eds.), *Policy and practice in bilingual education: Extending the foundations* (pp. 40–62). Clevedon, UK: Multilingual Matters.

Skutnabb-Kangas, T. (1999). Linguistic diversity, human rights, and the "free" market. In M. Kontra, R. Phillipson, & T. Várády (Eds.), *Language: A right and a resource approaches to linguistic human rights*. (pp. 187–222) Budapest: Central European University Press.

Smitherman, G. (1981). Introduction. In G. Smitherman (Ed.), *Black English and the education of Black children and youth: Proceedings of the National Invitational Symposium on the King decision* (pp. 11–31). Detroit, MI: Center for Black Studies, Wayne State.

Spring, J. (1994). *Deculturation and the struggle for equality: A brief history of the education of dominated cultures in the United States*. New York: McGraw-Hill.

Tatalovich, R. (1995). *Nativism reborn? The official English language movement and the American states*. Lexington, KY: University of Kentucky Press.

Tollefson, J. W. (1991). *Planning language, planning inequality*. New York: Longman.

Tollefson, J. W. (1995). Introduction: Language policy, power, and inequality. In J. W. Tollefson (Ed.), *Power and inequality in language education* (pp. 1–8). Cambridge: Cambridge University Press.

Toth, C. R. (1990). *German-English bilingual schools in America: The Cincinnati tradition in historical context.* New York: Lang.

U.S. Senate (1906/1974). The *San Francisco Chronicle* on segregation of Japanese school children. From editorial, November 6, 1906, as quoted in Senate document no. 147, 59th Cong., 2nd Sess. (1906), p. 30. Reprinted in S. Cohen (Ed.), *Education in the United States: A documentary history, Vol. 2* (p. 2972). New York: McGraw-Hill.

U.S. Senate (1943/1974). Description of Education in the Internment Camps. From Miscellaneous Documents, 1-142, 78th Cong. 1st Sess. Document No. 96. Segregation of loyal and disloyal Japanese (1943), p. 11. Reprinted in S. Cohen (Ed.), *Education in the United States: A documentary history, Vol. 2* (p. 2977). New York: McGraw-Hill.

Weinberg, M. (1995). *A chance to learn: A history of race and education in the United States,* 2nd ed. Long Beach, CA: California State University, Long Beach University Press.

Weinberg, M. (1997). *Asian-American education: Historical background and current realities.* Mahwah, NJ: Lawrence Erlbaum.

Wiley, T. G. & Lukes, M. (1996). English-Only and standard English ideologies in the United States. *TESOL Quarterly, 30*(3), 511–535.

Wiley, T. G. (1996a). Language planning and language policy. In S. McKay & N. Hornberger (Eds.), *Sociolinguistics and language teaching* (pp. 103–147). Cambridge: Cambridge University Press.

Wiley, T. G. (1996b). *Literacy and language diversity in the United States. Language in education: Theory and practice.* McHerny, IL: Center for Applied Linguistics and Delta Systems.

Wiley, T. G. (1998a). The imposition of World War I Era English-Only policies and the fate of German in North America. In T. Ricento & B. Burnaby (Eds.), *Language and politics in the United States and Canada* (pp. 211–241). Mahwah, NJ: Lawrence Erlbaum.

Wiley, T. G. (1998b). What happens after English is declared the official language of the United States. In D. A. Kibbee (Ed.). *Language legislation and linguistic rights* (pp. 179–194). Amsterdam: John Benjamins.

Wiley, T. G. (1999a). Comparative historical analysis of U.S. Language Policy and Language Planning: Extending the foundations. In T. Huebner & K. A. Davis (Eds.), *Sociopolitical perspectives on language policy and planning in the USA* (pp. 17–37). Amsterdam: John Benjamins.

Wiley, T. G. (1999b). Ebonics: Background to the current policy context. In J. D. Ramírez, T. G. Wiley, G. DeKlerk, & E. Lee (Eds.), *Ebonics in the urban debate* (pp. 8–19). Long Beach, CA: Center for Language Minority Education and Research (CLMER). California State University, Long Beach.

Wiley, T. G. (in press). Language policy and English-Only. In E. Finegan & J. R. Rickford (Eds.), *Language in the USA: Perspectives for the 21st century* (Cambridge: Cambridge University Press).

Wolfram, W., Adger, T. C., & Christian, D. (1999). *Dialects in schools and communities.* Mahwah, PA: Lawrence Erlbaum Associates.

Wright, E. (1980). School English and public policy. *College English, 42,* 327–342.

4

Reflections on Language Policies in Canada: Three Examples

Barbara Burnaby
Memorial University of New Foundland

Canada is a polyglot country with 11 different Aboriginal language families, two official languages (English and French), and over 100 other languages actively used by immigrants and their descendants. Language policy making in Canada is divided for political and practical reasons according to three groups of languages: the official languages, other immigrants' languages, and Aboriginal languages. This chapter examines an example of language policies for each of these three categories: federal official language policies for managing French-English group relations; Ontario's programs for managing access to English language training for immigrants; and educational programs using the Cree language as a medium of instruction on the east coast of St. James Bay. The analysis illustrates important differences in the treatment of these groups and demonstrates that some policies may have little impact on language behavior, that language may be a symbol in struggles over issues other than language, and that local control can be a crucial factor in language education programs for linguistic minorities.

OFFICIAL LANGUAGE STATUS IN FRENCH-ENGLISH
GROUP RELATIONS

The first example sketches the history of relationships between the English and French languages since Canada was formed as a country in 1867. The role of language as a symbol in French-English relations is traced and the effectiveness of major legislation in supporting actual language use is analyzed.

In 1867, the time of the signing of the British North America Act, Canada's original constitution, a major political focus was on establishing provisions to take into account citizens of British and French origins. According to Neatby (1992), in the 19th century the legal expression of rights for the "English" and the "French" populations focused on religion rather than on language or other possible differences. The 1867 Act gave equal status to French and English in the federal parliament and courts, and in the legislature and courts in Quebec. Also, educational jurisdiction was given to the provinces. Through the later 19th century and first half of the 20th century, changes in the structure of the economy, secularism, and waves of immigration resulted in the anglicization of the economy in Quebec, as in the rest of the country. As a result, francophone control and the use of French in the economy were marginalized (Beaujot, 1998; Wardhaugh, 1983), the federal bureaucracy became 90% English (Wardhaugh, 1983), and immigrants assimilated to English rather than French (Neatby, 1992).

Throughout the 1960s, the "Quiet Revolution" in Quebec entailed demands for the French language rights stipulated in the British North America Act (Neatby, 1992). In 1963, the federal government established the Royal Commission on Bilingualism and Biculturalism to look at relations among linguistic groups in the country; its main result was the declaration in 1969 of English and French as Canada's official languages. The Official Languages Act made English and French the languages of the federal parliament and bureaucracy, created the Office of the Commissioner of Official Languages, and established rules for language rights in education. In 1970, the federal government established the Official Languages in Education (EOL) program, which has provided financing for language minority schooling (i.e., schools in French for francophones outside of Quebec and in English for anglophones in Quebec) and for second official language programs in school (i.e., core French and French immersion classes outside of Quebec, and *anglais langue seconde* in Quebec) (Peat, Marwick & Churchill, 1987). Although the federal government has no mandate with respect to education, its official language legislation provided the legal basis for federal funding for schools.

With this funding—and fueled by parent enthusiasm—French immersion and core French programs burgeoned in anglophone areas of the country, from kindergarten to the end of high school, throughout the 1970s. The ability to speak both official languages was widely thought to be a great economic advantage, especially for young people. There is not and never has been any comparable federal funding for immigrant children learning English as a second language (ESL) or French as a second language (FSL) as their first official language. Although the federal government made a verbal gesture towards immigrant groups by acknowledging their potential interest in maintaining their original languages, the federal priority was on the second official language rather than any non-official language, especially as medium of instruction. Federal authorities resisted pressure to fund non-official language teaching in the school system. Thus any deviation of federal attention outside Quebec from support of the status of French, such as support for ESL for immigrant children or funding for immigrant languages, was avoided.

With the political focus on French-English relations, language and culture became a sensitive matter for those who had investments in other cultures and languages. In the face of a backlash against the declaration of official languages, on October 8, 1971, the federal government declared itself, by policy but not legislation, to be multicultural (rather than just English/French bicultural) within a framework of bilingualism. The original policy included, as its fourth tenet, that "the government will continue to assist immigrants to acquire at least one of Canada's official languages in order to become full participants in Canadian society" (Saouab, 1993, p. 4). However, there were no further funds from the federal government for ESL or FSL for immigrants under the name of multiculturalism. In a more pluralist vein, the multiculturalism policy did open the door of the state for some support for cultural and linguistic diversity, including some language activities in schools.

Throughout the 1970s, there was a great deal of political action with respect to the establishment of French language rights under provincial jurisdictions. Quebec declared itself officially monolingual in French and worked particularly towards making French the language of education (except for children of certain anglophone backgrounds) and in the workplace. At one point, the resulting tensions and political actions were so extreme that the Canadian prime minister invoked the War Measures Act to restore calm in Montreal. Public reaction was strongest with respect to the education provisions (Labrie, 1992). Court cases ensued and incidents arose over many issues, for example, the language of air traffic control.

From this point, the conflict began to change in character. Going into the 1980s, the federal government's political struggle with Quebec and other francophone populations expanded from language (since this battle was effectively won to the extent that it could be through legislation) to include the sovereignty of Quebec. In 1982, the federal Constitution Act was passed, replacing the British North America Act of 1867, and giving the country a home-grown constitution. Linked to it was the new Canadian Charter of Rights and Freedoms which constitutionally entrenched many of the language rights for English and French in the Official Languages Act, but added nothing to support substantially any other language; nor did it ensure the right to learn one of the official languages for immigrants who did not already speak French or English. The Charter did include a backhanded gesture of support in one clause stating that it was to be interpreted "in a manner consistent with the preservation and enhancement of the multicultural heritage of all Canadians" (clause 22). The clause mentions culture but not language. There is also a clause prohibiting discrimination on the grounds of race, national or ethnic origin, color, religion, sex, age or mental or physical disability. The Charter changed somewhat the way in which decisions could be made in Canada because one could now challenge laws and policies through the courts on the basis that they did not meet the standards of the Charter. An essential factor in this important legislation is that Quebec refused to sign, although all of the other provinces did. Currently, almost two decades later, Quebec has yet to sign although major political battles continue to arise over the Charter. Moreover, Quebec lost a provincial referendum aimed at gaining majority popular support for a renegotiated relationship with Canada. The issue of language is now rarely heard.

What have been the effects of these major legislative moves upon the French language? According to Beaujot (1998), francophones in Quebec have improved their social mobility and access to economic structures, and most children of non-French speaking parents in Quebec go to French medium schools. Francophone parents are more likely to pass their language on to their children, knowledge of French has increased outside of Quebec (especially among younger people), and the proportion of non-French mother tongue speakers in Quebec who can speak French doubled in 15 years. On the other hand, French as a mother tongue and home language has continued to decline at the national level. Although French has increased proportionally in Quebec, this is due to the departure of non-francophone groups from the province as much as it is to growth in the number of French speakers. Beaujot (1998) and Veltman (1998) describe ways in which French medium schooling has been less than effective in getting non-francophone children to switch to French. Moreover, non-francophone immigrants who arrive in Quebec as adults are unlikely to learn French. Veltman argues that Quebec was sending messages to immigrants and others during the Quiet Revolution in the 1950s and 1960s that francophones intended to control their own destiny, and that it was this climate even more than the legislation which followed that brought about changes in the language situation.

This example shows the rise and fall of the role of language as a central symbol in the federal preoccupation with French-English relations in Canada. For comparative purposes, it is interesting to note that this choice of symbol is not paralleled in the United States in the 1950s to 1970s, where race was a high profile issue instead. In addition, the example demonstrates the limitation of even massive legislation in the regulation of popular language choices (Burnaby & Ricento, 1998; Veltman, 1998). Finally, the size of groups (francophones are about one-quarter of the Canadian population) matters more than rhetoric about rights and needs of smaller groups.

MANAGEMENT OF ACCESS TO ENGLISH LANGUAGE TRAINING FOR IMMIGRANTS IN ONTARIO

In the second example, the history of provision of ESL training for adults is outlined for Ontario, Canada's largest immigrant-receiving province. (French as a second language is little in demand among immigrants in Ontario.) About 12% of Canadians reported on the 1991 census that they had a mother tongue other than English or French. In Ontario this sizeable group has significant need for learning English. In order to explore government priorities and programs for ESL training, the analysis focuses on agencies providing ESL training rather than on those who receive it.

From early days in Canada, accommodation for immigrants who did not speak English had been in the hands of non-governmental organizations (NGOs) (Burnaby, 1998a; Pal, 1993), school boards, and individual citizens. Federal policy created in 1947 a series of programs called the Citizenship and Language Instruction and Language Textbook Agreements (CILT) to fund adult ESL in school boards and NGOs through provincial departments of education. One part of the program paid the entire costs of textbooks for citizenship and language classes while the other paid half of direct costs for instruction. The ostensible focus was preparing immigrants with the language, knowledge (and perhaps allegiance) to pass the citizenship test, but it is difficult to know how this intention was actually translated to instruction in classes. It is virtually impossible to trace the expenditures under this program, nor can we tell what volume of programming on ESL and orientation training generated through CILT was actually delivered. Certainly demand for both ESL and settlement information by immigrants exceeded supply. Constitutionally, the federal government stood well back from the provincial responsibility for deciding the educational content of such programs and providing actual service.

In 1967, the federal government, concerned about human resources for the country's booming economy, built an emphasis into the Immigration Act not only on the selection of the most suitable workers, but also on cooperation with the provinces in bearing the costs of immigration. It created what will be called here the Manpower Program, providing funding for a range of full-time occupational and pre-occupational training for immigrant and other Canadian adults. In taking this step, the federal government came close to trespassing on the provincial governments' constitutional right to manage education; it avoided doing so by having the provinces provide the training purchased for students chosen by federal officials (Thomas, 1987). ESL for immigrants comprised a considerable proportion of training offered. ESL students received about 24 weeks of full-time training with a living allowance. These programs were in very high demand by immigrants because of the training allowance and the possibility of being sent for further training after the basic ESL course was finished.

The province of Ontario had to find ways to implement these federal initiatives as well as handling immigrant children in the school system. The Ministry of Education did not have a policy on accommodating immigrants, nor did it have experts among its staff in this field. It was up to the school boards to deal with specific issues such as ESL. There was little expertise among teachers and administrators about ESL other than experience gained by individuals in actually working with immigrant students (Mewhort et al., 1965). NGOs continued to provide and develop expertise and models for dealing with ESL and settlement from their own experience.

For settlement-oriented interventions for adult immigrants in general and with the incentive of CILT funding, in the late 1950s, the provincial government created a unit that will be called here the Citizenship Branch, which initiated, among other things, professional support for ESL teachers, such as newsletters, conferences, and textbooks for adult ESL. Also in the 1960s, it piloted ESL classes for immigrant parents and preschool children, taught by volunteers who were trained by ESL and preschool program supervisors under contract. In school boards, a good deal of what became adult ESL in evening and adult day classes started with adaptations of adult basic education and business classes. The Toronto Board of Education had three adult day schools for academic subjects and basic business courses. In 1965, one school was dedicated to teaching ESL to adults on a full-time basis. Other adults took ESL in evening classes in schools. In 1958, the Ministry of Education started a summer program to train ESL teachers. It employed the expertise of members of the Citizenship Branch, many of whom had had experience in teaching adult ESL. Throughout the 1960s, the students in these courses were mostly people intending to teach adults, although a growing number of elementary and secondary teachers took the course (Mewhort et al., 1965). The focus on teachers of adults was clear, for example, since students were not required to have a teaching certificate.

Thus expertise for deciding what kinds of interventions would be effective was scarce at most levels in this educational scenario. The people who had and were developing experience in the field were the front-line personnel in the NGOs and the schools. Academia had no appropriate pedagogical solutions. Theories about second language teaching for adults being developed in the United States and Britain had limited influence because they were too closely tied to specific linguistic and psychological theories and were developed mainly for adults learning English as a foreign language overseas or in American or British universities.

In 1970, the Citizenship Branch supported the creation of TESL Ontario, an organization of ESL teachers and other interested parties to support the provision of ESL to immigrants. Until about 1978, the Branch provided a good deal of the funding to keep this organization and its conferences going. In 1973, TESL Ontario studied provisions in TESL teacher training and standards. The summer programs funded by the Ministry of Education and conducted by the Branch continued, but questions were raised about the ways in which certified teachers who took the course would be credited towards continuing certification. Eleven other ESL teacher training courses in post-secondary institutions were in place or about to begin, increasing the need for coordination of program offerings and standards. An additional complicating factor was the decision made about that time to require elementary school teachers to have an undergraduate degree (to take effect in 1980). This decision necessitated the creation of standards by which teachers would be credited with specialized learning. The final outcome for ESL, starting in about 1976, was the evolution of the old Ministry of Education summer course in ESL into the three-part Additional Qualification program in ESL, still existing today, taught by the faculties of education. By completing all three parts of this program, a certified teacher becomes an ESL specialist. The impact of this program was substantial in that school boards and other institutions could use it to assess candidates for teaching positions in ESL; many began to require it as a basic qualification. These developments were, in effect, the professionalization of ESL teachers and their integration into the schools, with significant but lesser impact on the colleges and NGOs.

Also in the 1970s, the province divided education and training delivery into two and then three Ministries: one with responsibility for the schools;

a second with responsibility for post-secondary, mainly credit education and training, but also including the Manpower adult ESL programs in the colleges; and a third with responsibility for mainly non-credit training relating to the labor force, including adult literacy and private sector interests. All three of these jurisdictions still included adult non-credit programs for immigrants and others. In 1980, the Ontario Ministries of Education and Colleges and Universities published a discussion paper about continuing education, that is, non-credit formal education that is neither elementary/secondary nor post-secondary (colleges and universities). This paper focused rather narrowly on the need for employment-related training and adult literacy. It did not mention ESL. An underlying political issue was which ministry(ies) would have the fiscal burden for continuing education. Over the next six years, adult literacy as a purported damper on the economy became a high profile issue, both federally and provincially. Then in 1986, the Ontario Ministry of Colleges and Universities published *Continuing Education Review Project—Project report: For adults only* (Ontario Ministry of Colleges and Universities, 1986). It established separate responsibilities for secondary schools, colleges, and universities with respect to adult literacy, ESL and FSL, Franco-Ontarians, older adults, and people with special needs. It ensured that school boards could not charge a tuition fee for adult basic education or ESL and that universities and colleges would be restricted in the amount they could charge. A clear distinction was drawn between credit and non-credit courses; ESL and adult literacy were largely in the latter category. A result of this division of responsibilities was that people teaching adult non-credit courses did not have to be certified teachers. Although the report comments about the need for well-trained ESL teachers, it does not specify suitable qualifications.

Coordination in the arcane and complex system of language training funding and delivery has been a constant problem (e.g., Burnaby, 1992; Canada Employment and Immigration Advisory Council, 1991). The federal ESL Manpower program had been criticized on a number of serious grounds, including discrimination and poor quality (Burnaby, 1998b). Therefore, in 1983, the Canada Employment and Immigration Commission (CEIC) sent out a discussion paper proposing to amalgamate the Manpower program and CILT, thereby creating one new program. The main component would be a general purposes program for all newcomers immediately after their arrival in Canada. Stipends would not be available, but services such as child care and transportation might be arranged. A second smaller component would be made available for those who needed specific language training before they could enter the labor force (CEIC, 1983). The delivery model for this proposed program was that it would contract directly with NGOs or any other educational institutions rather than going directly through a provincial government. Such a change would permit the federal government to: (1) make its own decisions about service programs and delivery agencies; (2) avoid the wage scales of unionized teachers in provincial educational institutions; and (3) keep delivery agencies competitive and accountable on one-year contracts while being reimbursed less for sustained administrative costs. In 1986–1987, CEIC launched a pilot of the general program for newly arrived immigrants, called the Settlement Language Training Program, which was judged to be successful, except that delays in financing caused severe problems for some of the delivery agencies (Burnaby, Holt, Steltzer, & Collins, 1987). Meanwhile, the CILT program was eliminated, thus reducing the federal programs from two to one. The federal government was gaining very little recognition for its expenditures through CILT and had virtually no control over what the provinces would charge back against the program.

Despite this experiment in a more general yet flexible federal language training program, the federal government revamped the Manpower program in the late 1980s. Then, in 1990, the federal government introduced a new immigration plan that included a completely revised adult language training program. This new program replaced the Manpower program with the current Language Instruction for Newcomers to Canada (LINC) for all immigrants in their first three years in Canada, and Labour Market Language Training (LMLT), a smaller, more restricted program for LINC graduates. Delivery agencies and their teaching programs are selected as they were for the Settlement Language Training Program, that is, through annual competition of proposals from any suitable agency (colleges, school boards, NGOs, private agencies) (Immigration Canada, 1993), thus bypassing the community colleges unless they can come in with a competitive bid. In addition, all immigrants who want to enter the program are assessed at a special center on the basis of national language benchmarks, including one level for those not literate in their first language. These benchmarks also relate to curriculum so that the content of programs across the country can be coordinated. After assessment, immigrants are given a list of local programs which could serve their needs.

This program has been criticized in that it only serves immigrants in their first three years in the country, that its annual proposal and reporting structure causes a great deal of stress for delivery agencies, especially small organizations, and that the national benchmarks may be a good description of language levels, but do not address the many kinds of diversity (particularly lack of literacy skills) that immigrant language learners bring to the classroom (Cray, 1997; Goldstein, 1993). Flemming (1998) objects to the benchmarks on the grounds that they are a throwback to the era of experts imposing on teachers' autonomy and professionalism, and adds that they represent potential dangers if they are proposed as a reliable indicator of what actually is needed in ESL classrooms.

In 1998, a study was commissioned of all adult ESL/FSL services in Ontario (Power Analysis Inc., 1998). Among training providers that serve adult immigrants (rather than universities and private sector firms that largely serve foreign students), LINC programs accounted for 39% of all the Ontario programs, and 48% of the programs combined LINC with ESL supported from other sources. It is unfortunately not possible to determine the extent to which LINC classes took over the load from the Manpower program. Community agencies provided most of the LINC and half of the combined LINC/ESL programs. School boards offered almost all of the ESL programs, about 35% of the combined LINC/ESL programs, but very few of the LINC-only. The ESL-only classes were about 80% non-credit. Classes typically had about 17 students; almost all had continuous intake of students; a quarter were multilevel classes; and few used alternate forms of delivery. Four percent of students had no education at all and 13% had not reached high school (Power Analysis Inc., 1998). Women comprised 69% of the students. Except for the class sizes, these educational conditions are significantly challenging (Cray, 1997).

As for the teachers, school boards employed 70% of the LINC/ESL instructors while community agencies employed only 10% because the boards supply many of the teachers to agencies for the classes. For all types of programs, 86% of the teachers were women, 35% were not native speakers of English, and 56% considered themselves fluent in another language as well as English. Although they were almost universally highly qualified, the teachers averaged 20.6 hours a week; only 29% were permanent employees; the average hourly wage was $28.65; 40% had no benefits (most of those who did had only sick days); and 42% belonged to a union. The teachers and administrators agreed that funding was by far the biggest problem (Power Analysis Inc., 1998).

Whatever the strengths and shortcomings of LINC, the federal government plans to devolve all its responsibility for adult ESL programs for immigrants to the Ontario government, as it already has in British Columbia and Manitoba. Work continues federally at the Centre for Canadian Language Benchmarks, now a federal agency at arms' length from the government, with respect to how these standards will be used by the provinces. In preparation for the devolution of the federal ESL enterprise to Ontario, the province simplified its own operations related to adult ESL. It closed down, by 1996, all of the ESL programs in what was called the Citizenship Branch, except for those which are settlement-related, such as access to the professions and trades in Ontario. An office within the Ministry of Education and Training is preparing to coordinate all adult language training for immigrants. Measures for school board accountability for adult ESL and literacy are under consideration. Also TESL Ontario was funded to produce a set of standards for non-credit adult ESL instructors in Ontario. In research for this project (Sanaoui, 1996, 1997, 1998), it became clear, as it did in the Power Analysis Inc. (1998) report, that current teachers of adult non-credit ESL are generally very well qualified. The resulting standards will be used in the current LINC process and future provincial programs in choosing among proposed programs and in accountability efforts.

In sum, then, the federal government started in the 1940s to fund the provinces for ESL for adult immigrants through NGOs and school boards for settlement purposes, and in the 1960s through community colleges for labor development. As economic problems arose in the 1980s, it sought to reduce its costs by contracting adult ESL, not through the provinces but directly to delivery agencies, thus largely bypassing union wage standards and the power of the provinces themselves. As a result, the federal government has transferred its entire enterprise of ESL delivery for adults in Ontario to community programs, mainly school boards and NGOs, most with challenging teaching conditions. The employment conditions for the teachers under LINC (and other adult ESL) are highly unfavorable, despite teachers' high qualifications, and funding is precarious. Federal adult ESL delivery is being devolved entirely to the province in Ontario.

Like the federal government, the Ontario government began by dealing through the Ministry of Education with educational programs for adult immigrants through school boards and NGOs, then expanded its programs in the 1960s into other areas under the Citizenship Branch and other government bodies, but is in the process of reconsolidating most of these activities again under the Ministry of Education. The Ministry has fiercely and effectively guarded itself against any changes that would impinge on the Education Act directly and its legislated responsibility for the qualifications of teachers. Teachers of non-credit adult ESL through school boards do not have to have the same credentials as those teaching regular school programs. The school boards' continuing education programs more closely resemble those in NGOs rather than schooling under the Education Act. (One partial advantage that they have over NGOs in the competition for training dollars is a somewhat more secure infrastructure to sustain them in the competitive process as long as the boards consider it worthwhile to continue to compete.) The Citizenship Branch and the school boards originally were creative in supporting NGOs and developing outreach programs on language and settlement, but the Citizenship Branch was closed down in the mid-1990s in anticipation of the creation of one blanket provincial ESL and settlement program.

In this process, both levels of government were instrumental in the early professionalization of ESL teachers, but eventually deprofessionalized teachers of non-credit ESL programs and allowed their job conditions to deteriorate. Since the flow of money in the 1980s slowed down and the federal government began to fund on a competitive basis, both mainstream and immigrant group-specific NGOs and school board adult ESL programs have increasingly struggled under the competitive and accountability exigencies of current adult ESL funding (Owen, 1999). Such circumstances for adult ESL are reported as similar in the United States (Chisman, Wrigley & Ewen, 1993).

POLICY (AND LACK OF IT) IN ABORIGINAL LANGUAGE EDUCATION

People who report themselves as ethnically Aboriginal in Canada comprise about one percent of Canada's population. The 10,000 Cree on the east coast of James Bay mostly speak their ancestral language as a mother tongue (unlike about 75% of Aboriginal people in the country), and are thus a small linguistic and cultural minority embedded in the population of Canada within layers of other groups with their own linguistic and cultural agendas and struggles. How the Cree people chose Cree as the language of instruction in their schools is worth documenting and exploring, given: (a) the small size of the group; (b) the great sociolinguistic differences between Cree and most other languages in the country; and (c) the rarity of the use of a language other than English or French as medium of instruction in formal schooling. The use of Cree in schools is a striking example of resistance to well-ingrained beliefs underlying most instances of colonial language imposition on minority language groups. Such widely held beliefs include the following: English is best taught monolingually; the earlier English is taught, the better the results; and the more English is taught, the better the results (Phillipson, 1992). Such beliefs conflict with the 1953 UNESCO declaration that it is best to teach a child in his or her mother tongue, at least for the first few years of schooling (UNESCO, 1953), as well as Cummins' contention that early mother tongue development supports not only the learning of the mother tongue but the second language as well (Cummins, 1991). These basic positions clash in the Cree School Board debate over language and culture learning.

In the early 1990s, nine Cree communities on the eastern shores of James Bay and inland began work on a pilot project to use Cree as the language of instruction (CLIP) for Grade 1 in two communities. In the past decade, the communities have extended use of Cree so that Cree is now the main language of instruction up to Grade 4 (the target level) in most of their schools. Under Cree leadership, the Cree School Board initiated CLIP as an experimental alternative to English or French as medium of instruction. English or French is taught as a subject of instruction and the medium of one or two subjects (such as art and physical education) starting in Grade 2. At Grade 4, the main medium of instruction becomes English or French, but a number of subjects, such as Cree literacy, Cree culture, and moral instruction, continue to be taught in Cree. Schools in the first two communities involved, Chisasibi and Waskaganish, have had cohorts of students who have reached Grade 4 through CLIP. Other communities joined the program in subsequent years. After the first few years of the pilot, Cree School Board authorities made the program compulsory in the communities as long as they had the personnel to staff the Cree medium program.

In the past several hundred years, the Crees east of James Bay, traditionally hunters and gatherers, altered their economy through the fur trade to include trapping. After the federal Indian Act was signed in 1876, these Cree people were identified legally as Indians, and their administrative affairs were handled by the federal government. They generally learned English if they acquired a European second language. Toward the middle of this century, the Crees began settling permanently into communities on the coast and inland, becoming more involved in wage labor occupations, although many still practice traditional occupations full- or part-time (Tanner, 1981). Given the geographic isolation of the area, Cree are still greatly in the majority in that part of northern Quebec.

In the 19th century, Christian missionaries and Cree from the Ontario side of James Bay introduced a syllabic system of writing Cree that was developed for Ojibwe by an English missionary in the 1840s (Nichols, 1996). For more than a century, people in the James Bay area have used syllabics mainly to write letters and for Christian observances. People were taught to use syllabics through the church or by family members, usually when they became adults; few read it well enough to recover new meaning from unknown text (Burnaby & MacKenzie, 1985; MacKenzie, 1985; Valentine, 1995).

Formal schooling in the European style was late to come to the James Bay east coast. Old federal policies favored paying Christian organizations to provide education for Aboriginal children. Starting in the 1940s, many children from this area were taken away to residential schools, a practice now deeply resented in the James Bay communities (Bobbish, 1996). Some children were away from their families for as long as nine years. In the 1960s, in the tradition of many mission schools, at least some Cree was used as subject or medium of instruction in local schools (Preston & MacKenzie, 1976). The provincial curriculum of Quebec was the nominal standard, but there was no mechanism for coordination among and within schools. Preston and MacKenzie, in reviewing this situation in 1976, point to the basic problem in education in the area as lack of decision making (power or assertiveness) from the community level. Most of the certified teachers in the late 1960s and early 1970s were non-Aboriginals from outside the Cree communities. A few Crees enrolled in a special one-year teacher training program in Montreal in 1969–1970. From 1969 to 1976, the Department of Indian Affairs and Northern Development (DIAND) provided training for Cree people to become teacher aides. These people often were given full control over early elementary grade classrooms (Preston & MacKenzie, 1976), and sometimes taught those classes almost entirely in Cree. In many cases, those with teacher aide training became the instructors of Cree literacy as a subject of instruction (Tanner, 1981).

At the national level, as discussed above, in the 1960s the focus of politics was on relations between francophone and anglophone Canada, couched largely as a language issue. The 1969 Official Languages Act was passed and Quebec passed legislation which put severe restrictions on using any language other than French as the medium of instruction in schools in the province. Also, in order to assert its sovereignty and for economic reasons, the Quebec government began to pay attention to the vast northern region of its territory which had, up to that time, largely been administered by the federal government. In 1969, in a debate linked to the issue of anglophone-francophone relations, then-Minister of Indian Affairs and Northern Development, Jean Chrétien, tabled a White Paper in Parliament proposing that the Indian Act be abolished, on the grounds that it was racist, and instead recommended that the people designated as Indians under the Act be henceforth treated as any other citizens. Aboriginal response to this proposal was swift and almost completely negative. The most prominent statement, called *Indian Control of Indian Education* (National Indian Brotherhood, 1972), demanded that the federal government retain fiscal responsibility for Aboriginal education but that control should be given to the parents of Aboriginal children. In the document, detailed requirements were set out for the central role of Aboriginal languages as medium and subject of instruction in education for first and second language learners (pp. 14–16). The rationale for Aboriginal language education was that it would lead to better comprehension of content in the early grades, better identity reinforcement, and reversal of overall trends towards Aboriginal language loss.

In the early 1970s, Aboriginal language use was clearly declining. According to the census, the percentage of people who identified themselves as being of Aboriginal ancestry and having an Aboriginal language as a mother tongue dropped from 75.7% in 1961 to 57.1% in 1971

(Burnaby & Beaujot, 1986, p. 36). With very little coordination, Aboriginal languages were beginning to be introduced as subjects of instruction (as first or second languages) in various places across the country. Wasacase (1976) and Kirkness (1976) promoted a more ambitious model of Aboriginal language instruction in which the Aboriginal language would be the medium of instruction in the first few years of school, while English was slowly introduced until it was the medium for about half the school day by Grade 4. This model was ambitious because the Aboriginal languages had virtually never been used before in western style education; pedagogical approaches, trained teachers, curriculum, materials, and school support services appropriate for them had never been developed. In Manitoba in the early 1970s, this approach was implemented in several communities in the north where children came to school speaking an Aboriginal language. The program survived for a number of years, particularly in one community, but was reduced to subject of instruction eventually. In Ontario, in concert with the Manitoba initiative and also reflecting the French immersion model, an Ojibwe community on Manitoulin Island had an Ojibwe medium of instruction program for English speaking Ojibwe children for several years (Wasacase, n.d.). In neither of these cases did local people have control over their children's education nor were their initiatives linked administratively to the authority of a school board.

In Quebec in the early 1970s, a similar model to Wasacase's and Kirkness' was promoted by Gagné (1979) for Aboriginal languages in that province. In 1972, the Native North American Studies Institute was created under the leadership of the Quebec office of DIAND, which promoted the training of Aboriginal teachers to teach through the medium of their languages in their schools (Bourque, 1979; Gagné, 1979). From 1973 to 1976, the Institute offered summer programs at La Macaza, Quebec, to train teachers under the auspices of the University of Quebec at Chicoutimi. The first Crees who attended this program had been Cree language teachers. An emphasis in this program was on Aboriginal language materials development and underlying linguistic work, such as dictionaries and orthography standardization. The need became evident for Aboriginal language speakers trained in research and development, so a program was created to train "technolinguists" in both linguistics and education methods. After several years, the main program was organized into Stream A (for teachers to teach through the medium of their Aboriginal language) and Stream B (for teachers to teach Aboriginal children through English as a second language) (Preston & MacKenzie, 1976). Also, from 1973–1976, an exceptional undertaking, the Cree Way Project, was conducted out of Waskaganish, a community in the James Bay Cree area, to produce teaching materials and resources, mostly in Cree, for schools. The intent was to make available classroom materials that reflected the local language, culture, and approach to learning. This productive operation was at arms length from government school authorities (Preston & MacKenzie, 1976; Tanner, 1981).

As part of its interest in asserting sovereignty over arctic Quebec, the Quebec government decided to exploit the economic potential of the broad rivers which flow westward into James Bay by building hydroelectric dams. This meant negotiating with the federal government and the Crees and the Inuit in this area to work out its jurisdiction. In the end, two large areas were identified, one for the Crees and the other for the Inuit, each to be administered under a locally controlled government rather like that of a municipality. Within the Cree Regional Authority thus created, the Cree School Board was formed in 1978. It operates basically as a regular provincial school board, but is released from a number of provincial regulations to permit, among other things, the use of Cree as a medium of instruction in schools (Tanner, 1981). Given the rigor with which Quebec has implemented its law to have French as the medium of instruction for almost all children in the province, this concession was not inconsiderable. Since the late seventies, most Cree School Board communities offer both French or English as options for medium of instruction. From 1976, McGill University took over teacher training for the Cree School Board, including supervision of teachers-in-training in their home communities, and over the years, the University developed a system of offering many of its courses in the communities as well. The Stream A and Stream B system was maintained.

The new Cree School Board was given considerable latitude through the James Bay Agreement to create curriculum based on local language and culture within the basic curriculum framework for Quebec schools. It commissioned a position paper (Curriculum Development Team, 1979), which proposed four potential program types, ranging from no Cree medium instruction to all Cree medium instruction from kindergarten to the end of high school. The position paper also included an extended discussion of how Cree cultural elements could be incorporated into the curriculum and the need for Cree language and materials development to support a Cree medium program. The Council had already allowed for the teaching of Cree literacy as a subject of instruction, and for Cree to be the medium for moral and religious instruction and for physical education (Tanner, 1981). At the same time, the Katavik School Board, the sister Inuit school board to the Cree School Board created by the James Bay Agreement in arctic Quebec, began a gradual increase in the use of Inuktitut up to Grade 4. Use of Inuktitut was extended community by community, grade by grade, through the use of classroom assistants and teachers-in-training, while more teacher training, research, and curriculum development continued

(Stairs, 1985). This model still exists at Katavik. Also, between 1982 and 1987, the Innu (Montagnais) community of Betsiamites on the north shore of the St. Lawrence River experimented with an Innu medium of instruction program with transition to French from pre-kindergarten to the Grade 3 level. The program was terminated after the final year of the first cohort, despite extensive teacher, materials, and curriculum preparation (Drapeau, 1992).

Although the Cree School Board worked toward the development of Cree medium of instruction with gradual transition to English or French, there were immediate problems with this approach. Tanner, an anthropologist, was hired in 1981 to research the background of the issue and to survey parents' attitudes. His summary of grounds for opposition to the program included: Cree-speaking teachers with full certifications to teach in regular classrooms (i.e., not just Cree as a subject of instruction) were trained to teach in English or French, not Cree; only two of 11 teachers knew the Cree writing system; materials were scarce and curriculum inadequate; and parents expected English or French to be taught from the beginning to prepare children for later school demands (Tanner, 1981). Tanner found that parents in communities with more traditional economies tended to prefer the options with more Cree, while those with less traditional economies tended towards more English/French. Parents were particularly worried about their children becoming literate in Cree before English or French (see also Drapeau for similar concerns in Betsiamites). Like Preston and MacKenzie in 1976, Tanner focused his analysis on the need for clear and consistent goals for the language program and problems resulting from lack of integration with the goals of the rest of the school curriculum.

Between 1981, with Tanner's report, and 1993, when the CLIP program was initiated in two communities, the use of Cree in the Cree School Board schools remained little different from what it had been in the early 1970s. However, other changes were taking place that could alter the conditions for Cree medium instruction. Work begun at La Macaza and called for by the Curriculum Development Team (1979) on orthography standardization and training of technolinguists continued through various phases, resulting in a dictionary, teacher support materials, and a great deal of awareness of language issues on the part of local teachers and curriculum support professionals (MacKenzie, 1985). The teacher training programs continued to certify local people as fully credentialed teachers, who then gained experience in the schools. In the early 1990s, a language teachers' specialization was initiated within the teacher training program. The original intent of Stream A as a program for teachers to teach in Cree as a medium of instruction gained interest, and the new specialization offered support for the literacy and pedagogical needs of B Stream teachers contemplating Cree medium teaching. Teachers and pedagogical coun-selors at the Cree School Board participated in the development of an ESL language arts program for Aboriginal children in northern communities (Burnaby et al., 1986–88). This program served not only as a set of mate-rials for use in Cree School Board English classrooms but also as a model of language arts and curriculum design. A document was produced out-lining the Cree values and knowledge that community members agreed should be part of school education. These values were integrated with the framework of the Quebec Ministry of Education's (MEQ) curriculum. In addition, the communities settled economically, politically, and socially into their new situation under the Grand Council of the Crees.

About this time, Bobbish (1996, originally written in 1992), Director of Education Services of the Cree School Board, described the Crees as con-cerned about diminishing levels of Cree language maintenance. He also noted that: parents' acceptance of English-French medium education had not resulted in much educational success; Cree had been further weak-ened by the advent of electronic media in the communities in 1975; chil-dren's Cree identity had been weakened by immersion from an early age in an irrelevant curriculum; Cree language and culture taught as subjects of instruction were just add-ons to the curriculum; and teaching children literacy in Cree syllabics was ineffective because the children were not adequately fluent in oral Cree first (pp. 245–247).

In December, 1988, the Council of Commissioners of the Crees decided to implement its education plan by creating a Cree language policy. Also, a group of people in Chisasibi strongly lobbied the Cree School Board to institute a school program using Cree as the language of instruction, at least for the first few grades. In 1992 a pilot Cree-medium program was planned for the communities of Chisasibi and Waskaganish. For a year, teachers were prepared; a curriculum combining the MEQ's framework, the Cree values curriculum, and a language arts approach was created; and materials were developed, adapted, or translated. The evaluation of the first year (1993–94) noted the success of the program but listed predictable issues yet to be dealt with such as the need for more literature in Cree; language support for the teachers; community education to involve other teachers, parents and others in the program; the need for various normal educational supports (e.g., methods of student evaluation); better planning for future years and revisions; and better integration with other school programs (Burnaby et al., 1994). In the second year, Grade 2 levels were added in the original schools and Grade 1 was started in various others. The evaluation for that year expressed similar overall satisfaction with the program and general needs as well. The program has continued in this vein. After the first few years of success as a pilot, the Council of Commissioners decided to make the program mandatory in all its schools except where there was not sufficient qualified personnel to staff it.

In sum, after decades of painful submersion in highly assimilative forms of education, the Cree leadership and communities have been able to create a unique situation for themselves that promises to lead toward their stated goal for their children of both succeeding in mainstream formal education and retaining their language and culture. The success of the program is due to several factors. First, important mainstream institutions had some of same goals as the Crees, such as Cree language and cultural development, training for Cree subject and language teachers and community language workers, and support for orthography and literacy work. Second, the politics of language in Quebec and in national politics, Quebec's expansion into the north, and the James Bay Agreement and the resulting formation of the Cree Regional Authority undoubtedly contributed to the outcome. Third, effective Cree leadership took the situation in hand and made the best of the possibilities for local control. In particular, the decision to take advantage of economy of scale by having their own school board for nine communities was crucial. This decision helped win parents' support for the School Board's second attempt to make Cree the language of instruction. In addition, the Board wisely launched a pilot project to build further confidence in the instructional model, particularly in having Cree as the first language of literacy. If we are to hope for more examples of this kind of creative synthesis of diverse language and cultural elements in education, then we need to learn from this example of effective local control, development of human resources, unique cultural attitudes to language and literacy, and economies of scale in educational administration.

CONCLUSIONS

These three examples serve to illustrate the complex interface between language and governance. As shown here, sweeping federal policies do not necessarily affect language behavior, even when the policies are widely publicized and the focus of intense national debate. Moreover, language can be used as a symbol in struggles that are really over something else, and governments may manipulate employees (especially if they are women or visible minorities) and clients (especially if they do not have the vote). The Cree example demonstrates that local control makes a major difference in minority language situations (though it is not a panacea), and that mainstream initiatives may help minority projects. Finally, the size of the population may affect the ability of local leaders to mobilize support for locally controlled initiatives.

REFERENCES

Beaujot, R. (1998). Demographic considerations in Canadian language policy. In T. Ricento &
  B. Burnaby (Eds.), *Language and politics in the United States and Canada: Myths and realities*
  (pp. 71–83). Mahwah, NJ: Lawrence Erlbaum.

Bobbish, J. (1996). The future of the Cree language. In J. Maurais (Ed.), *Quebec's aboriginal
  languages: History, planning and development* (pp. 244–249). Clevedon: Multilingual Matters.

Bourque, V. (1979). *Amerindianization Project report 1972–1979*. Quebec City: Department of
  Indian and Northern Affairs.

Burnaby, B. (1992). Official language training for adult immigrants in Canada: Features
  and issues. In B. Burnaby & A. Cumming (Eds.), *Socio-political aspects of ESL in Canada*
  (pp. 3–34). Toronto: OISE Press.

Burnaby, B. (1998a). English as a second language for adult immigrants. In S.M. Scott,
  B. Spencer & A. Thomas (Eds.), *Learning for life: Canadian readings in adult education*
  (pp. 283–295). Toronto: Thompson Educational Publishing.

Burnaby, B. (1998b). ESL policy in Canada and the United States: Basis for comparison. In
  T. Ricento & B. Burnaby (Eds.), *Language and politics in the United States and Canada: Myths
  and realities* (pp. 243–267). Mahwah, NJ: Lawrence Erlbaum.

Burnaby, B. & Beaujot, R. (1986). *The use of Aboriginal languages in Canada: An analysis of 1981
  census data*. Ottawa: Social Trends Analysis Directorate and Native Citizens Directorate,
  Department of the Secretary of State.

Burnaby, B., Faries, E., Fietz O., & McAlpine, L. (1994). *Cree Language of instruction grade one
  program: Report of external evaluators*. Chisasibi, Quebec: Council of Commissioners of the
  Cree School Board.

Burnaby, B., Holt, M., Steltzer, N., & Collins, N. (1987). *The Settlement Language Training Program: An assessment (Report on behalf of the TESL Canada Federation)*. Ottawa: Employment
  and Immigration Canada.

Burnaby, B. & MacKenzie, M. (1985). Reading and writing in Rupert House. In B. Burnaby
  (Ed.), *Promoting Native writing systems in Canada* (pp. 57–81). Toronto: OISE Press.

Burnaby, B., McInnes, J., Guebert, L., Izatt, M., Speares, J., & Upper, M. (1986–88). *Circle: An
  ESL and reading program for Cree and Ojibwe speaking children*. Markham, Ontario: Fitzhenry
  and Whiteside.

Burnaby, B. & Ricento, T. (1998). Conclusions: Myths and realities. In T. Ricento & B. Burnaby
  (Eds.), *Language and politics in the United States and Canada: Myths and realities* (pp. 331–343).
  Mahwah, NJ: Lawrence Erlbaum.

Canada Employment and Immigration Advisory Council. (1991). *Immigrants and language
  training*. Ottawa: Canada Employment and Immigration.

Canada Employment and Immigration Commission. (1983). *A discussion paper on a new framework for immigrant language training*. Ottawa: CEIC.

Chisman, F,. Wrigley, H. S., & Ewen, D. T. (1993). *ESL and the American dream*. Southport, CT:
  Southport Institute for Policy Analysis.

Cray, E. (1997). Teachers' perceptions of a language policy: "Teaching LINC". *TESL Canada
  Journal, 15*:1, 238.

Cummins, J. (1991). Interdependence of first- and second-language proficiency in bilingual children. In E. Bialystock (Ed.), *Language processing in bilingual children* (pp. 70–89).
  Cambridge: Cambridge University Press.

Curriculum Development Team. (1979). *Position paper: Bilingual education, Cree as a language
  of instruction*. Val d'Or, Quebec: Council of Commissioners of the Cree School Board.

Drapeau, L. (1992). *Rapport final sure le projet-pilot de Betsiamites: Étude longitudinale (1982–1990)*.
  Montreal: Département de linguistique, Université du Québec á Montréal.

Flemming, D. (1998). Autonomy and agency in curriculum decision-making: A study of instructors in a Canadian adult settlement ESL program. *TESL Canada Journal, 16*(1), 19–35.

Gagné, R. (1979). The maintenance of Native languages. In J. Chambers (Ed.), *The languages of Canada*, (pp. 115–129). Montreal: Didier.

Goldstein, T. (1993). Working with learners in LINC programs: Asking ourselves some questions. *Contact: Newsletter of the Association of Teachers of English as a Second Language of Ontario, 18*(2), 12–13.

Immigration Canada (1993). *Immigration consultations 1993: The Federal Immigration Integration Strategy in 1993: A progress report*. Ottawa: Employment and Immigration Canada.

Kirkness, V. (1976). *Manitoba Native Bilingual Program: A handbook*. Ottawa: Indian and Northern Affairs, Education and Cultural Development.

Labrie, N. (1992). The role of pressure groups in the change of status of French in Quebec since 1960. In U. Ammon & M. Hellinger (Eds.), *Status change of languages* (pp. 17–43). Berlin: De Gruyter Verlag.

MacKenzie, M. (1985). Spelling reform among the James Bay Cree. In B. Burnaby (Ed.), *Promoting Native writing systems in Canada* (pp. 49–55). Toronto: OISE Press.

Mewhort, D. S., Milloy, A. B., Sweetman, N. A., & Gore, G. M. (1965). Untitled report. Toronto: Board of Education of the City of Toronto, Office of the Director of Education.

National Indian Brotherhood. (1972). *Indian control of Indian education*. Ottawa: National Indian Brotherhood.

Neatby, B. (1992). Introduction. In Office of the Commissioner of Official Languages, *Our two official languages over time* (pp. iii–ix). Ottawa: Office of the Commissioner of Official Languages.

Nichols, J. (1996). The Cree syllabary. In P. T. Daniels & W. Bright (Eds.), *The world's writing systems* (pp. 599–611). Oxford: Oxford University Press.

Ontario Ministry of Colleges and Universities. (1986). *Continuing Education Review Project—Project Report: For adults only*. Toronto: Ontario Ministry of Colleges and Universities.

Owen, T. (1999). *The view from Toronto: Settlement services in the late 1990s*. Paper presented at the Third National Metropolis Conference, Vancouver, British Columbia.

Pal, L. A. (1993). *Interests of state: The politics of language, multiculturalism, and feminism in Canada*. Montreal and Kingston: McGill-Queen's University Press.

Peat, Marwick & Partners & Churchill, S. (1987). *Evaluation of the Official Languages in Education Program: Final report*. Ottawa: Peat, Marwick & Partners.

Phillipson, R. (1992). *Linguistic imperialism*. Oxford, England: Oxford University Press.

Power Analysis Inc. (1998). *Study of ESL/FSL services in Ontario: Final report*. London, Ontario: Power Analysis Inc.

Preston, R., & MacKenzie, M. (1976). *A comprehensive study of the educational needs of the communities comprising the Grand Council of the Crees (of Quebec)*. Val d'Or, Quebec: Grand Council of the Crees of Quebec.

Saouab, A. (1993). *Canadian multiculturalism*. Ottawa: Library of Parliament, Research Branch, Supply and Services Canada.

Sanaoui, R. (1996). Characteristics of instructors teaching non-credit adult ESL in Ontario: A progress report on TESL Ontario's research study. *Contact, 21*(2), 29–30.

Sanaoui, R. (1997). Professional characteristics and concerns of instructors teaching English as a second language to adults in non-credit programs in Ontario. *TESL Canada Journal, 14*(2), 32–54.

Sanaoui, R. (1998). *The development of a protocol and uniform standards for the certification of instructors teaching non-credit ESL to adults in Ontario: Phase 3: Draft report on the Steering Committee's recommendations*. Toronto: TESL Ontario.

Stairs, A. (1985). The developmental context of Native language literacy: Inuit children and Inuktitut education. In B. Burnaby (Ed.), *Promoting Native writing systems in Canada* (pp. 33–48). Toronto: OISE Press.

Tanner, A. (1981). *Establishing a Native language education policy: A study based on the views of Cree parents in the James Bay region of Quebec.* Val d'Or, Quebec: Grand Council of the Crees of Quebec.

Thomas, A. M. (1987). Government and adult learning. In F. Cassidy & R. Faris (Eds.), *Choosing our future: Adult education and public policy in Canada,* Symposium Series 17 (pp. 103–130). Toronto: OISE Press.

UNESCO. (1953). *The use of vernacular language in education.* Paris: UNESCO.

Valentine, L. (1995). *Making it their own: Severn Ojibwe communicative practice.* Toronto: University of Toronto Press, Anthropological Horizons Series.

Veltman, C. (1998). Quebec, Canada, and the United States: Social reality and language rights. In T. Ricento & B. Burnaby (Eds.), *Language and politics in the United States and Canada: Myths and realities* (pp. 301–315). Mahwah, NJ: Lawrence Erlbaum.

Wardhaugh, R. (1983). *Language and nationhood: The Canadian experience.* Vancouver: Star Books.

Wasacase, I. (n.d.). *Bilingual "immersion" Native language Ojibwe pilot project, West Bay, Ontario.* Ottawa: Department of Indian Affairs and Northern Development.

Wasacase, I. (1976). Native bilingual-bicultural education programs. *Dialogue, 3*:1, 2–8 (publication of the Indian and Eskimo Affairs Program of the Department of Indian and Northern Affairs).

III

Language Policy and Governance

The chapters in Part III explore the following critical issue: How do state authorities use language policy for the purposes of political and cultural governance? In order to answer this question, two chapters in this section use the concept of "governmentality." While the term "government" usually refers to a macro-level concern with state authorities and particular political and administrative structures, "governmentality" focuses on the micro-level of how power functions at the level of diverse practices. That is, the focus is on the strategies and techniques by which state authorities seek to enact programs and policies. But governmentality does not mean "implementation," a concept that implies a willful effort to carry out a planned program. Rather, governmentality refers to the complex array of forces (administrative, legal, financial, professional) and techniques that regulate individuals and groups with respect to state authority.

The chapters in this section examine language policy within the framework of governmentality. This perspective means that language policy analysis is not just a question of how particular policies promote or restrict particular languages, but rather, in Pennycook's words, "how debates around language, culture, and education produce particular discursive regimes." In Chapter 5, Pennycook examines language policy in Hong Kong within the discursive framework of colonialism. Educational language policies in colonial Hong Kong were directed towards preserving particular understandings of local cultures and languages and the promotion of particular languages *as means of social regulation*. Pennycook examines in particular the role of education in constructing Hong Kong Chinese as "docile," a crucial component in British governance of the colony. In his provocative conclusion, Pennycook extends his analytical approach to

other contexts, arguing that language policies—even when they are de-
bated within a discourse of "pluralism" and "cultural diversity" in liberal
democracies—are often part of a broad range of forces for control and
techniques for governance.

In Chapter 6, Helen Moore's analysis of language policymaking in
Australia in the 1990s also makes use of the concept of governmentality, in
this case to examine the successful effort by conservatives in Australia to
reassert the dominance of English and to roll back progressive policies promulgated in the 1987 National Policy on Languages. Moore describes how
conservative politicians and other state authorities managed to limit the
influence of linguistic minority communities and professional language
educators by defining them as "factions," thereby limiting their ability
to influence policies ostensibly designed to promote the "national" interest. Moore's analysis of the intense debates that preceded policy decisions
demonstrates how language policymaking in Australia during the 1990s
was fundamentally determined not by pedagogical aims and concerns, but
by political struggles. Her analysis shows further that minority communities and educators who wish to play a role in shaping language policies in
education must learn to become effective advocates within policymaking
processes that are "fraught with politics."

In Chapter 7, Donahue's complex and wide-ranging analysis is concerned with the politics of the Official English movement in the state of
Arizona in the United States. The chapter begins with a discussion of
anomie in American politics. In Official English controversies, citizens are
asked to make important decisions about language policy with little information about the role of official languages, the consequences of voter
initiatives, or constitutional constraints on language policies. The result,
in Donahue's words, has been "a frustrating sense of anomic normlessness." In such circumstances, the Official English movement leads many
citizens to support destructive and unconstitutional values, while shifting attention away from serious educational issues. Donahue analyzes
Official English by using "solipsism" as a central explicating concept. By
"solipsism," Donahue refers to "conditions under which the individual
has uncertain information" about the formation of the self and uncertain
knowledge about the relationship between the individual and the larger
community. He argues that the fractured and disrupted public discussion
of the Official English controversy is an example of a broader phenomenon:
the failure of education to offer formative connections between the individual and the community, thus resulting in isolated, solipsistic citizens.

Donahue places stakeholders in the Official English controversy within
three major ideological camps: the right-of-center group pluralist ideology; the left-of-center core-periphery ideology; and a centrist ideology.

Despite intensely felt differences among proponents of these views, Donahue shows that none of the participants in Arizona articulated a substantive ideological position, and that voters as a result were "pitted against each other" without regard to achieving a workable language policy for the state. Donahue then places this controversy within the broader history of public policy debate in the United States, specifically within the two competing ideologies of *Liberalism* and *Communitarianism*. In a brief analysis of how these ideologies are articulated in public policy debates in inconsistent and non-systematic ways, Donahue shows that citizens are left with ideologically incoherent public policy discussion. Donahue's concern is that under conditions of anomie, the manipulation of ideological confusion offers extraordinary opportunities for dominant groups to sustain their advantage. He is particularly critical of the liberal emphasis upon the solipsistic Self, which in his view is easily isolated and manipulated. Finally, Donahue asks how citizens may become better able to counter such forces and to decide important matters of language policy in an informed and coherent manner. He proposes a critical approach to education based upon the principles of *discipline, attachment*, and *autonomy*. Only through critical education will citizens be able to undertake the "aggressive analysis . . . cerebral and skeptical," that language policy requires.

5

Language Policy and Docile Bodies: Hong Kong and Governmentality

Alastair Pennycook
University of Technology, Sydney

Language policy has always been about far more than choosing which language to use in government, education, or the law. In addition, language policy involves the use of languages for purposes of cultural governance, or governmentality. Looking principally at colonial language policy in Hong Kong, I shall show how language policy was linked to a discursive construct of Hong Kong Chinese as politically passive (as docile political bodies), and simultaneously part of an attempt to bring about such docility through conservative educational curricula (as docile cultural bodies). I will argue that language policy is a crucial cornerstone of cultural governance that both reflects and produces constructions of the Other. This understanding of language policy has significant implications not just for Hong Kong in the present but for all contexts of language policy.

This approach to language policy is based on three interrelated principles: Foucault's notion of governmentality, his concept of docile bodies, and language policy as cultural politics. As developed by Foucault in his later work (e.g., 1991), the notion of governmentality focuses on how power operates at the micro level of diverse practices, rather than macro regulations of the state. Indeed, in the notion of governmentality, these micro and macro relations are elided. As Dean (1994) explains: "Rather than a theory of the state, Foucault proposes to analyze the operation of governmental power, the techniques and practices by which it works, and the rationalities and strategies invested in it" (p. 179). Rose (1996) explains further:

> As an array of technologies of government, governmentality is to be analyzed in terms of the strategies, techniques and procedures through which different authorities seek to enact programmes of government in relation to the materials and forces at hand and the resistances and oppositions anticipated or encountered. Hence this is not a matter of the implementation of idealized schema in the real by an act of will, but of the complex assemblage of diverse forces (legal, architectural, professional, administrative, financial, judgmental), techniques (notation, computation, calculation, examination, evaluation), devices (surveys and charts, systems of training, building forms) that promise to regulate decisions and actions of individuals, groups, and organizations in relation to authoritative criteria (p. 42).

The notion of governmentality, then, is significant for a number of reasons. First, it moves the analysis of governance away from the intentional and centralized strategies of government authorities toward the multiplicity of ways in which practices of governance may be realized. Thus our attention is shifted away from the state as an intentional actor that seeks to impose its will on the people, and instead much more localized and often contradictory operations of power are highlighted. The notion also implies that in order to understand the regulation of public life, we need to look not so much at laws, regulations, policing, or dominant ideologies, but instead at discourses, educational practices, and language use. Finally, the notion of governmentalilty sheds light on the ways in which the alleged shift from authoritarian government to liberal government, while on the one hand allowing greater democratic rights and freedoms, on the other hand may be accompanied by increasing forms of governmentality as the technologies of government diversify.

In the colonial context, the notion of governmentality focuses less on the formal modes of colonial and state control such as the military, law and bureaucratic apparatuses, and more on the formations of culture and knowledge produced by colonialism (see Cohn, 1996), as well as the growing number of localized moments of government in a diversity of practices and in a diversity of contexts. In language policy, therefore, the issue is not so much one of mapping out the formal policies that promote or restrict the use of certain languages, but instead how debates around language, culture, and education produce particular discursive regimes. Arguments for education in one language or another are thus not merely rationalizations of larger economic or political goals, but rather need to be understood within a broader cultural and historical field. In the context of Australia, for example, it may be possible to produce a genealogy of "protectionism" from the operation of the Aborigines Protection Board in the late 19th century to the work of linguists in the late 20th century. Thus this paper focuses on colonial language policy not so much as a site of particularly authoritarian modes of governance, but rather as a context that sheds light on the continuity of forms of governance and the increasing modes of governmentality in the change from colonial to other forms of government.

The second notion that guides this study is Foucault's "docile bodies." Mapping changes in European penal practices in the 18th and 19th centuries, Foucault examines the apparent liberalization of techniques of incarceration and punishment, such as the change from public hanging (and drawing and quartering) to more gentle and private means of execution. Although such changes appear to represent a more humane and liberal treatment of offenders, they also entailed increasing modes of surveillance, epitomized by the "panopticon," in which prisoners increasingly become subjected not merely to the assumed gaze of the warder but also to their own practices of self-monitoring. As particular forms of architecture, scheduling, and social organization in prisons, hospitals and schools were developed, and as particular regimes of knowledge grew up about "deviant" behavior, an array of disciplinary practices gradually came into being that helped construct the docile body.

> Thus discipline produces subjected and practiced bodies, "docile" bodies. Discipline increases the forces of the body (in economic terms of utility) and diminishes these same forces (in political terms of obedience)... If economic exploitation separates the force and the product of labour, let us say that disciplinary coercion establishes in the body the constricting link between an increased aptitude and an increased domination (Foucault, 1979, p. 138).

While the construction of docile bodies is only one aspect of governmentality, I am highlighting it here because of its particular salience in Hong Kong, where the physical production of docile bodies through the promotion of opium was replaced by educational and discursive means to construct the physically productive but politically passive Chinese body.

Finally, the third principle guiding my argument is that language policy is primarily cultural policy. By this notion, I do not mean simply that language and culture are connected and thus that language policy will always have cultural implications, nor that they are reducible to each other (and virtually isomorphic), but rather that language policies are fundamentally linked with political governance, educational curricula, and systems of morality; in short, they are about cultural opportunities and preferences. Thus arguments in favor of one language or another are part of broader moral and political visions. The central point is that language policy is concerned with what can be achieved culturally through language. Language policies are cultural policies, addressing questions of language within a far broader cultural field. To illustrate this argument, I shall look briefly at the development of language policies in different parts of the British empire, before turning to focus in more detail on the construction and regulation of docile bodies in Hong Kong.

COLONIAL LANGUAGE POLICIES AND THE REGULATION OF POSSIBILITY

One standard critical approach to language policy argues that colonialism should be seen as the first phase in linguistic imperialism (Phillipson, 1992). In this view, a cornerstone of colonial rule was the promotion and enforcement of colonial languages. Yet while the broader economic dictates of empire and the imperializing ideologies of Anglicism (pro-English policies) clearly played important roles within the empire, language policies were also tied to Orientalist views on the need to preserve colonized cultures in a pristine state of precolonial innocence, as well as to local conditions of control. Education was seen as a crucial means for more effective governance of the people, and language policy was one mechanism for effectively providing such education. As W. Fraser wrote in a letter to the Chief Secretary of the East India Company, W.B. Bayley, in 1823:

> It would be extremely ridiculous in me to sit down to write to the Government or to you a sentence even upon the benefit of teaching the children of the Peasantry of this country to read and write. I shall merely observe that the greatest difficulty this Government suffers, in its endeavours to govern well, springs from the immorality and ignorance of the mass of the people, their disregard of knowledge not connected with agriculture and cattle and particularly their ignorance of the spirit, principles and system of the British Government (Bureau of Education, 1920, p. 13).

Viewing education in the service of the (colonial) state was common during this period of expansion of educational provision both in Britain and its colonies. In the middle of the 19th century in Australia, the Reverend James Clow argued that "as the educated citizen is much more valuable to the State than an uneducated one, the State should do all in its power to further education" (Blake, 1973, p 24). As Smith explains in the context of education in Papua New Guinea: "Within the colonial context the type of education provided for subject peoples can be seen more as serving the requirements of those who provided it rather than those for whom

it was provided" (Smith, 1987, p. vii). While this may be the case for all
societies (education has always been provided largely in the interests of the
providers), it is particularly evident in colonial contexts, where "rulers and
ruled are separated not only by economic and political position but often
by other features such as race, colour, language and culture. Education,
then, was a means of political, economic and social control in the colonial
state" (p. vii).

Although the mechanism for ensuring that education instilled an understanding of the "spirit, principles and system of the British Government"
was sometimes to be found in policy providing an education in English, it
was far more widespread through the provision of education in vernacular
languages. The development of language policies in Malaya can be seen
to have followed a tendency to "play safe" and promote local languages
rather than English. In the 1884 report on education (Straits Settlements),
E.C. Hill, the Inspector of Schools for the colony, explained his reasons for
opposing an increase in education in English: "As pupils who acquire a
knowledge of English are invariably unwilling to earn their livelihood by
manual labor, the immediate result of affording an English education to
any large number of Malays would be the creation of a discontented class
who might become a source of anxiety to the community" (p. 171). This
commonly held position is echoed by Frank Swettenham's argument in the
Perak Government Gazette (6 July, 1894): "I am not in favour of extending
the number of 'English' schools except where there is some palpable desire
that English should be taught. Whilst we teach children to read and write
and count in their own languages, or in Malay ... we are *safe*" (emphasis
in original). As Loh Fook Seng (1970) concludes, "modern English education for the Malay then is ruled out right from the beginning as an unsafe
thing" (p. 114).

Although frequently couched in terms of a moral duty, the promotion
of vernacular education for the Malay population was closely linked to
questions of social control and local economic development. As George
Maxwell (Chief Secretary to the Government of the Federated Malay States,
1920–26) said in a speech in 1927, the main aims of education in Malaya
were "to improve the bulk of the people and to make the son of the fisherman or peasant a more intelligent fisherman or peasant than his father
had been" (Maxwell, 1927, p. 406). In an article on vernacular education
in the State of Perak, the Inspector of Schools, H.B. Collinge, explained
the benefits of education in Malay as taking "thousands of our boys ...
away from idleness," helping them at the same time to "acquire habits
of industry, obedience, punctuality, order, neatness, cleanliness and general good behaviour." Thus, after a boy had attended school for a year or

so, he was "found to be less lazy at home, less given to evil habits and mischievous adventure, more respectful and dutiful, much more willing to help his parents, and with sense enough not to entertain any ambition beyond following the humble home occupations he has been taught to respect." Not only does the school inculcate such habits of dutiful labor; it also helps colonial rule more generally, since "if there is any lingering feeling of dislike of the 'white man,' the school tends greatly to remove it, for the people see that the Government has really their welfare at heart in providing them with this education, free, without compulsion, and with the greatest consideration for their mohammedan sympathies" (cited in Straits Settlements, 1894, p. 177).

While one aspect of this vernacular education was to promote loyalty, obedience, and acceptance of colonial rule, another dimension was tied to the Orientalist interests of many of the scholar-administrators who were closely connected to educational policies. In Malaya, Swettenham, who warned against the teaching of English in Malaya, "earned his Knighthood on the strength of his ability to understand the ignorant unspoilt Malay" (Loh Fook Seng, 1970, p. 114). Another orientalist administrator, Wilkinson, "believed as many an Englishman has believed before him and since that the native must not be taken away, must not be uprooted from his fascinating environment, fascinating to a brilliant Malay scholar" (Loh Fook Seng 1970, p. 114). Thus, as Loh Fook Seng suggests: "Much of the primitive Malay education that continued to be supplied by the British Government was in no small degree due to this attempt to preserve the Malay as a Malay, a son of the soil in the most literal sense possible" (p. 114).

Orientalism has, of course, been understood as a central aspect of colonialism since Said's (1978) classic study. Singh describes the apparent paradox that lay at the heart of this colonial study of other languages and cultures: "On the one hand, the Orientalists as civil servants shared the standard colonial belief in the superiority of Western knowledge and institutions. On the other hand, these Indologists 'rediscovered' a glorious India by identifying a certain resemblance between East and West in a shared ancient past" (Singh, 1996, p. 71). It was from amid these paradoxical studies of Indian, Malay and Chinese cultures that conservative policies for the preservation of culture and knowledge—as defined by these colonial scholars—emerged, and, most importantly, policies to promote conservative forms of education were developed. Language-in-education policies in British colonies were thus directed toward the preservation of Orientalist understandings of local cultures and the promotion of vernacular education as a means of social regulation. Both components of this policy may be seen as aspects of governmentality—means to regulate possibilities for colonial subjects.

CHINA AND CULTURAL FIXITY

In order to explain colonial language policy in Hong Kong, it is important to locate British attitudes toward their colonial subjects within the broader context of shifting attitudes toward China. The question here is an extension of Yao's (1999) for Singapore: "What was the nature of colonial encounters in 19th-century Singapore which condensed the contradictory and unstable representation of the Chinese into different positions of 'fixity'" (p. 103). The concept of "fixity," derived from the work of Bhaba (1994), highlights the notion of the stereotype not just as an overgeneralization but rather as an historically located strategy of fixing the Other. In his critical discussion of Bhaba, Thomas (1994) points out that "it is generally presumed that colonial discourses depict colonized people pejoratively; yet, just as some sexist imagery can, at least superficially, exalt and celebrate women, attractive and even sympathetic constructions of colonized peoples may admire or uphold them in a narrow and restrictive way" (p. 54).

Drawing on these observations, I am interested not so much in how negative images of the Other are (re)produced, but how images of the Other become fixed. Thus, as Yao (1999) illustrates, European images of Chinese gradually settled on various fixed types and characteristics, though not without degrees of ambivalence. On the one hand, there were the "coolie" laborers, who were admired for their ability to work but denigrated for their immorality, especially their use of opium: "To the colonial authorities in 19th-century Singapore ... the Chinese coolies appeared as both immoral and hardworking, partial to decadent sins and pleasures, yet capable of doing all those unpleasant tasks other natives refused" (p. 118). On the other hand, the wealthier merchant class, particularly the Straits Chinese, were admired for their business acumen, their close cooperation with British rule, and their adherence to Chinese traditions. For 19th century Singapore, then, Chinese were assigned to two "communities:" "the drug sodden coolie labourers on the one hand, the virtuous and wealthy Chinese merchants on the other" (p. 103).

Such images, particular to Singapore on one level, were also part of a larger discursive framework in East Asia. For example, describing the colonial stereotype constructed of Malays during the colonial period, Alatas (1977) notes that foreign writers concluded "that the Malays are easy-going; that they are sensitive to insult; that they are prone to violent outbursts; that they are good imitators, lacking originality in thought and culture; that they are fond of idleness; but loyal to their chiefs and kings; that they are polite; that they are morally lax; but that they lack incentive or initiative for acquiring wealth; and that they are treacherous and wily" (p. 115).

My particular interest here is the cultural fixing of the Chinese. According to the Brockhaus *Conversations-Lexicon* published in 1852: "Hard work, politeness, the love of peace and mildness are the hallmarks of the Chinese character. Nothing is more sacred to him than the love of a child or the fidelity of a subject. On the other hand, lust, gluttony, deceitful cunning in trade and traffic, cowardice and false flexibility, an intolerable national pride, rigid adherence to tradition, pitilessness, vindictiveness, and corruptibility form a strong dark side" (cited in Mackerras, 1989, p. 61). Such fixity has considerable continuity, thus allowing Bonavia (1982) in his book, *The Chinese*, to write, "They are admirable, infuriating, humorous, priggish, modest, overweening, mendacious, loyal, mercenary, ethereal, sadistic, and tender. They are quite unlike anybody else. They are the Chinese." (p. 16)

Describing the development of Western images of China, Kiernan (1969) points out that it has been "a very long process, quickening in its later stages, that turned the fabled Cathay of Europe's half-buried memories into a solid, humdrum China pervaded by an aroma of nightsoil" (p. 146). Generally, Mackerras (1989) suggests that "the dominant images of most periods have tended to accord with, rather than oppose, the interests of the main Western authorities or governments of the day. There has indeed been a "regime of truth" concerning China, which has affected and raised "the status of those who are charged with saying what counts as true" about that country" (p. 263). The early period of writing on China (from Marco Polo to the 16th century) was often full of admiration: "At the end of the sixteenth century, Europe may have believed it could teach the Chinese, but it was still prepared to admire them" (p. 27). According to Yao (1999), up until the end of the 18th century, "there was great enthusiasm for China, for its practical philosophy and for its arts, which flowered into the exuberant European mimicry seen in the style known as chinoiserie" (p. 104).

Around the late 18th and early 19th century, however, this image shifted as a result of "the rise of European, and especially British, imperialism from the time of the Industrial Revolution. For the first time Britain became a leader as a formulator of Western images of China" (Mackerras, 1989, p. 43). While contact with China during the preceding centuries had been limited to small scale missionary activity and trading, from the middle of the nineteenth century until the fall of the Qing dynasty the main activities were "imperialism, profit, and conversion to Christianity" (p. 264). In this period, China began to be seen as a country from which the West had nothing to learn, stuck far behind in the upward march of progress, and only able to progress if it adopted modern Western practices. In this period "the 'Orientalist' approach to China reached its height, when Europe colonized not only parts of China, but also knowledge about it" (Mackerras, 1989, pp. 44–5). Crucial in this process was the arrival of British Protestant missionaries, with their condescending and negative views towards China, and the larger body of knowledge that was being established as part of the great colonial archive of knowledge about the Other: "The idea of China as a stagnant oriental despotism, which even a strong opponent of the capitalist system such as Karl Marx advocated, was used to justify Western intervention to force change upon a reluctant China" (p. 264). As Yao (1999) describes the change: "The infatuation now more frequently turned into a critical depreciation of China; her social, economic and political systems were decried for their conservativism, for being immobilised by the weight of tradition and history" (p. 104).

These constructs became part of the general knowledge about China. The descriptions of China to be found in encyclopedias such as *Encyclopaedia Britannica*, for example, were "extremely condescending, regarding China as an exotic, backward, only semi-civilized, and in some ways rather barbaric country" (p. 60). In *The Popular Encylopedia* (no date, circa 1891), Chinese people are described thus:

> In thickness of lips, flattened nose, and expanded nostril, they bear a considerable resemblance to the negro. In bodily strength they are far inferior to Europeans . . . The Chinese are very deficient in courage. In their moral qualities there is much that is amiable. They are strongly attached to their homes, hold age in respect, toil hard for the support of their families, and in the interior, where the worst kind of foreign intercourse has not debased them, exhibit an unsophisticated simplicity of manners which recalls the age of the patriarchs. In the great mass these qualities are counterbalanced or rather supplanted by numerous vices—treachery, lying, and numerous abominations (p. 312).

It was during this period that some of the central and lasting images of China developed, including those of "hordes" of crowded and filthy Chinese. In his book *Asia's Teeming Millions* (1931), Etienne Dennery dwelt at length on the "Crowds in the great Chinese cities, half sunk in dirt and mud, swarming like ants in dark, narrow winding alleys, in which the sickening stench of decaying meat or putrid flesh ever lingers" (cited in Spurr, 1993, p. 88). This view of the teeming hordes of China was linked, as Kiernan (1969) points out, to the concept of the "Yellow Peril." Most important for my focus, however, was the image of the passive Oriental caught in a static history. In the middle of the 19th century, Marx referred to China as "a giant empire, containing about one-third of the human race, vegetating in the teeth of time" (1858, p. 216). As John Stuart Mill argued (cited in Metcalf, 1996), "Oriental" societies were "brought to a permanent halt for want of mental liberty and individuality" (p. 32).

The image of a stagnant China, peopled by passive subjects and despotic rulers, has continued into the present. Writing in 1960, Perham suggests that "the continuity of China's civilization and its extension over such a vast area and population through millennia of virtual isolation from the rest of the world, had bred in the people both conservativism and complacency" (1960, p. 291). Spurr (1993) argues that this view of China as unchanging and conservative has continued to justify imperial intervention as well as modern development policies: "The argument that development—meaning economic and political modernization—is not compatible with Oriental passivity simply reformulates the Hegelian notion of the imperishability of the Oriental world, which can be conquered and subjugated, but never energized from within" (p. 73). As Blaut (1993) shows, such images of a static and unchanging China persist today in current textbooks on China (pp. 106–7). Indeed, so far did the earlier admiration for Chinese arts, culture, and invention shift, by the beginning of the 20th century the very possibility of invention was being denied them. According to an article on Chinese education in *A Cyclopedia of Education* published in 1911 (Monroe, 1911), Isaac Headland, professor in the Imperial University, Peking, explains that:

> there is nothing in the Chinese course of study in the way of mathematics or science, or indeed in any line of thought, which will tend to develop the thinking faculties, such as reason or invention, and hence these faculties have lain dormant in the Chinese mind. They have never invented anything. They have stumbled upon most of the useful, practical appliances of life, and among these upon the compass, gunpowder, and printing, and, though noted for their commercial astuteness, have lacked all power to develop them into a commercial success (p. 635).

Headland repeated this assertion in his 1912 book, *China's New Day*: "Reason and invention have remained dormant in the Chinese mind. They have never invented anything" (cited in Spurr, 1993, pp. 104–5).

This view of the docile Chinese mind extended into the domains of language, literature, and education. The Chinese language was viewed in negative comparison to Indo-European languages. For many writers, "the Chinese language, monosyllabic, isolated, non-inflectional, incapable of generating prefixes and suffixes, and divided between speech and writing, was very much a primitive form of a linguistic system" (Tong, 1993, p. 29). Contrasting Chinese with Sanskrit, Humboldt was able to conclude that

Chinese was necessarily inferior since it "lacks imagination, is like mathematics in being purely designative and lexical" (cited in Tong, p. 38). The prevailing view of Chinese language and literature is exemplified by an entry on Chinese literature in the *New Standard Encyclopedia* of 1940:

> The Chinese language is monosyllabic and uninflectional ... With a language so incapable of variation, a literature cannot be produced which possesses the qualities we look for and admire in literary works. Elegance, variety, beauty of imagery—these must all be lacking. A monotonous and wearisome language must give rise to a forced and formal literature lacking in originality and interesting in its subject matter only. Moreover, a conservative people ... profoundly reverencing all that is old and formal, and hating innovation, must leave the impress of its own character upon its literature (cited in Brown, 1980, p. 127).

Similarly, Chinese educational practices were derided as imitative and passive. In his education report for 1865, Frederick Stewart, headmaster of the Central School in Hong Kong wrote: "The Chinese have no education in the real sense of the word. No attempt is made at a simultaneous development of the mental powers. These are all sacrificed to the cultivation of memory" (p. 138). Such views were commonly held by many colonizers who worked in Hong Kong or China. The Rev. S.R. Brown, Headmaster of the Morrison Education Society School, wrote in a report in 1844 that Chinese children are usually pervaded by "a universal expression of passive inanity ... The black but staring, glassy eye, and open mouth, bespeak little more than stupid wonder gazing out of emptiness." This view is linked to Brown's view of Chinese schools, where a boy may learn "the names of written characters, that in all probability never conveyed to him one new idea from first to last." Despite this lack of education, the Chinese boy also comes "with a mind to be emptied of a vast accumulation of false and superstitious notions that can never tenant an enlightened mind, for they cannot coexist with truth" (cited in Sweeting, 1990, p. 21). The principal characteristics of Chinese boys are "an utter disregard of truth, obscenity, and cowardliness" (p. 22).

Such views reemerged in the 1882 Commission on education in Hong Kong. According to the Bishop of Victoria (Hong Kong): "You know the way they learn; they memorate [sic], they hear the Chinese explanation, and this goes on from morning to night for years, and they get the classics into them" (Report of the Education Commission, 1883, p. 6). Moreover, "when a Chinaman goes to school he is given a little book, and he just simply sits and pores over it, not understanding the meaning of a character, and he goes on growing and getting other books which he does not understand at all, and at the end, when he is in his teens, he begins to have some explanation given to him" (p. 11). This view can be found again in an article by Addis (1889) on education in China: "In truth Chinese education is—*pace* the sinologues—no education at all. It is no 'leading out of' but a leading back to. Instead of expanding the intelligence, it contracts it; instead of broadening sympathies, it narrows them; instead of making a man honest, intelligent and brave, it has produced few who are not cunning, narrow-minded and pusillanimous" (p. 206). He goes on: "The truth is that if the comparative test be applied, almost the only merit which can be claimed for Chinese education is that it strengthens the memory" (p. 206).

Addis then compares the poor state of Chinese education with Hong Kong, where "half a century ago the island was peopled by a few half savage settlers steeped in ignorance and superstition" but where "a foreign Government, by the impartial administration of wise and just laws, has made this dot on the ocean so attractive" (pp. 206–207). Here, then, we can observe very clearly the conjunction between general images of Chinese passivity and more particular constructions of the passive Chinese learner. This construction of the docile Chinese student is a crucial aspect of the construction and regulation of Chinese bodies in the context of language policy. Such a construction on the one hand justifies colonial education. In the same way that an image of a static, despotic China was used to justify the colonization of regions of China, so the image of static minds was used to justify enforced education. On the other hand, such images need to be understood not merely as justification, but also in terms of their productive power: Language-in-education policy produces its own constructions of the docile mind and body. In order to understand language policy as cultural policy in Hong Kong, it is important to examine two crucial aspects of Hong Kong history that are significant in the construction of the docile Chinese body: opium and political unrest.

THE CONSTRUCTION AND REGULATION OF DOCILE BODIES

The role of opium in the development of Hong Kong has been largely ignored by British colonial historians (Trocki 1990). As Yee (1992) points out, "compared to the infamies of World War II, which still prey upon the Germans and Japanese, the supply of opium to China which led to the addiction and death of countless hundreds of millions has been neglected" (p. 47). Yet Hong Kong developed as a direct result of the imperial trade in opium. The British (and others, including the Americans) developed a lucrative route from England to India, where they traded for opium, across the Indian ocean to the coastal ports of China, where they traded opium for tea, silk and other Chinese goods in demand in Europe, and then back to England. According to Freuchen (1957, cited in Yee), it would be more appropriate to refer to the famous and romanticized sailing ships of the 19th century not as tea clippers, but as "opium clippers."

As a result of the first "Opium War" (1840–1842), during which the British attacked Guangzhou in retaliation for the destruction of large quantities of opium, Hong Kong was "ceded" to the British, along with a $6 million reparation. Hong Kong then developed rapidly as a trading port, with many of its most well known companies directly involved in the opium trade. According to the Auditor-General's report for 1845, there were eighty opium clippers registered in Hong Kong, which had become "the world's opium centre handling 75% of India's opium crop" (Yee, 1992, p. 38). The trade in opium was to remain dominant in Hong Kong's development until the Japanese invasion in 1942: "The deliberate application of its cultivation within the territory and in Singapore and other British colonies; its sale locally and as an export staple for more than two-thirds of Hong Kong's history (1841–1942) cast an indelible blight upon British history in the territory and Asia" (Yee, 1992, p. 41).

Many colonial historians have argued that Britain was averse to the opium trade and that the Opium Wars were not really about opium. According to Cantlie (1906), for example, the war of 1840 "is frequently styled the Opium War, but that is a mere misnomer. The war was the result of 200 years of insult, injury, and wrong heaped upon British subjects by the Chinese. It was not, in fact, until starvation and annihilation stared the British community in the face that the Government came to their aid" (p. 503). Despite such claims, other historians such as Trocki (1990), have documented "incredibly determined efforts by the Colonial Office . . . and the British economic community in the colonies to oppose anything that might decrease the opium revenue or otherwise shift the tax burden." Trocki suggests further that "any argument that the imperial system did not rely on opium and was not, in the pathogenic sense, systematically dependent on the drug is simply not in accordance with the facts" (1990, p. 237). It is against this background of imperial trade and interests that the governance of Hong Kong needs to be seen, for while the British empire's dependence on opium was a massive boost for imperial trade, and while the enforced addiction to opium in mainland China created both economic dependency and physical incapacity, the prevalence of opium in Hong Kong was not conducive to the development and governance of a productive workforce.

A second important historical question concerns acts of resistance to colonial rule in Hong Kong. One aspect of the docile Other is to construct the colonized as willing and passive recipients of colonial rule. The construction of Hong Kong stresses the social and political stability of the colony, the political acquiescence and passivity of the population, and the supposedly ubiquitous interest in financial rather than political questions. According to Tsai (1994), however, this view ignores "a long series of tensions and crises in which the Chinese people in Hong Kong expressed their displeasure with and hostility toward the British colonial authorities" (p. 9). According to Young (1994), "the common view that Hong Kong has always enjoyed political stability is a historical myth" (pp. 135–136). Several large-scale incidents suggest a fairly turbulent history and a populace that is anything but docile and acquiescent: the mass celebrations after the 1911 Revolution in China, which, as Tsai suggests, marked a shift from anti-foreign sentiment to Chinese nationalism; the tramway boycott of 1912–1913; the "May Fourth" boycott of 1919, sparked by protests in China against the refusal of the European powers to return Qingdao to China in the Versailles Treaty; and the massive general strike and boycott of 1925–1926, which came close to ruining Hong Kong financially. Many of these incidents have been dismissed either as the products of purely economic concerns or as the result of "outside agitation." Yet the elements of anti-foreign, anti-government, and anti-colonial politics in many of these demonstrations suggest otherwise. Discussing the 1925–1926 strike/boycott, for example, Chan (1994) argues that "in all its essential aspects, the 1925–26 movement was a nationalistic protest against imperialism, using economic means for political ends, not vice versa" (p. 46).

CHINESE EDUCATION AS "SOCIAL INSURANCE OF THE BEST KIND"

Language-in-education policies must be seen against this background: a strong imperial interest in maintaining Hong Kong as a trading port, with a major interest in opium, and the need to maintain social order in a population that frequently showed violent antiforeigner and anti-colonial sentiments. Chinese colonial subjects were constructed as passive imitators, but anti-colonial riots threatened British rule and therefore had to be suppressed. Chinese workers were incapacitated by opium addiction, yet a hard-working labor force was needed to maintain the development of this opium-dependent colony. One challenge, therefore, was to develop language-in-education policies as part of larger colonial governance that could continue the discursive construction of the docile Chinese while regulating both the anti-colonial sentiments and the opium induced docility: Could education provide politically docile but physically active bodies?

For Frederick Lugard, governor of Hong Kong from 1907 to 1912, who faced "several big subjects—Opium, Subsidiary Coinage, Riots, and

Hong Kong University" (letter to his wife, cited in Mellor, 1992, p. 23), the answer was to close down the opium trade and to develop a university in which "the training of character and the provision of moral instruction" was to be based on residential colleges, playing fields and an education through English (in Mellor, 1992, p. 138). Following other Anglicist colonial administrators who favored the promotion of English, Lugard was known for his development of the colonial theories of indirect rule and the dual mandate. In his most important work, *The Dual Mandate in British Tropical Africa* (1926), Lugard emphasized the importance of understanding "that Europe is in Africa for the mutual benefit of her own industrial classes, and of the native races in their progress to a higher plane; that the benefit can be made reciprocal, and that it is the aim and desire of civilised administration to fulfill this dual mandate" (p. 617). Lugard remained steadfastly convinced that while Britain could gain materially from its colonies, the trusteeship of the world had been left in British hands so they could spread the benefits of its civilization: "I am profoundly convinced that there can be no question but that British rule has promoted the happiness and welfare of the primitive races . . . We hold these countries because it is the genius of our race to colonise, to trade, and to govern" (p. 618–9). Writing about the use of English at Hong Kong University, he similarly praised the imperial mission:

> In conclusion I would emphasize the value of English as the medium of instruction. If we believe that British interests will be thus promoted, we believe equally firmly that graduates, by the mastery of English, will acquire the key to a great literature and the passport to a great trade. On the one hand we desire to secure the English language in the high position it has acquired in the Far East; on the other hand since the populations of the various provinces in China speak no common language, and the Chinese vocabulary has not yet adapted itself to express the terms and conceptions of modern science, we believe that should China find it necessary for a time to adopt an alien tongue as a common medium for new thoughts and expressions—as the nations of the West did when Latin was the language of the savants and of scientific literature—none would be more suitable than English (1910, p. 4).

While such views might be taken as epitomizing colonial rule, there are two important issues to consider here. First, colonial administrators went far further than policies designed simply for financial benefit; rather they saw themselves as fulfilling a moral duty to the world. This is important because it suggests that colonial discourse was not merely a rationalization for, or a product of, imperial expansion and exploitation, but rather operated at a separate level that might indeed be in contradiction with material imperial goals. These thinkers were at the forefront of the "frenzy of liberal reform known as the 'civilizing mission'" (Singh, 1996, p. 89). This liberalism, as Metcalf (1996) points out, was informed by a

"radical universalism:" "Contemporary European, especially British, culture alone represented civilization. No other cultures had any intrinsic validity. There was no such thing as 'Western' civilization; there existed only
'civilization.' Hence the liberal set out, on the basis of this shared humanity, to turn the Indian into an Englishman" (p. 34). Moreover, this liberal
interventionist view of civilization was to form one of the central discourses
throughout the colonial period: "Macaulay and Mountbatten, the last
viceroy, were ... linked indissolubly together as the beginning and the
end of a chain forged of liberal idealism" (Metcalf, 1996, p. 233).

Second, while Lugard's views, like Macaulay's before him, have long
been considered the most influential in colonial policy, as I have argued
elsewhere (1998), they were in fact far less influential in the context of
local educational policy. They produced a grand rhetoric of empire that
still has echoes in some current images of English and international relations, but their ideas were out of touch with language and education
policies which tended to favor vernacular education for colonial governance. Thus, in spite of earlier Anglicist orientations of some 19th century
governors of Hong Kong, and in spite of the brief but powerful presence
of Lugard, language education policies shifted towards vernacular education. E. J. Eitel, Inspector of Schools in Hong Kong from 1879 to 1897, a
former German missionary, and a "sound orientalist and sinologist" (Lethbridge, 1895/1983, p. vii), who had written a dictionary of Cantonese and
books on Buddhism and *Fengshui*, was most concerned that education
should give students sufficient grounding in morality. Although he clearly
supported the teaching of English, he also argued that students in the
village schools were getting a better education than those receiving a secular education in English. By studying Chinese classics, students learn "a
system of morality, not merely a doctrine, but a living system of ethics."
Thus they learn "filial piety, respect for the aged, respect for authority, respect for the moral law." In the government schools, by contrast, where
English books without religious education were used, "no morality is im-
planted in the boys" (Report of the Education Commission, 1883, p. 70). The
teaching of Chinese, Eitel argued, is "of higher advantage to the Government" because "boys strongly imbued with European civilization whilst
cut away from the restraining influence of Confucian ethics lose the benefits of education, and the practical experience of Hongkong is that those
who are thoroughly imbued with the foreign spirit, are bad in morals"
(p. 70).

Hong Kong educational policy was also a reaction to local conditions
of unrest. The setting up of Hong Kong University (1912) by Governor
Lugard, for example, needs to be seen against the background of the 1911
revolution in China. Indeed this revolution and the increased sense of

nationalism among the Chinese was to have profound effects on Hong Kong's schools. While the government was promoting vernacular education for its conservative ideals, there was also concern that this same vernacular education was encouraging pro-Chinese and anti-colonial national sentiment. As Chan (1994) points out, "to counter the Chinese revolution's undermining impact on the conservative ideas and traditional values taught by Hong Kong's several hundred vernacular schools, which to that point had remained unassisted and uncontrolled by the government, Governor May enacted in August 1913 the Education Ordinance, which required every school to register with the director of education, conform to government regulations, and submit to official inspection" (p. 32). This educational ordinance, which, according to Sweeting (1992) represents "the high-water mark of colonial power and authority over education" (p. 45), signaled the move not merely to support but also to regulate vernacular education.

Following the massive 1925 strike and boycott of goods in Hong Kong, R.H. Kotewall (CO 129/489) pointed directly to the schools as the source of problems and recommended increased supervision: "Obviously the first remedy is an increased watchfulness in the schools. Special care should be exercised in the supervision of the vernacular schools in particular, for these can the more easily become breeding grounds for sedition" (p. 455). His recommendations extended to changes in Chinese school curricula: "The Chinese education in Hong Kong does not seem to be all that it should be. The teaching of Confucian ethics is more and more neglected, while too much attention is being paid to the materialistic side of life ... In such a system great stress should be laid on the ethics of Confucianism which is, in China, probably the best antidote to the pernicious doctrines of Bolshevism, and is certainly the most powerful conservative course, and the greatest influence for good" (pp. 455–456). Thus, "money spent on the development of the conservative ideas of the Chinese race in the minds of the young will be money well spent, and also constitutes social insurance of the best kind" (p. 456).

Kotewall's view was supported most actively by the Governor, Sir Cecil Clementi, a long-term colonial administrator in Hong Kong and a scholar of Chinese folk songs. Inviting senior Chinese literati to Government House in 1927, Clementi addressed them in Cantonese, asking them to help him to develop a curriculum that would emphasize traditional morality and scholarship, a curriculum based on orthodox Confucianism emphasizing social hierarchy and subservience to patriarchal authority (Luk, 1991). Clementi's goal was to counter the rising tide of Chinese nationalism by emphasizing traditional notions of hierarchy and loyalty. Thus "appeal was made to the cultural tradition of the native people to help safeguard foreign rule against the growth of nationalistic feelings among the younger generation" (Luk, 1991, p. 660). Often far more important, therefore, than the civilizing zeal of English teaching was the conservative use of vernacular education, developed and implemented by colonial administrators and Orientalist scholars. These were the crucial tools of governmentality through language-in-education policies. Conservative Chinese education was the colonial route to the making of docile bodies.

LANGUAGE POLICY AND GOVERNMENTALITY

The particularity of the colonial context might suggest that the relationship between language policy and governmentality outlined here has limited applicability to current policies in liberal democracies. While it is certainly the case that language policies need to be understood within their own social, cultural, geographical, economic, and political contexts, an important argument here is that there are also striking continuities in the ways in which modes of governmentality have develope 1. Goodall (1995) argues in the context of Australia that the conventional interpretation of colonial race relations assumes improved relations and decreasing restrictions. In this interpretation, the 19th century saw the greatest restrictions on Aboriginal Australians, but these restrictions were gradually reduced as more enlightened policies of "protection," "welfare," and "self-determination" were adopted. As Goodall argues, however, it would be mistaken to assume that such policies actually entailed less control. Rather the history of race rela.ions in Australia is marked by "the increasing control which the government has tried to exercise over Aboriginal people" (p. 58).

This understanding of increased modes of surveillance brings into question two widely held views of language policy: That more liberal and pluralistic approaches to language policy necessarily have less governmental implications; and that mother tongue or vernacular education is necessarily preferable to education in other languages. The arguments I have presented here do not deny the value of mother tongue education or state intervention in language policies in some contexts. Rather, I am arguing that the model for understanding the relationship between language policy and broader political concerns needs to move away from an understanding of language policy as the imposition or denial of particular languages. A more fruitful perspective may be to view language policy in term of governmentality, by highlighting the complex relationships among language policies, cultural politics, curriculum, educational practice, and the modes of surveillance of the liberal state.

REFERENCES

Addis, C. S. (1889). Education in China. *The China Review*, XVIII, 205–212.

Alatas, S. H. (1977). *The myth of the lazy native*. London: Frank Cass.

Bhaba, H. (1994). *The location of culture*. London: Routledge.

Blake, L. J. (Ed.). (1973). *Vision and realization: A centenary history of state education in Victoria*, vol. 1. Melbourne: Education Department of Victoria.

Blaut, J. M. (1993). *The colonizer's model of the world: Geographical diffusionism and eurocentric history*. New York: The Guilford Press.

Bonavia, D. (1982). *The Chinese*. Harmondsworth: Penguin.

Brown, H. D. (1980). *Principles of language learning and teaching*. Englewood Cliffs, NJ: Prentice Hall.

Bureau of Education. (1920). *Selections from educational records, Part 1, 1781–1839*. (H. Sharp, Ed.). Calcutta: Superintendent of Government Printing.

Cantlie, J. (1906) Hong Kong, in *India, Ceylon, Straits Settlements, British North Borneo, Hong-Kong*. London: Kegan Paul, Trench, Trabner & Co.

Chan Ming K. (1994). Hong Kong in Sino-British conflict: Mass mobilization and the crisis of legitimacy. In M. K. Chan (Ed.), *Precarious balance: Hong Kong between China and Britain, 1842–1992* (pp. 27–58). Hong Kong: Hong Kong University Press.

CO (various years). Colonial Office Documents (unpublished).

Cohn, B. (1996). *Colonialism and its forms of knowledge*. Princeton, NJ: Princeton University Press.

Dean, M. (1994). *Critical and effective histories: Foucault's methods and historical sociology*. London: Routledge.

Eitel, E. J. (1895). *Europe in China*. Kelly & Walsh/Luzac & Company. Reprinted in 1983 by Oxford University Press, Hong Kong.

Foucault, M. (1979). *Discipline and punish: The birth of the prison*. New York: Vintage Books.

Foucault, M. (1991). Governmentality. In G. Burchell, C. Gordon & P. Miller (Eds.). *The Foucault effect: Studies in governmentality* (pp. 87–104). Hemel Hempstead: Harvester Wheatsheaf.

Goodall, J. (1995). New South Wales. In A. McGrath (Ed.), *Contested Ground: Australian Aborigines under the British Crown* (pp. 55–120). St. Leonards, NSW: Allen & Unwin.

Kiernan, V. G. (1969). *The lords of human kind: European attitudes towards the outside world in the imperial age*. London: Weidenfeld and Nicolson.

Lethbridge, H. J. (1895/1983). Introduction. In E. J. Eitel, *Europe in China*. Hong Kong: Oxford University Press.

Loh Fook Seng, (1970). The nineteenth century British approach to Malay education. *Jurnal Pendidekan 1*, no.1, 105–115.

Lugard, F. D. (1910). *Hong Kong University: Objects, history, present position and prospects*. Hong Kong: Noronha.

Lugard, F. D. (1926). *The Dual Mandate in British Tropical Africa* (third ed.). Edinburgh: William Blackwood and Sons.

Luk Hung-Kay, B. (1991). Chinese culture in the Hong Kong curriculum: Heritage and colonialism. *Comparative Education Review 35*, no. 4, 650–668.

Mackerras, C. (1989). *Western images of China*. Hong Kong: Oxford University Press.

Marx, K. (1858). The opium trade. *New York Daily Tribune*, 5433, Sept 20, 1858, (pp. 213–216). New York: International Publishers.

Maxwell, G. (1927/1983). Some problems of education and public health in Malaya. In H. Kratoska (Ed.), *Honourable intentions: Talks on the British Empire in South-East Asia delivered at the Royal Colonial Institute 1874–1928*. Singapore: Oxford University Press.

Mellor, B. (1992). *Lugard in Hong Kong: Empires, education and a Governor at work, 1907– 1912*. Hong Kong: Hong Kong University Press.

Metcalf, T. (1996). *Ideologies of the Raj*. Cambridge: Cambridge University Press.

Monroe, P. (Ed.). (1911). *A Cyclopedia of Education*. New York: The MacMillan Company.

Pennycook, A. (1998). *English and the discourses of colonialism*. London: Routledge.

Perham, M. (1960). *Lugard: The years of authority 1898–1945*, (vol. 2). London: Collins.

Phillipson, R. (1992). *Linguistic imperialism*. Oxford: Oxford University Press.

Popular Encylopedia, The (no date, circa 1891). London: Blackie and Son Ltd.

Report of the Education Commission appointed by His Excellency Sir John Pope Hennessy, K.C.M.G . . . to consider certain questions connected with Education in Hong Kong, 1882. (1883). Hong Kong: Hong Kong Government.

Rose, N. (1996). Governing "advanced" liberal democracies. In A. Barry, T. Osborne & N. Rose (Eds.). *Foucault and political reason: Liberalism, neo-liberalism and rationalities of government* (pp. 37–64). London: UCL Press.

Said, E. W. (1978). *Orientalism*. London: Routledge and Kegan Paul.

Singh, J. (1996). *Colonial Narratives/Cultural Dialogues: "Discoveries" of India in the Language of Colonialism*. London: Routledge.

Smith, P. (1987). *Education and colonial control on Papua New Guinea: A documentary history*. Melbourne: Longman Cheshire.

Spurr, D. (1993). *The rhetoric of empire: Colonial discourse in journalism, travel writing, and imperial administration*. Durham: Duke University Press.

Straits Settlements. (Various years). *Straits Settlements Annual Departmental Reports*. Singapore: Government Printing Office.

Sweeting, A. E. (1990). *Education in Hong Kong, pre-1841 to 1941: Fact & opinion*. Hong Kong: Hong Kong University Press.

Sweeting, A. E. (1992). Hong Kong education within historical processes. In G. A. Postiglione (Ed.), *Education and society in Hong Kong: Toward one country and two systems* (pp. 39–81). Hong Kong: Hong Kong University Press.

Thomas, N. (1994). *Colonialism's culture: Anthropology, travel and government*. Oxford: Polity Press.

Tong, Q. S. (1993). Myths about the Chinese language. *Canadian Review of Comparative Literature*, March–June, 29–47.

Trocki, C. A. (1990). *Opium and Empire: Chinese society in colonial Singapore, 1800–1910*. Ithaca, NY: Cornell University Press.

Tsai Jung-fang. (1994). From antiforeignism to popular nationalism: Hong Kong between China and Britain, 1839–1911. In M. K. Chan (Ed.), *Precarious balance: Hong Kong between China and Britain, 1842–1992* (pp. 9–25). Hong Kong: Hong Kong University Press.

Yao Souchou. (1999). Social virtues as cultural text: Colonial desire and the Chinese in 19th- century Singapore. In P. Chew & A. Kramer-Dahl (Eds), *Reading culture: Textual practices in Singapore* (pp. 99–122). Singapore: Times Academic Press.

Yee, A. H. (1992). *A people misruled: The Chinese stepping-stone syndrome*. Singapore: Heinemann Asia.

Young, J. D. (1994). The building years: Maintaining a China-Hong Kong-Britain equilibrium. In M. K. Chan (Ed.), *Precarious balance: Hong Kong between China and Britain, 1842–1992* (pp. 131–147). Hong Kong: Hong Kong University Press.

6

"Who will Guard the Guardians Themselves?"[1]
National Interest Versus Factional Corruption in Policymaking for ESL in Australia

Helen Moore
Ontario Institute for Studies in Education
Ontario, Canada

> The attempt to secure popular government from the corrupting effects of certain kinds of faction provides the conditions in which other powerful forms of factional corruption can be expected to take root. A liberal government may well be concerned to defend the conduct of government against the impact of faction—but, since any government will be corrupted by faction, it will also seek to mobilize that concern for factional purposes (Hindess, 1997b, p. 266).

> *H: The issue is, I think, the distinction between ESL and literacy, and whether it's a real distinction...*
> *G: It's a real distinction to insiders. To outsiders, it has no reality at all.... By outsiders, I mean employers and [pause] yes, well, basically, well, all of us [very softly] (Extract from interview data).*

---

[1] My title is a translation of the Latin "*Sed quis custodiet ipsos custodes?*" (Juvenal, *Satires* 347) quoted in Allington & Woodside-Jiron (1999, p. 10). The third and fourth sections of this chapter are an updated version of Moore (1996a).

For language policy in Australia, 1991 was a turning point, not the least for teaching immigrants and their children English as a second/additional language (ESL; see Appendix A for a list of acronyms). During the 1970s and 1980s, under successive federal governments of different political persuasions, ESL education was legitimized as a specific policy and pedagogical concern. ESL development was portrayed as a long-term process involving oral and written skills across all areas of the curriculum and in the public domain, and integrally related to learners' competence in other languages (e.g., Campbell & McMeniman, 1985; Galbally, 1978). The *National Policy on Languages* (NPL) (Lo Bianco, 1987) described ESL as "adding a language to an existing linguistic repertoire" and argued strongly that it could not be separated from issues of mother tongue development (pp. 85 ff.).

In 1991, the NPL was replaced by *The Australian Language and Literacy Policy* (ALLP) (Department of Employment Education and Training, 1991). The ALLP located ESL within the goal that "all Australians should develop and maintain effective literacy in English to enable them to participate in Australian society" (vol. 1, p. 4). Specific federal policy interest in ESL was limited to immigrants in the year following their arrival (18 months for some children). Policy relating to languages other than English was seen as entirely separate from and irrelevant to ESL. The view of ESL as a sub-category of English literacy became the basis for program and funding descriptions, accountability procedures, curriculum development, and further policymaking. By 1996, ESL (aside from teaching new arrivals) had disappeared in a new National Literacy Plan. The federal policy focus was now English literacy "benchmarks" and the early years of schooling (Department of Employment Education Training and Youth Affairs, 1998).

Most ESL educators, among whom I count myself, argued against this policy shift, seeing it as a return to the pre-1970s marginalization and stigmatization of ESL learning needs (Davison, 1999; Lo Bianco, 1998;

I thank Chris Davison, Alan Davies, Barry Hindess, Howard Nicholas, Ross Garnaut Alan Williams, and the History of the Present group at the University of Toronto for their helpful comments; my anonymous interviewees for their time and insights, including the government officials who accepted that my analysis might appear unsympathetic to them; and Jim Tollefson for exemplary and patient editorial work.

The interview data is from six government officials and three ESL educators/administrators (from a total of 51 interviews). Interviewees are identified from within or outside DEET if relevant to the discussion. Transcripts are edited to include punctuation and eliminate pauses, repetitions, and grammatical infelicities unless these seemed to be significant. Conventions are as follows:

G	government official/bureaucrat
E	educator
H	author
...	one or more words deleted
Underlining	emphasis by the speaker
[]	author's comment/correction

McKay, 1998). The epigraph to this chapter sums up policymakers' responses to these arguments: ESL, as distinct from (English) literacy, had "no reality at all"; ESL claims were "just unsustainable . . . because it's special pleading and out of kilter with general government policy." Given the previous policy legitimation of ESL, the new representation of its claims as special pleading was confusing to many, including myself. But no matter how broadly we tried to present our concerns, the accusations of partisanship persisted.

In this chapter, I explore how these accusations became possible, using material from interviews with educators and government officials. My analysis draws from recent theoretical work by Barry Hindess, a political scientist, who examines "factions" in the context of Foucault's (1991) notion of "governmentality."

LIBERAL GOVERNMENT AND THE PROBLEM OF FACTIONS

From a Foucauldian perspective, "government" is practiced in many different ways by a wide variety of agencies. Government acts indirectly. In contrast to domination, government is an "art" or "activity" requiring "calculations" about how to shape, guide, correct, and modify individual and group behaviors, and practical techniques based on these calculations (Burchell, 1996, p. 19). It is fruitless to assume or search for a single controlling agency or structure that constitutes the "State" or for which government is a carrier:

> The forms of power that subject us, the systems of rule that administer us, the types of authority that master us do not find their principle of coherence in a State nor do they answer to a logic of oppression or domination or the other constitutive oppositions of liberal political philosophy [e.g. state/market, domination/freedom, public/private, compulsory/voluntary]. . . . The force field with which we are confronted in our present is made up of a multiplicity of interlocking apparatuses for the programming of this or that dimension of life (Rose, 1993, p. 286).

This perspective is often interpreted as obviating "a focus on the intentional and centralized strategies of government authorities" (Pennycook, this volume). However, I see it as actually inviting study of the "interlocking apparatuses" centered on the government of nation states. Thus, we can probe how politicians and bureaucrats (henceforth "state authorities") use their distinctive positioning and coordinating roles "to regulate the conduct of large numbers of individuals and of a variety of private and public institutions" (Hindess, 1997c, p. 14).[2] These agents work together

---

[2]This paper is part of a larger project that also considers ESL educators' understandings and contribution to government.

and with others:

> not through the direct imposition of force, but through a delicate affiliation of
> a loose assemblage of agents and agencies into a functioning network. This in-
> volves alliances formed not only because one agent is dependent upon another
> for funds, legitimacy or some other resource that can be used for persuasion or
> compulsion, but also because one actor comes to convince another that their
> problems or goals are intrinsically linked, that their interests are consonant,
> that each can solve their difficulties or achieve their ends by joining forces or
> working along the same lines (Miller & Rose, 1993, pp. 83–84).

Modern government, as practiced by state authorities and other agents, rests on claims that it benefits those who are governed. State authorities take their work to be "conducting the affairs of the population in the interests of the whole" (Hindess, 2001, p. 42). Liberal government as practiced in Western democracies constructs these interests in terms of the particular "art" of limiting intrusions on the assumed "natural" freedoms of those who are governed (i.e., their autonomy) and instituting methods for developing these freedoms (Hindess, 1996).

However, the assumption that the governed are and should be autonomous creates a problem for liberalism: "A government of free persons is a government of persons who are free . . . to organize politically in the attempt to influence, or even to dominate, the law-making and other powers of central government" (Hindess, 1997c, pp. 21–22). Those organized for this purpose are seen as "factions" whose political activity is a "damaging infection" undermining the common interest (Hindess, 2001, p. 46). Finding ways to defend "the proper purposes of government from the impact of partisan politics" is an important duty of state authorities (Hindess, 2001, p. 46).

The professions present just this problem. State authorities install and empower professional experts and rely on their contributions to understanding and regulating social processes. But it is precisely these experts' autonomy (i.e., their perceived distance from state authorities and any type of coercive force) that makes their truth claims credible (Rose, 1993). To the extent that the disciplines and professions maintain distance from state authorities and rest their claims on their particular domains of enquiry and professional codes of conduct, they constitute potential factions. Thus, the reliance of state authorities on groups such as the professions "may well co-exist with a desire to undermine their status as independent centers of government control" (Hindess, 1997c, p. 21).

One way in which state authorities have sought to protect themselves from factions, both within their own ranks and beyond, is by removing "significant areas of public provision from the realm of political decision" and relying instead on "suitably organized forms of market interaction" (Hindess, 2001, p. 46). For example, as will be seen later, the ALLP was followed by an extension of competitive contracting for the delivery of adult ESL programs in Australia. State authorities justified this move by claiming that the natural processes of the marketplace would eliminate the (supposed) feather-bedding and inwardness of lazy government officials and self-serving state-protected ESL teachers (i.e., factions) (Moore, in press).

In this chapter, my concern is with policymaking, that is, the technique used to produce the categories by which state authorities administer, fund, and generally recognize governmental programs and thereby give them institutional existence. State authorities legitimate these policies in terms of the national interest. Using the ALLP and the initiatives that followed as a case study, I examine how this policy and its associated notions of the common good were developed by particular groups in pursuit of quite specific goals and interests.

These groups were what might be called factions. However, as Hindess (2001) points out, accusing state authorities of seeking "partisan advantage" (p. 46) is a tactic as old as that of state authorities labeling their opponents in this way. Inevitably, the processes by which governmental alliances are formed, maintained, resisted, and destroyed are intensely and inevitably political and partisan. Under liberal forms of government, partisan dispute can be expected to flourish (Hindess, 2001). Labeling alliances and counter-alliances as factions does nothing to prevent partisanship. Rather, these accusations, from whatever side, reveal the political nature of the argument (Hindess, 2001).

According to Hindess (1997b), the politics surrounding threats to nation states' mythical and "imaginary cultural and moral unities" drive contemporary concerns about factions. These threats include "the movement of people, narcotics, cultural artifacts and distinctive lifestyles across national boundaries" (Hindess, 1997a, p. 36). It is to be expected that politics will be intense around policies for the education of immigrants and their children.

CONSTRUCTING THE NATIONAL INTEREST: ECONOMIC RESTRUCTURING

The ALLP was developed in the middle years of a 13-year period (1983–1996) of a federal Labor government. The main policy objective of this government was "economic restructuring," seen as a program involving state authorities in cooperation with trade unions, business, and industry.

The economic restructuring alliance was formed in the context of Labor's accession to office on the promise of responsible government based on "consensus." The promise was a potent one for an electorate still in shock from a previous Labor government (1971–1975) that had ended in a constitutional crisis over the Prime Minister's dismissal by the Governor-General, followed by a Liberal-National coalition government (1975–1983), itself dogged by industrial disputes, youth unemployment, and a major economic downturn (1982–1983).

At the heart of this promise lay an "accord" between Labor and the centralized governing body of the trade union movement, with whom Labor was traditionally allied. The unions agreed to avoid strikes, regulate wage demands, and streamline job classifications and promotion paths. In return, employers conceded moderate wage increases, improved working conditions, and universal superannuation benefits. To workers, employers, and the general electorate, Labor offered (and delivered) tax cuts, lower inflation, improved social security benefits, and, until recession struck in 1990–91, increased employment and falling unemployment levels.

The commitment to consensus engendered new policymaking and implementation hierarchies. Decisions and recommendations to the Cabinet were made in centralized ad hoc bodies and new committees containing representatives from national organizations deemed to be key policy stakeholders: business, trade unions, social service providers, and Commonwealth and State/Territory political and bureaucratic managers. Their decisions were given implementable form in subcommittees and working parties, also made up from these stakeholders and, where seen as relevant, other advisors.

These structures provided the grounds for the government's claims to both strong leadership and consensual policymaking. By the same token, however, those who lay outside the partnership of state authorities, employers and workers (as expressed though trade unions) became "objects" of policy intervention, and, in the case of immigrants for example, the "disadvantaged." Their ways of naming themselves, understanding their realities, and staking their claims lost the legitimacy they had gained under both previous Labor and Liberal-National governments (Yeatman, 1990, p. 158).

Although formulated in ways that reflected local concerns and history, economic restructuring can be seen as one version of a much wider change in governmental understandings about society and the economy (Rose, 1999). For much of the 20th century (and prior to this), economic theory and practice assumed *national* economies to be naturally self-regulating systems (Hindess, 1998). In the last quarter of the 20th century, this assumption eroded in the face of growing international trade, new technologies facilitating foreign investment, large-scale financial movements that destabilized international trading relations, and new accounting technologies that allowed national economies to be understood through "increasingly disaggregated econometric models" (Hindess, 1998, pp. 218–219). It is now the *global* economy that is seen as naturally self-regulating.

When national economies were understood to be relatively self-contained, growth was assumed to be a resource for projects aimed at "a larger national unity" (Hindess, 1998, p. 222). However, because global economic growth does not necessarily entail benefits for any one national economy, this assumption has become a relic of "the extravagant state" (Hindess, 1998, p. 221). Benefits (or penalties) are now perceived to flow from how one nation *is placed in relation to others* as the global system grows, and the imperative for governments is "to do better than their competitors, or at least to keep up with the pack" (p. 222). This imperative reverses the previous relation between economic growth and the nation's social projects. So, for example, education, health, and welfare are assessed in terms of their "bearing on economic life," not simply with reference to "the availability of resources, but also in terms of their consequences for promoting or inhibiting the pursuit of national economic efficiency" (Hindess, 1998, p. 223). This shift of understanding constitutes a potentially new national cultural and moral unity: "The only way to avoid becoming a loser—whether as a nation, firm or individual—is to be as competitive as possible" (Hirst & Thompson, 1996, p. 6, cited in Hindess, 1998, p. 212).

Labor's economic restructuring aimed to install this national ethos. Policy was directed to stimulating group and individual initiative and productivity through privatization, income tax reduction, relaxing controls on overseas investment, and removing tariffs and farm subsidies. To the same end, the public sector applied "'leading edge' business practices" to service delivery: "Competition, market incentives, and negotiation" were implemented at the local level, while the center took responsibility for "product definition" and "accountability protocols" (Marginson, 1997, p. 89). The new ethos became known by its critics as "economic rationalism" and its attendant structures and procedures as "corporate managerialism" (Considine, 1988; Marginson, 1992). Insofar as groups' and individuals' understandings lay outside the new cultural, moral, and political vision of policy makers, they were either irrelevant or a threat.

PROVIDING NATIONAL LEADERSHIP

In 1987, John Dawkins became minister of a newly expanded and reorganized federal Department of Employment, Education, and Training (DEET). His ambition was to place education at center-stage in economic restructuring, and had been announced in an earlier paper, jointly authored with a prominent trade union official. The paper proposed that "new forms of national leadership in education" were essential to Labor's commitment to taking "control of our own economic destiny" and to "a just and equal society" (Lingard, Porter, Bartlett, & Knight, 1995, p. 44). This leadership should go "beyond the provision of grants of money to schools, school authorities and tertiary institutions" and should "be concerned with the objectives of education and the structures through which it is provided and with the adequacy of our total educational efforts" (p. 68).

Exerting national leadership in education could not proceed independently of the eight States/Territories. Although they are dependent for transfer grants on the federal government (known as "the Commonwealth"), which has almost exclusive rights of taxation, the States/Territories jealously assert their constitutional authority over all non-university education. This authority is potentially eroded by grants that the Commonwealth earmarks for particular priorities, but since such grants supplement untied grants, they are never refused. On the argument that immigration is a Commonwealth responsibility, school ESL had received earmarked funds since 1970, and adult ESL was almost entirely dependent on special Commonwealth funding. An important bargaining chip was the prospect of the Commonwealth untying its earmarked grants but maintaining funding levels.

The consensus model provided the process and structures for enacting these politics. Previous semiautonomous policymaking and advisory bodies were abolished. The Australian Education Council (AEC), which consisted of the Commonwealth and State/Territory education ministers and chief executive officers of State/Territory education authorities, was reinvigorated as the apex of a pyramid of new committees, councils, and working parties whose chairmanship and membership reflected the consensus alliance (Lingard et al., 1995).

For the members of these bodies, educational reform to promote economic restructuring demanded new definitions of skills, educational content relevant to industry-defined needs, and new accountability procedures. The discourse of "outcomes" met these requirements. Outcomes simultaneously bridged the commonsense understandings of committee members (cf. Jones & Moore, 1993), promised that their goals could be met, and accorded with other public sector reforms. Outcomes became a key intellectual and practical technology that translated notions of industrial productivity—or, more broadly, of "enterprise"—into educators' work practices, self-governance, and the governance of their students (cf. Miller & Rose, 1993, p. 97 ff.).

In the school sector, outcomes took shape from 1991–1993 in the AEC's guideline curriculum *Statements* and assessment *Profiles* for eight key learning areas. These guidelines were adopted in toto by most States/Territories and used as a basis for further curriculum work in others. In the post-secondary non-university sector, the National Training Agenda was launched in 1989, its centerpiece being the Australian Standards Framework. This framework represented outcomes as the "competencies" required for the career paths authorized through the accord reforms. The same framework was used for accrediting non-university courses and recognizing credentials. Course accreditation was enforced and extended through DEET effectively restricting its special purpose funding to accredited courses.

Universities' legal autonomy allowed them to resist the Standards Framework, although they could not ignore the fact that by 1995 almost all the professions (and over half the remaining workforce) had used it to develop competency specifications (Curtain & Hayton, 1995; Gonczi, 1994). Depicting universities' resistance as motivated by self-interest and backwardness, the chair of the AEC's Employment and Skills Formation Council, Laurie Carmichael (former trade unionist and member of the Communist Party), predicted the demise of "my mystical academic friends, who believe you can only learn to think in a way bestowed by them in universities. There'll be a convergence of work and learning, and the convergence of the workplace into both a work and learning place will have developed to such a degree that academic witchcraft will finally disappear" (The Australian, 2 June, 1992, cited in Taylor & Henry, 1994, p. 114).

THE ALLP AS A NATIONAL POLICY

The opening sentence of the ALLP focuses on national concerns: "Australia's national identity is explored, expressed and enlivened through language" (Department of Employment Education and Training, 1991, vol. 1, p. iii). The policy document is subsequently described as presenting "the Commonwealth Government's proposals for a national collaborative effort to improve our language and literacy achievements in the 1990s" (Department of Employment, Education, and Training, 1991, vol. 1, p. vii).

The terms "national" and "collaborative" reflect the new consensual structures and processes by which policies and projects were now legitimated. The existence of these structures also enabled the ALLP to be distinguished from the NPL. Despite the latter's title as a "national" policy, a DEET officer explained:

> The NPL was essentially a Commonwealth policy . . . the ALLP was in fact a genuinely national policy to the extent that the goals and objectives were actually signed off by all Education and Training Ministers.

This distinction exemplifies the increasingly "high semantic overload" placed on the descriptors "national" and "collaborative" by the new structures and processes (Lingard et al., 1995, p. 48). *National* could variably mean "the highest level of abstraction or consensus; the lowest common denominator or consensus; derived from constituent individuals or groups; and inclusive of *all* constituent units" (Lingard et al., 1995, p. 47). *Collaborative* also had variable meanings. It was "used by the Commonwealth in an attempt to incorporate the States into its own agenda" and "by the States to resist this process and to assert their primacy in determining school policy" (Lingard et al., 1995, p. 48). Despite the aura of calm, firm, and widespread agreement embodied in these descriptors, the national collaborative processes that produced both the national *Statements* and *Profiles* for schools and the National Training Agenda were intensely conflictive, constantly vulnerable to destabilization (Lingard et al., 1995; Marsh, 1994), and played out in select closed forums.

National collaboration over the ALLP was no different. Gilding (1996, pp. 1–2) reports that, in 1991, when the Commonwealth minister brought the ALLP—intended as "a comprehensive national policy"—to the AEC, he experienced "a rude shock": "State and Territory ministers were hostile" because of the Commonwealth's failure to negotiate "policy or program commitments" (p. 1). A "fiery meeting" ensued, in which the minister "managed to secure commitment to four broad national goals" (p. 2). Three further years of negotiation were required before all ministers endorsed the "National Collaborative Adult English Language and Literacy Strategy" (p. 2). As we shall see, these negotiations required a complete reworking of the arrangements for funding and managing adult ESL programs (Martin, 1999).

In education, once "outcomes" had been agreed on as the key to reform, the decisive politics were between those representing the Commonwealth and States/Territories, with the other players available for co-option into their agendas. For the Commonwealth minister and his officials, part of these politics entailed simply holding the States/Territories to the actual process that allowed policies and projects to be described as national and collaborative. As described by one DEET officer:

> *Dawkins wanted national collaboration and he got... [the States'] agreement on that. But as part of the price, perhaps, of getting their agreement to national collaboration, the Commonwealth, through its officials and so on, had to step right back, and essentially play a passive role, and allow the States to work out the details of that collaboration. Because if they were going to agree to collaborate at all, it had to be on their terms, with their officials leading the charge.*

Holding some States to this process was not at all straightforward. Predictably, they had their own agendas:

> *Most of the State players were quite committed to working toward a genuinely national thing. ... The problem with the bigger States is that they often really*

don't feel the need to participate in anything that's genuinely national. They can do their own thing and bugger the rest of the country. This is part of the problem of living and working in a federal system, from my perspective as a Commonwealth person [laughs].

Despite these frustrations, both sides understood the Commonwealth's power. As described by a State government official, in the AEC "all notionally participate as equals, but the Commonwealth is the dominant player, having the resources to give it leverage and using its resourcing powers to pursue agendas for reform which are often unpalatable to the States and Territories" (Gilding, 1996).

Policy directions for ESL were formulated within the domain of education. However, the political imperatives of the consensus alliance and Commonwealth–State relations meant that the expertise and concerns of most participants in AEC forums were not primarily directed to educational content, much less language issues. In fact, this content seemed mostly irrelevant and trivial to these players. An example of this dynamic was described by an ESL educator as follows:

The Steering Committee was made up of very senior people from government departments, industry boards, and unions. . . . All they see is a big wad of paper and a list of academics who've said something about it. So they think it's fine. . . . [As one said], he was impressed at the thickness of it [i.e. a particular project], and that this was really good. And then after all this back-slapping, I had to speak to this picky, nasty paper that the ESL field had put together. And it was really dismissed, people were really sort of snide and angry about it. . . . "How dare they? . . . How little vision people have! Isn't it pathetic?" And then we went off and had lunch.

ESL AND DEPARTMENTAL POLITICS

Commonwealth leadership in education was not confined to maintaining national collaborative processes. The various agents that could speak in the name of the Commonwealth, in this case those representing DEET, had their own agendas. In regard to the ALLP, the DEET minister's speech to launch the policy indicated these agendas:

This policy brings together a number of strands of policy that have been separately administered, separately put together in the past and now this is our attempt to try and make a coherent whole out of these various strands of policy and various programs. And the starting point is that Australia is a nation of many cultures but Australia has but one national language, that being Australian English (Dawkins, 1991, p. 1).

The minister's focus on policy fragmentation and English amazed many language educators. For them, the outstanding characteristic of the NPL, which his own department administered, had been its application of a coherent set of principles to language issues. In regard to English, the minister's assertion seemed gratuitous: The NPL had declared English to be "the national language of Australia" and had affirmed "the legitimacy and importance of the functions which are fulfilled by English" (Lo Bianco, 1987, p. 71). The minister's point about English had to be read in relation to *other* languages: In place of the NPL's equally strong affirmation of the social, cultural, and economic benefits of widespread societal multilingualism (pp. 73–76), the minister described languages other than English as "foreign" and endorsed their value in promoting trade with Asia.

Although surprising, the minister's refusal to acknowledge the NPL, his focus on fragmentation and his positioning of English were purposeful. These purposes related to ministerial and departmental ambitions, the AEC strategy, administrative arrangements, and inter-departmental rivalries. I now consider each of these ingredients in the politics shaping policy for ESL.

Ambitions

As we have seen, the minister's early policy paper signaled his leadership ambitions in education.[3] The NPL had made languages an object of explicit policymaking before Minister Dawkins gained the education portfolio. Language policy offered an opportunity for asserting leadership, but a new take was needed.

DEET readily adopted its minister's commitment to leadership. As described by one government official: *"DEET was looking to rise in the pecking order. They weren't in the pantheon of coordinating Departments but they wanted to profoundly influence and shape the government's policy."*

As already indicated, the need for "vision" gained salience. A DEET officer explained: *"As public servants, we are here to serve a Commonwealth government agenda and, through that, the agendas of our own individual ministers. Sometimes these need [pause] a degree of vision."*

From outside the department, DEET and its minister's vision appeared somewhat differently:

> There was in DEET a sort of heroic streak, in my perception, where it was gung-ho, ripper, "Let's mow down all before us, because here's the New World order." It was a mega-department that had bashed up the old Education Department [i.e. the department that had been restructured], which was educationally oriented and focused. The staff saw their department as ... having a very hard edge to it and it was going to save the country.

---

[3]Minister Dawkins later became Treasurer. He retired from politics when it became clear that his political career would go no further.

In 1989, the way forward was provided by an NPL report on adult literacy (Wickert, 1989). "Illiteracy" was transparently interpretable as hindering economic restructuring. Despite the author's protests at this extrapolation, the report was sensationalized in the media as identifying one million illiterate Australians. The subsequent 1990 International Year of Literacy and the NPL's Adult Literacy campaign called for action. In 1991, the end of NPL's three-year funding cycle offered the opportunity for a new policy, which became the ALLP.

Using the 1989 literacy report, the DEET discussion paper leading to the ALLP played into anti-immigrant sentiment (whose development will be elaborated below) by implying that immigrants had gained more than their fair share: "The difference in funding for adult ESL programs compared to adult literacy programs" could be explained largely by the hitherto hidden adult literacy need among English speakers, which was "two to three times as great" as ESL needs (Department of Employment Education and Training, 1990, vol. 1, p. 17). At the same time, the minister took every opportunity to disavow the NPL's pluralism, a notable example being his description of it as "a dog's breakfast" (Australian Literacy Federation, March 8, 1991). These tactics drove a wedge through ESL's previous linkages with bi/multilingualism, eliminating what one government official described as its "soft" and "wet" dimensions. Instead, legitimized in the ALLP as part of "language and literacy," and under the firm leadership of DEET and its minister, ESL had been allocated its place in economic restructuring.

The AEC

The policy approach to ESL was also shaped by ministerial and departmental tactics in the AEC. In regard to schools, the committee developing the *Statements* and *Profiles* had already determined that ESL was part of the subject English and was steadfast in this designation, despite representations from ESL educators that it replaced distinctive ESL concerns for bilingualism and across-the-curriculum content with traditional English/Language arts content and assumptions (Moore, 1996b). Accepting this decision held no pain for the Commonwealth. The tied grant to the States/Territories for school ESL had always been so loosely monitored that it was impossible to tell whether and how it was actually spent on ESL. In 1992, during the national curriculum development process, a "scathing" Auditor General's report criticized DEET's failure to monitor the outcomes of this grant (Cahill, 1996, p. 53). A simple solution was to abandon it. As a DEET officer explained: "*We were essentially backing right out of kids' responsibilities at that stage.*" In 1994, the ESL school allocation, apart from intensive courses for new arrivals, was subsumed within a National Equity Program.

The program set broad goals but gave State/Territory education systems greater discretion over federal funding. Long-term ESL requirements subsequently disappeared from federal government policymaking (Michel, 1999).

The minister's atomistic prioritization of English also followed from the AEC's focus on "outcomes" in both school and post-school sectors. Outcomes cut the ground from under "mystical," "wet" arguments that learners' other languages made ESL learning distinctive. A DEET officer explained:

> Employers would simply say "I don't care where you come from or what your background is. I want to know what you can do. If you were born in this country or born overseas, that's irrelevant. What can you deliver? What English language and literacy skills do you have?"

As the same person continued, the AEC's understanding of outcomes made educators' traditional emancipatory claims seem selfishly extravagant:

> If you want to say "Look, I'm trying to develop this particular individual, I should have open go, as much resources as I need reasonably to develop that person educationally,' then governments will say 'Well, the public aren't prepared to pay that sort of money."

Policy Coherence and DEET Administration

The minister's sense of the need for "a coherent policy whole" reflected the administrative complexities in his own very large department, which managed Commonwealth education grants to the States and universities, unemployment benefits and job placement, and various ad hoc programs.

These latter programs were the means by which the federal government responded to electoral concerns with initiatives in education. Consequently, these programs had inherently uncertain life spans. In adult education, the required flexibility was achieved by short-term contracting (in some cases for six weeks; before 1994, never longer than 12 months). Contracts were won by competitive bidding by Colleges of Technical and Further Education (TAFE) and community and private profit-making agencies.

Within DEET, ongoing policy initiatives spawned different sections managing these programs. Fragmentation was further exacerbated by regionalization. Regional offices drew up course specifications in line with various centrally determined program guidelines matched against local training needs as indicated by unemployment figures, and allocated and monitored contracts. In Melbourne, for example, a city of about three million people, approximately five regional offices made their own separate decisions about course types and focus.

The minister's desire to eradicate incoherence was well placed in regard to DEET-funded courses, not least in ESL. Short-term competitive contracting meant that students were rarely sure that courses would run in any given venue. Demand was impossible to chart because people frequently applied for multiple courses and/or enrolled in unsuitable courses for fear of missing out. Providers did not know the outcomes of contract bids until the last minute, so they could not plan ahead or advertise courses in a timely way. Classes often ran with small numbers and were made up of highly disparate students. Teachers were often hired at short notice, and ESL courses were frequently taught by teachers with minimal or no ESL qualifications. Professional development was generally an individual responsibility. Instability meant teacher morale was often low and teaching resources were minimal.

By the late 1980s, DEET's priorities were directed toward counteracting mounting unemployment. Funds increased dramatically for "labor market training," giving a sense of urgency but no room for tackling incoherent course provision. As a DEET officer explained, the department's "clients" were now "all job seekers." Although "there's nothing for non-English speaking background people as such," "language and literacy," legitimated by the ALLP, was, however, relevant:

> The department would say "If you've got English language and literacy difficulties, which is not the same as being non-English speaking background or English-speaking background, we will address that need." But they didn't want to differentiate against people's backgrounds or their learning needs. They were running such a massive system in labor market programs, they couldn't get down to that level of refinement.

"Learning needs" were nevertheless differentiated in some ways:

> The only way in which the department tended to separate them [i.e. clients] out would be the very disadvantaged—at some stage they used to have this concept of the very disadvantaged and the less disadvantaged. That was a queuing mechanism. And then... [in 1994] we got that concept of the long-term unemployed as going to the head of the queue.

Likewise, the reluctance to consider "backgrounds" was selective: "*The department doesn't actually target people. Apart from Aboriginal people. And single parents, but the single parents can be male or female. But they're only special purpose things. And there's a few support programs for people with disabilities.*"

In the TAFE system, consistent attention to adult ESL learning needs relied on State systems' and colleges' discretionary use of recurrent funding. By 1991, the TAFE colleges' recurrent funding ($274 million) was just slightly more than half DEET's labor market training budget ($464 million), making them highly dependent on DEET short-term contracts (Marginson,

1997, pp. 169–170). (In 1995–96, the labor market training budget increased to $2.1 billion [Keating, 1994]). Courses providing ESL and adult literacy were taught in departments or sections whose names and mandates encompassed as wide a scope as possible to attract funding. This imperative worked against distinct ESL and/or English mother tongue adult literacy programs, much less specialist departments or sections, although a few existed. Consequently, to the extent that DEET officials had contact with educational providers, the general term "language and literacy" accorded with their conception of program designation and management (cf. Smith's, 1990, "ideological circle"). As expressed in the epigraph to this chapter, the distinction between ESL and literacy had no reality for "all of us." As another DEET officer added: *"Frankly, I never really understood why they [i.e., some ESL educators] were so resistant to the idea of looking holistically at a group with language needs."*

In this administrative context, the development of the ALLP, and a small Language and Literacy branch within DEET to implement it, could be seen as a victory for those looking to keep language issues on the policy map. A member of the branch gave some indication of the internal politics the policy generated:

> *It's worth saying what an enormous struggle it was, within the public policy context, to have separately identified funds for the adult English language and literacy needs of unemployed people.... To actually acknowledge that you needed to support... [these] learning needs was not readily agreed to.*

While a victory for the ALLP's architects, the separate identification of language and literacy funding was not straightforward. The total figure was considerable ($333.33 million by 1993–1994) but was compiled from allocations to existing programs. Very little was new money ($45.11 million in the first year) and (in contrast to previous NPL funding) projections for future years were not committed. Despite the emphasis on unmet English mother tongue literacy needs, increases in this area were a small proportion of the total budget ($25.45 million for 1991–1992).

Likewise, although the Language and Literacy branch was responsible for implementing the ALLP, it had no authority over these programs, nor did it have the mandate to address the fundamental problems for adult ESL and literacy provision that lay in short-term contracting, regionalization, and program designation. The main work of branch officers lay in further policy development, allocating small research grants, and representing the department in relevant inter-departmental and inter-institutional conferences and committees, including AEC subcommittees.

As a small and newly created part of a mega-department, the branch was powerless to shape departmental culture. The policy "whole" of language and literacy became yet another ingredient in the mix of DEET concerns, while the administrative incoherence faced by providers and students intensified as labor market training funds increased.

Policy "Strands" and Inter-Departmental Rivalries

Although DEET's policy preoccupations and administrative structures made its responsibilities for ESL at best irrelevant and at worst an embarrassment, ESL was an important tool in giving substance to DEET claims to leadership. Most notably, it was the allocation to existing ESL programs (in 1991–1992, $243.77 million, i.e., 80% of total funds) that saved the ALLP budget from looking decidedly thin. The bulk of these funds were for school ESL in the form of transfer grants to the States/Territories. As we have seen, DEET had foregone a leadership role here, in return for national collaboration.

In adult ESL, approximately $89 million of the ALLP budget (in 1990–1991) was for the Adult Migrant English Program (AMEP). The AMEP was administered, not by DEET, but by an entirely separate department which was responsible for immigration (henceforth "Immigration"—the department's name varied during the period under discussion). The AMEP was part of Immigration's "settlement" mandate (Moore, in press). The provocative inclusion of another department's territory within the ALLP budget, and its designation as "language and literacy," indicated that DEET aspired, if not to appropriate this program (as many within it feared), then at least to bring it within its policy vision.

Unlike DEET programs, the AMEP had a focused and stable management structure, underpinned by a Commonwealth–State agreement reached in 1951 and recurrent funding since 1978. The lack of other designated adult ESL provision meant that demand centered on the AMEP. Since its beginnings in the late 1940s, AMEP ESL courses had expanded and diversified in response to the complexity of settlement, educational, age-, gender-, and employment-related factors in the immigrant population. The program was supported by ESL-qualified teachers, quality teaching materials, and ongoing research and development. At the time of the ALLP, and in response to economic restructuring, the AMEP was in process of developing what became one of the first curriculum and assessment frameworks in *any* field to be accredited within the new procedures (Hagan et al., 1993). The program was also the most comprehensively monitored of any educational endeavor at any level in Australia and included the largest database on ESL learners in the world.

The quality of the AMEP did not protect it from DEET's ambitions but rather invited criticism of "softness" and wastefulness. Immigration's responsibilities and attendant lowly status in the departmental pecking order contributed fundamentally to the AMEP's vulnerability. Throughout the 1980s, the department's standing had been buffeted, starting with claims by prominent academics, fuelled by the media, that Australian culture was being undermined by "Asian" immigrants and "multiculturalism." In 1986, an influential government enquiry reported that "views representing hundreds and thousands of Australians" expressed "confusion and mistrust of multiculturalism [undefined], focussing on the suspicion that it drove immigration policy" (Fitzgerald, 1986, p. xii). The report recommended that immigration serve national economic interests, to which the department responded by reworking both visa criteria and the AMEP to focus on job skills. Nevertheless, it continued to be targeted as unsympathetic to economic restructuring and promoting threats to traditional Australian cultural unities based on race, language, and English institutions. The Immigration department itself also contained powerful individuals and groups with widely differing views on immigration, multiculturalism and the utility of the AMEP.

From the late 1980s onward as described by one government official:

They [Immigration] got knocked around every budget time... they couldn't convince Finance that they knew what they were doing.... DEET kept on undermining them. Dawkins was very smart... DEET basically ran their own game and did what they wanted to do, because they were a lot smarter at it.

With mounting unemployment and the 1990–1991 recession, pressure on the government to cut immigration numbers became irresistible. The various political forces, as they played out in the Cabinet, also enabled significant erosion of the AMEP. In 1992, unprecedented legislation restricted eligibility for AMEP tuition to low level learners in the period directly following arrival. At the same time, and to avoid the spectacle of students without courses and unemployed ESL teachers, a portion of DEET's increasing labor market training budget was earmarked for AMEP providers. By 1993, the overwhelming majority of adult ESL courses—although not designated as such—were funded through this budget and managed through DEET. DEET's vision had been realized.

These changes intensified existing problems and created new ones. DEET's administrative structures and the restriction of eligibility for the AMEP generated what one official described as "anarchy" in the Immigration department and, for overall provision, "*an absolute schimozzle... a giant administrative mess.*" The 1951 Commonwealth–State agreement on ESL provision was inoperable, engendering, as we have seen, a fiery State/Territory reaction in the AEC. Instability persisted throughout the three-year period in which new arrangements were negotiated, including a year in which the AMEP budget was under-spent by $27 million.

The influx of funds and students into DEET programs also highlighted DEET's rudimentary accountability procedures, which were almost entirely based on keeping *per capita* costs low. In 1990, the department had attempted to engage with this issue by commissioning a project to develop outcome measures for adult literacy courses. Intense hostility from professional associations prompted an evaluation of these measures, which was devastatingly critical (Freebody et al., 1993). An appropriate task for the Language and Literacy branch was to give its interpretation of "language and literacy" technological form:

> H: What would you say was the bottom line for you as the representative of the Commonwealth?
> G: Of DEET?
> H: Of DEET, yes . . .
> G: A single system for reporting across adult literacy and adult ESL.

In 1993, together with a new AEC-instituted body, the branch jointly funded production of the National Reporting System (NRS) for "adult English language, literacy and numeracy"[4] (Coates, Fitzpatrick, McKenna, & Makin, 1995). However, in 1994, at the end of the ALLP's projected funding period (and before completion of the NRS in 1996), under a different DEET minister whose interest in language issues was minimal, the Language and Literacy branch was dissolved. In 1996, the incoming conservative government abolished labor market programs as an ineffective extravagance and hence DEET funding for adult language and literacy. As a DEET official observed (without irony): *"The Commonwealth's interest in specific elements of the adult ESL and literacy field may, in fact, no longer be relevant."* The 1992 legislation that had restricted entitlements to the AMEP now protected this program, demonstrating that Immigration officials had been less inept than painted at the time. The AMEP was once again the main source of adult ESL, albeit limited to new arrivals.

Meanwhile, DEET's lack of interest in "kids' responsibilities" were reversed by its new Minister's aggressive promotion of a literacy policy for schools. Encompassing ESL, the policy offered no direction or incentive (quite the contrary) for accommodating these learners (Davison, 1999; Lo Bianco, 1998). As described by an ESL educator, *"ESL provision for children who need it is now very much a matter of chance."*

Although DEET's policies and programs might be seen as ephemeral, the politics of the 1990s had one consistent effect: The long-term and complex English learning needs of immigrants and their children had lost their reality on the Commonwealth policy map.

---

[4]The numeracy descriptors were separate.

ESL AS FACTIONAL CORRUPTION

National collaborative policies and projects, and the understandings on which they rested, were products of hard-fought political processes. Having reached decisions, the participants, with reason, did not want them unraveled. The diverse and conflicting interests thus formed alliances directed to convincing others to translate these political achievements into implementable form.

These processes were also political, but, as "consultations," they were differently so. The closed forums in which policies had been developed were replaced by processes that drew in as many interested parties as possible. Thus, for example, the NRS consultations were described by a DEET officer as involving "hundreds if not thousands" of people. However, as the officer explained, the aim was "communication." The contests that had generated policies and programs were not an option:

> Inevitably, there's going to be people whose noses are out of joint. The communication is very difficult in that context, making sure that people actually have a common understanding of what the objectives are, let alone what the outcomes might be.

The process by which people's noses went "out of joint" in regard to the school ESL *Profile* was described by an ESL educator as follows:

> The assessment *Profile* looked at students' immersion in English rather than giving a sense of them growing and developing as bilinguals. There was no reference to first language knowledge or cultural knowledge, or the learning that's involved in learning how to operate in a new culture, because the writers considered it was too hard within the constraints of the national curriculum project. . . . They were given a particular *Profile* to write for particular types of learners and they had to do it within the constraints of the structure of the National Curriculum Statements that had been written already. . . . And I guess that was an argument we were never really able to have, because whenever that comment was made, the people on the writing team would say "But that would be going beyond our brief."

This dynamic bred cynicism:

> They treated consultations largely as briefings and limited the extent to which you could provide input. When the final thing appears, there's a line in the acknowledgments saying "We've done this consultation with a large number of professionals" [laughing]. And you think "I think that was me." . . . And then there is that trick of saying in the final draft "We've incorporated these peoples' ideas." [laughing]. You look and say "Well, there's just this tiny little point. And yes, they have." So you can't say "Well they haven't," because in a very trivial and concrete way, that's true [laughing], but in a much more profound way it's so false.

Predictably, precluding debate fermented conflict:

H: So how do you see the debate about ESL and literacy . . . what's your memory of how that played itself out?
G: Ah, I just remember the brawls.

The content of these brawls centered on accusations of factionalism. For example, the most overt critic of the NRS development process was the largest AMEP provider, who had developed the curriculum and assessment framework adopted nationally in 1992. (A second large provider was more circumspect, conscious that the NRS steering committee chair headed the department of which they were part). Not without their critics among fellow AMEP providers and others in the ESL and literacy fields (including myself), this group was portrayed as the source of opposition and lacking support from their colleagues. Their motivation was attributed to resentment of challenges to their expertise and threats to their "curriculum markets and theoretical territory," while their failure to accept government policy was misguided and racist: "Because the Australian Language and Literacy Policy set an agenda of English literacy for all Australians . . . having separate frameworks for people from different backgrounds would have in fact been discriminatory" (Coates, 1996, p. 4).

Within the various advisory committees, those who questioned project directions were portrayed as personally insensitive to those engaged in the difficult task of furthering national goals. As described by an ESL educator:

There was a sense that we needed to support [the project director], a sort of personal level of support from the committee that I was very frustrated with, because I wasn't operating that way. . . . There seemed to be a network or club who were all very supportive and loyal but I felt that it wasn't the professional agenda that was driving that loyalty.

These factional accusations had considerable personal costs. As described by a government official: *"It was just extraordinary. Really capable people beating each other up. Capable and competent, being reduced to sobbing wrecks."*

FACTIONS: LEGITIMATE INTERESTS OR DAMAGING INFECTIONS?

The ALLP and subsequent policy directions did not derive from some ideal alternative to partisan politics. They were developed through the network of power centered on national economic restructuring. To the extent that this example is typical of the formation, maintenance, and disintegration of governmental alliances in the central coordinating arenas of nation states, it illustrates how these processes are inseparable from politics.

Inevitably, these political processes included some groups and individuals while excluding others. Those who were excluded, for example ESL educators, could be represented as a corrupting faction, although they were no more or less directed to their own particular concerns than was anyone else. In my experience and as far as my interview data indicate, the only basis for accusations of factionalism was this political work of inclusion/exclusion. ESL educators and others struggling against the exclusion of their concerns from the policy process may be assisted in maintaining direction if they recognize the function of these kinds of accusation.

The fact that government directed to the common good is always constituted by particular interests need not be grounds for cynicism. Myths embody the moral and cultural unities—the norms and ideals—intrinsic to governmentality and to being human. Although mythologies erode and change, it is not just a myth but a dangerous illusion that we can dispense with ideals, even if unattainable. Grounds for cynicism exist when the liberal democratic myth is used by some to exclude others from the inevitably political processes in which their "good" is crucially determined, and when the fear of factions is mobilized to disguise these politics.

APPENDIX

List of Acronyms

AEC   Australian Education Council.
ALLP   Australian Language and Literacy Policy (1991).
AMEP   Adult Migrant English (formerly Education) Program.
DEET   Department of Employment, Education and Training.
ESL   English as a Second Language.
NPL   National Policy on Languages (1987).
NRS   National Reporting System.
TAFE   Technical and Further Education (Colleges).

REFERENCES

Allington, R., & Woodside-Jiron, H. (1999). The politics of literacy teaching: How "research" shaped educational policy. *Educational Researcher, 28*(8), 4–13.
Burchell, G. (1996). Liberal government and the techniques of the self. In A. Barry, T. Osborne, & N. Rose (Eds.), *Foucault and political reason* (pp. 19–36). London: University College London Press.
Cahill, D. (1996). *Immigration and schooling in the 1990s.* Canberra: Bureau of Immigration, Multiculturalism and Population Research.
Campbell, W. J., & McMeniman, M. M. (1985). *Bridging the language gap: Ideals and realities*

pertaining to learning English as a second language. Canberra: Commonwealth Schools Commission.

Coates, S. (1996). *A strategic and educationally sustainable response to government requirements for accountability of adult English language and literacy programs*. Paper presented at the World Congress on Comparative Education Societies, Sydney, Australia.

Coates, S., Fitzpatrick, L., McKenna, A., & Makin, A. (1995). *National reporting system: A mechanism for reporting English language, literacy, and numeracy indicators of competence*. Canberra: Department of Employment and Training/Australian National Training Authority.

Considine, M. (1988). The corporate management framework as administrative science: A critique. *Australian Journal of Public Administration, 47*, 4–18.

Curtain, R., & Hayton, G. (1995). The use and abuse of a competency standards framework in Australia: A comparative perspective. *Assessment in Education, 2*(2), 205–224.

Davison. (1999). Missing the mark: The problem with benchmarking of ESL students in Australian schools. *Prospect: A Journal of Australian TESOL, 14*(2), 66–76.

Dawkins, J. (1991, September 2). *Transcript of John Dawkins, Minister for Employment, Education and Training, press conference re Australia's Language—The Australian Language and Literacy Policy [Media release]*, Canberra.

Department of Employment Education and Training. (1990). *The language of Australia: Discussion paper on an Australian literacy and language policy for the 1990s*. Canberra: Australian Government Publishing Service.

Department of Employment Education and Training. (1991). *Australia's language: The Australian Language and Literacy Policy*. Canberra: Australian Government Publishing Service.

Department of Employment Education Training and Youth Affairs. (1998). *Literacy for all: The challenge for Australian schools. Commonwealth literacy policies for Australian schools*. Canberra: DEETYA.

Fitzgerald, S. (Chair). (1986). *Immigration: A commitment to Australia. The report of the committee to advise on Australia's immigration policies*. Canberra: Australian Government Publishing Service.

Foucault, M. (1991). Governmentality. In G. Burchell, C. Gordon, & P. Miller (Eds.), *The Foucault effect: Studies in governmentality with two lectures by Michel Foucault* (pp. 87–104). Chicago: University of Chicago Press.

Freebody, P., Cumming, J., Falk, I., Muspratt, S., Doyle, S., Flaherty, J., & Lee, N. (1993). *A trialing and evaluation of the Adult Literacy and Numeracy (ALAN) scales*. Nathan, Queensland: Faculty of Education, Griffith University.

Galbally, F. C. (1978). *Migrant services and programs: Report and appendices. Vols. 1–2. Review of post-arrival programs and services for migrants*. Canberra: Australian Government Printing Service.

Gilding, N. (1996). *Strategic responses in ABE to contemporary changes in social, economic and educational policy—Collaborative strategic planning at state and national level - A commentary on the Australian Language and Literacy Policy*. Paper presented at the World Conference on Literacy, Philadelphia, PA.

Gonczi, A. (1994). Competency-based assessment in the professions in Australia. *Assessment in Education, 1*(1).

Hagan, P., Hood, S., Jackson, E., Jones, M., Joyce, H., & Manidis, M. (1993). *Certificates in spoken and written English I–IV*. Sydney: NSW Adult Migrant English Services/National Centre for English Language Teaching and Research, Macquarie University.

Hindess, B. (1996). Liberalism, socialism and democracy: Variations on a governmental theme. In A. Barry, T. Osborne, & N. Rose (Eds.), *Foucault and political reason*. London: University College London Press.

Hindess, B. (1997a). Anti-political motifs in Western political discourse: Explorations in modern antipolitics. In A. Schedler (Ed.), *The end of politics?* (pp. 21–39). Sydney: Macmillan.

Hindess, B. (1997b). Politics and governmentality. *Economy and Society, 26*(2), 257–272.

Hindess, B. (1997c). A society governed by contract? In G. Davis, B. Sullivan, & A. Yeatman (Eds.), *The New Contractualism?* (pp. 14–26). Sydney: Macmillan.

Hindess, B. (1998). Neo-liberalism and the national economy. In M. Dean & B. Hindess (Eds.), *Governing Australia: Studies in contemporary rationalities of government* (pp. 210–226). Cambridge: Cambridge University Press.

Hindess, B. (2001). Power, government and politics. In K. Nash & A. Scott (Eds.), *The Blackwell companion to political sociology.* Oxford: Basil Blackwell. pp. 40–48.

Hirst, P. Q., & Thompson, G. F. (1996). *Globalisation in question: The myths of the international economy and the possibilities of governance.* Oxford: Polity.

Jones, L., & Moore, R. (1993). Education, competence and the control of expertise. *British Journal of the Sociology of Education, 14*(4), 385–397.

Keating, P. J. (1994). *Working nation: Policies and programs.* Canberra: Australian Government Publishing Service.

Lingard, B., Porter, P., Bartlett, L., & Knight, J. (1995). Federal/state mediations in the Australian national education agenda: From the AEC to MCEETYA 1987–1993. *Australian Journal of Education, 39*(1), 41–66.

Lo Bianco, J. (1987). *National policy on languages.* Canberra: Australian Government Publishing Service.

Lo Bianco, J. (1998). ESL . . . Is it migrant literacy? . . . Is it history? *ACTA Background Papers, 2,* 15–21.

Marginson, S. (1992). Education as a branch of economics: The universal claims of economic rationalism. In D. Stockley (Ed.), *Melbourne Studies in Education 1992* (pp. 1–14). Melbourne: La Trobe University Press.

Marginson, S. (1997). *Educating Australia: Government, economy and citizen since 1960.* Cambridge: Cambridge University Press.

Marsh, C. J. (1994). *Producing a national curriculum: Plans and paranoia.* St Leonards, N.S.W., Australia: Allen & Unwin.

Martin, S. (1999). *New life, new language: The history of the Adult Migrant English Program.* Sydney: National Centre for English Language Teaching and Research, Macquarie University.

McKay, P. (1998). Discriminatory features for ESL learners in the literacy benchmarks. *ACTA Background Papers, 2,* 27–29.

Michel, M. (1999). "Wither" ESL? Post-literacy prospects for English as a second language programs in Australian schools. *Prospect, 14*(2), 4–23.

Miller, P. & Rose, N. (1993). Governing economic life. In M. Gane & T. Johnson (Eds.), *Foucault's new domains* (pp. 75–105.). London & New York: Routledge.

Moore, H. (1996a). Language policies as virtual reality: Two Australian examples. *TESOL Quarterly, 30*(3), 473–497.

Moore, H. (1996b). Telling what is real: Competing views in assessing ESL development. *Linguistics and Education, 8*(2), 189–228.

Moore, H. (in press). Although it wasn't broken, it certainly was fixed: Interventions in the Australian Adult Migrant English Program 1991–1996. In J. Lo Bianco & R. Wickert (Eds.), *Language and literacy policy in Australia: 30 years of action.* Melbourne: Language Australia.

Rose, N. (1993). Government, authority and expertise in advanced liberalism. *Economy and Society, 22*(3), 283–299.

Rose, N. (1999). *Powers of freedom: Reframing political thought.* Cambridge University Press.

Smith, D. (1990). *The conceptual practices of power: A feminist sociology of knowledge.* Toronto: University of Toronto Press.

Taylor, S. & Henry, M. (1994). Equity and the new post-compulsory education and training policies in Australia: A progressive or regressive agenda? *Journal of Education Policy, 9*(2), 105–127.

Wickert, R. (1989). *No single measure: A survey of Australian adult literacy.* Canberra: DEET.

Yeatman, A. (1990). *Bureaucrats, technocrats, femocrats.* Sydney: Allen & Unwin.

7

Language Planning and the Perils of Ideological Solipsism

Thomas S. Donahue
San Diego State University

INTRODUCTION: ANOMIE IN CONTENT AND PROCESS

Since the beginning of the 1980s, political interest groups like U.S. English and its offshoot organizations have played upon the vulnerabilities of the American citizenry to a late 20th century type of anomie, with resulting confusions between values for community and for the Self, and a broad insensitivity toward legal principles and traditions. The exploitation of anomic characteristics takes two forms, emphasizing content and then process. First, there is a focus on political issues with which the average American citizen is uncomfortable. Diverse interest groups, including political action groups and proponents of views from the religious right, have attempted to gain influence by crafting confusing and disputatious positions on such issues as American identity as opposed to complex multicultural and multilingual ethnic identities, allegedly "common sense" simplifications of educational policies, and the need for frugal government spending in perilous economic times. Second, through vigorous assertions and counter-assertions, individuals seeking political leadership can promote emotional divisions, masking or diverting attention from larger social problems that are difficult and real. When anomie is a given, unscrupulous persons can achieve leadership by manipulating both the content and the process of debate. Such persons proceed by fostering and then exploiting confusion about a wide array of issues concerned with the modern nature of community and the Self—matters about which most people have only the most slender information.

Any description of anomic political characteristics is complicated by the fact that in a given election year, most voters may be deprived of any rational perspective for judging what happens around them. At a time when most ideological views are based on an orthodox pragmatism, the judgments of American voters become neutralized when complex issues such as language policy are placed in poorly defined and discussed contexts. Further, when professional politicians shun responsibility for placing events in perspective and providing informed and informing leadership, American citizens become particularly vulnerable to the stresses of mixed and mismatched ideological positions—the "Lego Effect" detailed below.

Typical of such ideological mismatching is the Official English issue. In the last 20 years, the highly specialized academic and public policy discipline of language planning has become politically foregrounded through a series of ostensibly grass-roots voter initiatives. Often, language planning is conducted through a set of formal procedures, including the formulation of goals, the codification of resources, the elaboration of language source materials, the implementation of goals through private and public incentives for change, and the monitoring and analysis of results (cf. Eastman, 1983). The practice of real politics disregards or discards such procedures. In a variety of American states, citizens have been asked to declare English as an official language, yet the voters ordinarily have never been informed about what an official language is, or what it is supposed to do, or whether or not there are constitutional constraints protecting affected citizens. Ultimately no one realizes his or her will, or gets his or her way, and a frustrating sense of anomic normlessness prevails. I shall examine the issue of English as an official language in Arizona as a case in point.

The Office English debate in Arizona was long and agonized, with a variety of larger issues occupying the background. At the most serious level, the Official English controversy attests to the anomic nature of the modern political process, a process which can lead a large portion of the voting public to accept nontraditional, extra-legal, and unconstitutional values. Further, we will see that the Official English controversy has diverted public attention away from other serious concerns: What are the real conflicts between the needs of minority groups and those of the governing state? What are the tradeoffs between the development of personality and Self on the part of the citizens, and the need for political stability and fiscal responsibility in the state? What is our current view of the interaction between Self, community, and government? If it is possible to manipulate a political issue from motives of ambition, duplicity, or division, who does such things, and why? What are the risks for political and educational policy when the practice of ordinary process politics is used to slow the response to genuine needs?

This chapter will investigate the Official English controversy in Arizona by using the philosophical meaning of "solipsism" as an explicating concept. In conventional terms, solipsism means that only the Self exists, and that reality can only begin with the perceiving Self. In a practical application for our purposes, solipsism refers to a variety of conditions under which the individual has uncertain information about the influence of the outside world upon the Self, and uncertain knowledge about the ways in which a Self is formed at all. If we can identify a political situation in which individuals have an ideological commitment to a sense of Self, but in which at the same time anomie is a basic condition of life—such that individuals have no certain identity, or no defined direction for personal development—then we have a most interesting setting for the formation and manipulation of political opinion. Beyond that, we will have identified a complex and paradoxical condition in which education occurs in a social vacuum, and persons are utterly vulnerable to outside political forces. This chapter proceeds with an analysis of such a condition and it builds arguments which suggest changes in policies and practices for the future. After a review of the facts of the Arizona controversy, the chapter discusses alternative interpretations of the Official English issue. The discussion proceeds with an attempt to locate the controversy amid the liberal/libertarian and communitarian traditions of political thought. The chapter concludes with a recommendation for "Applied Communitarianism" in future language and education policies.

OFFICIAL ENGLISH IN ARIZONA

After years of nationwide and then statewide controversy about naming English as an official language, the citizens of Arizona in 1988 voted for Proposition 106, a proposed addition to the Arizona Constitution. The central requirement of the Proposition asked that the English language be used as "the language of the ballot, the public schools and all government functions and actions" (see Appendix). Ten years later, on April 28, 1998, the Arizona Supreme Court ruled as follows:

> We hold that the Amendment violates the First Amendment to the United States Constitution because it adversely impacts the constitutional rights of non-English-speaking persons with regard to their obtaining access to their

government and limits the political speech of elected officials and public employees. We also hold that the Amendment violates the Equal Protection Clause of the Fourteenth Amendment to the United States Constitution because it unduly burdens core First Amendment rights of a specific class without materially advancing a legitimate state interest (Paragraph 2 of the summary of the opinion by Justice James Moeller).

The position of the Arizona Supreme Court is notably firm and direct, and this opinion (at least for this time and place) settles the issue of whether or not it is constitutional for Arizona to require the use of a language, with no exceptions, for the conduct of official business.

The Facts of the Case

The case began in October 1987, when Arizonans for Official English began to circulate a petition proposing an amendment to the state constitution which would require that all state and local employees conduct government business exclusively in English. On November 8, 1988, with a 50.5% positive vote, the people of Arizona passed that initiative [for the text of the Amendment, see the Appendix]. Two days after election day, Ms. Marie-Kelley F. Yniguez, a state employee who handled medical malpractice claims against the state, brought suit against the state of Arizona and Governor Rose Mofford in the District Court, seeking to have the new law declared unconstitutional because it violated the first and 14th amendments of the U.S. Constitution. With this suit, there began a complex series of events which unfolded in the following sequence (adapted from the discussion by Justice James Moeller):

1. Ms. Yniguez left her state job for other employment in 1991.
2. Judge Paul Rosenblatt of the District Court asserted declaratory relief on her behalf on February 6, 1990; he found that the amendment was "facially overbroad," and it violated freedom of speech guarantees of the first amendment of the U.S. Constitution. The District Court also ruled that a "narrow construction" of the amendment (which would give the Amendment only the force of a recommendation from the public) was not possible.
3. Governor Mofford chose not to appeal, but Arizonans for Official English, headed by Mr. Robert Parks, proceeded with an appeal, which the District Court denied.
4. In January 1994, Judge Jeffrey Cates of the Maricopa County Superior Court issued a ruling that upheld the legality of the Official English amendment.

5. The Ninth Circuit Court of Appeals reversed the 1990 denial of the District Court [item 3 above] and permitted a group called Arizonans Against Constitutional Tampering to represent the interests of plaintiffs and appellees against the amendment. In addition, the Court of Appeals allowed the intervention of the Arizona Attorney General so that a "narrow interpretation" of the amendment might be considered.
6. The State of Arizona filed an assertion of mootness because Ms. Yniguez had left her job.
7. The Court of Appeals rejected the mootness claim and declared that Ms. Yniguez retained continued standing to seek additional declaratory relief.
8. Arizonans for Official English chose to appeal the original District Court finding that the Amendment was unconstitutional, and Ms. Yniguez appealed that court's denial of nominal damages.
9. On December 7, 1994, a panel of the Ninth Circuit Court of Appeals concurred that the Amendment violated any public employee's freedom of speech and was "unconstitutional in its entirety," and that Ms. Yniguez was entitled to damages. The entire court agreed with the panel.
10. Arizonans for Official English appealed to the U.S. Supreme Court, which vacated the Ninth Circuit ruling for two reasons: There was no case because Ms. Yniguez was no longer an employee of the State of Arizona, and the case should have gone next to the Arizona Supreme Court.
11. The Arizona Supreme Court ruled in April, 1998 that the amendment violates the First Amendment to the U.S. Constitution and that it violates the Equal Protection Clause of the 14th Amendment to the U.S. Constitution.
12. Arizonans for Official English appealed this ruling to the U.S. Supreme Court, which refused to hear the appeal on January 12, 1999.

The Political Atmosphere Surrounding the Amendment

In an earlier treatment of the English as an Official Language controversy, Donahue (1995) argued that public opinion on this issue had been mobilized in three divergent directions. From a right-wing perspective, adherents of the Group Pluralist Theory believe that ethnic diversity in a given population is inherently destabilizing. To serve separate political needs of minority groups and to facilitate the development or emergence of leadership elites in such groups is risky and ultimately dangerous. Thus the

support of general policies for distinct mother-tongue language maintenance, and the specific funding of bilingual education in any form, undermines the peace and security of the state. Sharply divergent from this position is the centrist, or the Cultural Pluralist perspective. The centrist view
maintains that in a state with a well-developed and strong legal culture,
diverse identities and separate ethnic affiliations constitute an immensely
strong social resource. All individuals in such a state are dependably enriched by the thinking and the reasoning of people unlike themselves.
Those assuming a left-wing stance argue from a Core-Periphery perspective: there exists an elite Core formed by business interests of any and all
sizes, and it becomes their mission (and that of their political epigones)
further to disempower and disenfranchise persons who are already pe-
ripheralized through their membership in minority language cultures.

The English as an Official Language movement, under the leadership
of the interest group U.S. English, grew in power and influence throughout the 1980s, and the hold on the public imagination by this vanguard
group and its issue did not seem to be substantially undermined by the
revelation that the founder of U.S. English was motivated primarily by a
fear of Latino fertility and of Latino immigration into the United States
(see Donahue, 1995). Our principal interest at this point lies in an examination of the orchestration of public sentiment on this issue during the vexed
12-year span of this case in Arizona. When any public statements reflect
a motive of partisan ideology (as was the case with Arizonans for Official
English) or a mission to provide community leadership (as was the apparent case with the *Arizona Republic*, a Phoenix newspaper), it is important to
describe the underlying value system of the actors for the duration of this
issue. Of particular interest are the subsurface views regarding the individual citizen and his or her entitlements, as contrasted with any concept
of community needs, and the optimal ways (if these exist at all) to serve
them. The central thematic focus in this inquiry involves an emphasis on
Self, and specifically on the ways a Self is formed separate from community
influence, as opposed to the formative experience for Self found inside or
within communal influence.

THE RANGE OF OPINION: RIGHT, THEN LEFT AND CENTER

The history of public opinion on the English as an Official Language issue
in Arizona can be traced in the letters to the editors and in the ideological stance of columnists in the two newspapers in Arizona's capital city:
the *Phoenix Gazette* and the *Arizona Republic* (hereafter PG and AR, respectively). The earliest accounts, reporting from the time that the English-
only initiative began, contrast the right-of-center with the left-of-center

positions. In a United Press International (UPI) story of 9/11/1987, Mr. Robert Park (described as a "retired criminal investigator for the U.S. Immigration and Naturalization Service"), in his capacity as the Chairman of Arizonans for Official English is quoted as saying that the proposed voter initiative is "unifying because English is our common language," while current policies "to have the government run in more than one language" are "costly, divisive, and not what the people of the United States want, especially Arizona." Contrary opinions, offered by State Senator Peter Kay and other state legislators, together with "Hispanic leaders and other elected officials, including the chairman of the Navajo Tribe," labeled the initiative "divisive" and "too restrictive and reactionary."

At every legal twist and turn from this point forward, right-of-center opinion falls within the category of Group Pluralist ideology. When the initiative qualified for the ballot (as Proposition 106, the proposed 28th article for the Arizona constitution), Mr. Park savored his victory by assuming a more statesman-like position: he declared that those hoping to "promote and preserve our common bond" have been inappropriately characterized as "narrow-minded bigots" (UPI, 8/5/88). After victory at the polls, and the immediate suit by Ms. Yniguez, Mr. Park allowed himself to become spiny in reaction: "I think their goal is multilingual government" (AR, 11/16/88). When Governor Mofford refused to appeal the 1990 decision of Judge Rosenblatt, Mr. Park showed a skill for counterattacking with his opponent's rhetoric: "Not to appeal is to disenfranchise all voters" (AR, 2/14/1990). In the following month he declared: "It is chaos to conduct official government business in a language other than English" (AR, 3/27/1990).

As court appeals proceeded over time, the Group Pluralist ideology began to move in new directions. Writing for the Arizona Republic on July 21, 1993, Stefan Halper criticized the Clinton administration for conducting an American citizenship ceremony in Spanish. Halper complained that the symbolism of such a procedure disregarded the advice of John Quincy Adams (who required that new Americans "must cast off the European skin"), and instead played to a current sensibility to "denounce the idea of a melting pot." In addition to a "lack of respect" for the presently established American citizenry, he argued there were portentous issues of "cost and inconvenience" in providing multilingual services, and he warned ominously of the possibility of ethnic leadership elites: "those who would benefit from ethnic separatism have found a voice in the media." Later that summer, in a column entitled "'Ethnic Pride' Tears us Apart," Ernest W. Levefer undertook a rhetorical counteroffensive: it is not merely true that ethnic assertiveness is "disquieting," it is actually the case that this "new tribalism is clearly racist" in a way that offends the memory of Martin Luther King, Jr. (AR, 8/6/1993). With that remark, Lefever positioned himself among that extraordinarily clever subgroup of right-of-center citizens who can invoke remarks by the Reverend King to support nearly any cause.

Amid the court appeals of 1994, the *Arizona Republic* began to publish letters from citizens supporting the initiative. T. E. Winters expressed a fear of ethnic divisiveness, and declared that the "gradual encroachment of other languages into our official business will soon give us separate groups who cannot communicate;" thus Official English was "necessary to prevent us having the problems of Canada, Belgium, Finland, Switzerland, India, [and] Yugoslavia" (AR, 2/12/1994). Other writers found the amendment necessary to "prevent confusion and promote the 'American Dream'" (AR, 6/13/1994), or cautioned the readers to "look to Canada and its multiple language problems," or to "consider the Netherlands, where military officers must give commands in four different languages" (AR, 6/22/1994). Others felt that Official English was a "unifier" and quoted the experience of an immigrant parent who learned the language from elementary school textbooks (Ms. Frieda Rothbart in the AR, 6/28/94). Still others wrote of specific problems and expected the amendment to provide a different form of rescue: "the dangerous wedge is the uncontrolled flood of immigrants who, for whatever reason, refuse to do what all other international immigrants have done to be assimilated into American culture: Learn English!" This writer continues: "Do the words parasites, criminals, welfare cheats, street gangs, drug dealers, dilution of the quality of U.S. education, fatal injuries by unlicensed (and uninsured) alien drivers ring a bell? There is a basically simple answer to the illegal-immigration problem. Close the U.S. borders for a depth of three miles, secured by the military" (AR, 8/20/1994). On the same day another writer complains that "a vast majority of Hispanic illegal immigrants are illiterate and can't read Spanish either . . . How about the cost of welfare and health and schooling? How about the cost in crime and the incarceration of the illegal-immigrant criminal population?"

After the Ninth District Court of Appeals struck down the amendment in December, 1994, the Group Pluralist category of reaction at first was diffuse and only slightly moderated: "Look at the expense to the taxpayers if we have to print every official notice in several languages . . . we should ask Congress to expedite a federal constitutional amendment making English the official language of the entire land" (AR, 12/23/1994). Or consider: "whatever happened to majority rules?" (AR, 12/28/1994). Within a month, opinion became sharpened: "We must not turn this great country into a place where people from other countries arrive illegally and insist that they bring with them all of the divisive attributes that make their home countries so undesirable a place to live that they wish to leave. We cannot allow the Balkanization of the United States with dozens of different official languages" (AR, 1/1/1995). The writer believes further that persisting with a non-English language shows disrespect to English speakers of the past: "How dare we so denigrate their efforts, their work, and their sacrifices to say that learning the English language is too great a burden for the privilege of becoming a citizen of the United States of America?" (AR, 1/1/1995). Still other reaction offers a temperate retreat to earlier positions: "our mission is the preservation of our common bond through our common language: English . . . let's not have this country experience the plight of Canada that is split over the use of two languages" (AR, 1/9/1995).

When the Ninth District Court delivered its judgment, Mr. Park's attitudes at first took on a more ingratiating tone. He declared that the proposed amendment was merely about the "Language of Government," and that there was a prospect that "ethnic tensions will exacerbate" because "monolingual English speakers may not be employable in many government offices if it [the decision against official English] stands" (AR, 10/11/1995). While the case was under appeal to the U.S. Supreme Court, however, he chose to dissemble about his feelings: "The 9th Circuit has a dismal record with the Supreme Court when in one year it was reversed 26 straight times. When reviewed, this latest decision will surely follow suit" (AR, 4/13/1996). Other letter writers reassert the ethnic dimension: "What part of logic, or civics, don't you understand? English is the language of our founding fathers and original settlers" (AR, 8/28/1996). Months later the same author (Mr. Fred J. Gorchess) explains that position: "Logic dictates the need of a common language for economic and cultural reasons" (AR, 12/14/1996).

When the U.S. Supreme Court vacated the judgment of the Ninth District Court, Mr. Park was elated: "It means we won" (AR, 3/4/1997). As the Arizona Supreme Court considered the case, the orthodox Group Pluralist arguments reappeared: "If a nation does not conduct its affairs in one accepted language, there emerge two or more groups of people who cannot communicate with each other and who steadily grow apart . . . [we must] avoid the development of a fragmented and divided society" (a guest opinion from Mr. Terry Winters, AR, 4/23/1997). Mr. Park began a practice of quoting his opposition and then offering a testy response, often in a nativist mood. He quoted Martha Jimenez, an attorney for the Mexican American Legal defense and Education Fund, as follows: "[The] Official English campaign is not about language, but about power—raw political power—and control, which in its broadest sense means control of the future direction of the country . . ." Mr. Park's response: "Americans, she has that absolutely correct" (AR, 4/19/1997). When President Clinton remarked that "We want to become a multiracial, multiethnic society. We're not going to disintegrate in the face of it," Park's riposte was: "We do? When were you asked?" (AR, 7/28/1996) As the time approached for the Arizona Supreme Court's decision, Mr. Park vacillated between extreme views. In an initial position, he turned his opposition's rhetoric against itself: "The fact is, there is no constitutional right for individuals to receive government services in a particular language, a doctrine that courts historically have supported. To grant such a right would turn the First Amendment on its head" (AR, 11/23/1997). Within three months he announced that he would try to gain John McCain's seat in the U.S. Senate because "I see no other practical way for the people of Arizona to tell the federal government that they are fed up with Washington's failure to curb runaway immigration" (AR, 2/3/1998). After the final defeat, when the U.S. Supreme Court refused to hear the last appeal, Mr. Park remarked "This has been a really torturous adventure" (AR, 1/11/1999).

An examination of this politicized rhetoric over the last five years of the Official English debate shows that the proponents of the Arizona amendment became more desperate for any sort of confirmation of their position, and more strained in their eagerness for any victory, however small. In time, the shrillness of their arguments showed that their collective *amour-propre* was wearing thin, and any positive turn of events took on the aspect of personal vindication. Once personal involvement is set aside, the most remarkable characteristic of the Group Pluralist position is that the only sense of national identity consists in extending nativist affections toward the original speakers of English, together with according serial forms of contempt toward non-speakers of English. Beyond those sentiments, no vision of community underlies the appeals to logic, abstract principle, and a sense of satisfied Self in the Official English rhetoric. Indeed, no concept of Self or of human personality at all exists in any identifiable form at any spot in the rhetoric. A participant in this argument is to gain a sense of satisfaction from the argument alone, and not from anything promised afterwards to any person should the argument succeed.

On the Left

Proponents of the Core-Periphery model insist that those active in any other place in the political spectrum have an interest in marginalizing immigrants: newcomers in the state are placed only in the lowest-wage jobs, and they are permitted restricted or at best token participation in the political system. In Arizona, political leaders with left-of-center views circulated an alternative initiative to the Official English proposal in the last months of 1987. Because the Official English amendment was "too restrictive, too costly for the taxpayer, and too divisive for the state,"

Representative Armando Ruiz organized the Arizona English coalition, which circulated an initiative proposing that "It shall be the official policy of the state of Arizona to promote proficiency in English, the common language of the United States, while recognizing Arizona's unique history, languages and diversity" (UPI, 10/9/1987). This modest alternative proposition did not receive sufficient signatures to qualify for the November 1988 ballot; but two days after the initiative won, Ms. Maria-Kelly Yniguez was ready with her challenge in court. Despite occasional bitterness over the haste to litigate—Ms. Yniguez was accused by columnist John Kolbe of having been "recruited by Hispanic activists to file the lawsuit" (PG, 4/3/1996)—the leadership elite contesting the amendment appeared to conduct themselves in moderation and quiet self-control. Sometimes political columnists were deft but quite plainspoken, as was the case with Roger E. Hernandez:

> If non-Hispanic politicians had bowed to demagoguery, every state and country as a whole would have English as the official language. Allowing such an insult to bilingual people would be (as de Tocqueville warned) giving in to mob rule, precisely the danger from which Congress and state legislatures are supposed to protect citizens. Yet I do not believe the millions of Americans who voted for this are driveling racists. Rather, they are victims of a campaign of disinformation created by anti-Hispanic groups like English First and U.S. English (PG, 5/6/1993).

Even in moderation, it is apparent that critics arguing from this area of the spectrum did not hesitate to articulate the issue basically in terms of ethnic discrimination directed toward specific groups.

General sympathy with a Core-Periphery sentiment was quite rare in public debate on this issue. In a letter to the editor, Mr. Robert Altizer declared that "the drive to make English the official language of government is nothing more than a callous attempt to usurp power for the language majority and to deny it to language minorities. It's cloaked in high-falutin sentiments, but it's just another way to say ethnic cleansing" (AR, 11/26/1995). Tom and Barbara Dugan saw a parallel with the loss of Celtic languages in America: "Our ancestors came from Scotland and Ireland to escape the kind of repression that now seems the 'right way to do things.'... They were forbidden to speak, read, or write in their native tongue and had to make English their 'official' language.... If you can't see the parallels of what happened then and now, you better brush up on your history books" (AR, 4/27/1996). For the most part, the general citizenry resisted a Core-Periphery view. Yet as time passed, there emerged a vague discomfort with right-of-center excess, beginning with various lurking suspicions around the time of the 1996 elections ("you can practically feel the malaise," according to Amy Moritz of the National Center for Public Policy Research [AR, 6/23/1996]) and persisting in some quarters until the present time.

Because the Core-Periphery view was deployed through defensive countermoves in the Official English issue, it is impossible fully to describe a practical vision of any healthy, positive, and productive community values which might lie under the surface of this political position. Nor is it the case that this particular left-of-center posture masks any values that might yield a sense of personality or Self specifically or of the social construction of Selfhood generally. Here we see politics conducted in an anomic vacuum. It gradually becomes apparent that the arguments and counterarguments which underlie political moves in process, just as is the case with all agonistic behaviors, may only imperfectly represent the principles which motivate them.

The View from the Center

The most consistent centrist position on the Official English issue throughout this period was articulated early by the governors of the state of Arizona, and this position was supported by the two state capital newspapers, the *Phoenix Gazette* and the *Arizona Republic*. Governor Rose Mofford decided not to appeal the challenge by Ms. Maria-Kelly Yniguez in 1988. Her view was that state employees needed to "serve the public," and if by not supporting an appeal she became vulnerable in office, she remarked "I may be breaking the law, but if it's grounds for removal from office then I'm breaking the law" (UPI, 11/29/1988). In January, 1989, Attorney General Bob Corbin offered a narrow interpretation of the amendment. Although the amendment required that the state "Shall deliver services in English and in no other language," Mr. Corbin held that Proposition 106 "does not prohibit the use of other languages when they are reasonably required in the day-to-day operation of government" (UPI, 1/24/1989). This particular interpretation failed to restore civic quietude, and the court challenges continued. In 1994, Governor Fife Symington was known to oppose the amendment even though he was named a defendant when the case was moved from the District Court under Judge Rosenblatt to the Maricopa County Superior Court under Judge Jeffrey Cates (AR, 1/25/1994). At this point, when Judge Cates ruled that the amendment was constitutional, the *Arizona Republic* took a vigorous position in an editorial: "The beast was back... what the amendment did was invite divisiveness and bigotry to take off their hats and stay awhile in Arizona. Whether by court action or repeal, this amendment needs to be removed from the Constitution" (AR, 1/29/1994).

In succeeding editorials, the *Arizona Republic* persisted with a stalwart and plain-dealing demeanor: After announcing that "diversity is one of this country's greatest strengths, and fear of diversity is one of its greatest curses," an editorial on 5/31/1994 asserts that the amendment "is divisive. Insulting. And unconstitutional." Later that year, Ms. Linda Valdez, an editorial writer for that newspaper, responded to (among other readers) those people "who call up and insult me on the basis of my last name. They say 'Mexicans are the problem.' They think the latest wave of immigrants is inferior." Ms. Valdez reacted with a rather becalmed Cultural Pluralist's attitude: "Official English would be silly if it weren't so hurtful to some people. It sees English and the American culture as frail things that are imperiled by newcomers. America is not in danger of losing her soul or character as she embraces yet another group of people who want to make their futures and their fortunes here" (AR, 6/3/1994). Supporting this view, but with a more assimilationist perspective, was a strongly phrased letter from Ms. Edith Ray:

> It is time that we set aside all of the "isms" of racial, political, and the radical actions of special-interest groups. We are Americans. That should mean that, yes, English is our official language. It should also mean that each culture can keep its language, customs and traditions within its homes and families. How can this not do anything but make us stronger . . . [Some people] are helping us understand that America should not be a melting pot, but a "smelting pot," where we can all learn to work together and still maintain our individuality and the influences of our distinct cultures (AR, 6/25/1994).

After the opinion of the Ninth District Court of Appeals in 1994, Governor Symington was satisfied with the finding of unconstitutionality, and the centrist view of the *Arizona Republic* declaimed that the opinion was "a blast of flag-waving patriotism that ought to blow this assault on free speech and diversity to smithereens . . . . It was an echo of a 1923 U.S. Supreme Court ruling in which a Nebraska statute that prohibited the teaching of German in Schools was struck down. Civic cohesiveness cannot be pursued by coercion. Not in a democracy. Not then. Not now" (AR, 12/12/1994).

From this point forward, the newspapers' position remained consistent. When the Republican Party showed sympathy for the Official English issue before the 1996 election, the *Arizona Republic* maintained "along with being unconstitutional, history proves that English-only laws are unnecessary and un-American" (AR, 9/23/1995). The newspaper approved of the finding of unconstitutionality by Justice Stephen Reinhardt for the full Ninth Circuit Court of Appeals because the law "turned out to be a textbook on what's wrong with mandating how people talk in a nation

that respects free speech" (AR, 10/6/1995). When the case was on appeal for the first time to the U. S. Supreme Court, the newspaper declared
"beside the constitutional problems with the law, it is demonstrably un-
needed"(AR, 3/29/1996). After the Supreme Court returned the case, or as
the editorial writer phrased it, "threw the whole mess back to Arizona," the
newspaper remarked "Confused? Conflicted? Well, then, Official English
has done its job" (AR, 3/5/1997). Before the Arizona Supreme Court ruled,
the *Republic* still welcomed provocative views in its letters to the editor.
Mr. Antonio Hurtado asked: "By denying the constitutionality of an official language, our courts would continue to respect individual freedom
of speech and allow language choice. Our constitution says we shouldn't
discriminate on the basis of one's race, nationality, religion, gender, sex-
ual preference, political affiliation or handicap. How about language?"
(AR, 12/10/1997). Then, in approving the decision of the Arizona Supreme
Court, the editorial writer was encouraged to ventilate: "Official English
was the product of a system that allows dumb ideas to become law. It was
defeated because the same system gives people the power to attack idiocy
and defend their rights" (AR, 4/29/1998).

It is remarkable that throughout the history of court challenges and the
swelling of public opinion between those challenges, the citizenry typically stayed patient with what may be termed Process Politics. Experts
in the legal system had their own views, but preferred to keep an individual distance as events lurched along: "By most lawyers' accounts (but
never for attribution), there is more than a little legal politics at work here"
(PG, 4/3/1996). Yet even as the Cultural Pluralist/centrist position took
shape and asserted itself, it is remarkable to see that no one had a fully
evolved idea of what the community is, or what it does, or how individual
lives are to be formed within it. The centrist position throughout this debate was pragmatic in its appeal to calm and quietude. Beyond that there
seemed to be no defined ideological depth in much of what was thought
and said.

The explosive debates occurring during the official English controversy
throughout the United States showed that no one achieved a workable
centrist position and many persons with influence played hob with the
truth if they had to. Indeed, there seemed to be no consistent ideological
substance in the issue, and many local politicians operated on the assumption that the Truth is what you can get the people to believe. The penulti-
mate effect was that meaningful debate was neutralized. Voters of a variety
of ideological persuasions were pitted against each other, with a personal
sense of compensation through adhering steadfastly to a belief being the
only outcome (cf. Donahue, 1995). The ultimate effect was that public opinion was divided, conquered, and scattered amidst a form of ideological

spindrift, and voters were distracted through a variety of manipulated issues during a time in which government policy in the United States (and
in England) was directed toward an upward redistribution of wealth.

I propose in what follows to examine this issue from a different set of
political perspectives. In the next section of this chapter, I link the ideologies
underlying the Official English debate to broader traditions in American
political thought. Once we have examined the ideologies anew, it will be
possible to gauge the nature and extent of their use by leadership elites to
manipulate the voting public.

LIBERALISM AND COMMUNITARIANISM

For most of this century, public policy debate has been influenced by two
competing ideologies: liberalism and a collection of views which has become known as communitarianism. A narrowed version of right-wing
"liberalism" (sometimes better understood as a group of borrowed views
from nineteenth century libertarianism) has dominated thinking for the
past 35 years. In the 20th-century application of liberal principles, it is axiomatic that the major role of the state is to secure and guarantee the rights
of individual persons as they act autonomously out of self-interest. Thus
individuals are responsible economically and socially only for themselves
and any other specific persons they choose, and it is generally held that
persons with such a disposition are under the principled rule almost exclusively of macro- and micro-economic laws unless they agree otherwise.
Specifically, such persons are under no obligation (through their taxes) to
attend to the unmet needs of others in society. Indeed in an extreme view
(as stated by Margaret Thatcher) the only moral laws are economic ones,
and "there is no such thing as society" (Bird, 1999, p. 15). In opposition to
this collection of views there have risen the communitarians, who believe
that individuals grow and mature in interactive social circumstances, and
that as an ordinary function of normal social bonds individuals develop
responsibilities and obligations to help meet the needs of other persons.

Political difficulties emerge from the fact that the average citizen is un-
aware of the tenets and corollaries of liberalism and communitarianism.
Other difficulties arise from the fact that many political leaders have not
chosen to commit themselves to a described and consistent ideology in one
camp or the other; and still other leaders have chosen to confuse Liberalism
and Communitarianism, with injurious effects to political life generally and
to most voters specifically. In academic circles, there is a growing understanding that each of these two political theories is not yet fully formed, and
that rigorous attempts to systematize and articulate sound philosophical

principles for each view reveal that both bodies of thought show inconsistencies and incoherencies.

Liberalism/Libertarianism

We must begin with the understanding that on the right wing, the underlying ideology supporting our modern political quandary is a derived, trickled-down, and applied form of libertarianism. In a recent analysis of the origins of libertarian thought, Bird (1999) shows that current thought in libertarian/liberal individualism theory holds fast to two basic principles: every person can claim self-ownership, and everyone is granted inviolable rights. Professor Bird's treatment in *The Myth of Liberal Individualism* traces the history of libertarian views in modern American political theory to two separate streams of thought. There is first, a tradition of elaboration upon an "aggregative asymmetrical" set of ideas and values which are derived from the work of John Stuart Mill. Next, there is an "associative symmetrical" value system which has come to apply concepts from Kant, Rousseau, and Marx in a distinct matrix of analysis. Bird's remarks upon these separate streams in our intellectual history, and of the problems of conflict and irresolution contained within them, is of crucial importance to understanding the notion of solipsism in this chapter; in the pages immediately following I will present a wider discussion of his ideas.

Bird labels the John Stuart Mill tradition (as elaborated further by Lomasky, 1987) an "aggregative asymmetrical" value set because in this view there is no personality principle attached to individuals: persons may be thought of as individuals or members of a group, but there is no need to attend to individual distinctions or to the uniqueness of separate beings. Persons (or agents) are in an asymmetrical relationship with the value system of the state, in that as citizens they receive but are not bound to reciprocate the values of the state in return. Beyond this one-way, state-to-citizen "service conception" of public agency, additional specific values in this tradition include the following, as contrasted with the Kant-Rousseau-Marx set of values (see Bird, 1999:190–191):

John Stuart Mill Tradition	Kant-Rousseau-Marx Tradition
1. rightness in a value scheme is only a property of outcomes (that any is, have services been delivered properly to the right people?);	1′. rightness in a value scheme is a "property of processes," (that is, in process one must ask whether or not the value of individuals was respected);

2. persons have self-ownership, and as such they are "the exclusive owners of their bodies, lives and personal assets and resources, and are free to make of them what they will" (p. 33);

2'. individuals are presumed to act from a capacity for "self-command";

3. rights in the Millian tradition are in fact "violable and alienable" (p. 190), and can be compromised or bartered away for purposes of security or to serve a greater good;

3'. all rights are by definition inviolable and inalienable;

4. any value is judged in the way it relates to individuals;

4'. any value is measured by its worth with regard to individuals;

5. neutrality is preserved in judging personal values; and public morality is "restricted to interpersonal affairs."

5'. neutrality is not preserved with respect to the judging of personal values; and

6'. as a corollary to the symmetry of the expressivist principle specifically, public morality is viewed as "continuous with intrapersonal morality."

In comparison, Bird's analysis of the Kant-Rousseau-Marx tradition of liberal individualist thought holds that the basic identifying properties are associative and symmetrical: in the first instance, individuals are thought of as separate and sentient beings relating on a personal level to others in a community. Next, they have a symmetrical or two-way relationship with the values of the state because as human agents they accept those values and reciprocate them or "express" them to others and to the state. Other characteristics of this tradition differ from the Millian value set as seen above (cf. Bird 1999:191).

Bird's analysis of these separate streams of thought shows that the legacy of liberal individualist ideas from the past is fraught with contradictions and inconsistencies, and that modern politicians have been, so to speak, shopping impulsively and inconsistently as they try to furnish their ideologies with useful substance in any form. It is obvious, as we proceed with our discussion, that Professor Byrd provides a significant analysis by demonstrating the critical conflicts between the concepts in 2 and 2' and 3 and 3' above. Yet for our purposes it is more important to bring into focus the view that liberal individualism is in fact a politically reified form of solipsism. Such a concept of Self as isolated from the formative influences of community is primitive by every measure, as we will see below. In a political sense this concept has a simplistic property with the strongest appeal to those leadership elites who wish to exert influence among, and then manipulate the most naïve of their followers.

Communitarianism

Communitarian thought arose as an alternative to the extreme reaction to social and economic determinism which underlies and informs the arguments by Mill. In the modern articulation of the communitarian position, sociologists like Etzioni (1997) and philosophers like Khatchadourian (1999) build upon the work of such highly respected proponents as Bell (1993) and Sandel (1982, 1996). A communitarian view emphasizes the positive results to be obtained from cultivating a broad-based moral sense and a system of altruistic values in a community; the consistent position taken in this line of thought is that an emphasis on individual autonomy cannot guarantee anything other than amoral behavior, while a collectivist system of organization promotes a moral perspective in which the whole is greater than the sum of its parts. In the most basic terms, the reaction to Libertarianism has surfaced in the criticism that Libertarianism

1. devalues, neglects, and/or undermines community, and community is a fundamental and irreplaceable ingredient in the good life for human beings;
2. undervalues political life; viewing political association as a merely instrumental good, it is blind to the fundamental importance of full participation in political community for the good life for human beings;
3. fails to provide, or is incompatible with, an adequate account of the importance of certain types of obligations and commitments (those that are not chosen or explicitly undertaken through contracting or promising), such as familial obligations and obligations to support one's community or country;
4. presupposes a defective conception of the self, failing to recognize that the self is "embedded" in and partly constituted by communal commitments and values which are not objects of choice,
5. wrongly exalts justice as being the "first virtue of social institutions," failing to see that, at best, justice is a remedial virtue, needed only in circumstances in which the higher virtue of community has broken down (Buchanan, 1989, pp. 853–3; cf. Sharpe, 1999, p. 121).

As a reaction to those in the Liberal/Libertarian camp, in recent times Communitarianism has developed a stronger set of systematic principles. Bellah et al. (1996) offered a more rigorous definition of the term "community":

> We use [the term] in a strong sense: a community is a group of people who are socially interdependent, who participate together in discussion and decision-making, and who share certain practices . . . that both define the community and are nurtured by it. Such a community is not quickly formed. It almost always has a history and so is also a community of memory, defined in part by its past and its memory of its past (p. 333.)

Etzioni (1997) has proposed a new "Golden Rule" that would support a better understanding of the differences between the two systems: "Respect and uphold society's moral order as you would have society respect and uphold your autonomy" (1996, p. xviii). Khatchadourian (1999) proposes that since only communal life can satisfy "certain basic psychological needs, among which are a basic need for love, for belonging and acceptance, and for achievement or recognition" (p. 5), it becomes the responsibility of any community to develop a *telos* that will deepen the meaning of person-to-person bonds and promote methods to "further the interests and goals" (p. 9) of each citizen. In establishing a set of values for public education and for language policy and language teaching, the Communitarian line of reasoning has an extraordinarily strong appeal to linguists and specialists in the sociology of language who are interested in language maintenance and bilingual education.

Yet the difficulty persists, as Buchanan correctly argues, that in its emphatic criticism of opposing views, Communitarianism on its own has not thoroughly developed and articulated a "philosophical theory of the good, a theory of objective value" (1989, p. 857.) Further, as Phillips (1993) argues, Communitarians may have a psychologically simplistic notion of what a constituted "Self" actually is. The Self is not only a social product of a person's experiences and circumstances from the earliest years; it may also be an entity formed *in opposition*. Indeed, in the formation of Self in most cultures, there may come a time when an individual constructs a Self *separately* from, and in *strong reaction* against the social forces in his or her background, rather than in compliance with those forces.

In practical terms, American voters have been affected adversely by the non-systematic character of the two views. In election season, they are left in a condition of life in which their voting impulses are ideologically incoherent, with the result that even with well-motivated political propositions there is extreme difficulty in predicting positive outcomes for any initiative which is begun with a beneficent intent. For instance, at election time voters are led to believe that all taxation is a form of theft, and that a person's major ethical obligation is to keep one's real property free from those taxes which might serve the underemployed and unworthy (that is, a large proportion of one's fellow citizens). There is a great potential for abuse in a random selection of the ideas from these schools of thought, particularly when those ideas are issued with a scattershot "sound bite" approach. With a most useful image, Bird warns specifically of an *ad libitum* approach to political practice that "assumes that history somehow deposits concepts and ideas like Lego bricks that the theorist can mix and match at will according to his needs. But historical concepts and ideas are not like this" (1999, p. 165).

THE LEGO EFFECT

We may thus call the effort to mix, match, and force-fit ideological principles to emerging political needs the *Lego Effect*. This concept refers to attempts to play upon *a priori* political concepts in a deconstructed fashion in a way that permits, and in fact invites, a variety of manipulations from those in power. For the most part, the Effect is designed to win a surface sentiment of agreement from the electorate, as long as the citizens do not examine an utterance too closely and choose not to suspect duplicity on the part of their leaders. The Lego Effect works most efficiently in that ideal world in which voters' positive liberties (those beyond political constraints) are expanded at the same time that their negative liberties (those reined in by political constraints) are accepted as personally unintrusive. As applied to ballot choices, the Effect will have produced the best results when the voter acts with the conviction that his or her ballot choice will stimulate incentives for the weakest and least productive among the citizenry, and at the same time will allow for taxes to be reduced, all the while providing beneficent results for society generally and for the education of the young specifically. The Effect, in short, is part of a created atmosphere near election time; it is an ideologically induced Nirvana in which voters make choices out of self-interest and at once stop thinking about the consequences of those choices.

APPLIED COMMUNITARIANISM, LANGUAGE POLICY, AND EDUCATION

I offer another perspective in an attempt to provide a way out of this politicized dilemma. To find a strong and coherent application of the most cogent principles of communitarianism, we need only review the work of one of the earlier major figures in modern sociology. The treatment which is most useful for our purposes is that of Cladis (1992), with his analysis of the contemporary relevance for the philosophy of education of Emil Durkheim. In his treatise on *Moral Education* (1961), Durkheim spoke of the need for three principled outcomes in the influence of a society upon its young: Beginning with their earliest educational experiences, children optimally are to form a sense of discipline, attachment, and autonomy. In modern terms, discipline involves a sense of Self and an amount of patience as social forces move that Self in a perceived direction, and at the same time an awareness that the direction promotes the "values and goals of moral individualism" (Cladis, 1992, p. 200.) Thus, the purpose of discipline is to produce a personality which is "enriched and stayed by the stable yet flexible intellectual and moral traditions of an age" (201). The concept of attachment stipulates that young persons develop a respect for the "beliefs, practices, and institutions" of the culture which is in the process of shaping them (p. 201). Attachment involves a capacity to analyze what constitutes a philosophical good in the surrounding culture, and to develop a personal affinity and loyalty toward it. Autonomy as a young person matures takes the form of a personal sense of free moral choice in one's life. An individual achieves rationality, and upon developing an understanding of his or her relation to the surrounding culture, the young person can then make personal decisions that are worked out in freedom from "external motivations such as threats or rewards" (p. 204).

Durkheim's analysis commands respect because it requires that young people identify, with a critical awareness, the social forces at work in their lives, but at the same time they are to establish a sense of Self that is separate from those forces. As persons mature in time, they are to achieve what Riesman called in his classic, *The Lonely Crowd*, a sense of inner-directedness: What is valuable from the past is to be recognized and cherished, yet what is harmful must be acknowledged and cast away. When individuals are educated to attempt independence from narrowing deterministic pressures, they develop a capacity to produce moral choices which may yield a broad array of beneficial results.

A Critical Linguistics Approach

As we work with the concepts of discipline, attachment, and autonomy, it becomes desirable to develop an approach from critical linguistics. The developing field of language acquisition is in the process of improving our understanding of the ways children acquire their phonological, morphological, syntactic, semantic, and rhetorical systems as they mature. It is useful at this point to redirect a question from the field of language acquisition. We must now ask: What do we learn concerning the optimal conduct of our lives from the way we acquire language? The answer to this question will be of the greatest importance as we seek a political framework for education generally and for language policy specifically.

It is commonly understood through scholarship and common experience alike that language is learned in a social setting, through interactions with parents and siblings, together with friends from within an age span of 18 months younger than the child to 18 months older. Because it is physically impossible to acquire all of the social and geographical dialects of a language, an individual learns a reduced portion of a language, marked by the narrowed social circumstances of class, gender, ethnicity, political identity, and location of birth (Donahue, 1985). As a person matures, he or she continues to develop within a variety of distinctive historical, material, and deterministic constraints; the greater or lesser sense one may have of developing an autonomous Self depends on whatever ideas his or her personal culture may pass along. There is in an obvious sense a distinctly modern peril: An exclusive libertarian emphasis on the autonomous and indeed solipsistic Self exacerbates the prevailing condition of social anomie. But beyond that, a sense of personal autonomy may come easier for a person who is bicultural and bilingual, because in this condition an individual finds a personally expressive center, and then chooses the language which must meet the immediate social demands of the outside world. At all times from infancy through old age, and in an attempt to satisfy a variety of expressive demands, under ideal conditions a person's vocabulary and articulation skills grow and develop as his or her social roles grow and develop. As a person's education progresses, a more sophisticated growth of language skills allows one to carry on increasingly demanding social responsibilities; if one has the time and the good fortune to pursue them, his or her language skills facilitate the development of additional forms of intelligence, including mathematical, spatial, kinetic, musical, and other social modes of thought.

Yet individual autonomy and self-ownership are specific philosophical constructs, and they are not guaranteed to appear in the formation and development of mind. In fact, no guarantees exist: instead, there is only a constant pressure to develop one's expressive potential in order to find and then occupy a place in a socially interactive group. A person's success in developing verbal facility is increased with membership in what Wenger (1998) has identified as one or more *communities of practice*. Language fluency and increasing skills in social interaction are helped by the personal growth which occurs in one's work, whether in the lowliest job or in the most respected sort of professional career. In a community of practice, the expressive individual becomes aware of a new responsibility in his or her life: As one matures under the influence of extremely strong social forces, an individual must at the same time gain personal control over the extent to which those forces interfere in order to wield power in his or her own life. All of a person's mature life thus becomes a continuous exercise in social learning, during which a person has the task of assimilating the "rhythms by which communities and individuals continually renew themselves" (Wenger, p. 262).

WHAT WE HAVE LEARNED: THE CORE-PERIPHERY THEORY REVISITED

We may acknowledge that the major components of current political thought in liberalism/libertarianism and in communitarianism are ill-formed and non-systematic, and that the basic tenets are inconsistent and poorly understood. If in addition we accept the view that anomie is the ordinary condition of modern life, then we are forced to conclude that the manipulation of ideological confusions can preserve an extraordinary advantage for those in power. It is axiomatic in such a view that some of those in political power can sustain their positions by purposely confusing the public and private ideological certainties of the citizens. Official English in Arizona is such a case.

Responsible modern citizens must react with an aggressive analysis of any public policy initiative which undertakes language planning or educational reform. Any urged reform must be scrutinized for the likelihood of a positive outcome for the general public. More specifically, all citizens must protect the potential of others to develop a fully empowered, autonomous, and skeptical Self in the same way that they have been accorded such a right in the past. In addition, we must be especially cautious about the use of coercive language near election times in a modern democracy. As is apparent in the Arizona case, we must suspect that individuals occupying extreme political positions have willfully oversimplified their public policy views, and in their adherence to ideology either do not or cannot intellectually absorb principles of the law; indeed, political extremes produce positions which are unfit to form policy for language use or for education.

We may then proceed with the understanding that a critical linguistics approach to analyzing political and educational policy requires that we identify and attempt fully to characterize all ideological strains which underlie election initiatives. If we see that the ideas are incoherent, or inconsistent and mismatched, we must suspect manipulation by those in power. Such a response to the history of events in the English Only initiative in Arizona shows that a theoretically liberal emphasis on the autonomy of the Self and on Self-ownership has a variety of inherent risks for leaders and citizens alike. An undeveloped and naïve Self is merely solipsistic, and such a Self can be easily isolated and politically manipulated; the worthier Self is a sophisticated one, seeking lifelong a proprietary identity which is cerebral and skeptical, rather than narrow and emotional. Only the thoughtful and fully developed individual holds citizenship in a polity of which liberals and communitarians alike may be proud.

APPENDIX: PROPOSITION 106—ARTICLE 28
OF THE ARIZONA CONSTITUTION

Section 1. English as the official language; applicability

(1) The English language is the official language of the state of Arizona.
(2) As the official language of this state, the English language is the language of the ballot, the public schools and all government functions and actions.
(3) (a) This article applies to:
  (i) The legislative, executive and judicial branches of government.
  (ii) All political subdivisions, departments, agencies, organizations, and instrumentalities of this state, including local governments and municipalities.
  (iii) All statutes, ordinances, rules, orders, programs and policies.
  (iv) All government officials and employees during the performance of government business.
(b) As used in this article, the phrase "this state and all political subdivisions of this state" shall include every entity, person, action or item described in this section, as appropriate to the circumstances.

Section 2. Requiring this state to preserve, protect and enhance English
This state and all political subdivisions of this state shall take all reasonable steps to preserve, protect and enhance the role of the English language as the official language of the state of Arizona.

Section 3. Prohibiting this state from using or requiring the use of languages other than English; exceptions

(1) Except as provided in subsection (2):
   (a) This state and all political subdivisions of this state shall act in English and in no other language.
   (b) No entity to which this article applies shall make or enforce a law, order, decree or policy which requires the use of a language other than English.
   (c) No governmental document shall be valid, effective or enforceable unless it is in the English language.
(2) This state and all political subdivisions of this state may act in a language other than English under any of the following circumstances:
   (a) To assist students who are not proficient in the English language, to the extent necessary to comply with federal law, by giving educational instruction in a language other than English to provide as rapid as possible a transition to English.
   (b) To comply with other federal laws.
   (c) To teach a student a foreign language as a part of a required or voluntary educational curriculum.
   (d) To protect public health or safety.
   (e) To protect the rights of criminal defendants or victims of crime.

Section 4. Enforcement; standing. A person who resides in or does business in this state shall have standing to bring suit to enforce this article in a court of record of the state. The legislature may enact reasonable limitations on the time and manner of bringing suit under this subsection.

REFERENCES

Bell, D. (1993). *Communitarianism and its critics*. Oxford: Oxford University Press.
Bellah, R. N., Madsen, R., Sullivan, W. M., Swidler, A., & Tipton, S. M. (1996). *Habits of the heart*. 2nd ed. Berkeley: University of California Press.
Bird, C. (1999). *The myth of liberal individualism*. Cambridge: Cambridge University Press.
Buchanan, A. E. (1989). Assessing the communitarian critique of liberalism. *Ethics, 99*, 852–882.
Cladis, M. S. (1992). *A communitarian defense of liberalism*. Stanford: Stanford University Press.
Donahue, T. S. (1985). What the sociology of language has to say about American dialectology, in R. A. Hall, Jr. (Ed.), *Proceedings of the eleventh LACUS forum* (pp. 460–471). Columbia, SC: Hornbeam Press.
Donahue, T. S. (1995). American language policy and compensatory opinion. In J. W. Tollefson (Ed.), *Power and Inequality in Language Education* (pp. 112–141). Cambridge: Cambridge University Press.
Durkheim, E. (1961). *Moral education*. Trans. by E. K. Wilson & H. Schnurr. Glencoe: Free Press.
Eastman, C. M. (1983). *Language planning: An introduction*. San Francisco: Chandler and Sharpe.

Etzioni, A. (1997). *The new golden rule*. New York: Basic Books.

Khatchadourian, H. (1999). *Community and communitarianism*. New York: Peter Lang.

Lexis-Nexis. For articles from the *Arizona Republic*, the *Phoenix Gazette*, and United Press International (UPI).

Lomasky, L. (1987). *Persons, rights, and the moral community*. Oxford: Oxford University Press.

Phillips, D. (1993). *Looking backward: A critical appraisal of communitarian thought*. Princeton: Princeton University Press.

Riesman, D. (1961). *The lonely crowd*. New Haven: Yale University Press.

Sandel, M. J. (1982). *Liberalism and the limits of justice*. Cambridge: Cambridge University Press.

Sandel, M. J. (1996). *Democracy's discontent: America in search of a public philosophy*. Cambridge: Belknap Press.

Sharpe, B. (1999). Advice from a Tocquevillian liberal: Arendt, Tocqueville, and the liberal-communitarian debate. In P. Augustine & D. McConkey (Eds.), *Community and political thought today* (pp. 121–132). Westport, CT: Praeger.

Wenger, E. (1998). *Communities of practice: Learning, meaning, and identity*. Cambridge: the Cambridge University Press.

IV

MANAGING LANGUAGE CONFLICT

The two chapters in this section examine the following critical issue: How do language policies in education help to create, sustain, or reduce political conflict among different ethnolinguistic groups? Examining two states characterized by significant ethnolinguistic diversity, Selma K. Sonntag and James W. Tollefson explain why India and Yugoslavia took radically different directions in language policy conflict in recent years. As Sonntag shows in Chapter 8, in North India, the symbolic politics of language for both Nepali speakers in West Bengal and Urdu speakers in Uttar Pradesh took precedence over gaining the right to use the languages in education. Despite the existence of significant social cleavages along linguistic lines, the politics of language in education in North India has generally not led to widespread calls for dissolution. In part, Sonntag shows, this is because state and federal authorities have found acceptable ways to accommodate the demands of linguistic minorities without ceding full control of policymaking authority. Moreover, throughout the public policy debate, both majority and minority leaders remained committed to a democratic political solution within the federalist and liberal framework that has characterized India since the 1940s.

In contrast, in Yugoslavia, leaders of the Serbian population (the largest group in a united Yugoslavia) decided that it was in their interest to force linguistic minorities to either accept Serbian domination or a military solution. As Tollefson shows in Chapter 9, the willingness of Serb leaders under Slobodan Milošević to use their political power and control of the armed forces to rescind minority language rights and force linguistic minorities out of policymaking authority meant the end of pluralist policies and the political system of ethnolinguistic self-management that dated back to the 1950s. Thus the destruction of Yugoslavia was brought about not by the ethnolinguistic diversity of the country, but rather by the imposition of Serbian centralism and the end of pluralist language and nationality policies. Yet the progressive system of language policies and language rights did not disappear completely; it has been reformulated by the newly independent state of Slovenia, the first region to successfully break from Serbian control.

8

Minority Language Politics in North India

Selma K. Sonntag
Humboldt State University

With reportedly over 1,500 mother tongues in India, language policy is by necessity complex, multilayered, and frequently ambiguous. Hindi, spoken by about 40% of the population, was designated the official language of India by the Constituent Assembly upon independence (Austin, 1966). The government is constitutionally committed to spend resources for its spread and development. English, the former colonial language, has "associate" official language status, prolonged indefinitely by the 1967 Government of India Official Language Act. Also ensconced in the Constitution is a list, or "schedule" (Schedule VIII), of major languages of India, frequently referred to as India's national languages. The latest constitutional amendment to Schedule VIII, in 1992, added three more languages to the list, bringing the total to 18. The three new Schedule VIII languages are Konkani (spoken in Goa on the west coast), Manipuri (spoken in part of the area of India sandwiched between Bangladesh and Burma), and Nepali (spoken in the finger of India that juts up to Tibet between Nepal and Bhutan). The Schedule is an example of ambiguous language policy: it is unclear exactly what Schedule VIII listing confers on a language or its speakers (see Gupta, Abbi & Aggarwal, 1995).

India is a federal system composed of 26 states. A fairly drawn-out process of reconfiguring state boundaries along linguistic lines began in the

1950s, was codified in the States Reorganization Act of 1956, and continued with the early 1970s redrawing of state boundaries in the northeast. So today state boundaries conform more or less to major linguistic boundaries, although far from perfectly or consistently. Within each major linguistic state, multilingualism is prevalent. Each state thus has its own language policy, designating usually the most widely spoken language as its official language and sometimes conferring secondary official language status on (a) significant minority language(s) within the state. Official language status entails at least limited administrative use of the language(s) by the state government.

In education, India has adopted the so-called "three language formula." This controversial policy in its simplest form encourages regional or state language instruction at the primary level, with the federal union official language (Hindi) and English being added to the curriculum in mid-primary years. Students from Hindi-dominant states are encouraged to learn a South Indian language, but may choose Sanskrit or Urdu (closely related to Hindi) instead, feeding accusations of Hindi linguistic chauvinism frequently made by non-Hindi speakers. Minority language students whose mother tongue differs from the dominant and official language of the state in which they reside are in essence offered a four-language formula, with mother-tongue instruction combined with the state's dominant language as medium in early primary years (Agnihotri & Khanna, 1994; Nayar, 1969, pp. 152–163).

Such a complex, multilayered, ambiguous language policy lends itself to an intriguing critical analysis of minority language politics. In this article, I propose to examine the relationship between the symbolic politics of language and the practical pedagogical import of minority language use in education in the context of North India. Two cases of minority language demands will be compared and contrasted: those of (1) Nepali speakers in the Darjeeling area of West Bengal; and (2) Urdu speakers in Uttar Pradesh. In both cases, the symbolic politics of official recognition for the minority language has taken precedence over minority language use in education. But the trajectory of demands and accommodation has differed between the two, with Nepali receiving state-level recognition decades before receiving federal (Union level) recognition, and Urdu following the sequence in reverse, with federal recognition preceding state recognition. It will be argued that these two North Indian cases reveal much about the political context of language policy in federal liberal democracies. The administrative unit responsible for language policy (federalism), the ideological context in which the policy is justified (liberalism), and the process through which the policy is formulated (democratic) all temper the strategies adopted by linguistic minorities in India to safeguard their interests.

NEPALI IN DARJEELING

The Darjeeling area was incorporated into British India during the first half of the 19th century, as a result of wars and intrigues between India's colonial rulers and the kingdoms of Nepal, Sikkim, and Bhutan (Subba, 1992) (see Fig. 8.1). Under the British, migration to the Darjeeling area to work in the tea plantations increased dramatically. Autochthonous Tibeto-Burman groups such as the Lepchas and Bhutias were overwhelmed by other, immigrant Tibeto-Burman groups such as the Rai, Limbu, Tamang, Magar, and Gurung, as well as Indo-Aryan groups such as the Nepali castes of Bahun (Brahmin) and Chhetri (Kshatriya).

The British had wanted Darjeeling town proper as a hill retreat from the swelter of Calcutta. Scottish missionaries plied their trade as well in these highlands. The combination left Darjeeling with the educational legacy of English-medium boarding schools for elites and missionary schools for locals. The missionaries used both Hindi and Nepali, closely related Indo-Aryan languages, in their schools. By the 1930s, the British colonial government officially sanctioned Nepali as the medium of instruction for the local population, despite misgivings voiced by the Lepchas and Bhutias (Sen, 1989; Dewan, 1991; Bagahi & Danda, 1982). Darjeeling became the literary center for Nepali in the first half of the 20th century, while cultural creativity within the kingdom of Nepal stagnated under the oppressive rule of the Ranas (Hutt, 1988).

By the time of India's independence, then, Nepali was established as the lingua franca of the Darjeeling area's diverse and migrant population. Darjeeling was the Indian portion of a Nepali linguistic area, spanning the whole of the kingdom of Nepal to the east, the kingdom of Sikkim to the north, the southern portion of the kingdom of Bhutan to the northeast, and beginning to spread eastward into Assam following the expansion of tea plantation production. Upon independence, the Bengal presidency of the British Raj was partitioned between India and (East) Pakistan. The new West Bengal State of India slivered northward to include the Darjeeling area. In 1975, acting upon the "invitation" of Sikkim's legislative body, India annexed the kingdom and Sikkim became India's 22nd state. Darjeeling was no longer the northern frontier of India or the indisputable center of the Nepali language in India (Timsina, 1992, p. 40).

Today, Nepali is the official (and dominant) language of the state of Sikkim, while in West Bengal it is a minority language with official status in the Darjeeling area, although it is spoken by far more people in West Bengal (over 700,000 in West Bengal compared to about 200,000 in Sikkim). However, in West Bengal, Nepali speakers make up only 1.3% of the population, while in Sikkim they make up 62.5% (Beg, 1996, p. 126).

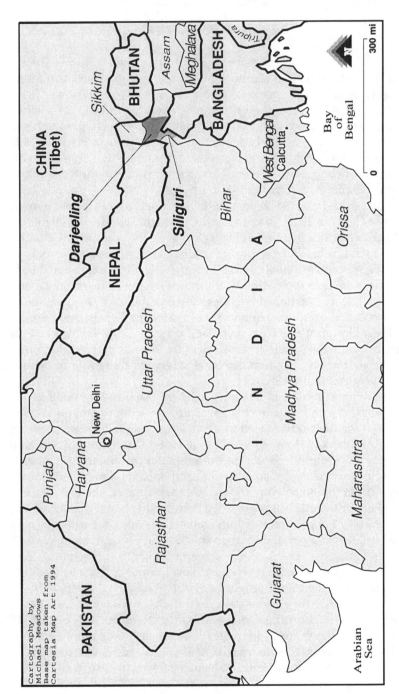

FIG. 8.1.

168

The trajectory taken by the Nepali language to its current status has been fraught with politics: the politics of communism and national liberation fronts; petitions and censuses; citizenship and foreignness; and violent demonstrations and parliamentary maneuvers. Even the naming of the language has been a political landmine.

In the charged atmosphere of the 1950s, when the momentum for reorganizing state boundaries along language lines was becoming insurmountable (King, 1997), the Nepali speakers of Darjeeling petitioned for separate administrative status from West Bengal (Datta, 1993, p. 147; Samanta, 1996, pp. 84–85; Timsina, 1992, p. 38). But Nepali was not deemed a major language of India (it was not a Schedule VIII language) and serious consideration of the Nepali speakers' request was not forthcoming. In defeat, the Nepali speakers focused their attention on the West Bengal State level, requesting official status for Nepali in the Darjeeling area. The West Bengal State government hesitated, in justification pointing to the 1951 census figures, which were dubiously low for Nepali speakers. With the 1961 census depicting much more realistic figures, the West Bengal State government relented and amended its official language act in order to designate Nepali as an official language for the hill districts of Darjeeling (Subba, 1992, pp. 94–96). The Nepali speakers, however, felt that this was a grudging concession: it had taken political protests and the recommendations of a state-sanctioned "enquiry committee" to get the amendment in the first place, and then its implementation was lackluster (Subba, 1992, p. 96).

Reading between the lines of the 1961 report of the Darjeeling Enquiry Committee, which lists not only the committee's recommendations but also remedial action taken by the state government, one senses what we might call the "democratic frustration" of Darjeeling residents. That is, the state indeed responds to democratic pressure, but its responses are cosmetic—not necessarily because it is "playing politics," but because of limited resources. It is easy to pass a state act officializing a language, but it is much harder to staff health centers with health providers who "have overcome the language difficulty and have a sympathy for rural hill people," as the Committee recommended (Government of West Bengal, 1961, p. 7). It is laudable that 307 primary schools in the Darjeeling area used Nepali as the medium of instruction in 1961, as the Committee's Report noted. But the state government's unwillingness or inability to meet basic infrastructure and transportation needs or to develop sustainable cottage industries, despite the Committee's recommendations to do so, reaffirmed the continuation of the Committee's observation that most of these schools were poorly staffed and attended, with little prospect for employment or upward mobility for those who did attend. Official language status should have triggered a demand for state government civil servants with the requisite language skills, but the slow implementation of the 1961 amendment probably dampened such an effect. Of course, the triggering of any such demand would have been limited to the Darjeeling area; proficiency in Bengali was still a prerequisite for government jobs in the state capital, Calcutta (Subba, 1992, pp. 182–183). More effective than officializing Nepali would have been to implement "reservations," or quota affirmative action, for the hills people of Darjeeling, another of the committee's recommendations that was summarily dismissed by the state government (Government of West Bengal, 1961, p. 20).

In short, Darjeeling remained peripheral, not only geographically and culturally but politically as well. A Darjeeling-based party, the Gorkha League, was established in the 1940s and had limited success in post-independence India (Franda, 1970). Until 1967, state politics in West Bengal were in firm control of the Congress party, as they were at the federal union level. In 1967, a coalition of non-Congress parties, under the United Front, came to power in West Bengal. At the same time, national and even international attention focused on the sliver of West Bengal that links the Darjeeling area to the rest of the state, where the Maoist Naxalite movement erupted. The movement drew support from scheduled castes and tribes that had migrated to the area to work in the southern belt of tea plantations, and thus was comprised of a different mix of migrant labor from the Nepali speakers found on tea plantations north of the 14-mile wide Siliguri corridor (Franda, 1971). The Naxalite movement profoundly changed not only West Bengal politics but perhaps more importantly relations between West Bengal and the federal union—relations that an astute politician from a minority group might be able to manipulate to his advantage. This indeed was the case when Subash Ghising led the Gorkha National Liberation Front (GNLF) in a showdown in the 1980s with the West Bengal State government, with the Union (federal) government attempting to appear as the mediator.

Ghising had inherited a muddled set of language demands. In the 1970s, rather ephemeral cultural-linguistic groups formed to demand federal recognition of Nepali by seeking its inclusion in Schedule VIII (Subba, 1992, pp. 96–97). In both the late 1970s and early 1980s, the state government, run by the Communist Party of India (Marxist), or CPI(M), passed resolutions in support of this demand (Timsina, 1992, p. 41; Munshi & Chakrabarti, 1979). The federal government either feigned prolonged hesitation, as under Indira Gandhi in the early to mid-1970s, or rejected the demand outright, as did the first non-Congress government at the Union (federal) level, in power from 1977–1980. Indeed, in 1977, the Janata coalition Prime Minister, Morarji Desai, in rejecting the demand for inclusion in Schedule VIII, implied that Nepali speakers in India were not Indians, claiming "You people came to India to join the army and to live in different parts of India.... We give you an inch and you want it all" (quoted in Timsina, 1992, p. 41). Such accusations aggravated the acute "sense of insecurity" felt by the Nepali-speaking minority (Munshi & Chakrabarti, 1979, p. 708). Adding to the muddle was Sikkim's accession in 1975 to India. Ghising's strategy was to explicitly repel the affront that the Nepalese in India, and by extension, the Nepali language, were foreigners. Nepali was indeed a foreign language, he declared; but Nepali was not spoken by the people of Darjeeling. Gorkha bhasa, or Gorkhali, was the language of the Darjeeling area and it was an Indian language (see Dey, 1992). Historically Gorkha bhasa is one of several terms, along with Gorkhali, Khas Kura, Parbatiya, and Nepali, that have been used to designate the Indo-Aryan language of the southern flank of the Himalayas (Hutt, 1988, pp. 32–33; Gurung, 1992). But the term "Gorkha" increasingly became associated with the brave and loyal Himalayan regiment of the (British) Indian army (Subba, 1992, pp. 55–56). By distinguishing a "Gorkha" language ("bhasa" means language) from Nepali, Ghising distanced himself politically from the Sikkimese language demands and portrayed a "more Indian than thou" image.

Ghising's demand was not for usage of Nepali (already in effect in education since the 1930s and in official venues since the 1960s–1970s, as noted above), but for the symbolic recognition of Gorkha bhasa as a *bona fide* Indian language by its inclusion in Schedule VIII. Indeed, one observer (Josse, 1992b, p. 11) noted, when the language was included in 1992, that "many [in the Darjeeling hills] found it difficult to enumerate what difference the granting of constitutional status to Nepali would henceforth make to their lives in a concrete way." Despite negligible practical import, the symbolic significance of Schedule VIII inclusion is substantial. In fact, practical import in education was willingly sacrificed during the GNLF-led agitation for their demands in the 1980s, when schools were forced to shut down because of the violence (Subba, 1992, pp. 214–218). Any language included in Schedule VIII is a national language of India. To demand its inclusion is a declaration of loyalty to the Indian nation-state and a "plea" for "integration" (Munshi & Chakrabarti, 1979, p. 706). As expressed by one of the leaders of a cultural group pressing for Schedule VIII inclusion in the late 1970s: "The legitimate claim for inclusion of Nepali in the Eighth Schedule of the Constitution is reflective of the expressed intent and strong desire on the part of Nepali speaking Indian citizens, to associate themselves, in full measure, in the mainstream of national life" (quoted in Munshi & Chakrabarti, 1979, p. 706). Moreover, the "national" languages of India, i.e., those in Schedule VIII, are identified as the source languages on which Hindi should draw for its development and enhancement.

Ghising and the GNLF, despite its egregious name, were "clamoring" for acceptance and integration in the Indian nation by establishing their "Indian" credentials (see Munshi & Chakrabarti, 1979, p. 708). This integrationist ideology also permeated the GNLF's demand for clarification of citizenship rights. This demand stemmed from the plight of Nepali-speaking refugees fleeing "sons of the soil" movements in Assam and Meghalaya in the early 1980s (see Fig. 8.1). These refugees heightened the Darjeeling Nepali speakers' sense of insecurity. Ghising worried that a 1950 India-Nepal treaty could be interpreted as conferring only residency rights for the Nepali speakers of Darjeeling, thus opening the door to expulsion and exclusion as had happened to the Nepali speakers further east. Ghising wanted explicit and secure Indian citizenship rights for the Darjeeling Gorkhas, who were neither Nepali speakers nor "Nepalese" according to Ghising, the latter terms implying loyalty to and citizenship of Nepal. Ghising repeatedly confirmed loyalty to the Indian state (BuraMagar, 1994, pp. 179, 189). He demanded "(a) abrogation of the Treaty, and (b) the creation of Gorkhaland, which would show that 'we are not here in India in accordance with the 1950 Indo-Nepal agreement, but we have been here in this land since the 12th century'" (Government of West Bengal, 1986, p. 18).

Citizenship, i.e., membership in a polity irrespective of race or ethnicity, is the hallmark of liberal democracies (see Kymlicka, 1995, pp. 174–176). In addressing the issues of citizenship and recognition of their language as Indian, Ghising and the GNLF were making liberal democratic demands for integration into a liberal democracy. In essence, Ghising was calling both the state and union governments' bluff: If indeed India is a liberal democracy, then the GNLF's demands should be easily accommodated. The federal government repeatedly interpreted the GNLF's demands as legitimate ("Blow Hot," 1988, p. 26). However the state government of West Bengal perceived the GNLF's demands as a direct threat, casting them in "anti-nationalist" terms (Dussar, 1986, p. 44). Ghising astutely played off the two sides in this political triangulation. At least partly because of the distrustful relations between the CPI(M) West Bengal State government and the Congress Union government which Ghising was able to manipulate, the GNLF ended up with a degree of self-government through the establishment of the Darjeeling Gorkha Hill Council (DGHC) in 1988. Ghising bargained hard for the addition of "Gorkha" to the official designation of this self-government council, once again reflecting the symbolic importance of the nomenclature issue (see "Accord endorsed," 1988, p. 114). In terms of practical import, the DGHC was probably the most significant of the concessions won, more so than the clarification of citizenship status or inclusion of Nepali in Schedule VIII. The purview of the DGHC includes primary education, and Ghising was successful in pushing through a rider in the West Bengal State Assembly that "Gorkha bhasa" (and not Nepali) is the official language of the DGHC (Josse, 1992b).

Ghising was, however, unsuccessful at pushing the "Gorkha bhasa" designation at the federal level. Instead the Chief Minister of Sikkim and his wife received credit in 1992 for inclusion of Nepali (not Gorkha bhasa or Gorkhali) in Schedule VIII ("Due honour," 1994). For once Ghising had not outmaneuvered his political rivals. Nor did he demonstrate his normal degree of political astuteness when his GNLF "attacked the homes of pro-Nepali language leaders" and threatened to expel from the electoral roles those who claimed Nepali rather than Gorkha bhasa as their spoken language (Josse, 1992a, p. 11; Samanta, 1996, p. 150).

Despite such repressive tactics, Ghising successfully taps the sentiments of his supporters, which are a majority in the Darjeeling area: the GNLF has consistently won a majority of seats on the DGHC ("Ghising Takes All," 1994). Those sentiments are for integration. Why would a cultural and linguistic minority press for integration? In the United States, it is widely assumed that the possibility of attaining the economic "American Dream" pushes minorities toward integration. In India, such an explanation carries less weight given India's economy, although India may be slightly better than Nepal in providing for the basic needs of its citizenry. A more fruitful explanation may be the nature of the system: India is an incredibly diverse federal liberal democracy. The system responds to and accommodates minorities who make liberal demands that are supported by voting constituents and are articulated by politicians who comprehend the vagaries of federal-state relations. As an international news magazine ("Land fit for Gurkhas," 1988, p. 31) noted at the height of the GNLF-led agitation, "[w]hat most people take to be signs of imminent disintegration [in India] may actually be part of the process of integration." The significance of this suggestion may be gleaned from identifying what India is *not*. India is not an explosive powder keg like some areas of Eastern Europe, despite remarkable similarities in ethnolinguistic configurations. Brubaker (1996, p. 57) describes the "deeply conflictual" and "potentially explosive and in some cases actually explosive" triadic relationship between nationalizing states, national minorities and external national "homelands" of the minorities in Eastern and Central Europe. We see the same possible configuration in India, with India engaging in nation-building and its national minorities such as the Nepali speakers in Darjeeling having a nearby homeland (in this case, Nepal) toward which appeal for protection and identification may be directed. Yet in India, rather than making such an

appeal, the national minority is bending over backwards to become part
of the mainstream nation!

URDU IN UTTAR PRADESH

Of course, Nepal is a politically and economically weak external national
homeland. India's primary regional rival, Pakistan, carved out of British
India upon independence, is a much more formidable external national
homeland to which India's Muslims and Urdu speakers could appeal. The
dangerous prospect of a triadic relationship between India, its Muslim minority, and Pakistan ratcheting up to an explosive level seems substantial
in recent years, with the electoral victories of the "nationalizing" Bharatiya
Janata Party (BJP) at both state and federal levels in India, the razing of the
mosque at Ayodhya in Uttar Pradesh and the ensuing riots, and the civil
war in Kashmir bringing India and Pakistan to the brink of nuclear catas-
trophe. An examination of the language issue allows us to step back from
these recent sensational events and develop a more contextual analysis.

Urdu is an Indo-Aryan language, syntactically identical to Hindi but
with a heavy dose of Arabic- and Persian-derived vocabulary. It evolved
along with the Moghul dynasty in India, beginning as early as the 11th
century. Written in the Arabic script, the literary gloss of Urdu differs from
Hindi (written in the Devanagri script), but on the colloquial level the
two languages, Urdu and Hindi, are virtually indistinguishable. Mahatma
Gandhi advocated the adoption of "Hindustani," the colloquial amalgam
of Urdu and Hindi, as the national language in his efforts at Hindu-Muslim
reconciliation. His idea was defeated in the Constituent Assembly, with
Hindu revivalists succeeding in pushing through a Sanskritized Hindi
as the official language (Austin, 1966). In the decades leading up to independence, the revivalists, through the press, literature, and, probably
most importantly, school textbooks, embarked on a "nationalizing" agenda
(Kumar, 1990). Language politics were at center stage: "The enormous
nationalist programme of the north Indian literati to provide independent
India with a national language became a victim of the religious and cultural
split in the Hindi heartland. In this process, a catalyst's role was played
by the breakup of a joint language [into Urdu and Hindi]" (Kumar, 1990,
p. 1255). The location of the revivalist movement was what is now the state
of Uttar Pradesh (U.P.).

Uttar Pradesh was deeply affected by the partition of the British Raj into
India and Pakistan. The Muslim League, the standard-bearer for partition,
was primarily based in U.P. The partition itself led to massive and tragic
refugee flows across the new border, with many of the "mohajir" (Muslim

refugees from India to Pakistan) coming from what was then called the United Provinces. It was these mohajir who came to power in the new Pakistan, with M. A. Jinnah, from U.P., taking the reins. Urdu, the language of the mohajir, became the official language of Pakistan, taking priority over the languages indigenous to the territory of Pakistan, such as Punjabi, Pushto, Sindhi, and Baluchi in West Pakistan, and Bengali in East Pakistan.

Language politics, then, were fundamental, and still are, to what in India is called communalism, i.e., the conflictual relations between the majority Hindus and the national minority of Muslims, and infuse India-Pakistan relations. In education in particular this has been manifest. Although the first education minister in Jawaharlal Nehru's government of newly independent India was Muslim, state governments in the "Hindi belt" of north India took steps to severely limit Urdu as a medium of instruction (Gani, 1978). When the Hindi-Urdu controversy flared up in education again in the 1970s in U.P., Hindi protagonists claimed that "Urdu [was] responsible for the partition of India," in the past and, contemporarily, "Urdu was threatening the national unity of India" (Mayank, 1980, p. 23).

The controversy in the 1970s was over the three-language formula. Chief ministers (executive heads) of the state throughout the 1970s cautiously promoted Urdu in education, through the appointment of Urdu teachers in the mid-1970s, and through the government-backed initiative in the late 1970s to open up the choices of the third language of the formula (the first and second being Hindi and English) to any language in Schedule VIII. In effect this would have rescinded a state statutory provision of Sanskrit being the third language, and lead to Urdu being a serious contender for students. (Urdu had been listed in Schedule VIII since its initial adoption at the Constituent Assembly.) However, "the fear of the Hindu backlash" forced the state government to back down (Mayank, 1980, p. 22).

Not only at the state level but also at the federal level, the "practical" pedagogically-based approaches of the 1970s to the accommodation of Urdu speakers, such as that of the Gujral Report on Urdu, were abandoned in the 1980s for the symbolic politics of language. Seeking to renew her popular support after the embarrassing defeat of her dictatorial denouement, Indira Gandhi's 1980 party manifesto advocated granting "second official language status" to Urdu in U.P. (Sonntag, 1996). The 1980s then was a decade of oscillating movement on the symbolic politics of Urdu, with the practical import, particularly in education, being drowned in the inundation of linguistic communal politics. In 1984, only after much political theatrics, Urdu was declared the "second language" (i.e., minus the "official" label). A renewed attempt to add the "official" designation succeeded in 1989, accompanied however by violent protests and subsequent challenge in the courts (Sonntag, 1996). As one commentator has noted, it is a "strategic error" to "deman[d] second official language status for Urdu . . . instead of making a minimal demand . . . for the provision of teaching of Urdu as a required subject from primary through secondary school" (Khalidi, 1995, p. 142). The 1980s were without doubt the decade of linguistic drama in U.P.

The 1990s were hardly less dramatic, although the language issue was eclipsed by the more forthright religious divide, most visibly apparent in the on-going controversy over the Ayodhya mosque. Politically, during the 1990s in U.P., Hindu nationalist (i.e., BJP) governments alternated with leftist populist governments. The latter explicitly and openly courted the Muslim (and Urdu) vote. (Urdu speakers make up approximately 9.7% of the population in U.P.; see Beg, 1996, p. 128.) In the educational realm the communal conflict in U.P. manifested itself in controversies over national symbols in the curriculum. For example, a recent flare-up involved the BJP-controlled state government mandating recitation of an identifiably Hindu nationalist song in state schools ("Discordant Notes," 1998). Once again, the practical import of education was sacrificed to the symbolism of the controversy.

CONCLUSION

Clearly the conflict over Urdu is more intense and potentially explosive, with greater ramifications for liberal democracy in India as a whole, than that over Gorkhali/Nepali. It conforms more to Brubaker's analysis of nationalizing states, national minorities, and external national homelands. The battles over Urdu have mainly raged at the state level, with state action impacting significantly the practical import of minority language use, particularly in education. Indeed, Khalidi (1995, p. 144) claims that there are no state-run Urdu primary schools in Uttar Pradesh. Yet the Urdu case, like that of Gorkhali/Nepali, shows the significance of the symbolic politics of language. Urdu was constitutionally ensconced from the beginning as a "national language" of India by its inclusion in Schedule VIII. That sacrosanct status has worked to deflate India-wide conflict over Urdu, despite the anti-Urdu "nationalizing" activities of state governments. Urdu controversies therefore tend to be "contained" within a state, with Urdu language politics and conflict differing greatly between states in terms of both timing and degree (see Sonntag, 1996, for a comparison of Urdu politics in U.P. and Bihar). Although the liberal inclusiveness of Schedule VIII status is often mitigated by the exclusiveness of state governments in the case of Urdu, there is immense variation at state level, contingent upon electoral politics. In U.P. politics, the Muslim vote has become critical to the success of alternatives to the "nationalizing" agenda of the BJP. The U.P. case of Urdu reveals again, as in the Darjeeling case, that it is the symbolic-practical tension of language policy in a federal liberal democracy that provides the most fruitful context for critical analysis.

REFERENCES

Accord endorsed, An. (1988). *Frontline* (September 3–16), 113–115.

Agnihotri, R. K., & Khanna, A. L. (1994). Language-in-education policy in India. In Omar N. Koul (Ed.), *Language development and administration* (pp. 64–73). New Delhi: Creative Books.

Austin, G. (1966). *The Indian constitution: Cornerstone of a nation.* Bombay: Oxford University Press.

Bagahi, S. B., & Danda, A. K. (1982). NE-BU-LA: A movement for regional solidarity. In K. S. Singh (Ed.), *Tribal movements in India, Vol. 1* (pp. 339–348). New Delhi: Manohar.

Beg, M. K. A. (1996). *Sociolinguistic perspective of Hindi and Urdu in India.* New Delhi: Bahri Publications.

Blow hot, blow cold. (1988). *Frontline* (February 6–19), 25–28.

Brubaker, R. (1996). *Nationalism reframed.* Cambridge: Cambridge University Press.

BuraMagar, H. B. (1994). *Is Gorkhaland a reality or simply mirage?* Kathmandu: Mrs. Puspawati BuraMagar.

Datta, P. (1993). *Regionalisation of Indian politics.* New Delhi: Sterling.

Dewan, D. B. (1991). *Education in the Darjeeling Hills.* New Delhi: Indus Publishing Co.

Dey, S. (1992). Ghising's baffling stand on Nepali. *Times of India* (Bombay edition, August 11), 12.

Discordant notes. (1998). *India Today* (International edition, December 7), 22–23.

Due honour. (1994). *Rising Nepal* (Kathmandu edition, March 31), 4.

Dussar, S. (1986). Gorkhaland and Bengali nationalism. *Frontier* (Calcutta), *19*, 8–10 (October 11–25), 42–45.

Franda, M. F. (1970). Intra-regional factionalism and coalition-building in West Bengal. *Journal of Commonwealth Political Studies, 8*, 3 (November), 187–205.

Franda, M. F. (1971). *Radical politics in West Bengal.* Cambridge: The M.I.T. Press.

Gani, H. A. (1978). *Muslim political issues and national integration.* New Delhi: Sterling Publishers Pvt. Ltd.

Ghising Takes All. (1994). *Indian Express* (New Delhi edition, January 5), 8.

Government of West Bengal. (1961). *Recommendations of the Darjeeling Enquiry Committee and action taken and other comments thereon.* Alipore, West Bengal: West Bengal Printing Government Press.

Government of West Bengal. (1986). *Gorkhaland agitation: The issues (an information document).* Calcutta: Director of Information, Government of West Bengal.

Gupta, R. S., Abbi, A., & Aggarwal, K. S. (Eds.). (1995). *Language and the state: Perspectives on the Eighth Schedule.* New Delhi: Creative Books.

Gurung, H. (1992). Review: Frontier to boundary. *Himal 5*, 3 (May–June), 40–41.

Hutt, M. J. (1988). *Nepali: A national language and its literature.* Kathmandu: Ratna Pustak Bhandar.

Josse, M. R. (1992a). Recognition of Nepali in India: Implications. *The Independent* (Kathmandu edition, September 30), 11.

Josse, M. R. (1992b). Recognition of Nepali in India-II. *The Independent* (Kathmandu edition, November 11), 11.

Khalidi, O. (1995). *Indian Muslims since independence*. New Delhi: Vikas.

King, R. D. (1997). *Nehru and the language politics of India*. Oxford: Oxford University Press.

Kumar, K. (1990). Quest for self-identity: Cultural consciousness and education in Hindi region, 1880–1950. *Economic and Political Weekly* (June 9), pp. 1247–1255.

Kymlicka, W. (1995). *Multicultural citizenship*. Oxford: Clarendon Press.

Land fit for Gurkhas, A (1988). *The Economist* (July 16), 31.

Mayank. (1980). Urdu: A victim of linguistic racialism. *Secular Democracy, 13*, 4 (April), 22–23.

Munshi, S. & Chakrabarti, T. K. (1979). National languages policy and the case for Nepali. *Economic and Political Weekly, XIV*, 15 (April 14), 701–709.

Nayar, B. R. (1969). *National communication and language policy in India*. New York: Praeger.

Samanta, A. R. (1996). *Gorkhaland: A study in ethnic separatism*. New Delhi: Khama.

Sen, J. (1989). *Darjeeling: A favoured retreat*. New Delhi: Indus.

Sonntag, S. K. (1996). The political saliency of language in Bihar and Uttar Pradesh. *The Journal of Commonwealth and Comparative Politics, XXXIV*, 2 (July), 1–18.

Subba, T. B. (1992). *Ethnicity, state and development: A case study of the Gorkhaland Movement in Darjeeling*. New Delhi: Vikas.

Timsina, S. R. (1992). *Nepali community in India*. Delhi: Manak.

9

Language Rights and the Destruction of Yugoslavia

James W. Tollefson
University of Washington

In multilingual states, language policies in education often play a central role in state efforts to manage language conflict. When competing language groups seek to further their social, economic, and political agendas within the educational system, language policy in education may be a crucial component in state efforts to favor one language group over another, or to reduce the potential for social conflict. A key to the success of language policies in education is public acceptance, not only among groups affected by policies but also among groups such as teachers who play a role in implementing policies. One challenge facing state authorities in many countries is the need to develop rationales for policies—that is, to make proposed policies appear to be a natural outgrowth of the historical situation. Thus, language policies are often linked to powerful ideologies of nation and national identity (Fairclough, 1989).

This chapter examines the relationship between language policies and ideologies, particularly focusing on the role of ideologies in legitimizing language policies. The particular case to be examined is the debate over language rights in Yugoslavia from the end of World War II until the breakup of the country in the 1990s. I will focus in particular on language policy in Slovenia, the northernmost region in Yugoslavia and the first to break away to form an independent state. The case of Slovenia reveals the complex interaction between policy and ideology: Ideologies not only constrain the formulation of policies, they are also central to public discussion and public acceptance of policies (Tollefson, 1991).

IDEOLOGY AND POLICY: SOME GENERALIZATIONS

Two generalizations about ideology are important for this analysis of language policy in Slovenia. First, as Schmidt points out (1998), in most places, language policy conflict is conditioned by the two powerful discourses of *equality* and *nationalism or national unity*. These discourses are sometimes in conflict and sometimes mutually reinforcing, but in any case they tend to force public debate to focus on the role of policies in achieving or sustaining "national unity" and the degree to which policies affect the "equality" of ethnolinguistic groups. As we shall see, in Yugoslavia during the 1980s, the political discourse of nationalism and equality, long associated with language policies dating back to the 1950s, became fundamentally altered.

Second, it is important to recognize that ideologies of language are linked to other ideologies that can influence and constrain the development of language policies. For instance, monolingual standard language ideology in the United States (Lippi-Green, 1997) is linked to related discourses of immigration and assimilation that involve complex ideological narratives of "the melting pot" in American history. Alternative ideologies, such as "cultural pluralism," must confront not only the monolingual ideology of standard English, but these powerful, related discourses as well. In Yugoslavia, ideologies of language were closely linked with powerful ideologies of nationalism and democratic centralism.

Schmidt's typology of language policies (1998) provides a useful framework for describing the range of language policy options available to policy makers in Yugoslavia and elsewhere. Schmidt lists four types of language policies:

1. In a monolingual or *centralist policy*, national security and national unity are linked with a dominant language, and the dominant ethnolinguistic group sustains its control of political and economic power by rationalizing the exclusion of other languages from public domains, particularly education. Centralist policies often rely upon a standard language ideology and a discourse of nationalism and national unity (Schmidt, 1998).
2. A policy of *assimilation* encourages subordinate groups to adopt the language of the dominant ethnolinguistic group as their own. In many states (e.g., the United States), assimilationist policies are rationalized

by both a discourse of national unity (e.g., the American "melting pot") and a discourse of equality (e.g., "equal opportunity").

3. A policy of *pluralism*, which encourages linguistic diversity and has as a central value tolerance for different languages and ethnolinguistic groups, is often associated with a discourse of equality, though it may also be associated with a discourse of national unity, as in Yugoslavia before 1980.

4. A policy of *linguistic nationalism* is often implemented through the political/administrative framework of confederation. Linguistic nationalism usually entails, though is not limited to, state legitimation of several languages in their separate geographical regions. For a brief period Yugoslavia moved toward this type of policy, but it was never fully realized.

It is important to note that particular ideologies and discourses need not be associated with particular language policies. For instance, a discourse of equality may be associated with monolingual policies that reward language shift among subordinate language groups (e.g., in the United States; see García, 1995), but in other circumstances it may support policies that block access to employment and to political participation (e.g., guest-worker policies in Germany). Similarly, a discourse of nationalism/national identity may be used to justify policies that block real assimilation and sustain patterns of segregation (e.g., in apartheid South Africa; see Cluver, 1992), or it may be associated with language maintenance programs and efforts to encourage widespread multilingualism (e.g., in Australia in the 1980s; see Moore, this volume).

EXTENDING PLURALISM: LANGUAGE POLICY IN YUGOSLAVIA, 1945–1980

In general, language policy in the post-World War II state of Yugoslavia (1945–1991) shifted from a policy of pluralism, which was rationalized by complex ideologies of national unity and linguistic equality during the period 1945–1980, to a fundamental struggle over Serbian efforts to impose a centralist policy during 1980–1991. Following background information about the population and language situation in Yugoslavia, I present an analysis of this ideological and policy shift, and then examine Slovenia's efforts to develop new policies of pluralism after achieving independence in 1991.

Created under the terms of the Treaty of Versailles in 1918, Yugoslavia was characterized from the beginning by significant ethnolinguistic diversity. Serbs were the largest group, making up about 40% of the population, while Croats comprised about 20%, Macedonians and Slovenes less than 10% each, and 15 other nationalities smaller proportions of the population (see Table 9.1). Important historical, cultural, and linguistic differences distinguish these groups. Slovene and Croatian regions were part of the Austro-Hungarian Empire, while much of Serbia, Bosnia, and other regions in the south were under Turkish rule. The northern populations of Slovenes and Croats have important historical ties to the Roman Catholic church, while Serbs are historically Orthodox, and two million Moslems lived in Bosnia and elsewhere. In all censuses since World War II, citizens have been asked to state their "nationality," thus declaring officially the significance for citizenship of their ethnolinguistic identity (see Sentić & Breznik, 1968). (Some individuals classified themselves as "Yugoslav," a complex term with varying social and political significance [Tollefson, 1981].)

Perceptions of ethnic differences in Yugoslavia were largely congruent with important linguistic differences, as language was one of the crucial factors (along with religion) forming the complex web of national identification. Although Serbian and Croatian are mutually intelligible, important lexical, grammatical, and phonological differences mark individuals as speakers of one variety or another, including regional dialects (see Rugarski & Hawkesworth, 1992). Slovenes and Croats write with the Roman alphabet, while Serbs and others in the south use Cyrillic. Other large language groups speak distinct languages that are mutually unintelligible, including the Slovenes, Macedonians, Albanians, and Hungarians. Smaller ethnic groups, each speaking its distinct language, include Italians, Germans, and Romanians. The most commonly spoken second language in Yugoslavia was Serbo-Croatian, widely used for communication among groups with different primary languages.

The constitutions of Yugoslavia under Tito (1953 and 1974) distinguished between "nation" (*narod*) and "nationality" (*narodnost*). The nations were the national groups associated with the six republics (i.e., Serbs, Croats, Slovenes, Montenegrins, Macedonians, and Moslems [a national rather than religious term under the Constitution]). That is, the nations were those groups for which the area of Yugoslavia was the homeland and which numerically dominated each of the six republics. The nationalities were other groups whose source regions were outside Yugoslavia; they were often majorities in particular communes (e.g., Italians along the border with Italy). Two nationalities had special intermediate status. The Albanians were granted semi-autonomous status in the province of Kosovo in the Republic of Serbia; the Hungarians were granted the semi-autonomous province of Vojvodina in Serbia. This complex, multileveled politico-administrative

TABLE 9.1

The Major Nations and Nationalities of Yugoslavia Before the Breakup
(in thousands)

	Yugoslavia	Bosnia	Montenegro	Croatia	Macedonia	Slovenia	Serbia	Vojvodina	Kosovo
Serb	8136	1320	20	532	45	42	4861	1107	210
Croat	4428	758	8	3454	3	56	31	109	8
Moslem	2000	1629	78	24	39	13	151	5	59
Slovene	1754	3	1	25	1	1712	8	3	0
Albanian	1731	4	37	6	378	2	72	4	1277
Macedonian	1341	2	1	5	1281	3	29	19	1
Montenegrin	577	14	399	10	4	3	77	43	27
Hungarian	427	1	0	25	0	9	5	385	0
Yugoslav	1216	326	31	379	14	26	271	167	1

Source: Statistički koledar Jugoslavije, 1988.

system was designed so that all nations and most nationalities were able to further their interests within particular geographical-political-administrative units (the federal government, republics, semi-autonomous provinces, and communes). The aim of this organization was to ensure that the nations and nationalities remained committed to a united Yugoslavia that would be widely perceived as protecting their interests.

In the first years after World War II, Yugoslavia followed the Stalinist model of state centralism, but the split between Yugoslavia and the Soviet Union and other factors (such as disastrous agricultural production) resulted in the end of Stalinism and the development of an increasingly decentralized system of state authority and economic organization that was called "self-management" (see West, 1994). In language policy, *pluralism* became the dominant approach to managing language conflict, beginning with important constitutional changes enacted in 1953.

The constitutional changes of 1953 began a process lasting until the late 1970s, in which Yugoslavia under Tito institutionalized a principle of *duality* of group loyalty and affiliation (cf. Joó, 1991). Two kinds of loyalty were required of citizens: state loyalty and nationality (or ethnolinguistic) loyalty. The principle of state loyalty was concerned with the maintenance of a unified political state (Yugoslavia), and was linked with discourses of national unity, economic development, the external Soviet threat, and democratic centralism. Nationality loyalty was concerned with maintenance of the major languages and cultures, and invoked discourses of equality and language and cultural rights. Thus language policy debate from 1953 until the early 1980s was associated with both a discourse of national unity and a discourse of ethnolinguistic equality.

Under the system of self-management, the major nationalities were proportionately represented in state organs. That is, it was not individual citizens who participated democratically and exercised rights, but rather the nations and nationalities, through their representatives in positions throughout the state system. Thus identification with one's ethnolinguistic group was essential for effective political participation. Because ethnolinguistic loyalty was associated with a discourse of language and cultural rights, political participation was ideologically linked with language and cultural rights as well. The major focus of language rights legislation involved language in education, in the courts, and in other areas of public life, as well as preservation and development of cultural institutions such as publishing houses, theater groups, and writers' associations functioning in a wide variety of languages.

Pluralism entailed powerful legal protections for language. In general, the period of 1953–1980 was characterized by increasingly detailed policies at the federal, republic, and communal levels designed to guarantee language maintenance and use for a wide range of languages, including Serbian, Croatian, Macedonian, Slovene, Hungarian, and Albanian. Language policies affecting the nations and nationalities were formulated and implemented at all three administrative levels: the federal system, the republics, and the communes. At the federal level, policies were spelled out in the Constitution of Yugoslavia, while the republic constitutions and fundamental laws of the republics and the communes spelled out detailed language policies as well. In addition, specific laws regulating language use for the benefit of linguistic minorities were adopted in multilingual communes. For instance, in the Italian and Hungarian communes in Slovenia, language rights for Italians and Hungarians were ensured in education, in the courts and legislative bodies, and in broadcasting and the media. Legislation was so detailed, for example, that notices on public kiosks in the bilingual communes were required to be bilingual (in Slovene and Italian or Hungarian). Such guarantees were designed to protect Italian and Hungarian from the much larger Slovene and Serbo-Croatian groups.

In education, the main principle was that every individual has the right to education in his or her native language (Vukobratović, 1976). This principle was implemented fully in the republics and semi-autonomous provinces, where national groups had a complete range of elementary, secondary, and tertiary educational institutions in their languages. For the nationalities, the situation was variable. Italians, for instance, could attend Italian-medium primary and secondary schools in Slovenia, but no tertiary institutions operated in Italian, and outside the bilingual communes, Italians had no special language rights (Tollefson, 1981). The spread of schools in the languages of the smaller nationalities was particularly strong from the 1950s until the mid-1960s. In some local bilingual areas, speakers of the dominant language (e.g., Slovene) were required to learn the minority language (e.g., Italian). Thus the implementation of pluralism in education entailed significant efforts (successful in many bilingual areas) to bring about reciprocal bilingualism.

IDEOLOGICAL CONFLICT: FROM PLURALISM TO SERBIAN CENTRALISM, 1980–1991

The policy of linguistic pluralism was largely dominant by the time of important constitutional revisions in 1974. These revisions codified pluralism in a new federal constitution, as well as in new constitutions at the regional (republic) and local (communal) levels. After 1974, however, three factors began to undermine pluralism and to prepare Yugoslavia for the assertion of centralist policies in the 1980s:

1. Economic crisis in the 1970s. Severe recession in the 1970s led to regional conflict over economic issues and resistance to long-standing policies designed to strengthen the economic position of areas in the less developed south (e.g., Kosovo and Bosnia). With the weaker economy, Slovenes and Croats were particularly reluctant to continue subsidizing what they considered to be inefficient industries in other republics (Türk, 1991).
2. Weakening of federal power in Belgrade in the years immediately before and after Tito's death in 1980. With the loss of Tito's leadership, regional authorities gained increasing power as federal officials in Belgrade failed to solve the country's economic problems. This process of shifting power to the regions increasingly led to policy stalemates at the federal level (Glenny, 1992) and was abruptly halted with the rise to prominence in the mid-1980s of Serbian leader Slobodan Milošević.
3. The rise of Serbian nationalism. Under the leadership of Slobodan Milošević, Serbian nationalism undermined pluralism by giving priority to Serb interests at the federal level, thereby shifting the role of the federal government in Belgrade: While the federal government under Tito had sought to block the rise to prominence of any particular nation or nationality, under Milošević Belgrade came to represent Serb interests alone.

Although these processes temporarily strengthened regional authorities, the success of Serbian nationalism and the assertion of Serbian-dominated centralism eventually brought an end to pluralism by around 1988. In response, Slovenia, Bosnia, Croatia, and Macedonia came to view confederation (and, later, independence) as the most desirable alternative to Serbian centralism.

Serbian Centralism and Language Policy Conflict in Slovenia

The rise of Serbian nationalism under Slobodan Milošević had direct impact upon language policy conflict during the decade leading up to the wars in Yugoslavia (i.e., 1981–1991). As the movement for Serbian hegemony intensified during the 1980s, Slovenia, Croatia, Bosnia, and Macedonia increasingly came to believe that a new, highly decentralized confederation was the only way to preserve their ethnolinguistic autonomy guaranteed under the pluralist constitution of 1974. In response, Serbian leaders sought to prevent the process of national emancipation through confederation. The result was that Slovenes and others were faced with the choice between acceding to Serbian centralism or seeking independence, which, they correctly feared, would lead to civil war (Denitch, 1996; Glenny, 1992). A key component of the campaign by Serb leaders to impose Serbian centralism was a series of Serb-initiated changes in language policy in education.

In 1983, federal education authorities in Belgrade, largely comprised of Serb nationalists loyal to Milošević, sought to impose a new national school curriculum. The so-called "common core" curriculum was to replace the regional curricula that had been largely under the control of regional (e.g., Slovene) authorities. The proposed federal curriculum required that approximately half of the literary texts to be studied in school would be mandated by federal authorities, and half would remain under the control of educational authorities in the republics and communes. When the proposal was made public, critics argued that it was designed to give increased attention to Serbian language, literature, and history in schools throughout the country. In Slovenia, many Slovene intellectual leaders responded by organizing groups to resist the proposal and to maintain Slovene control over schools in Slovenia. (For a critical view of Slovene reaction, see Wachtel, 1998). Most prominent among these groups was the Commission for the Protection of the Freedom of Thought and Writing of the Slovene Writers' Society, which led opposition to the proposed new curriculum.

The organization of Slovene writers was also instrumental in leading opposition to the Memorandum of the Serbian Academy of Sciences and Arts (Mihailović & Krestić, 1995). The Memorandum elicited intense public debate across Yugoslavia when it was leaked to the press in 1986. Written by an influential group of Serb intellectuals (including linguists and other social scientists), the Memorandum was widely viewed as providing the framework for a reorganized political system in Yugoslavia (see Tollefson, in press). The Memorandum included a detailed analysis of the "severe crisis" facing the country and the need to resolve that crisis in order to avert "a catastrophic outcome" (Mihailović & Krestić, 1995, p. 95). According to the Memorandum, the cause of the economic and political crisis was the policy of pluralism, particularly the range of ethnolinguistic rights enshrined in the 1974 Constitution. Claiming that "the present-day political system of Yugoslavia is increasingly contradictory, dysfunctional, and expensive" (p. 105), the Memorandum proposed as a solution to the crisis new restrictions on the autonomy of the republics and nations/nationalities, as well as changes in language policy. Asserting that "we must throw off the ideology that lays primary emphasis on ethnic and territorial considerations" (p. 105), the Memorandum favored a national educational curriculum, and specifically criticized language policies protecting Albanian in Kosovo and Croatian in Croatia. Moreover, the Memorandum argued that Serbian and Croatian varieties should be unified (presumably under a Serbian model) in order to protect the Serb minorities outside Serbia in Bosnia and Croatia. The Memorandum also proposed new policies to promote Serbian-medium education in Serb areas outside Serbia, though no parallel policies were proposed for members of other nations living outside their home republics.

The Memorandum was also significant for its impact upon the discourse of language and nationality. Under Tito, public discussion of language policy was constrained by the dual principles of state and nationality loyalty. Thus advocates for particular policies were not permitted to express "ethnic chauvinism" or other forms of public criticism of national groups (Tollefson, 1981). The Memorandum, however, "launched a new and virulent vocabulary, which in the next few years imbued the public discourse" (Udovički & Torov, 1997, p. 89). This new discourse, evident in such phrases in the Memorandum as "genocide against the Serbs" and "Serbian holocaust," gradually became part of the public vernacular of nationalism in Serbia, particularly in the media, and played an important role in shaping public discussion of language and nationalism.

The intense reaction to the Memorandum in Slovenia and the continuing activism by Slovene writers and other intellectuals gradually shifted language politics to the forefront of public political discussion in Slovenia. In addition to the writers' group, explicitly political groups such as the Human Rights Council of the Socialist Alliance turned their attention to linguistic human rights. With an increasing number of cultural and political groups in Slovenia discussing the issue of language rights, all that was needed to mobilize masses of Slovenes over the issue of language was a sufficiently dramatic public event.

In June, 1988, the Yugoslav Army provided that event with the trial of four Slovene journalists accused of treason. The Slovenes, including Janez Janša, a journalist from the periodical *Mladina* who later became Minister of Defense in independent Slovenia, were tried in military court for publishing articles about possible corruption in the Army. The trial, held in Ljubljana, the Slovene capital, was conducted in Serbo-Croatian rather than Slovene, the defendants' language, despite explicit guarantees under the Slovene Constitution that defendants should be tried in their own language. The Army's decision to require the accused to defend themselves in Serbo-Croatian conveyed the message that pluralist policies ensuring Slovene language rights were no longer applicable. In other words, the trial marked the explicit end of the federal policy of linguistic pluralism. The result was a series of huge demonstrations in Ljubljana, out of which was formed the Committee for the Defense of Human Rights, which played a central role in defending Slovene language rights and later in the push for constitutional changes to democratize Yugoslavia and to create a Yugoslav confederation (see Lee, 1989).

In December, 1988, an additional major event was a set of Serbian-imposed amendments to the federal constitution that curtailed language and cultural rights in the Albanian semi-autonomous province of Kosovo and the Hungarian semi-autonomous province of Vojvodina (for an account, see Pipa & Repishti, 1989). Among other actions, Serb leaders shifted the medium of instruction in schools in Kosovo from Albanian to Serbian and purged Albanian-speaking teachers and administrators from the educational system, despite the fact that the population was approximately 90% Albanian. Slovenes were so alarmed by these actions that it became politically impossible for leaders of the Slovene League of Communists to continue their public commitment to salvaging the old pluralism. Thus, even the Slovene communists joined the movement for confederation, as an alternative to the now obviously defunct system of pluralism. Milan Kučan, a key leader of the Slovene communists, began to argue in meetings of the League of Communists (the Yugoslav Party at the federal level) for a new confederation of largely independent states.

Faced with mounting evidence that Serbian leaders in Belgrade would be satisfied with nothing less than the replacement of pluralism with a new Serbian centralism, the Slovene parliament in late 1989 adopted a series of constitutional changes that began to move Slovenia toward formal confederation. In March, 1990, the Parliament adopted additional amendments guaranteeing the language rights of the Italian and Hungarian nationalities in Slovenia. In April, 1990, the first free multiparty elections were held; they resulted in a landslide victory for Demos, the united opposition parties. For the rest of 1990, Slovene officials pleaded with Serbian leaders in Belgrade to adopt formal confederation. When it became clear that this option was not acceptable to Milošević, the separation of state and nationality, which had been sustained in Yugoslavia through the principle of dualism, became impossible. As a result, Slovenes voted overwhelmingly for independence in a December, 1990, plebescite. Finally, the Slovene Declaration of Independence was adopted on June 25, 1991 (see Blaustein & Flanz, 1992). The document itself was a model of pluralism, pledging Slovenia to a wide range of measures to protect the ethnolinguistic rights and identities of Italians and Hungarians, the main minorities in Slovenia. The Declaration also reiterated Slovenia's support for language minorities elsewhere in Yugoslavia, including the Albanians in Kosovo, who were by then living under Serbian-imposed martial law.

A major result of Slovenia's conflict with Serbia during the 1980s was that pluralist policies were moved to the center of Slovene political discussion. These policies were linked to a developing ideology of internationalism that emphasized Slovenia's links with Western Europe, the integrated capitalist world economy, and liberal democracy. In other words, the rise of Serbian nationalism stimulated the Slovene independence movement, which evoked a powerful ideology of Slovene internationalism in order to justify independence and new economic and political links with Western Europe. This ideology of internationalism had significant implications for language policy. Most importantly, a pluralist language policy became one of the ways that Slovenia sought international support for independence and made its case for entrance into the European community (see Council of Europe, 1993).

Thus the evolving crisis involved a fundamental shift in Serbian political discourse, ended the separation of state and nationality, moved the national question to the center of state politics, and forced both the ruling elite and opposition leaders in Slovenia and elsewhere to place language questions at the forefront of state policy (e.g., see Vučelić, 1991). The disintegration of the Yugoslav state created the opening for the rise of a new political ideology in Slovenia. This new ideology involved demands for (1) political pluralism, (2) political institutions in which conflict could be mediated without threat to ethnolinguistic identity, (3) the legitimacy of the Slovene national question, and (4) links between Slovenia and Western Europe rather than the Balkans (Bibič, 1993).

Why did language rights, linguistic pluralism, and proposals for confederation/independence come to dominate Slovene political culture just prior to independence? Four historical and structural factors help to explain the appeal of linguistic pluralism and confederationist policies in Slovenia in the late 1980s:

1. The homogeneity of the population of Slovenia (more than 90% Slovene). Unlike Bosnia and Kosovo, where significant Serb minority populations opposed regional confederation, Slovenia's relatively homogenous population made it feasible for Slovenia to move toward confederation and ultimately independence without major internal conflict.

2. The particular nature of Slovene political culture, in which active political involvement of diverse social groups was commonplace. In the first multiparty elections in April, 1990, for instance, candidates for the legislative assembly represented the full spectrum of Slovene society, including cultural organizations, the writers' association, professional and occupational groups, farmers, students, and environmentalists, as well as traditional activists such as the Human Rights Council of the Socialist Alliance and representatives of the Italian and Hungarian minority populations. Such diverse political groups

involved in decision making at the highest levels of Slovene political culture helped to ensure that pluralist policies would be adopted.

3. Slovenia's preeminent economic position in Yugoslavia, with the highest per capita income, highest rates of literacy and employment, and a percentage of national income that was generally twice its proportional share (Lah, 1972; *Statistični bilten*, n.d.; Tollefson, 1981). Slovenia's relative wealth, which was widely perceived in Slovenia as associated with a distinct Slovene culture, made it likely that Slovenes would want to preserve their autonomous political and economic institutions.

4. Slovenia's high degree of what Brym (1989) calls "institutional completeness," which refers to the number and types of formal organizations. In culture, politics, education, and the economy, Slovenes for many decades had operated a full range of institutions in which the Slovene language is used. In general, a greater degree of institutional completeness means a greater effect of ethnolinguistic group membership on socioeconomic standing. With Slovenia's preeminent position in the economy, Slovenes had powerful economic incentives to identify themselves in ethnolinguistic terms and to preserve those institutions that they had come to associate with their economic success.

These factors meant that Slovenes could realistically envision a confederation that would further their economic and political interests. Indeed, as the movement for Serbian domination increased in the late 1980s, many Slovenes began to believe that their economic well-being and ethnolinguistic survival could *only* be protected in a new Yugoslav confederation. When it became clear that Serb leaders would not accept a confederation, Slovenes (like minorities elsewhere in Yugoslavia) were left with independence as the only viable option for retaining their pluralist language policies.

LANGUAGE POLICIES IN INDEPENDENT SLOVENIA: THE NEW PLURALISM

Unlike Serbia, the Slovene independence movement did not entail an aggressive and ethnocentric Slovene nationalism; instead, independence was fundamentally associated with the ideology of internationalism. One reason may have been that the groundwork for pluralism was established by the internationalism of Yugoslav communism, particularly its emphasis upon language and nationality rights. But widespread hostility to communism in Slovenia and the rise of ethnocentric nationalism elsewhere in

Yugoslavia suggest that this is an inadequate explanation. Instead, two particular historical-structural factors may help to explain the unique appeal of internationalism in Slovenia:

1. The small size of Slovenia. For centuries under the political domination of larger groups, Slovenes had developed an intense awareness of the extraordinary difficulty of maintaining a distinct identity and achieving some degree of political autonomy. As a result, most Slovenes viewed as unrealistic any ideology that would hold out hope of Slovenia's complete separation from more powerful surrounding states. It was widely assumed that some form of economic (perhaps also political and military) alliance would be necessary for an independent Slovenia (see Hribar, 1991).
2. Widespread perception in Slovenia that independence entailed enormous risks. The risk of independence not only involved the likelihood of war with the much more powerful Serbian-led Yugoslav army, but also fundamental questions about the viability of Slovenia as an independent economic and political unit in Europe. During the late 1980s, the practical problems of surviving as a small state in Europe had consumed economic and political analysts in Slovenia (Horvat, 1993). The intense public discussion of the feasibility of independence led to a sober consensus that strong political and economic ties with Western Europe were essential if Slovenia hoped to survive as an independent state. This widespread concern for the future was mitigated by the ideology of internationalism, which emphasized Slovenia's historical ties with Western Europe as part of Austro-Hungary, its relatively developed democratic political institutions, and its economic links with Italy, Germany, Austria, and elsewhere in Europe (Klopčič, 1993). In other words, internationalism provided the rationale for an independent Slovenia.

Perhaps the most dramatic evidence of the link between pluralism, internationalism, and independence was the public attention Slovenia gave to its pluralist language policies in its campaign to be admitted to the European Community. For instance, in a document outlining the policy of pluralism, the director of the Slovene Government Bureau for Ethnic Communities argued that general provisions for pluralism were being practically implemented through a wide range of legal protections (Winkler, 1994). When Council of Europe investigators visited Slovenia to decide whether new state institutions met the standards of Western European democracies, Slovenia's pluralist language policies received particular attention. In the investigators' report, these policies were called a "model" for all of Europe:

> Slovenia scores high in all respects. It has modern legislation in civil and penal law—and in many other areas—and modern institutions, some of which do not yet exist in all Council of Europe member states (Constitutional Court, ombudsman and special representatives of minorities in elected bodies) . . . Under these circumstances, it must be said that both [Italian and Hungarian minority] communities are rather privileged . . . Slovenia . . . fully protects the rule of law and fundamental rights and freedoms. The way it protects the rights of minorities is a model and an example for many European states (both East and West) (Council of Europe, 1993).

Thus Slovenia's commitment to pluralism became a mechanism by which Slovene political leaders were able to remove Slovenia from a Serbian-led Yugoslav state and move independent Slovenia toward closer political and economic ties with Western Europe. This process has been so successful that when a meeting of Balkan states was held in 1997, Slovenia refused to send a representative, declaring that Slovenia was not a Balkan state.

The new Constitution of independent Slovenia, adopted in December, 1991, is a model of pluralist ideology. Although the Constitution explicitly links Slovenia's independence with the "permanent and inviolable right of the Slovene nation to self-determination," the document commits independent Slovenia to linguistic pluralism: Slovenia "protects and guarantees the rights of the autochthonous Italian and Hungarian ethnic communities." (All quotations from the Constitution of Slovenia are from the English translation by Blaustein & Flanz, 1992, pp. 1–35). This general guarantee of pluralism in Slovenia is linked with Slovenia's commitment to the protection of Slovene minorities in neighboring Italy and Austria: Slovenia "looks after the autochthonous Slovene ethnic minorities in neighboring states, Slovene emigrants and migrant workers, and promotes their contacts with their homeland."

In a section on official languages, the Constitution guarantees that Italian and Hungarian are official languages (with Slovene) in regions where Italians and Hungarians reside. This policy of declaring officially bilingual districts repeats the traditional formula for protecting language rights in specified geographical areas that was used throughout Yugoslavia from the 1950s until the 1980s (see *Osnovne in srednje šole* . . . , 1976; Tollefson, 1981; Zorn & Pleterski, 1974). The importance of official language status is emphasized further in the Constitution when language is specifically linked to human rights. Along with race, sex, religion, political conviction, and nationality, language is one of the categories given official human rights protection.

In addition to general statements of principle, the Constitution (as well as other statutes; see Jesih, 1994) includes a number of specific guarantees of linguistic pluralism. For instance, any individual arrested or imprisoned "must be notified immediately of the reason for the loss . . . of liberty in the person's mother tongue or in a language which the person understands." Italians and Hungarians are guaranteed the right to use their languages in government offices in the bilingual districts. An entire section (article 64) is devoted to "special rights" for Italians and Hungarians in Slovenia. Publicly funded education in Italian and Hungarian is guaranteed; one provision suggests that education in Italian and Hungarian (as well as Slovene) will be required of Slovenes living in the bilingual districts ("the law shall determine the regions in which bilingual education is compulsory"). Article 64 also declares that laws affecting the linguistic minorities may not be passed "without the consent of the representatives of the national communities." Additional provisions in the Constitution require that at least one Italian and one Hungarian delegate be elected to the 90-member Slovene assembly. Finally, an ombudsman and a constitutional court are established as guardians of the rights of citizens, particularly of linguistic minorities.

In addition to constitutional provisions, Slovene authorities have adopted a wide range of measures to implement the policy of pluralism. These measures include election procedures that ensure Italian and Hungarian involvement in administering elections in bilingual regions, special seats for Italian and Hungarian representatives on community councils, and a provision permitting Italians and Hungarians residing outside bilingual districts to register and vote in the bilingual districts (for details, see Tollefson, 1997). In education, Slovene-Hungarian bilingual programs in ten elementary schools and one secondary school in the Prekmurje region enroll Hungarian and Slovene students. The policy of using Slovene and Hungarian throughout the school day is implemented by bilingual teachers who use Slovene for certain lessons (e.g., in science, with additional Hungarian vocabulary introduced at the end of lessons), and Hungarian in other lessons (e.g., regional European history). In the Italian region, elementary and secondary schools are either Slovene or Italian, with the other language taught as a required subject. Court procedures in bilingual districts are conducted in the language of the defendant (if Italian or Hungarian), with prosecutors and juries required to speak the language as well. Due to a shortage of legal personnel fluent in Hungarian, however, implementation of this provision is inconsistent in Hungarian districts. Government offices in bilingual districts are required to function bilingually, with a variety of local laws requiring bilingualism in notices, public announcements, signs, and public records.

Thus, the first constitution of independent Slovenia and additional laws reassert the pluralist approach to language policy that dominated language policy in Yugoslavia from the 1950s until the 1980s. In part, this reassertion of pluralism was a response to Serbian nationalism, which continued to threaten the regions of former Yugoslavia. An additional factor was the ideology of internationalism that had come to play a major role in Slovene politics after 1988. In other words, the new pluralism was Slovenia's expression of its links with multilingual, multicultural Europe and its commitment to liberal democracy.

The Role of English and German in Contemporary Slovenia

The ideology of internationalism and pluralist policies have had impact upon the rapidly changing role of languages other than Slovene. While Slovenia was part of Yugoslavia, the primary concern for Slovene nationalists and for Slovene language policymakers was the relationship of Slovene to Serbo-Croatian. With virtually no support among Slovenes for extending Serbo-Croatian into Slovene social life, the Slovene language was secure under the Titoist policy of pluralism. In independent Slovenia, however, English and German have rapidly expanded into domains of use previously reserved exclusively for Slovene. For instance, English is widely used in advertising and the mass media. The spread of English and German is not generally perceived to be a problem, but rather is widely viewed as a reflection of the ideology of internationalism and the integration of Slovenia into the European community (Paternost, 1997; Toporišič, 1997).

Perhaps the most important change in the use of languages other than Slovene is the rapid spread of English in the educational system, where English is now introduced in the third year of elementary school. In addition, a major program of teacher training is aimed at improving English language instruction at all levels. Moreover, the popularity of English-language culture, especially videos, television, radio, and music, have led to a rapid expansion of English in the language of young people. All of these changes have elicited opposition among some Slovene nationalists (Toporišič, 1997).

In part, the spread of English in Slovenia reflects the general importance of English in Europe. As Phillipson and Skutnabb-Kangas (1996) point out, "English is being vigorously promoted as the royal road to democracy, a market economy, and human rights" (p. 431; also see Berns, 1995). But *local* forces in Slovenia are equally important. The Slovene ideology of internationalism, with its links to the Slovene independence movement, gives special impetus to the use of English and German. In other words, the use of other languages in Slovenia is an outgrowth not only of international political and economic forces that favor English, but also of recent events in Slovenia that have brought the ideology of internationalism to the forefront of Slovene public life.

According to some Slovene nationalists, one risk to the Slovene language is that it may gradually be displaced by English (Toporišič, 1997). They fear that as the spread of English continues and the domains of use for Slovene become increasingly restricted, a "diglossic division of labor" (Phillipson & Skutnabb-Kangas, 1996, p. 446) may restrict Slovene to the home, family, and local concerns. Although it is impossible to predict the future language situation in Slovenia, at this early stage in the history of independent Slovenia, there is some evidence that public use of Slovene has diminished in important domains (Toporišič, 1997). Thus a major concern of Slovene nationalists is that the Slovene independence movement, Slovenia's pluralist approach to language policy, and the ideology that supports it have ironically served to further the use of languages other than Slovene (see Gjurin, 1991; Toporišič, 1991, 1997). In response, there is some evidence that Slovene nationalists may assert a new ideology of Slovene linguistic centralism and attempt to rescind constitutionally protected policies of linguistic pluralism (Toporišič, 1997). Whether such a movement is successful will depend in large part upon the continuing appeal of the ideology of internationalism. As long as Slovenia prospers under its association with Western European capitalism, Slovene nationalists are likely to be unsuccessful in such efforts. Should Slovenia sink into serious recession, however, then the ideology of internationalism may lose its appeal, and Slovene nationalists may gain support for a policy of exclusive Slovene language rights.

CONCLUSION: LANGUAGE POLICY AND LANGUAGE RIGHTS IN YUGOSLAVIA

In efforts to gain support for policies, state institutions and interest groups often develop and manage complex ideologies that provide rationales for policies. In Yugoslavia, as we have seen, the Titoist ideology of pluralism supported detailed federal, regional, and local policies to protect language rights. With the rise of the ideology of Serbian nationalism, alternative Serbian-initiated centralist policies were proposed. These centralist policies elicited intense resistance in Slovenia and elsewhere. Following several years of conflict, Slovenia's successful separation from Serbia resulted in pluralist policies in independent Slovenia that were supported by the Slovene ideology of internationalism.

Similar links between ideology and policy exist elsewhere. For instance, Wiley and Lukes (1996) explore two interrelated ideologies of language in the United States: The ideology of English monolingualism, which portrays language diversity as the alien result of immigration and a threat to state security; and the ideology of standard English, which positions speakers of different language varieties within a hierarchy of social and economic privilege that favors speakers of the standard variety. Moreover, the ideology of English monolingualism is associated with the ideology of individualism and social mobility (Wiley & Lukes, 1996). Thus the ideological justification is created for English-only centralism, as well as related policies that rescind bilingual education (see Wiley, this volume). In Yugoslavia, the tensions between Serbian nationalist ideology and Slovene internationalism finally could not be managed; dissolution became the only option.

The recent history of language rights in Yugoslavia also highlights the important differences between individual and group rights. Under Tito, the system of national rights had a territorial basis: individuals' rights depended upon their membership in groups whose rights were ensured within particular geographic areas of the country. This approach to rights is fundamentally different from citizenship rights that are extended to individuals without regard to ethnolinguistic identity or geography. One reason for Milošević's success in mobilizing Serbian popular opinion in support of Serbian nationalism was that Serbs living outside the national territory of Serbia (in Bosnia and Croatia) did not have the same language and national rights as Serbs living inside Serbia. Thus Milošević was able to exploit this issue to achieve his political goals.

Finally, the destruction of Yugoslavia demonstrates the potential for the symbolic politics of language to mobilize populations and shape public opinion. In Yugoslavia between 1981 and 1991, public debates about language rights and language policy helped to define and to shape options, not only in language policy, but in the larger issues of state reorganization that preceded the wars. In part through intense, public language policy debates, Yugoslavia was changed from a pluralist, multinational state that was widely perceived as meeting the needs of most nations and nationalities, to one where proposals for Serbian-centralist policies ensured intense social, political, and, finally, military conflict.

REFERENCES

Berns, M. (1995). English in the European Union. *English Today*, 11 (3), 3–11.

Bibič, A. (1993). The emergence of pluralism in Slovenia. *Communist and Post-Communist Studies, 26,* 367–386.

Blaustein, A. P., & Flanz, G. H. (1992). Constitution of the Republic of Slovenia, 23 December, 1991; Declaration of Independence, 25 June 1991; and other documents. In *Constitutions of the countries of the world,* 1–74. Release 92–6. Dobbs Ferry, NY: Oceana.

Brym, R. J. (1989). *From culture to power: The sociology of English Canada.* New York: Oxford University Press.

Cluver, A. D. de V. (1992). Language planning models for a post-apartheid South Africa. *Language Problems and Language Planning, 16*, 105–136.

Council of Europe. (1993). *Report of the Committee on Legal Affairs and Human Rights in Slovenia*. AS/Jur (44) (March 22), 55.

Denitch, B. (1996). *Ethnic nationalism*. Minneapolis: University of Minnesota Press.

Fairclough, N. (1989). *Language and power*. London: Longman.

García, O. (1995). Spanish language loss as a determinant of income among Latinos in the United States. In J. W. Tollefson (Ed.), *Power and inequality in language education* (pp. 142–160). New York: Cambridge University Press.

Gjurin, V. (1991). *Slovenščina zdaj!* [Slovene now!] Ljubljana: Art agencija.

Glenny, M. (1992). *The fall of Yugoslavia*. New York: Penguin Books.

Horvat, B. (1993). Requiem for the Yugoslav economy. *Dissent* (summer), 333–339.

Hribar, V. (1991). The Slovenes and European transnationality. In N. Grafenauer (Ed.), *The case of Slovenia* (pp. 33–36). Ljubljana: Nova Revija.

Jesih, B., et al. (1994). *Ethnic minorities in Slovenia*. Ljubljana: Institute for Ethnic Studies.

Joó, R. (1991). Slovenes in Hungary and Hungarians in Slovenia: Ethnic and state identity. *Ethnic and Racial Studies, 14*, 100–106.

Klopčič, V. (1993). Cultural rights in multinational communities. In S. Devetak, S. Flere, & G. Seewann (Eds.), *Ethnic minorities in an emerging Europe* (pp. 200–203). Munich: Slavic Verlag Dr. Anton Kovac.

Lah, A. (1972). *The Yugoslav federation: What is it?* Belgrade: Medunarodna politika, Studies, 36.

Lee, M. (1989). The strange death of Tito's Yugoslavia. *Against the Current, 3* (6), 19–28.

Lippi-Green, R. (1997). *English with an accent: Language, ideology, and discrimination in the United States*. London: Routledge.

Mihailović, K., & Krestić, V. (1995). *Memorandum of the Serbian Academy of Sciences and Arts—answers to criticisms*. Belgrade: Serbian Academy of Sciences and Arts.

Osnovne in srednje šole na koncu šolskega leta 1974–1975 in začetka šolskega leta 1975–1976 (1976). Ljubljana: Statistical Office of the SR Slovenia, 37.

Paternost, J. (1997). Recent sociolinguistic struggles for language sovereignty among the Slovenes. *International Journal of the Sociology of Language, 124*, 185–200.

Phillipson, R., & Skutnabb-Kangas, T. (1996). English only worldwide or language ecology? *TESOL Quarterly, 30*, 429–452.

Pipa, A., & Repishti, S. (1989). Reflections on the Kosovo crisis. *Across Frontiers* (Winter Spring), 7–8.

Rugarski, R., & Hawkesworth, C. (Ed.). (1992). *Language planning in Yugoslavia*. Columbus, OH: Slavica Publishers.

Schmidt, R. J. (1998). The politics of language in Canada and the United States: Explaining the differences. In T. Ricento & B. Burnaby (Eds.), *Language and politics in the United States and Canada* (pp. 37–70). Mahwah, NJ: Lawrence Erlbaum.

Sentić, M., & Breznik, D. (1968). Demografske karakteristike etničkih, religioznih, i rasnih grupa. *Stanovništvo* (July–December), 142–183.

Statistični bilten. (n.d.). Belgrade: Federal Statistical Office, 255, 439–700.

Statistični koledar Jugoslavije 1988. (1988). Belgrade: Zvezni zavod za statistiko.

Tollefson, J. W. (1981). *The language situation and language policy in Slovenia*. Washington: University Press of America.

Tollefson, J. W. (1991). *Planning language, planning inequality: Language policy in the community*. London: Longman.

Tollefson, J. W. (1997). Language policy in independent Slovenia. *International Journal of the Sociology of Language, 124*, 29–49.

Tollefson, J. W. (in press). The language debates: Preparing for the war in Yugoslavia, 1980–1991. *International Journal of the Sociology of Language.*

Toporišič, J. (1991). *Družbenost slovenskega jezika: Sociolingvistična razpravljanja* [The social aspect of Slovene: Sociolinguistic studies]. Ljubljana: Drzavna založba Slovenije.

Toporišič, J. (1997). Slovene as the language of an independent state. *International Journal of the Sociology of Language, 124,* 5–28.

Türk, D. (1991). Slovenia and Europe: A case for a new design. In N. Grafenauer, *The case of Slovenia* (pp. 91–94). Ljubljana: Nova Revija.

Udovički, J., & Torov, I. (1997). The interlude: 1980–1990. In J. Udovički & J. Ridgeway (Eds.), *Burn this house: The making and unmaking of Yugoslavia* (pp. 80–107). Durham, NC: Duke University Press.

Vučelić, M. (1991). *Razogvori sa epohom* [Conversations with the epoch]. Novi Sad: Politika.

Vukobratović, B. (1976). The constitutional law bases for ensuring equality in education in the languages of the nationalities in the Socialist Republic of Croatia. Paper presented at the International Symposium on the Establishment of Nationality Equality in Education, Novi Sad, Yugoslavia.

Wachtel, A. B. (1998). *Making a nation, breaking a nation: Literature and cultural politics in Yugoslavia.* Stanford, CA: Stanford University Press.

West, R. (1994). *Tito and the rise and fall of Yugoslavia.* New York: Carroll and Graf.

Wiley, T. G., & Lukes, M. (1996). English-only and standard English ideologies in the U.S. *TESOL Quarterly, 30,* 511–536.

Winkler, P. (1994). Introduction. In B. Jesih et al. (Eds.), *Ethnic Minorities in Slovenia* (p. 6). Ljubljana: Institute for Ethnic Studies.

Zorn, T., & Pleterski, J. (1974). Prispevek k problematiki sprememb v socialnih štrukturah koroških slovencev. *Razprave in gradivo, 6,* 106–119.

V

Language and Global Relations

The chapters in this section deal with the following critical issue: How are local policies and programs in language education affected by global processes such as colonialism, decolonization, the spread of English, and the growth of the integrated capitalist economy? In Chapter 10, Florian Coulmas traces the role of language in Japan since the Meiji era (1868–1911), with particular emphasis on how the Japanese language was linked with national unification, relations with the West, and later with the goals of empire. More recently, the increasing ethnolinguistic diversity of Japan, brought about by globalization and immigration, places new demands upon policy makers, who must simultaneously develop policies for new ethnolinguistic groups and respond to continuing concerns about the future of the Japanese language.

The articles by Sue Wright and Sook Kyung Jung/Bonny Norton deal explicitly with the major linguistic manifestation of globalization: the spread of English. In Chapter 11, Wright's historical analysis of language education in Vietnam shows that new policies to encourage English language learning are constrained not only by the economic and material limitations facing educational institutions in Vietnam, but also by the long association of foreign languages with political and military conflict between Vietnam and other countries. In Chapter 12, in their analysis of the new elementary English program in Korea, Jung and Norton are especially interested in teachers' response to the program. Their research in three schools in the Seoul area found that the government's efforts to promote the program were rather successful, particularly through a heavily funded program of teacher training. Teachers' resistance to the program was found to be the result of two factors: (1) concern that the emphasis on English would threaten the future of the Korean language; (2) the particular working conditions in specific schools where, for example, some English teachers were assigned additional duties not given to regular teachers, leaving them little time to undertake the materials preparation the new program requires.

In Chapter 13, Alamin M. Mazrui also examines the role of English as an international language, though his focus is on contexts in which English was introduced under colonialism and continues to dominate higher education. Mazrui contrasts the influence of English in Africa, where linguistic dependency has led to intellectual dependency, with its influence in Japan, where Japanese is used for a full range of intellectual discourse. Mazrui's goal is to promote decolonization: finding ways to reduce the linguistic and cultural dependency of African higher education on English and the West. To this end, he describes five strategies for decolonization: indigenization, domestication, and diversification of African educational institutions, as well as greater exchange of skills and resources within Africa ("horizontal inter-penetration") and greater influence of Africa upon the West ("vertical counter-penetration"). Mazrui's call for the "recentering of African languages in African institutions" is the most explicit statement of the worldwide concern for languages displaced by English—whether in Japan, Vietnam, Korea, or elsewhere. His proposal of strategies for decolonization parallels similar proposals in the chapters in Part VI of this book.

10

Language Policy in Modern Japanese Education

Florian Coulmas
Gerhard Mercator University, Duisburg, FRG

Identification, loyalty and effective citizenship depends on literacy and education in the one favoured language (Gellner, 1994, p. 60).

Japan has a tradition of considering both education and language a matter of government responsibility. With the emergence of a centralized modern state, a language policy took shape, which in the course of the past century generated a great deal of public debate and turned the Japanese language into a key symbol of Japan's ethno-national identity. During this period, both language and education figured prominently in discussions about Japanese nationhood and nationalism. Three main policy issues concerning language and education are examined in this overview of Japanese language policy from the Meiji era (1868–1911) until the end of the 20th century: language and modernization, language and empire, and language and democracy.

LANGUAGE AND MODERNIZATION

De Vries (1991) identified four aspects of modernization which trigger heightened activity in language planning. They are (1) the expanded role of a central government; (2) the development of a capitalist industrial system; (3) the expansion of communications media; and (4) the growth of ethno-nationalist movements. De Vries's focus is on the post-World War II system of nations, but his considerations apply equally to 19th century Japan, the first country ever to engage in deliberate modernization in the sense of emulating the West (Smith, 1965).

When in the 1850s American gun boats sailed into the Bay of Uraga south of Edo, present-day Tokyo, Japan was suddenly faced with the threat of Western imperialism. At the time, China had lost the ability to act as a sovereign state in the wake of the Opium War and India had been absorbed into the British Empire. The danger of suffering a fate similar to that of these two nations, which the Japanese greatly admired, was real and the Japanese were aware of it (Nagai, 1985). After almost three centuries of seclusion, Japan was in no position to resist Western pressure. Yet a generation of determined and foresighted leaders managed to preserve national independence and by embarking on a course of radical social reform transformed Japan into the first modern state outside the Western world. In the course of this great social transformation, which is generally called the Meiji Ishin or Restoration of Imperial Rule, drastic reforms were carried out in virtually all spheres of society. Along with administrative centralization and monetary and tax reform, Western institutions such as the Gregorian calendar were adopted and new structures created, such as conscription, rail transport, a family register, and a postal service. Nothing, however, was more important than education. As Horio (1988, p. 26) observed, the early Meiji leaders "fully recognized that education was the cornerstone upon which the whole process of national transformation would eventually come to rest." Far-reaching education reforms were initiated in the 1870s, which also witnessed the emergence of a consequential language reform movement, described in great detail by Twine (1991).

From the very beginning of the Meiji period, language was high on the agenda of reform-minded intellectuals. They realized that the extant system of languages and styles was a reflection of the obsolete social order: hierarchic, inflexible, and highly stratified. In their view, raising the level of popular education was essential for catching up with the West, which in turn was the only way to avoid subjugation by the West. This could not be accomplished if, in present-day parlance, knowledge transfer and diffusion had to rely on a cumbersome communication system. Vertical communication between the government and the general population, as well as horizontal communication within the general public, had to be improved if other reforms were to succeed. In the words of Cooper (1989, p. 72), "In the process of diffusion, . . . language planning, other social planning, and social, political, and economic change all influence one another as well as the direct agents of change who, in turn, influence potential adopters of a communicative innovation." In the first issue of the most influential enlightenment journal, *Meiroku Zasshi*, which spread knowledge of the West during the early Meiji years, Nishi Amane (1874) succinctly pointed out the connection between language reform and education: "Manifestly, the reform will simplify the difficulties of embarking on study." The immediate objectives of the language reform envisioned by Nishi and others were a script reform and a style reform concerning the relationship between the spoken and the written language. To appreciate the significance of these two issues and how they interact, it is necessary to review Japanese literacy practices at the beginning of the Meiji period.

Literacy Practices

The rather involved language system of Japan at that time was characterized by a range of very distinct spoken and written styles. In writing, four major varieties were in use: *kanbun*, *sōrōbun*, *wabun*, and *wakankonkōbun*. Government publications and other serious books were drafted in *kanbun*, the Japanese version of classical Chinese. Valued for its close association with officialdom, erudition, and upper-class education, *kanbun* was inaccessible to the lesser educated, not least because of the large number of Chinese characters it employed. There was, therefore, another Sino-Japanese style of writing for official and private correspondence of a more general nature, *sōrōbun*, so called for its characteristic copula verb *sōrō*. Like *kanbun*, it was derived from Chinese but over the centuries had drifted toward Japanese. At the beginning of the Meiji period, *sōrōbun* was written in a mixture of Chinese characters and syllabic *kana*. It was simpler than *kanbun* but still rather involved and difficult to master. *Kanbun* was Chinese, whereas *sōrōbun* incorporated as many Chinese as Japanese elements. Yet another written style was largely Japanese—*wabun*. Like *kanbun* and *sōrōbun*, it bore little resemblance to anyone's speech. *Wabun* was classical Japanese, based on 10th-century grammar and lexicon. Written entirely in *kana*, its graphic form was relatively simple, but it was separated from the vernacular speech by a gap of many centuries of linguistic evolution. The use of both Sino-Japanese and colloquial vocabulary was avoided. *Wabun* was used in literary prose and favored by nativist scholars (*kokugakusha*). In addition to these three styles a range of mixed varieties summarily referred to as *wakankonkōbun*, "Japanese-Chinese blend," or *kanamajiribun*, "mixed *kana* style," also were used. Like the others, *wakankonkōbun* had no proper counterpart in the spoken language, because writing in the spoken language was not expected.

Thus, when Japan's intellectual elite had convinced themselves that adopting Western ways was necessary for the sake of the country, they had no written language at their command that could be used easily to communicate new ideas to the general public. Japan's literary culture was highly complex and sophisticated, but it lacked a written style that was close to the spoken language, easy to learn, and intelligible without many years of formal education affordable only to the upper classes. This was in stark contrast to what the Japanese learned from the Dutch, the only Westerners allowed to maintain a presence in Japan since early in the 17th century. In the West, the Dutch told Japanese students of "Dutch Learning," vernacular languages had long replaced Latin as a separate written language for official and learned purposes. Enlightened scholars and politicians such as Fukuzawa Yukichi (1835–1901), the founder of Keio Gijiku University, Yano Fumio (1850–1931), editor of daily *Yūbin Hōchi Shinbun*, and Mori Arinori (1847–1889), the first Minister of Education, early on established a link between Western advances in science and technology and vernacular literacy. They believed that their own literacy practices were a stumbling block on the way to successful diffusion of new knowledge and social reform. Translation from Western languages into any of the written styles was difficult and gave rise to a sense of language crisis so acute that even the adoption of a Western language instead of Japanese was seriously discussed (Coulmas, 1990).

From the present point of view, such a suggestion appears outlandish, because Japan is now known as a linguistically highly homogeneous country with relatively few language problems. However, this current state of affairs is the result of decades of educational language planning. In the early Meiji years, intellectuals clearly perceived a language problem and sought remedies. They were the pioneers of language planning; the government followed. As Weinstein (1983, p. 62) observed, "writers, translators, poets, missionaries, publishers, and dictionary makers can shape language for political and economic purposes; their effectiveness may be greater than government." The Japanese intellectuals' contribution to language reform in Meiji Japan is a case in point. They favored a simpler writing system and closer correspondence between spoken and written language as means of advancing education and participation in public life by ordinary citizens. Greater uniformity in written styles was desirable so that a larger part of the populace would have equal opportunities to read.

Writing Reform

The complexity of the Japanese writing system at that time is undeniable. A great number of Chinese characters and the two syllabic *kana* systems were used separately and in various combinations, depending on the style. This made for varied and segmented literacy. Chinese characters played an overly important role, not just for communicating ideas but also for displaying the writer's erudition. No generally recognized standard for the use of Chinese characters existed, so that it was common for writers to use *kana* as reading aids printed in smaller size alongside Chinese characters to indicate pronunciation. It was thanks to these extensively used *furigana* that even members of the merchant and townsmen class could read highly Sinicised text that, however, they would not be able to write. Complicated orthography was a marker of social distinction.

To reduce the social gradient of literacy, various reform proposals were made concerning both the written style and the writing system. Three strategies for simplifying the writing system were discussed. The most radical proposal was to abandon Chinese characters all together and Chinese writing with them. This suggestion was first advanced even before the feudal regime of the Tokugawa Shogunate finally collapsed. In 1866, Maejima Hisoka, a scholar and minor government official, submitted a petition to the government entitled *Kanji gohaishi no gi*, "A proposal for abolishing Chinese characters." As a translator, he was keenly aware of the importance of unimpeded communication and knew from everyday experience how unwieldy was Japanese writing. His argument for breaking with Chinese provided for writing all texts in *kana*, which implied a more colloquial style, because Chinese characters were associated with Chinese-style writing. With his proposition, Maejima was ahead of his time. Another project of his relating to facilitating communication in Japan was more successful. As the founder of the Japanese postal service, he secured a place for himself in Japanese history books.

Maejima's original proposal was followed up by himself and others, such as Shimizu Usaburō and Nishi Amane. Like Maejima, Shimizu (1874) advocated the use of *kana*, giving his argument a slightly patriotic touch. In Europe and the United States, he observed, it was common to write in the national language. Japan should do likewise and discard Chinese letters. Nishi (1874), following an earlier suggestion by Nambu Yoshikazu, went a step further. He made an argument in favor of terminating the use of Chinese characters and writing Japanese not with *kana*, but with the Western alphabet instead. He thought that the alphabet was more convenient and that it allowed for writing and speaking to follow the same rules. He also argued that assimilating European knowledge would be facilitated by adopting an alphabetic writing system.

Many intellectuals and writers participated in the discussion about the abolition of Chinese characters in the early Meiji years, but in the end it did not convince many people. It was too bold a measure to be adopted. Few people in Japan had used alphabetic letters, although the alphabet had been known for centuries (Coulmas, 1994). Literacy, however, although spread unevenly, was relatively high, thanks to a closely knit network of *terakoya*, or writing schools. Various estimates put basic literacy by 1870 at

40–45% for boys and 15% for girls, rates that are comparable with Western European countries (Marshall, 1994). In combination, these conditions made it unlikely for these proposals to lead to specific policy measures, no matter whether they called for replacing Chinese characters by a *kana* orthography or for adopting the Roman alphabet. The fact that both Shimizu Usaburō and Nishi Amane wrote their essays in *kanbun* illustrates well the difficulties that every reform proposal was bound to meet at the time. Shimizu felt compelled to comment on this apparent discrepancy. His *kana* theory, he pointed out, was for the convenience of later generations. Old habits die hard, and writing systems are among the most conservative social conventions.

There was another reason, however, why a reformed written language without Chinese characters was hard to imagine. The sudden contact with the West brought with it the need for lexical innovation on an unprecedented scale. The Chinese language and script were an important medium of lexical enrichment (Seeley, 1991, p. 136). A flood of new words entered the Japanese language at this time. These were translations for words from Dutch, English, and other European languages. The advantage of using the Sino-Japanese lexical stratum in the form of Chinese characters for coining loan translations was that the unfamiliar concepts embodied in these words did not look unfamiliar, and hence, were more easily assimilated than direct loan words from European languages. In this way, the language crisis was not compounded by additional alienation.

Chinese characters thus continued to play an indispensable role in Japanese writing. In a third proposal for writing reform, this was taken for granted. Rather than advocating the adoption of a new script, its supporters called for regulating Chinese characters and reducing their number. In a practical treatise on writing, the educator and most famous of all enlightenment scholars, Fukuzawa Yukichi (1873), first suggested that the difficulties of reading and writing Japanese could be alleviated by reducing the number of Chinese characters in use. His hugely influential *Encouragement of Learning* expounded the vital necessity of raising the general level of education. Fukuzawa accordingly advocated practical skills for the advancement of ordinary people. In sharp contrast to other reformers, he practiced what he preached. In his 1873 book on writing, he demonstrated the feasibility of his proposal using less than 1,000 different characters. This text was intended for children, and, therefore, characters could be used only sparingly anyway. Fukuzawa, however, also expressed the opinion that general usage should be restricted to 2,000 to 3,000 different characters. A year prior to the publication of Fukuzawa's book for children, a government order, the Fundamental Code of Education (1872), called for universal literacy, an aim which made restricting the number of characters virtually imperative, unless, that is, they were to be replaced by a simpler script. It was Fukuzawa's proposal, then, which eventually determined the direction which Japanese writing reform would take. Setting the tone for later developments, the *Shinsen jisho*, a dictionary commissioned by the Meiji government that was published in 1872, contained 3,167 characters.

The Written Style

In the early Meiji years many scholars, writers, and officials understood the need for simplifying the written language, but no one had a clear idea of what the outcome would be. The government was in no mood to decree a specific scheme, particularly while it faced many reforms in other areas that required immediate action and continuous attention. Moreover, an official scheme not just presupposed very thorough knowledge about the status quo and the various options for improvement, it also bore the risk of provoking resistance on the part of those whose support the government needed, the intellectual elite. In retrospect, it seems prudent that rather than taking the lead by committing itself to one option or another, the government initially kept a low profile in the writing reform debate, allowing it to gravitate towards a practical solution.

While the government took a noncommittal stance, those who had proposed specific measures tried to gather support for putting them into practice. Maejima Hisoka in 1873 founded an all-*kana* newspaper, the *Mainichi Hiragana Shinbun*. Short-lived though it was, it helped promote the idea of *kana* writing. A number of support groups were formed to discuss strategies for advancing their case. In 1883, these groups united to form the *Kana no kai*, or *Kana* Club. At the same time, the supporters of a romanized script for Japanese engaged in various activities to win public backing. They too formed an association with a platform, the *Rōmaji kai*, or Romanization Club. Their bulletin, the *Rōmaji zasshi*, was first published in 1885, in roman letters, of course. Both clubs were places of debate and experimentation. A basic decision for either *kana* or roman still left plenty of room for determining definite and exhaustive orthographic rules. This issue was of considerable importance even if the ultimate goal of replacing the old script could not be accomplished. It was obvious that for lexicographic and other reference purposes, Japanese would be written in roman letters. As for *kana*, they had been used for writing Japanese all along, but a reform of orthographic rules was long overdue.

Another problem that was of great concern for both associations was the creation of a suitable colloquial style for writing. The task was twofold. The great variety of function-specific styles was to be replaced by a multipurpose style, and this new style was to approach colloquial speech. Writing was traditionally a highly cultivated art and not expected to be a close representation of the spoken language or serve a guiding function for it. Just as there was no unified written standard, the spoken language, too, lacked unification. Thus, the problem was not just selecting a style but creating one that would become both the focus of written Japanese and a leading paradigm for spoken Japanese. At issue, then, was not choosing one out of a number of existing styles but rather bringing about a convergence of written and spoken styles.

Once again, the credit for the language treatment, which, indeed, led to convergence within a very short period of time, goes to writers and other intellectuals rather than to the government. Their effort to find new forms for written expression crystallized into a language movement, which in the 1880s generated much public discussion. It was called *genbun itchi*, literally "unification of spoken and written language." As Takada (1989, p. 112) pointed out, naturalism in literature, which called for giving expression to one's inner feelings, was a driving ideational force in this movement. Novelists who were influenced by this literary current, which originated in Europe, were at the forefront of the movement toward a colloquial writing style. The publication in 1887 of Futabatei Shimei's novel *Ukigumo* ("Drifting Clouds") was a breakthrough now celebrated as the birth of modern Japanese prose. Other works written in colloquial style by novelists such as Yamada Bimyō and Ozaki Kōyō followed. These writers experimented with several different styles of colloquial Japanese and participated in theoretical debates about the unification of the spoken and the written language.

Calls for a "standard language" (*hyōjungo*) soon became more articulate. Okakura Yoshizaburō, who in 1890 first used the term, pointed out realistically that social and political factors rather than linguistic considerations were decisive in determining a standard (Sanada, 1987, p. 89). The speech of Tokyo was heavily favored, because the metropolis was the center of the feudal administration and attracted people from all parts of Japan. Various speech forms were assimilated, although a clear division existed between the "high-city varieties" of the upper classes and the "low-city varieties" of the common people. Some writers experimented with both forms, but eventually the speech of educated Tokyoites close to the "high-city variety" became the model of the new colloquial written style. Diffusion and acceptance of the new style was very rapid, although Chinese-style writing was kept alive in certain domains, such as the law, for several decades into the 20th century. By the turn of the century the new style, Modern Colloquial Japanese, was firmly in place. In 1903, the Ministry of Education adopted it for the textbooks of primary schools, thereby giving it a stamp of official recognition. The Ministry of Education also issued regulations aimed at standardizing *kana* usage, changing the complicated historical orthography to one based on actual pronunciation. More than a mere technicality, this measure was yet another step emphasizing the importance of the spoken language as a model for the written language. This was by no means the end of all the other written styles, but from that time on, the proponents of *kanbun*, epistolary *sōrōbun*, and the mixed Sino-Japanese style were fighting a losing battle.

Spearheaded by the literary avant-garde, the *genbun itchi* movement was a great achievement. It is no exaggeration to call it a crucial component of Japan's comprehensive modernization program during the final decades of the 19th century. Its initial success was facilitated by three factors. The first was an enlightened elite of intellectuals who at a crucial juncture in history threw their weight behind the reform, rather than obstructing it by insisting on use of difficult language as a means of defending their privileged status. Second, the language reform movement had as its audience an educated public characterized by a high level of schooling and literacy. By the turn of the century enrollment in elementary schools was virtually 100% for boys and for girls. Third, although a considerable variety of different dialects were in use, some of which were mutually unintelligible, the population of Japan nevertheless constituted a relatively homogeneous speech community in the sense that the vast majority recognized Japanese as "their" language. There was not much linguistic diversity involving minority languages. To be sure, for many centuries, Chinese and Chinese-derived styles had dominated written communication, but the literati were Japanese. In response to the mood of the times, these same literati turned their talents to crafting a national language for Japan.

LANGUAGE AND EMPIRE

Viewed from a slightly different angle, the deliberate unification of written and spoken Japanese as the objective of the *genbun itchi* movement reveals another aspect of modernization, the establishment of a national language. On their missions to Europe in the early Meiji years, the Japanese concluded that a common national language was one of the features of the modern European nation state, whereas a linguistic division along class lines was characteristic of feudal agrarian society. A modern state and a modern society needed a language suitable for universal communication, both vertical and horizontal. Unification within and demarcation in relation to the outside are two mutually related functions of language that in the age of nationalism became ever more important. In Japan, this age dawned early in the 1890s when two decades of fervent Westernization provoked a backlash. Japan was swept by a wave of anti-Western nationalism, which also had its effects on language attitudes and language planning. For instance, in this suddenly hostile climate, the Romanization Club in 1892 ceased its operations. More importantly, the Sino-Japanese War of 1894–95 served as a catalyst to revitalize the language reform movement, which was charged with a new meaning.

As Twine (1991, p. 163) has pointed out, it was at this time that Ueda Kazutoshi (1867–1937) returned from Germany, where he had studied linguistics and breathed the winds of linguistic nationalism that blew through Europe. Nishi Amane, in the title of his 1874 essay on writing Japanese with Western letters, had used the term *kokugo* or "national language." This term was then as new as the concept for which it stood. Because *kanbun*, Chinese was the language of prestige, the notion of a common language functioning as a bond and symbol of the nation was not part of the ideological horizon. When Nishi used the term, a national language was yet to be created. Twenty years later, Ueda Kazutoshi clearly realized the political significance of this development. He devoted his entire career to this cause, becoming the champion of the national language that he called the "spiritual blood of the people." Scholar and nationalist, he first made his case forcefully in his acclaimed *Kokugo no tame* ("For a National Language"), published in two volumes in 1895 and 1903. He argued that the national language was to be cultivated as a critical element of the national heritage. So far, the new language had two faces, the colloquial style for writing and the standard based in the educated speech of Tokyo. The reform debate had centered on these two themes. By adding linguistic nationalism as a third theme, Ueda did much to bring the other two under a common roof. Linguistic nationalism was a necessary component of the language reform movement, without which it could not have been successful. Every language reform involves inconveniences for the literary elite, who must part with old, established ways. They need incentives and promises or lofty ideals. When the initial enthusiasm for enlightenment ebbed, a tide of nationalism filled the ideological lacuna. In this sense, Ueda's precepts were timely.

Because Ueda called for a national language, it was only logical that he supported government responsibility for language planning. Ueda entered government service in the Ministry of Education, and together with some like-minded colleagues, worked tirelessly for the creation of a national body that would be charged with language planning. In 1900, a preparatory committee was appointed, and two years later the National Language Research Council (*Kokugo Chōsa Iinkai*) was established under the auspices of the Ministry of Education. Its main tasks were investigating the possibilities of a phonetic script, promoting a colloquial style for writing, and standardizing language. The Council was disbanded in 1913, and in 1920 the Interim Committee on the National Language (*Rinji Kokugo Chōsakai*) was put in its place. Its main achievement was the publication in 1923 of a "List of Characters for General Use," which comprised 1,963 Chinese characters. It continued its work until 1934 when the Deliberative Council on the National Language (*Kokugo Shingikai*)—which is still in existence—was formed. In 1937, it published the official *Kunreishiki* romanization.

After the government had formally accepted its responsibility for the fate of the national language by setting up the National Language Research Council, the themes around which the language reform movement had revolved during the previous two decades remained largely the same, but the tone of the discussion changed gradually (Lee, 1996). The term *kokugo*, "national language," along with other notions such as *kokudo*, "national land," and *kokumin*, "national people," were used more frequently and helped to raise the awareness that a national concern was at issue.

Language standardization was an important point on the agenda of the National Language Research Council and its follower agencies. After selecting a base for the standard—the speech of educated Tokyo dwellers—the main task was to make sure that it spread throughout the country. This educational goal was pursued in the schools along lines familiar because of similar developments in Europe, France, and Germany in particular (Fishman, 1973). It proved hard to install the standard without at the same time denigrating rural dialects, which were perceived not just as an impediment to mastering the national language, but as remnants of an old order and barriers to Japanese national integration. They had to be eradicated for all Imperial subjects to speak the same *kokugo* (Sanada, 1987, p 103). What was right for Japanese dialect speakers could not be wrong for Imperial subjects who spoke other languages. Therefore, the language standardization policy through schooling was implemented in Hokkaidō and Okinawa, where the *kokugo* was pitted against Ainu and Ryōkyōan, respectively (Uemura, 1969). At school, dialect tags (*hōgen fuda*) were employed to discourage use of the local language, a practice that was reminiscent of language education policy measures in certain European environments, Alsace-Lorraine of the 1920s for example (Jacob & Gordon, 1985). Like the *patois* of the Occitans, Bretons, and Corsicans in France, Ainu and Ryūkyūan thus came under pressure.

Traditionally, the territory of the Ainu, Hokkaidō, which the Japanese called Yezogashima (Yezo's island), was the last of the four main islands of Japan to come under Shogunal control. The Meiji government embarked on a policy of colonization and assimilation that was motivated by concerns over Russian designs and the desire to secure the empire's northern border (Salwey, 1913). To appreciate the significance of this question to the Japanese government, it is useful to remember the "Northern Territories" issue, as the Japanese call it. Since the end of World War II, four islands off Hokkaidō had been under Soviet and then Russian control. Japan claimed these islands, and the issue went unresolved. In the 19th century and after the Russo-Japanese war of 1904–05, the need to firmly integrate Hokkaidō into the Japanese state was felt even more urgently. These political conditions led to profound and irreversible changes in the demography and culture of rural Hokkaidō. Outnumbered on a large scale by Japanese settlers, the impoverished Ainu with their traditional ways and unwritten language were forcefully turned into Imperial subjects. Pressured by the government and drawn by economic necessity, they quickly shifted from Ainu to the Japanese language within a generation's time.

Like Hokkaidō, the Ryūkyū Islands were late to become part of the Japanese empire. At the crossroads of Chinese and Japanese influence, the Ryūkyū kingdom had preserved its precarious political status as a semi-independent entity until its formal annexation by Japan in 1879. The Meiji government then established Okinawa Prefecture, which marked the beginning of large-scale deterioration of Ryūkyūan. Compulsory education under central government control led to bilingualism first, followed by massive language shift. In the course of the 20th century, the *kokugo* replaced Ryūkyūan vernaculars almost completely.

To sum up this section, the modernizing state had no patience with what it considered outdated idioms. Compulsory education under the firm control of the central government was carried out, and there was never any doubt that this education had to be done in the medium of the preferred language, the *kokugo*. Such was the spirit of the times, and few people thought twice about it. Bilingual education was quite beyond anyone's educational philosophy, social policy, or budgetary potential. The exclusive use of Japanese in schools led to the suppression of regional dialects and the marginalization of minority languages at the southern and northern peripheries of the empire, but this was widely seen as a byproduct of modernization that was not just inevitable, but desirable.

The government's language spreading policy did not stop at Japan's borders. As a result of the Sino-Japanese War, Taiwan came under Tokyo's rule in 1885. The colonial administration did not lose time implementing the assimilationist policy (*dōka*) of the Japanese government. Schooling was considered the key, another indication of the enormous trust the Meiji government put in education. As Lee (1996, pp. 231, 245) has pointed out, Japanese language instruction in the name of *kokugo* rather than *nihongo* ("Japanese") played a critical role from the beginning. The Government-General's Common School Regulation of 1898 states that: "The common school should teach Taiwanese children ethics and practical knowledge, thereby cultivate in them qualities of Japanese citizenship, and also lead them to be well versed in the *kokugo*" (Miyawaki, n.d., p. 2). The same logic that guided Japan's language standardization policy at home was transferred to the overseas territories acquired in the course of the expansionist policies during the half-century from 1895 to 1945. Taiwan, including the Pescadores, was the first building block of the Greater East Asia Co-prosperity Sphere (*Dai Tōa Kyōeiken*) that was to be erected to secure Japan's supremacy in Asia. *Chōsen*, the Korean peninsula (1905), *Nan'yō*, the South Seas Islands (1914), and *Manchoukuo*, Manchuria (1932) were added step by step.

Initially, Japanese language education was a matter of practicality. The colonies had to be administered, the educational level of the population (which was far behind Japan's) had to be raised. When the Meiji government started to administer Taiwan, 95% of the population consisted of illiterate farmers (Tsurumi, 1984, p. 283). Schooling had to be provided for the Japanese who settled in Taiwan. Teachers had to be trained. The colonial government sought to duplicate the elementary school system that had proved to be such an effective means of social control on the mainland. Schools for the local population and Japanese nationals were segregated, although the doctrine of assimilation promised eventually to turn the Taiwanese into *kōmin*, or "imperial people." Both Chinese and Japanese were taught at school, but the latter was favored over the former, and in 1922 Chinese was made an optional subject.

In Korea, a protectorate since 1905 and formally annexed in 1910, the Korea Government-General tried to implement similar educational policies, stressing moral education and the importance of diffusing the national language. However, the situation was more difficult than in Taiwan. Although the Taiwanese elite perceived a Japanese education as a stepping stone to material wealth and social advancement, the Koreans put up much more resistance against assimilation, showing no signs of accepting the role the Japanese government had designed for them as part of the "New Order in East Asia." Rather, Japanese colonial rule became a catalyst for Korean cultural nationalism: "Koreans never saw Japanese rule as anything but illegitimate and humiliating" (Cumings, 1997, p. 141). While Taiwan was gradually turned into what many Japanese and Taiwanese considered a Japanese province, the colonial administration never managed to quell Korean defiance. Although Korean intellectuals had for centuries cultivated classical Chinese, to some extent to the detriment of Korean, Japan's language spread policy made them turn to Korean, which was written in the native Hangul alphabet and became a symbol of insubordination. By 1919, when Korea's last king died, the colonial Government-General had managed to establish a functioning education system, but as the demonstrations following the funeral made clear, "acceptance of

Japanese colonial education did not necessarily result in acceptance of Japanese culture and values, inculcation of which was the main purpose of that education" (Tsurumi, 1984, p. 302).

In the South Seas territories, too, Japanese language spread policy centered upon education. Instruction in the *kokugo* and Japanese ethics "served to mould the outlook of Micronesian youth and to instill in them a respect for Japan and its political institutions" (Peattie, 1984, p. 188). These efforts at imbuing in the Micronesian youths Japanese values were largely successful. Japan did not compete with an established educational system and, except for some missionary schools, there was not much in terms of formal education before the Japanese Navy occupied the islands in 1914.

Manchuria was the last of Japan's colonial acquisitions and in many ways the greatest challenge for its language spread policy. The close proximity to the Chinese heartland made it impossible to adopt a policy designed to replace the local language by Japanese. Instead, Manchuokuo was declared trilingual: Chinese (somewhat confusingly called Manchurian), Mongolian, and Japanese were all accorded formal status. Class hours in the three languages were on a par at entrance level, but time spent on Japanese was gradually increased. Japanese alone was the national language for the entire country, whereas Chinese and Mongolian were regional languages (Takasaki, 1995, p. 335).

As the Japanese colonial empire expanded, the Japanese language became an ever more important element of imperialist ideology. By the early 1930s, the *kokugo* was firmly linked with the *kokutai* or "national essence," as this key term of Japanese nationalism usually is translated. True to Ueda Kazutoshi's call "For a National Language," Japanese was bound up with the unique spirit of the nation (*minzoku koyū seishin*). Indeed, it was believed that the Japanese language had a soul, a spirit of its own called *kotodama* (Miller, 1982, p. 127ff). The uniqueness of Japanese, in which this mysterious spirit (reminiscent of 19th century German *Volksgeist*) resided, was one of the strongest-ideological topics of this time, surpassed in importance perhaps only by the 1890 Imperial Rescript on Education (*kyōiku chokugo*) that called for loyalty to the Emperor and obedience to the superiors. In Miyawaki's (n.d., p. 2) words: "These two elements, *kokugo* and the *kyōiku chokugo* dominated Japanese education until 15 August 1945."

The close association of moral education and Japanese language training was a crucial component of Japan's colonial rule, designed to achieve *hakko ichiu*, or to put "the eight corners of the world under one roof." Making Japanese the lingua franca of the empire was seen as crucial to accomplishing this goal (Lee, 1996, p. 287). As war progressed and Japan occupied other parts of Asia, the language spread policy became part of the overall war effort (Miyawaki, 1993; Kawamura, 1994). In 1942, the Council on the Construction of the Greater East Asia Co-prosperity Sphere proposed measures to make Japanese the common language of East Asia, *tōa kyōtsūgo* (Yasuda, 1999). There were grand designs for Japan and, indeed, for the Japanese language, which was to be not only the preeminent language of Asia, but a leading language of the world. A remark by linguist Ishiguro Osamu (1941) well reflects the mood of the time:

> According to England's Firth, the world's seven major languages are English, Hindi-Urdu-Hindustani, German, Russian, Spanish, Japanese, and Bengali. France's Tesnière lists Chinese instead of Hindustani. Japanese has thus been counted among the world's major languages for several decades. It is now set to become the world's number two language.

LANGUAGE AND DEMOCRACY

When Japan lost the Pacific War, the Greater East Asia Co-prosperity Sphere dissolved into thin air, and Japan's language spread policy was decommissioned along with the three million troops stationed on Asian battlefields. Aspirations for Japanese to become a world language were cast aside, replaced by the troublesome thought that the Japanese language and its convoluted writing system had contributed to the nation's catastrophic defeat. Wasn't the enemy at a greater advantage in communications thanks to the simplicity of the alphabet? This conjecture was seriously discussed after the war and played a role in determining the new language policy after 1945.

During the 1930s and 1940s, writing reform issues were generally put on the back-burner, as the ultra-nationalists who opposed any reform became more and more dominant on the political scene. Adopting the Western alphabet was completely out of the question, and tinkering with the characters was branded unpatriotic. Only when it became apparent that the numerous and complicated Chinese characters in the weapons nomenclature created serious problems did the Imperial Army in 1940 decide that characters used for technical terms must be simplified. Apart from this isolated step towards reform, the military and other conservative forces were remembered after the war for their unyielding insistence on the traditional writing system. Indeed, it was in the traditional system that important documents, such as the Imperial Rescript on Education had been redacted; writing reform, therefore, had been considered sacrilegious. As both Gottlieb (1995) and Unger (1996) have documented in admirable detail, it is because of this widely publicized tradition-before-utility stance by the militarists and ultra-nationalists that language policy became a matter of political contention in occupation Japan.

Writing Reform

For many Japanese, the defeat in the war was the defeat of the old order. Japan had to be rebuilt. Looking ahead rather than back was the order of the day. Under the guidance of the American-led occupation, various measures of re-education and democratic reform were carried out. Traditional institutions and values were called into question. The Emperor was forced to revoke his divinity, as a new constitution reduced him to a mere symbol of the nation and made the people supreme sovereign. As a result, the general climate was favorable for reform, including reform of the written language. Briefly, even romanization seemed a realistic possibility (Kitta, 1989). Proposals to this effect, however, were easy to attack as being pushed at the behest of the Americans, who could claim superior knowledge about many things, but not necessarily the national language. Aspirations for romanization thus came to nothing.

Yet there was a sense of a new beginning, which helped those gain the upper hand who thought that reshaping written Japanese to a more economic and efficient form of the language was the order of the day. The technical issues were the same as before, and the frontline in the debate was clear: Liberal proponents of simplification stood against traditionalist opponents. The link that had been forged in the later Meiji years between language and state, however, was not called into question. There was wide agreement that language policy was a government prerogative. The Education Ministry, its Japanese Language Section, and the Deliberative Council on the National Language (*Kokugo shingikai*) appointed by it remained the locus for discussing and deciding language policy. In the immediate postwar years, a new theme entered the debate: democracy. A transparent written language accessible to all was presented by reformists as a precondition for political participation and democratic citizenship. Reducing the number of Chinese characters thus became an imperative of social reform. Whatever force this argument really had is hard to assess, but by 1948 the Council, politically divided though it was, managed to produce a list of 1,850 characters called *Tōyō Kanjihyō* or "List of Characters for Interim Use." The title indicated to some that this list was a first step only, and that in the future the number of characters was to be further reduced. Bringing to a conclusion plans dating from the beginning of the century, this reform limited the number of characters and their Japanese and Sino-Japanese readings as well as their graphical form.

The 1948 reform was hailed by many liberal educators, but it was not the end of the story. As Tollefson (1991) has pointed out, language policy is an important part of state disciplinary power and therefore an area of political conflict. The story of writing reform in post-war Japan well illustrates this point. The reformists had their day in the unsettled postwar period, but once the occupation was over, the conservatives regrouped and under guidance of the Liberal Democratic Party worked to regain lost territory. A long sequence of amendments to the *Tōyō* list from 1966 to 1981 resulted in a new "List of Characters for General Use" (*Jōyō Kanjihyō*). Though it contains just 95 more characters than the earlier list, it marks a drastic change in policy, because the new list was given a different status. While the 1948 list was seen as a definite limitation, the 1981 list was described in its preamble merely as "a guide." Rather than setting an upper limit, the *Jōyō* list defined a basic standard. This opens the door to using Chinese character literacy as in the past—as an indicator of class and erudition— and as a social filter, for example, in university exams. Unger (1996) among others has argued that language policy is thus employed as a means of social control. In the past, he says, Japanese society was characterized by a double standard of restricted literacy for the poor and residents of rural areas and total literacy for the elites. This boils down to the contention that there is indeed a relationship between the complexity of a writing system and socioeconomic development.

Clearly, the institutionalization of the literacy standard through an officially sanctioned list provides the state with a means of social control. Indeed, state control over the written language is generally accepted in Japanese society, but of late a serious challenge to government authority has been mounted from an unexpected direction. During the 1990s, economic factors became increasingly important in shaping language use. Computer software that handles Chinese characters often does not conform with government-approved standards. Character lists drawn up by the Japan Industrial Standard Organization (JISO) and the International Standard Organization (ISO) include many more characters than the official *Jōyō kanji* list of 1981. Because developments in telecommunications are rapid, in their marketing decisions software makers pay little if any attention to government deliberations. Further, and perhaps even more crucially, software development moves in the direction of making active command of large numbers of characters expendable. Thus new technologies and market forces may well prove to be more important for future developments of the Japanese written language than policy decisions.

CHALLENGING THE MONOLINGUAL STATE

The economy made itself felt in yet another area of language policy in a way not anticipated and not desired by the political establishment. Ever since the Meiji reforms, ethnolinguistic homogeneity has been cultivated as a pivotal element of Japan's self-image. As a result, the unity of nation, state, and language was long taken for granted. The state functioned exclusively in the national language. However, as the winds of globalization hit Japanese shores, the monolingual state came under pressure. Within an international climate of increasing tolerance for minorities, the notion— long nurtured by nationalist politicians—that Japan had no minorities became untenable. Japan's internal diversity made its way onto the agenda of public discourse (Tanaka, 1991). Non-discrimination and language rights became topics of discussion (Tsuda, 1996).

As indigenous and immigrant minorities find a more assertive voice to publicize their grievances, the mainstream society is more prepared to listen. Estimates vary, but it is safe to say that at present all non-Japanese nationals taken together number close to two million, more than one-and-a-half percent of the resident population. The 600,000 Koreans left behind when the Japanese colonial empire was dismantled are the largest group. Under the assimilation policy of the colonial government, they were forced to adopt Japanese names and have always felt the effects of discrimination (Maher and Kawanishi, 1995). The second largest group are the Chinese, primarily immigrants from China, Taiwan, and Hong Kong (many of them illegal), who have flocked to Japan in growing numbers. Other groups include refugees from Vietnam, Cambodia, and Laos; Japanese "war orphans" (*zanryō koji*), children left behind in Manchuria in the final weeks of World War II and raised speaking Chinese; and labor immigrants from the Philippines, Bangladesh, and various other Asian countries. In the 1980s, Brazilians, Peruvians, and other Latin Americans of Japanese descent came to Japan to take up jobs the Japanese were no longer willing to do. "Asian brides," mainly from the Philippines, were imported to make up for an acute shortage of young women in the countryside. In recent years the language use of these groups has attracted the attention of sociolinguists (Koishi and Hirataka, 1998).

As workers from Asia and Latin America continue to be drawn to Japan by high wages and Japanese employers look for loopholes to avoid immigration restrictions, minority languages are becoming more visible in the media and in education. Multilingual radio stations, such as Tokyo InterFM, were created with programs in English, Chinese, Korean, Tagalog, Indonesian, Portuguese, Spanish, and Thai. At the same time, the term *kokugo* for Japanese has come under attack as being linked to exclusionist and intolerant attitudes. In the 1990s, several major universities have accordingly changed the names of their Japanese departments. *Kokubungakuka*, "Department of National Literature," became *nihonbungakuka*, "Department of Japanese Literature." More consequential changes have also taken place. In 1999, the resident Koreans accomplished a major policy aim when the government suspended the 1965 Ministry of Education policy of refusing to grant Korean-run schools official school status.

As a general trend, local governments have been more accommodating of linguistic diversity than the national government. Cities and towns with many resident foreigners and other non-Japanese have to deal with specific problems, often involving communication. The 1995 earthquake in Kobe, for example, made it clear to many civil administrators that there is considerable demand for information in a variety of languages (Sanada, 1996). A growing number of municipalities have since taken steps to provide interpretation and translation services in various departments and in other ways moved to recognize the existence of languages other than Japanese. The notion that a democratic society should make allowances for minorities and speakers of other languages is gaining ground, however slowly. The ideology of social and ethnolinguistic uniformity seems less attractive to many Japanese at the threshold of the 21st century than a generation ago.

To conclude, during the past decades Japanese society has become more open and more accommodating to outsiders. This is the result of many interacting factors. One is that democracy has become more firmly rooted in Japan. Another is Japan's wealth and close relations with many parts of the world through trade, academic exchange, tourism, and labor import. The demands of the economy open the door to pluralism, and demographic trends work in the same direction, as low birth rates make the relaxation of immigration restrictions inevitable. More political pressure and empowerment on the part of resident minorities also contribute to pushing Japan's language policy in a more liberal direction. People's attitudes change, partly in response to changing international currents of political thinking. The monoethnic nation state is out of fashion, at least in those countries that can afford to be a bit more generous with their minorities. For better or worse, Japan is one of them. Not that nationalism is dead—quite the contrary—but the need for an inwardly directed nationalism characteristic of the period of nation building and, in the case of Japan, the period of modernization, is less urgently felt at this time and accordingly has taken on a more domesticated form. When Japan first embarked on the course to become a modern nation state in the Meiji era, its leaders followed many Western examples, including language policies directed at standardization and assimilation. In this age of globalization, internal diversity and the question of how immigrants ought to be integrated (Yatabe, 1997; Suzuki, 1999) is once again a topic of public discourse. Although some still view it as a threat and potential source of disorder, others see it as a crucial component of successful participation in the global community.

REFERENCES

Cooper, R. L. (1989). *Language planning and social change.* Cambridge: Cambridge University Press.

Coulmas, F. (1990). Language adaptation in Meiji Japan. In B. Weinstein (Ed.), *Language policy and political development* (pp. 69–86). Norwood, NJ: Ablex.

Coulmas, F. (1994). Wie das Alphabet nach Japan kam. *Bild der Wissenschaft XI*, 90–100.

Cumings, B. (1997). *Korea's place in the sun: A modern history.* New York: Norton.

De Vries, J. (1991). Towards a sociology of language planning. In D. F. Marshall (Ed.), *Language planning: Focusschrift in honor of Joshua A. Fishman on the occasion of his 65th birthday* (pp. 37–52). Amsterdam: John Benjamins.

Fishman, J. A. (1973). Language modernization and planning in comparison with other types of national modernization and planning. *Language in Society 2*, 23–43.

Fukuzawa Yukichi. (1873). Moji on oshie [A lesson on writing]. In *Fukuzawa Yukichi Zenshū* 3 (1959, pp. 555–611). Tokyo: Iwanami Shoten.

Gellner, E. (1994). Nationalism and modernization. In J. Hutchison & A. D. Smith (Eds.), *Nationalism* (pp. 55–70). Oxford: Oxford University Press.

Gottlieb, N. (1995). *Kanji politics: Language politics and Japanese script.* London: Kegan Paul International.

Horio Teruhisa. (1988). *Educational thought and ideology in modern Japan.* Edited and translated by Steven Platzer. Tokyo: University of Tokyo Press.

Ishiguro Osamu. (1941). *Nihongo no sekeika* [World language Japanese]. Tokyo: Shūbunkan.

Jacob, J. E., & Gordon, D. C. (1985). Language policy in France. In W. E. Beer & J. E. Jacob (Eds.), *Language policy and national unity* (pp. 106–133). Totowa, NJ: Rowman & Allanheld.

Kawamura Minato. (1994). *Umi o watatta nihongo: Shokuminchi no 'kokugo' no jidai* [The Japanese language that crossed the seas: The era of the 'national language' of the colonies]. Tokyo: Seidosha.

Kitta Hirokuni. (1989). *Nippon no Rōmazi-undō 1889–1988* [Japan's romanization movement 1889–1988]. Tokyo: Nippon no Rōmazi-sha.

Koishi Atsuko & Hirataka Fumiya. (1998). *Fujisawashi oyobi Fujisawashi shūhen zaijū no burajiru shusshinsha no gengoshiyō jōkyō ni kansuru chōsa* [A survey of the language use of Brazil origin residents of the city of Fujisawa and neighboring areas]. Tokyo: Keiō Gijiku University.

Lee Yeounsuk. (1996). *'Kokugo' to iu shisō* [The idea of the 'national language']. Tokyo: Iwanami Shoten.

Maejima Hisoka. (1956 [1866]). Kanji gohaishi no gi [A proposal for abolishing Chinese characters]. In *Maejima Hisoka Jijoden* (pp. 153–159). Hayama: Maejima Hisoka Denki Kankōkai.

Maher, J. C., & Yumiko Kawanishi. (1995). On being there: Korean in Japan. In J. C. Maher & Kyoko Yashiro (Eds.), *Multilingual Japan*, (pp. 87–101). Clevedon: Multilingual Matters.

Marshall, B. K. (1994). *Learning to be modern: Japanese political discourse on education.* Boulder, CO: Westview Press.

Miller, R. A. (1982). *Japan's modern myth: The language and beyond.* New York: Weatherhill.

Miyawaki Hiroyuki. *Review of Japanese language policy in Asia until 1945.* Ms., n.d.

Miyawaki Hiroyuki. (1993). Maraya, shingapōru no kōminka to nihongo kyōiku [The imperialization of Malaya and Singapore and Japanese language education]. In *Kindai nihon to shokuminchi, 7, bunka no naka no shokuminchi* (pp. 193–208). Tokyo: Iwanami Shoten.

Nagai Michio. (1985). Education in the early Meiji period. In Nagai M., & M. Urrutia (Eds.), *Meiji Ishin: Restoration and revolution* (pp. 143–152). Tokyo: The United Nations University.

Nishi Amane. (1874). Yōji o motte kokugo o shosuru ron [An argument for writing Japanese with Western letters]. *Meiroku Zasshi*, 1 (no page numbers).

Peattie, M. R. (1984). The Nan'yō: Japan in the South Pacific, 1885–1945. In R. H. Myers & M. R. Peattie (Eds.), *The Japanese colonial empire, 1885–1945*, (pp. 173–210). Princeton, NJ: Princeton University Press.

Salwey, C. M. (1913). *The Island dependencies of Japan*. London: Morice.

Sanada Shinji. (1987). Hōjungo no seiritsu jijō [The formation of the standard language]. Tokyo: PHP.

Sanada Shinji. (1996). Hijōji ni okeru komyunikēshon. Kinkyūji gengo taisaku no kenkyū ni tsuite [Communication at times of emergency. Research on "Urgent language policy measures."] *Gengo*, 25, 1.

Seeley, C. (1991). *A History of writing in Japan*. Leiden: E. J. Brill.

Shi Gang. (1993). *Shokuminchi shihai to Nihongo* [Colonial rule and Japanese]. Tokyo: Sangensha.

Shimizu Usaburō. (1874). Hiragana no setsu [On hiragana]. *Meiroku Zasshi*, 7 (no page number).

Smith, W. C. (1965). *Modernization of a traditional society*. London: Asian Publishing House.

Suzuki Yuji. (1999). Tagengoshakai no jittai to kunō [The reality and problems of multi-lingual societies]. In *Tagengoshugi no kanōsei*, (pp. 11–18). Tokyo: Keio SFC Academic Society.

Takada Makoto. (1989). The development of Japanese society and the modernization of Japanese during the Meiji Restoration. In F. Coulmas (Ed.), *Language adaptation*, (pp. 104–115). Cambridge: Cambridge University Press.

Takasaki Sōji. (1995). 'Dai Tōa Kyōeiken' ni okeru nihongo [Japanese in the Greater East Asia Coprosperity Sphere]. In *Iwanami Kōza Nihon tsūshi* 19, 4 (pp. 346–362). Tokyo: Iwanami Shoten.

Tanaka Hiroshi. (1991). *Zainichi gaikokujin. Hō no kabe, kokoro no kabe* [Foreigners in Japan: Legal and mental barriers]. Tokyo: Iwanami Shoten.

Tollefson, J. W. (1991). *Planning language, planning inequality: Language policy in the community*. London: Longman.

Tsuda Mamoru. (1996). *Non-Japanese speaking defendants and the criminal justice system in Japan*. Paper presented at the International Conference on Language Rights, The Hong Kong Polytechnic University, June 22–24, 1996.

Tsurumi, E. P. (1984). Colonial education in Korea and Taiwan. In R. H. Meyers & M. R. Peattie (Eds.), *The Japanese colonial empire, 1885–1945*, (pp. 275–311). Princeton, NJ: Princeton University Press.

Twine, N. (1991). *Language and the modern state*. London: Routledge.

Ueda Kazutoshi. (1895, 1903). *Kokugo no tame* [For a national language]. 2 vols. Tokyo: Fuzambo.

Uemura Y. (1969). Okinawa no kokugo kyōiku [National language education in Okinawa]. *Kyōiku Kokugo* 18: 10–16.

Unger, J. M. (1996). *Literacy and script reform in occupation Japan: Reading between the lines*. New York: Oxford University Press.

Weinstein, B. (1983). *The civic tongue: Political consequences of language choices*. New York: Longman.

Yasuda Toshiaki. (1999). 'Kindai'ka no naka no gengo seisaku [The role of language policy for modernization]. In Shōji Hiroshi (Ed.), *Kotoba no nijūseiki* (pp. 78–92). Tokeo: Domes Shuppan.

Yatabe Kazushiko. (1997). Quelle intégration pour les immigrés? *Futuribles*, 216: 41–42.

11

Language Education and Foreign Relations in Vietnam

Sue Wright
Aston University

A study of the history of Indo-China makes it very easy to understand why foreign language learning has been problematic for recent governments of Vietnam. Four decades of conflict with five different enemies preoccupied the Vietnamese and soured relations with a large number of countries in the aftermath of the various wars. The languages of Vietnam's enemies disappeared from the school curriculum. Moreover, the enormous cost of keeping a large standing army and reconstructing the country after massive damage, together with a period of economic mismanagement, kept the education budget severely depleted. There has not even been enough money to make primary education universal and free. Thus, skill in many of the international languages was not only undesirable for patriotic reasons; it could not be afforded.

Nor was widespread language education necessary. The ideological division of the world and the isolation of Vietnam, gravitating in turn to one or another of the factions of the Communist world, limited the international networks in which the Vietnamese were involved and restricted both the desire and the need for foreign language acquisition.

When the Vietnamese government decided in 1986 to change political direction, liberalize the economy, and attract foreign investment, it was clear that it would also need to implement educational changes so that the Vietnamese population could benefit from these developments. If incoming companies could not recruit suitable staff from the autochthonous population, they would go elsewhere or, if allowed, bring in staff recruited abroad. Thus, in the past decade, improving foreign language skills among the population has become one of the prime requirements for Vietnam's successful incorporation in the world economic market. Yet this task has not been easy, given the weight of Vietnam's history. This chapter will examine how foreign language study in Vietnam historically has been a barometer of Vietnam's relations with other countries and how the foreign language curriculum has been directly affected by those relations.

THE MANDARIN LEGACY

The Chinese ruled Vietnam for 1,000 years, from 111 BC to 938 AD. During this time, they created a system of schools to train first their own children and subsequently the children of the Vietnamese aristocracy to staff the state bureaucracy, the mandarinate. Under the Tang dynasty (618–907), the competitive examination system was introduced. Education was in Chinese and followed the Chinese model. Outstanding students were sent to study in China.

In 939, Vietnam became independent. As a number of relatively stable feudal dynasties succeeded each other during the medieval period, the influence of China remained strong. An institution of higher education, Quoc Tu Giam, was established in Hanoi in 1076, in the first instance to teach the royal family. In the 13th century, this school, renamed Quoc Tu Vien, admitted commoners as well to prepare them for the mandarinate. Chinese remained the language of state; formal education was conducted in Chinese using Chinese text books (Lo Bianco, 1993). The Chinese system of competitive examination, which had lapsed, was also reintroduced at this time. The Van Mieu, the Temple of Literature, was of great importance as a center of Vietnamese literature and Taoist-Confucian thought (Pham Minh Hac, 1998). It was here in the course of the 13th century that scholars developed Nom, a script for the Vietnamese language based on Chinese characters. A complex diglossia resulted, with Chinese used as the written language appropriate for law and government, Nom used as the written form for Vietnamese culture, and the various (mutually intelligible) dialects used in spoken exchange (Nguyen Phu Phong, 1995).

From the 16th to 18th centuries, Vietnam was torn by civil strife. In the unstable conditions of this period, European adventurers and missionaries were able to gain a toehold in the country. The Portuguese arrived in 1516, with Dominican missionaries following in 1527, Franciscan missionaries in 1580, and the Jesuits in 1615. The Church had much greater success in penetrating Vietnamese society than the traders. Although the French were not the only Christian missionaries in Vietnam, their influence was the greatest, particularly after Bishop Pigneau de Béhaine recruited French adventurers to help put down the Tay Son rebellion and establish Nguyen Anh as emperor.

Taking the name Gia-Long, Nguyen Anh brought political unity to the country and founded a dynasty that would last until 1945. State power was centralized, as Gia-Long created a new legal code, strengthened the army, and invested in education. A national academy was built in the imperial city of Hue (Osborne, 1997). Gia-Long was open to French influence in that he saw, for example, the utility of fortresses constructed on the Vauban model. Nevertheless, in cultural and political spheres, French influence did not extend very deeply and was comprehensively rejected by Minh-Menh, Gia-Long's successor.

Minh-Menh was a Confucian scholar who built a solid administrative framework for the country and elaborated and extended the competitive examination system, using it to recruit his elites. Although the mandarinate was chosen by merit, certain families dominated, taking on the character of hereditary public servants. Their children inherited cultural capital (Bourdieu, 1989) that gave them greater opportunity to achieve the levels of scholarship necessary to succeed in the meritocracy. However, as Osborne (1997) argues, it was possible for a scholar with no connections to rise through ability alone. An advanced Vietnamese scholar in this period would master the Four Books that collated the precepts of Confucius and his followers, as well as other important works of the Confucian canon. Literacy was primarily in classical Chinese. Most scholars also had a knowledge of Nom that allowed access to the Vietnamese literary tradition.

Few among the elite, either emperors or mandarins, showed great interest in the ideas or languages permeating Asia from Western Europe. However, Christian missionaries had adapted the Roman alphabet so that it could be used to write Vietnamese. This endeavor is usually attributed to Alexandre de Rhodes, a French missionary working in Vietnam in the early 17th century, although the writing system is clearly based on other Romanized systems in Southeast Asia developed by Portuguese missionaries. Although Romanized Vietnamese is called *Quoc-Ngu*, or national language, in its first two centuries of existence it had very limited use, being the language of literacy for those converted to the Catholic faith and educated in the mission schools. It had, however, one vital advantage: It is much easier to learn than the ideograms based on Chinese.

THE FRENCH COLONIAL PERIOD

By the end of the 18th, century the French had lost their first colonial empire to the British and so the French government, seeking to redress the
balance in the race for colonies, looked to Vietnam as an area where French
commercial interests could be furthered and imperial ambitions realized.
This colonial interest in Vietnam coincided with the evangelical aspirations of the French Catholic Church, which was coming increasingly to see
Indo-China as its preserve. In return for Louis XVI's help in his bid for the
throne, Gia-Long had promised both exclusive commercial privileges to
the French and protection of Catholics. After his accession to the throne in
1802, he reneged on both these promises. Under his successor, Minh-Menh,
the persecution of Catholics was intensified. At first France was in no position to retaliate, but by 1843 part of the French fleet was permanently
deployed in Asian waters, and there were several clashes between French
forces and the Vietnamese. In 1862, the emperor, Tu Duc, was forced to sign
a treaty with the French, granting them religious, economic, and political
concessions. In 1867, the south of the country, which the French termed
Cochinchina, became a French colony. In 1883, Annam and Tonkin in the
north of present day Vietnam became French protectorates and in 1887
France created the Indo-Chinese Union, bringing together all the territory
they had acquired: the protectorates, Cambodia, and Cochinchina.

French colonialism was marked by the theory of assimilation and the
policy of direct rule. The French did not generally attempt to administer
their colonies through the existing ruling class and according to prevailing
social norms, as was largely the case during the British Raj in India. Indeed,
there was a desire to assimilate the regime to French ideals and to create
a francophone, francophile native administration. However much their
actual deeds may have belied this, the French subscribed wholeheartedly to
the idea that their colonialism was a *mission civilisatrice,* in which imperial
ambition could be made to benefit the colonized as well as the colonizers.
In 1898, Bishop Depierre, the bishop of Cochinchina, expressed this belief
in the following way:

> The precise honour of our country is to place intellectual, culture and moral
> progress above any other preoccupations. Instead of exploiting its subjects
> and pressuring them to death as is still done in the Indies and to some extent
> throughout the Anglo-Saxon world, Frenchmen have always made it a point of
> honour to bring to the nations in which they establish themselves their ideas,
> their civilization and their faith (quoted in Osborne, 1997, p. 42).

For the task of assimilation, France had a ready ally in the Vietnamese
Catholics, who had benefited from French protection and shared the same

belief system. Educated in mission schools, they had become literate in Quoc-Ngu. The Vietnamese Catholics provided the local work force of the new administration and native soldiers for the French army. In the south, where French influence and power were most concentrated, Confucian thought and Chinese characters waned as the mandarins withdrew. A small minority of French colonialists, such as Luro and Philastre,[1] regretted this, seeing many qualities to admire in the mandarinate; the majority of French colonialists, however, disagreed and the mandarinate is portrayed in much French contemporary writing as corrupt and inefficient (Osborne, 1997). Quoc-Ngu soon became the written form of Vietnamese throughout the French Indo-Chinese Union. Colonial policy was to use the Romanized script for Vietnamese as a first step to an eventual shift to French (Osborne, 1997). By 1878, only Quoc-Ngu and French were permitted in official documents. Thus colonization brought about the fall of the old Mandarin class and the rise of a new elite of French-speaking Vietnamese administrators.

The first civilian governor of Cochinchina, Le Myre de Vilers, appointed in 1879, carried out a number of policies aimed at promoting French culture and language. The French legal system was introduced; French medium education, begun in 1861, was extended; and a branch of the Alliance Française was established to further promote the learning of French. A few young Vietnamese were sent to France to complete their education so that they might return "in some way impregnated with our national genius, informed of the causes and effects of our civilization" (Le Myre de Vilers, 1908, quoted in Osborne, 1997, p. 50). When six Vietnamese were appointed to sit on the Colonial Council, the action was criticized because they could not speak French.

The term in the literature for the French-speaking elite required by the colonial regime is "collaborateurs," which may have a pejorative sense, depending on the stance of the author. Because of the language issue, it was perhaps inevitable that linguists would play a central role in the collaboration process. For instance, Petrus Ky and Paulus Cua, two noted linguists, were Catholics educated in the French missionary schools and literate in Quoc-Ngu. Ky was one of the first interpreters for the French, working both with the army in the south and with the negotiators of the treaties. He then taught in the Collège des interprètes, produced French-Vietnamese teaching materials, edited *Gia-Dinh Bao*, the French government sponsored

---

[1]Luro and Philastre were in the Service of Native Affairs in Cohinchina. They may have admired the Vietnamese, but they were nonetheless men of their time and committed to the colonial adventure, even if they wished conquest to be "by peace and good administration, by the propagation of our civilisation" (Luro, 1975, quoted in Osborne, 1997, p. 440).

newspaper published in Quoc-Ngu, and acted as an advisor to the French administration. Cua joined the French administration in the south in 1861 and remained a colonial civil servant until 1907. He was also a scholar, translating numerous Chinese texts into Quoc-Ngu and French. In 1896, he published a Quoc-Ngu dictionary. He too was closely associated with the newspaper, *Gia-Dinh Bao*.

Nevertheless, it is important not to overestimate the numbers of Vietnamese who were educated in French. French medium education continued to be available only to a tiny minority until the end of the colonial period. Although statistics are scarce and sometimes unreliable, this general point is incontrovertible (see Osborne, 1997).

The early colonial regime had started its education program rigorously, requiring each commune to provide one or two children to be taught Quoc-Ngu and French in government schools, yet there was scant enthusiasm among the Vietnamese. Communities often fulfilled their obligations by paying the children of the poorest families among them to attend. The bourgeois class still valued Confucian education, which continued in private establishments. In 1919, however, these were banned.

Having acquired a small core of French speakers for the administration of the colony, the French were concerned to develop education "horizontally not vertically," in the words of Governor General Merlin in 1924 (quoted in Pham Minh Hac, 1998, p. 4). Primary schools were the main concern, together with technical training colleges. These schools were to provide the workforce and medium-level technicians necessary for the colonial economy. The higher education sector remained small. From 1919, there was a university level Natural Science Faculty, and beginning in 1923, a Medical Faculty. A Legal Faculty opened in 1941 and Agriculture in 1942. These schools constituted the Indo-Chinese University. Enrollment in the 1939–1940 school year was only 582 students.

Despite Merlin's goal of extending participation in the school system, numbers remained low. Pham Minh Hac (1998) gives the figures in Table 11.1 for the public school system at the end of the colonial period.

TABLE 11.1

Public School Enrollment

1941–1942	Number of Schools	Number of Pupils
Senior secondary level	3	652
Junior secondary level	16	5,521
Primary level	503	58,629
Basic primary	8,775	486,362
Total		551,164

Source: Pham Minh Hac, 1998.

When the figures in Table 11.1 are taken together with private education (mainly Catholic establishments) and compared to the total population of 22 million, the restricted nature of education becomes clear. Only about 3% of the Vietnamese were in school in 1941–1942, the great majority enrolled only for three years, to a level that could not guarantee literacy in Quoc Ngu nor competence in French (see also Sloper & Le Thac Can, 1995).

Only a small Vietnamese elite was educated in French to secondary level. The traditional French practice was to deliver the same curriculum as in the metropole with the same rigor, to the same standards, and leading to competition in the same examinations. A small proportion of this group could progress to third-level education, either in France or in Indo-China. As events developed, it included both those who served the colonial power and those who would fight to depose it. Ho Chi Minh and many of the revolutionaries of his generation were educated in the French tradition. For instance, the Thang Long school, a private establishment set up in 1919 to increase the very limited provision for Vietnamese in Hanoi, functioned on the French model and was overseen by the colonial administration. Nonetheless, it became the nursery of the revolution, with a teaching staff that included Vo Nguyen Giap and Dang Thai Mai. In 1938, the group associated with this school created an organization to promote Quoc-Ngu (Nguyen Van Ky, 1997).

Dang Thai Mai, president of the Writers Association, expressed the complexity of the position for many of this group:

Although we fought the French we grew up with a life plan derived from French culture. We had schooled ourselves in French literature and art. We oriented ourselves according to European philosophy.... French literature, classic as well as modern, was close to my heart. I found in it the will to think things through and to analyse the human condition. I found high moral and ethical values (quoted by Weiss, 1971, p. 45).

At the other end of the spectrum, however, the vast majority of the population received no schooling. Most were peasants or workers on the tea, coffee, and rubber plantations, in the coal, tin, tungsten, and zinc mines, and in other industrial enterprises run by the colonialists. For most of these people, contact with the French was minimal. Of course, some Vietnamese did speak French in their capacity as servants, employees, and workers. However, for the vast majority, the language of contact was a Vietnamese/French pidgin, with a limited vocabulary and simple syntax, and documented in much French literature where the pidgin is reproduced (e.g., Delpey, 1964).

It would thus be erroneous to believe that the colonial period left a reserve of French language skills in Vietnam. In present day Vietnam, those who were educated through French are a very tiny and aging proportion of the population. Moreover, the colonial regime was a harsh one, the French colonialists notorious for low wages and inhuman treatment. The great majority of Vietnamese who served (rather than profited from) the French were unlikely to cling to an idiom associated with "so painful a period of social and political turmoil that even five decades later the scars still remain visible" (Nguyen Xuan Thu, 1993).

THE FRENCH WAR, 1945–1954

The seven decades of French colonial rule were marked by active defiance, revolt, and resistance. The harsh economic exploitation of the colony led to inevitable unrest that nationalists were able to harness. In the period between the two World Wars, the leaders of those who were opposed to French rule were a cohesive and increasingly revolutionary group.

When the metropole capitulated in 1940 and the French government collaborated with the Germans, the colonies followed suit. The Governor General accepted the Japanese occupation of Indo-China and continued to govern in collaboration with them. The only resistance in the country was led by Ho-Chi-Minh and the Viet Minh, which he founded in 1941. As the sole opposition to the Japanese, they were given a small amount of logistical support by the Americans.

In March 1945, under the pressure of the advancing Allied forces, the Japanese demanded that French troops in Vietnam be put at their disposal. When this was refused, they took over, declaring the country independent under the rule of their puppet, the emperor Bao Dai. The meeting of the Allies at Potsdam in July came to the agreement that the Chinese would liberate Indo-China from the north, the British from the south. When Japan capitulated in August 1945, the Allies had not yet arrived in Vietnam and thus there was a power vacuum. On September 2nd, Ho Chi Minh declared the independence of a united Democratic Republic of Vietnam. During September, Chinese, British, and Free French troops arrived in the country. When the French declared a colonial crisis, the country was divided between a reinstated colonial regime in the south and a Vietnamese nationalist regime in the north. After elections in the north in January 1946, confirmed Ho Chi Minh as leader, the French offered to recognize Vietnam's independence within the French Union, a newly conceived body which would replace the colonial system with a kind of commonwealth. However, what both sides understood by this was irreconcilable. Ho Chi Minh wanted a unified Vietnam; the French wanted to retain control in the south. In 1947, negotiations broke down and the French attacked Haiphong in the start of a campaign to retake the north by force (Aldrich, 1996). The Franco-Vietnamese war lasted until 1954, when the French were defeated at the battle of Dien Bien Phu. The Geneva Conference of 1954 divided Vietnam along the 17th parallel, pending national elections. Refusing to participate in the nationwide elections, Ngo Dinh Diem, the prime minister in the south, took power in a coup d'état. In the context of the Cold War, the communist regime of Ho Chi Minh in the north and the American-backed regime in the south were poised for conflict (Karnow, 1994).

COMMUNIST POLICIES AND CHINESE BACKING

In his Declaration of Independence, Ho Chi Minh promised that his government would combat famine, ignorance, and foreign aggression. To achieve the second aim, the revolutionaries started to establish basic education for the masses, with a goal of full literacy throughout the population. Literacy was to be in the national language, and Quoc-Ngu was the script to be used. Additional educational goals included free and obligatory schooling for the primary years, improvement in peasants' agricultural and technical skills, and an increase in the education of women.

Despite the war footing of the society and the incredible economic difficulties and pressures of the period, the government claimed moderate success in its main educational aims. The literacy campaign, begun in July, 1948, in the areas controlled by Ho Chi Minh's forces, included education for adults who had not received schooling as well as schooling for primary age children. Nineteen schools of secondary professional education were established between 1947 and 1950 to train teachers and agricultural specialists. Three university centers were set up: higher level teacher training in Thanh Hoa and Nanning,[2] and medicine and pharmacy in Viet Bac (Sloper & Le Thac Can, 1995). During the literacy campaign, a reported 10 million northerners became literate (UNESCO, 1979). During the nine years of resistance to the French, literacy levels in the national language rose to a reported 90% or more in the cities, lowlands and midlands of the north, although it needs to be understood that "literacy" covered a wide range of competence (Pham Minh Hac, 1995).

In terms of foreign language acquisition, the situation changed dramatically after 1947. Obviously knowledge of French was not an asset in the

---

[2]Nanning is actually in China, just across the border, a detail that underscores the close relationship between Vietnam and China at that time.

Viet Minh controlled areas. Bui Tin[3] (1995) recalls that possessing copies of Baudelaire and Lamartine was considered evidence of bourgeois leanings in the purges of the 1950s. He was accused of decadence because of his French medium schooling and was only saved by being able to prove that he had been a member of the Communist Party as early as 1945. As the People's Republic of China supported the Vietnamese Communists with military and civilian aid, there was a steady stream of cadres from Peking to advise the Vietnamese. Thus French was replaced by Chinese as the most desirable foreign language (Bui Tin, 1995). Chinese books, films and songs poured across the border. Young Vietnamese were encouraged to learn to read and speak Chinese, and a favored few were sent to university in China.

However, education to degree level, indeed past primary level, was a luxury in a society where the young were needed as soldiers. Bui Tin's memoirs refer to the fact that the political elite that took over from the Ho Chi Minh/Giap generation were generally uneducated in the traditional sense. They had been formed in prison and battle. Bui Tin sees many of the mistakes of the post war era as stemming from the lack of formal education among that group of political leaders.

THE AMERICAN WAR, 1955–1975

American involvement in Vietnam brought English into the linguistic equation. English had no presence in the area before World War II. The first contacts with English speakers in any numbers were with the Allied troops who appeared briefly in 1945. The next contacts were the American "advisers" who arrived to train soldiers to fight the Communists, beginning in January 1955.

From 1964, U.S. involvement in the war between the north and the south escalated. At its height, there were more than half a million U.S. troops in the country (figures from 1968). Obviously, a large number of Southern Vietnamese had to acquire some competence in English, including politicians and bureaucrats, as well as ordinary soldiers who fought with the GIs. Outside the barracks, drivers, shop keepers, servants, bar staff, and prostitutes who serviced the needs of the largely monolingual U.S. military were also pushed to accommodate to the English speakers. Anecdotal evidence suggests that the situation replicated the accommodation of the

---

[3]Bui Tin was a noted North Vietnamese soldier and journalist who documented the land reform purges, the fall of Saigon, and the Cambodian war before leaving Vietnam in 1990 in order to be able to comment freely on the situation in Vietnam.

French colonial period, with many South Vietnamese in lowly positions developing an English-Vietnamese pidgin to meet communication needs.

As the southerners adapted to the developing situation, the foreign language learning statistics for South Vietnam for the period 1958 to 1968 reveal the shift from French to English. In 1958–1959, 34,774 secondary pupils were learning French and 18,412 English. In 1968–1969, with more children being schooled, the number learning French had doubled to 76,628, but the number learning English had increased sevenfold to 112,657 (République du Vietnam, 1968–1969). The utility of French was still very evident; South Vietnam continued to employ it for administrative purposes. Nonetheless, the elite in Saigon saw the advantage in their children acquiring the language that gave access to American military and political influence. Outside the school system, there was a mushrooming of private English language schools hoping to profit from the need of so many to acquire some English (Crawford, 1966).

This is not to say that American involvement in Vietnam left significant numbers of English speakers. First, the period in which large numbers of English speakers were present on Vietnamese territory was very limited. (The Paris cease fire agreements ended U.S. military involvement in the war in March, 1973.) Second, the victory of the Communists and the fall of Saigon in 1975 led to a massive exodus of perhaps 100,000 people, though exact numbers are unclear (see Terzani, 1997). Finally, the violence of the war, including 1.5 million civilian deaths (Vietnam Courrier, 1982), fuelled a virulent anti-Americanism. Those who had acquired a smattering of English found it expedient to forget it quickly in the aftermath of the Communist victory.

After the victory of the north, the southern Vietnamese who had opposed the Communists were portrayed as *nguy* (puppets) under the influence of decadent "American imperialist" influences. The end of the war was to be seen as the defeat of the foreigner and the victory of all Vietnamese. Thus a key national goal of the post-war period was the need "to eliminate the enslaving decadent culture that destroys the old and beautiful traditions of the Vietnamese people" (quoted in Terzani, 1997, p. 176). Two carriers of this decadent culture were the English and French languages. Thus both disappeared from the educational system and from individuals' linguistic repertoire.

REUNIFICATION AND ISOLATION

Because of financial difficulties and the demands of reconstruction after the war education was severely under-funded in the first two decades after reunification. The lack of formal education of the majority of the leadership may also have led to education being a low priority. For whatever reasons, education was not generally a success in this period and the focus of the curriculum narrowed. After the 1981 reform, emphasis was on ideological and moral training first and acquisition of technical and scientific skills second (Pharm Minh Hac, 1998). The traditional humanities, including foreign languages were largely absent. Funding was never adequate. State investment was low, amounting to only 1% of GDP in 1989, much less than in neighboring countries such as Thailand (3.5%) and China (3.4%). Participation was never 100%. This stems in part from the fact that schooling is not free in Vietnam, and although the fees are modest, for the poorest families they are a considerable disincentive. Universal education has still not been achieved despite the National Assembly's 1991 law which aimed to make it so. Groups such as the hill tribes in the north and the fishing communities of the Ha Long Bay and Mekong Delta areas continue to have very low rates of participation. Finally, the average number of years of attendance remains low, only 4.5 years in 1990 (Chan Weng Khoon et al., 1997). The poor in both rural and urban areas do not stay in education long enough to acquire significant skills. Thus, the fight against illiteracy, apparently so successful in the early years of the revolution, has been undermined by new cohorts of young illiterates (Pham Minh Hac, 1998).

After 1975, education at all levels suffered from staffing difficulties. Teachers' pay was not enough for the teachers to support themselves or their dependents; a tradition evolved of teachers having other work to supplement their incomes. The deleterious effect that this has on their performance and commitment is recognized (Khoon et al., 1997). In addition, many teachers were under qualified for the work that they were doing in comparison with neighboring countries. In the late 1990s, only 30% of teachers had relevant qualifications; in the universities only 19% of the lecturing staff possessed postgraduate qualifications (Khoon et al., 1997).

The departure of thousands of Vietnamese by boat, beginning in 1978, and more recently by other means, had unplanned side effects on the nation's language skills. First, the "boat people" of 1978–1982 were disproportionately Vietnamese of Chinese origin; perhaps a half million of this group may have left (Bui Tin, 1995; Rigg, 1997). Although not all spoke one of the varieties of Chinese, many did, and as they left the country, so too did a pool of competence in Chinese and literacy in the Chinese script. Second, the boat people often came from the old bourgeois—the people most likely to be educated and perhaps to have received education in French and English.

Yet the language competence of the population was not of great official concern in the immediate post war period. By 1978, Vietnam was at war again, intervening in Cambodia to stop the genocide of the Pol

Pot regime and to counter the threat from Khmer Rouge incursions along the Vietnamese border. In 1979, war broke out also along the border with China. Though lasting only a few weeks, the war caused the two countries to sever relations, which were not renewed until November 1991. Thus Chinese joined French and English as the language of an enemy of the Vietnamese state. From 1975 to 1986, provision for these three foreign languages almost completely disappeared (though they were not banned). There were other priorities for the education system and no sufficient reason to institute large scale teaching of the languages of states with whom Vietnam had no diplomatic relations. A limited number of special secondary schools provided foreign language courses and one institute of higher education specialized in foreign languages. Outside the education system, the acquisition of a foreign language could be suspect. Language learning for the purpose of studying Confucian or Catholic teachings or to prepare for leaving the country clandestinely could bring retribution.

A continuing issue was the ideological and experiential gap between those who fought the war and those who did not. Bao Ninh's novel, *The Sorrow of War*, describes the distance between the guerrilla fighters and those who did not share their terrible experiences. The novel paints a bleak portrait of soldiers' lives as they struggled to come to terms with the legacy of their experiences. The narrator has contempt for the college graduate who spoke two foreign languages and lived "an easy life" (Bao Ninh, 1993, p. 56).

SUPPORT FROM THE USSR AND EASTERN EUROPE

One consequence of the American war was an increasing flow of aid, material, and advisors from the Eastern Bloc to Vietnam. Of particular interest for patterns of language use were the university scholarships granted to Vietnamese. Between 1965 and 1974, 26,000 Vietnamese gained first degrees in the Soviet Union (USSR) or Eastern Europe and 3,000 gained postgraduate qualifications (Vietnam Courrier, 1982). In the period 1975–1991, the USSR became the main supporter of an impoverished Vietnam, isolated from the Western capitalist world by the U.S.-led trade embargo, from China after the 1979 border war, and from the rest of its neighbors because of fears of Vietnamese expansionism after the invasion of Cambodia. The COMECON countries (communist trading block) became the principal trading partners of Vietnam and the sole providers of technical assistance and training.

Thus Russian became the most commonly taught language in the secondary school system. A number of "friendship schools" were set up to give school children some contact with the world outside Vietnam and to promote the learning of Russian and to a lesser extent the other Slavic languages. The only non-Slavic educational links in 1990 were those with Cuba and the Netherlands (Vietnamese Ministry of Education, 1990). Pham Minh Hac (1998) records that Vietnamese pupils were among those winning prizes for Russian-speaking in international competitions in 1987. Despite such achievements, the number of Vietnamese learning Russian was not large, and the number of pejorative terms for Russians coined in that period suggests that the Vietnamese never accepted them wholeheartedly.

The reliance of the Vietnamese on COMECON was so great that its collapse in 1991 nearly brought economic ruin to Vietnam. Trade aid relationships ceased and the Russian language quickly disappeared. Although prior to 1991 Russian was learned at secondary school level by the brightest pupils and many of the political and technological elite completed their studies in the USSR, there is little evidence that significant numbers of Vietnamese still possess this foreign language skill. Few of the present generation are now learning it. Indeed, teachers of Russian are being retrained (interview, Vietnamese Ministry of Education, 1999). Thus the large collection of Russian language books donated by Moscow to the National Library is now a resource impenetrable to many of the young students who use the library. In a study on higher education, Pham Thanh Nghi and Sloper note that study is difficult for this generation because "materials are either written in languages they do not understand or from ideological perspectives that are no longer dominant" (Pham Thanh Nghi & Sloper, 1995, p. 114).

DOI MOI AND THE END OF ISOLATION

In 1986, under the influence of Russia and following the pattern of Gorbachev's economic reforms, the Vietnamese introduced their own version of *perestroika*. Called *"Doi Moi,"* this change was to entail economic liberalization only, accepted as a necessity after a disastrous period of incompetent government and economic isolation that had brought the country close to famine. Like Deng Xiao Ping's reforms in China, *Doi Moi* did not include a political thaw. However, it did involve increased contacts with other countries, as Vietnam set out to build economic relations with the West. In consequence, the early 1990s witnessed exchanges between Hanoi and non-communist regimes on an unprecedented scale, including France and neighboring Thailand.

Commercial relations increased rapidly under a 1987 Foreign Investment Law that permitted foreign business to invest in joint ventures (Sadec Asia Pacific, 1999). From 1988 to 1995, capital flowed into the country from Taiwan, Hong Kong, South Korea, Japan, Australia, Switzerland, and

France (see Vietnam Investment Review figures, 1996; Nguyen Tri Dung, 1998). After ten years of liberalization, Vietnam had developed trade relations with more than 100 countries and direct investment from more than 50 countries.

Analyses of this rapid increase in international business in Vietnam cite two major difficulties. The first was a shifting legal environment, in which "officials trained in the universities of Eastern Europe or in the guerrilla camps of the war" were often out of sympathy with developments and interpreted legislation inconsistently and unsympathetically (Birolli, 1999; Carlson, 1998). The second difficulty was lack of foreign language competence. Investment analysts advising foreign businesses reported that those Vietnamese who had completed 12 years of national education were well prepared for technical work but had low levels of competence in the languages of potential investors (Carlson, 1998; Dickson, 1998; Sadec Asia Pacific, 1999). Nguyen Tri Dung suggests there were cultural as well as language barriers: "The lack of knowledge on business practices, laws and a poor knowledge of foreign languages are some of the main reasons many people fail to perform in foreign companies" (Nguyen Tri Dung, 1998, p. 10).

In the late 1990s, foreign investment slumped by as much as 40%, in part due to the Asian financial crisis (Pham Ha, 1998 Economist, 2000). However, in this period, Vietnam normalized its foreign relations: ASEAN (Association of South East Asian Nations) admitted Vietnam in 1995 and the United States established diplomatic relations after having lifted its trade embargo. Vietnam also became a member of AFTA (Asia Free Trade Area) and APEC (Asia Pacific Economic Cooperation). The language of business in these groups is mostly English or Chinese (Cantonese or Mandarin), leading to a demand for Vietnamese who speak these languages (CNN, 1996). This is not a demand that can be easily met.

THE RETURN OF ENGLISH AND FRENCH

Although in the latter half of the 1990s, the interest of most foreign investors in Vietnam decreased, investment from France tripled. The French were also present in Vietnam as participants in a large number of non-profit programs in medicine, psychiatry, dentistry, pollution control, environmental health, and sustainable development operated by non- governmental organizations and private associations. Indeed, the French government seems to be using the former colonial links between France and Vietnam to create a special relationship in the diplomatic and educational spheres. Its motivation stems from the French belief that former Indo-China can be cultivated as an area in Southeast Asia where Francophones can challenge Anglophone-dominated globalization. The French president, Jacques Chirac, was quite explicit:

> Asia, already a major center for economic development and world trade, will also realize its full political importance in the near future, fulfilling the promise of its ancient and wonderful civilizations, and truly reflecting its dynamism and its power... Francophonie already possesses a historic base in Indo-China and in the Pacific... Francophonie is perhaps above all a certain vision of the world. We are building a political association founded on a virtual community, that of the language that we have in common and which unites despite our cultural diversity... Our raison d'être stems from a conviction that in the 21st century language communities will be key actors on the international political stage (Chirac, 1997).

Chirac admitted that competence in French had been "eroded" among the Vietnamese, but was optimistic that French could be reintroduced. This optimism was based in no small part on the generous funding and vigorous efforts that the French government was making to extend French-medium education and French language learning in Vietnam.

For its part, Vietnam has seen membership in Francophonie as one of the ways out of isolation. (South) Vietnam had become a member of the first institution set up by Francophonie, ACCT, the agency for technical and cultural cooperation, at its creation in 1970. This historical link provided a rationale for representatives of the SRV (Socialist Republic of Vietnam) to attend the first Francophone Summit in 1986. Vietnam then became a full member of Francophonie and in 1997, hosted the 11th Francophone Summit, the first intergovernmental meeting to be held in Vietnam.

Membership in Francophonie was also one of the ways to gain aid for the Vietnamese educational system. In the 1997–1998 school year, the Francophone agency, AUPELF, financed 14,000 school children in 491 bilingual (French-Vietnamese) programs staffed by teachers from Francophone countries, principally France. These programs are generously funded, with new text books and audio-visual and computer technology that are largely absent in the Vietnamese system. Entry is by competitive examination, with scholarships available for families unable to fund extended education. The scheme has acquired a reputation for high standards and rigor, and there is intense competition to be admitted. The bilingual secondary streams lead into a university program in which, in 1997, 5,000 Vietnamese students were being taught medicine, management, law, basic science, agricultural science, engineering, and computer science through the medium of French. Moreover, these students are then eligible for work experience in a variety of Francophone businesses that are in partnership in the scheme and recruit from among the graduates. These companies include giants such as Alcatel, Rhône-Poulenc, Crédit Lyonnais, and Air France.

The goal of this program is that 5% of all those completing 12 years of schooling (6–18 years) in the full Vietnamese primary and secondary system should do so in a bilingual French-Vietnamese stream. To this end, AUPELF plans to augment the number of classes available by 125 per year through 2010. In addition, there are small numbers attending the Lycée Français and learning French with the Alliance Française. As the major funder of AUPELF, France now educates a greater number of Vietnamese than during the colonial period. Given present trends, it seems likely that French will continue to gain in importance in Vietnamese society.

COMPETITION FROM THE ENGLISH-SPEAKING WORLD

Although the French initiative has had some impact on language learning in Vietnam, English is the language that most Vietnamese wish to acquire. As the lingua franca of the ASEAN and APEC countries with which Vietnam does business and the language of globalization, it is widely perceived as having the greatest economic value. Australia is currently the major provider of long-term overseas scholarships and of English language training to teachers and personnel in key ministries in Vietnam, through AUSAID, the Australian agency for international development. More than 2000 Vietnamese students per year have studied in Australia in the last five years (for budgetary data, see Fatseas, 1998). The Australian International Education Foundation (AIEF) organizes links between universities and joint publications.

Despite the presence of government agencies from Australia and to a lesser extent other English-speaking countries, English language teaching is dominated by the private sector. International organizations have set up schools in the main towns and there has been a growth of small enterprises, often established by travelers who have decided to stay in the new *Doi Moi* Vietnam. These programs are of varying quality and often ephemeral. Their success and proliferation, despite their obvious deficiencies, are evidence of the strong feeling among the Vietnamese that English is now an important asset.

In the cash-strapped public education system, the main foreign language is English. There is no foreign language in the basic general provision, which now has well over 10 million pupils. There is a possibility for foreign language study in basic secondary (11–15 years), which has over four million pupils, although how far this part of the curriculum is fully implemented depends very much on the availability of teachers, particularly in English. In upper secondary, there are over one million 15–18 year-olds in education, the great majority studying a foreign language for three hours a week (Pham Minh Hac, 1998). The Ministry of Education and Training (MOET) recognizes that this is an area where staff with appropriate qualifications are urgently needed (personal communication, MOET, 1998).

MOET also recognizes that English pedagogy needs to be reviewed. The traditional emphasis on accuracy in the written language rather than the acquisition of fluency in the spoken language is inappropriate for many Vietnamese today (Lo Bianco, 1993). Given the importance of spoken fluency, there is growing likelihood that changes in pedagogy will be forthcoming.

CONCLUSIONS

The history of Vietnam has been marked by war and troubled relations with the outside world. Given the strong sense of national identity and diplomatic isolation in the post-1975 period, it is understandable that formal foreign language provision has been a low priority and that individuals until recently have not taken the personal initiative to acquire foreign language skills. However, as Vietnam industrializes, language learning is necessary if the country is to participate in international networks and profit fully from foreign investment. The need for high quality language education can only grow as Vietnam seeks to create a new kind of knowledge-based economy, where access to information is overwhelmingly in other languages, particularly English. Thus a sizeable investment and much effort is needed in foreign language education. This undertaking is understandably difficult. However, unless Vietnamese workers acquire the languages demanded by investors, *Doi Moi* is unlikely to succeed in bringing employment for the Vietnamese, except in the most modest roles.

The group that has begun to take advantage of the demand for language skills is the Vietnamese who left the country and are fluent in both Vietnamese and the language of their adopted country. In the late 1990s, the Vietnamese government abolished the heavy taxes on expatriate money, lifted other restrictions, and invited the overseas Vietnamese (Viet Kieu) to return. Of the two million overseas Vietnamese, the number returning is relatively small, and most returnees have kept their foreign passports as a precaution in case policies change and they are no longer welcome (Lamb, 1996). Since the Viet Kieu are primarily based in the United States, Australia, and France, most returnees have competence in the languages most in demand. As the children of the capitalist and bourgeois classes expelled by the revolutionaries, they also have access to capital for investment. Yet their return involves a risk: If they are perceived as the main beneficiaries of economic development, resentment and conflict could result.

In Vietnam, foreign language learning has always reflected historical events and been a barometer of waxing and waning relationships with other powers. This is, of course, the case in all foreign language learning, which inevitably reflects economic and political association. The interesting aspect of the Vietnamese case study is the abruptness of the changes and the very evident cause-effect relationships.

In the future, foreign language learning will no doubt continue to be a barometer of social change in Vietnam and play a central role in the important economic and political developments taking place. In a follow up visit to South-East Asia in January 2001 I encountered an informal opinion among English mother tongue journalists that the communication difficulties they had been experiencing in Vietnam appeared to be easing, and that more English speakers could be found among the younger members of the Vietnamese political and business elites than was the case a few years ago. When this can be confirmed and quantified, it will indicate the beginning of a new phase in this narrative.

REFERENCES

Aldrich, R. (1996). *Greater France: A history of French overseas expansion*. London: Macmillan.
Année du Vietnam. (1997). Un septième sommet francophone, March.
Bao Ninh. (1993). *The sorrow of war*. London: Secker and Warburg.
Birolli, B. (1999, August 18). Le lézard qui n'est pas devenu dragon. *Nouvel Observateur 12*, 48–49
Bourdieu, P. (1989). *La noblesse d'État, grandes écoles et esprit de corps*. Paris: Minuit.
Bui Tin. (1995). *From cadre to exile: The memoirs of a North Vietnamese journalist*. Chiang Mai: Silkworm Books.
Carlson, J. (1998). Vietnam: Great or not-so-great for foreign investment? *Vietnam venture group business and investment articles*. www.vvg.hcm/vn.com.
Chirac, J. (1997, November). Opening address to the 7th Francophone Summit, given by the President of the French Republic, Hanoi.
CNN. Vietnam looks to former enemies for investment. (1996, May 2)
Crawford, A. (1966). *Customs and culture of Vietnam*. Vermont: Tuttle.
Delpey, R. (1964). *Soldats de la boue*. Paris: PIC.
Dickson, C. (1998). Study of labour market and foreign enterprise in Vietnam. *Vietnam Commerce and Industry, 19/12*, 15–16.
Economist. Goodnight Vietnam. (2000, January 8), 74–76.
Fatseas, M. (1998). Education and training links between Vietnam and Australia. *Vietnamese Studies, 3*, 29–36.
Karnow, S. (1994). *Vietnam: A history*. London: Pimlico.

Khoon, C. W., Lin, A. L. Y., & Sin, P. C. (1997). Development of education, training and investment opportunities in Vietnam. In T. T. Meng, et al. (Eds.), *Business opportunities in Vietnam*. Singapore: Prentice Hall.

Lamb, D. (1996). Viet Kieu: A bridge between two worlds. *The Vietnam Review*, 1. 420–426.

Lo Bianco, J. (1993). Issues and aspects of Vietnam's language policy: Some reflections after a brief visit. *Journal of Vietnamese Studies*, 6, 24–32.

Nguyen Phu Phong. (1995). *Questions de linguistique vietnamienne*. Paris: Presses de l'Ecole française d'extrême-orient.

Nguyen Tri Dung. (1998). Ten years of renovation and Vietnam foreign investment. *Vietnam Studies*, 3 , 5–10.

Nguyen Van Ky. (1997). Le modèle français. In G. Boudarel & Nguyen Van Ky (Eds.), *Hanoi 1936–1996: Collection mémoires*, no. 48, 56–83.

Nguyen Xuan Thu. (1993). Education in Vietnam: An overview. *Journal of Vietnamese Studies*, 6, 5–23.

Osborne, M. (1997). *The French presence in Cochinchina and Cambodia*. Bangkok: White Lotus

Pham Ha. (1998). Practical foreign investment. *Vietnam Commerce and Industry*, 19/12, 13.

Pham Minh Hac. (1995). The educational system of Vietnam. In D. Sloper & Le Thac Can (Eds.), *Higher education in Vietnam: Change and response*. Singapore: Institute of Southeast Asian Studies.

Pham Minh Hac. (1998). *Vietnam's education: The current position and future prospects*. Hanoi: The Gioi Publishers.

Pham Thanh Nghi & Sloper, D. (1995). Staffing profile of higher education. In D. Sloper & Le Thac Can (Eds.), *Higher education in Vietnam: Change and response*. Singapore: Institute of Southeast Asian Studies.

République du Vietnam. (1968–1969). Evolution des effectifs des professeurs de langue vivante et des élèves choisissant le français ou l'anglais comme première langue vivante. *Annuaire statistique de l'enseignement*.

Rigg, J. (1997). *Southeast Asia: The human landscape of modernization and development*. London: Routledge.

Sadec Asia Pacific. (1999). Investment rating fact sheets. www.sadec.com/profile/viet.html.

Sloper, D. & Le Thac Can. (1995). Introduction. In D. Sloper & Le Thac Can (Eds.), *Higher education in Vietnam: Change and response*. Singapore: Institute of Southeast Asian Studies.

Terzani, T. (1997). *Saigon 1975: Three days and three months*. Bangkok: White Lotus.

UNESCO. (1979). *The elimination of illiteracy and the use of complementary education in the Socialist Republic of Vietnam*. Bangkok: Ministry of Education of SRV.

Vietnam Courrier. (1982). *Education in Vietnam*. Hanoi.

Vietnamese Ministry of Education. (1990). *45 Years of educational development in Vietnam*. Hanoi: Educational Publishing House.

Weiss, P. (1971). *Notes on the cultural life of the Democratic Republic of Vietnam*. London: Calder and Boyars.

12

Language Planning in Korea: The New Elementary English Program

Sook Kyung Jung and Bonny Norton
University of British Columbia

In teaching English, the emphasis should be laid not on accuracy but on successful communication and fluency, not on rote memory but on the acquisition of the language through actual use of it (Ministry of Education of Korea, Elementary English Curriculum [Lee, 1995]).

The dominant role of English in current international trade and computer communication makes English teaching and learning an important issue in the educational systems of many non-English speaking countries. Over the last decade, English proficiency has been actively promoted by the governments of many ESL (English as a second language) and EFL (English as a first language) countries striving to achieve modernization and internationalization (Pennycook, 1994; Phillipson, 1992; Tollefson, 1995). A government's wish to equip its citizens with improved English proficiency prompts many non-English speaking countries to introduce English education at an early age. It is reported (Ko, 1993) that English is an optional subject at the elementary level in over 50 countries, 25 of which have made it a mandatory school subject. For example, China starts English education from Grade 4, Thailand from Grade 1, France from Grade 2, Norway from Grade 3, and Israel from Grade 3 (Ministry of Education, 1997).

As Tollefson (1989) notes, in many non-English speaking countries, a learner's acquisition of English can be profoundly affected by a government's policy toward the role of English in the society and also by the procedure for implementing those decisions in its educational system. The formation of language policy for English teaching, however, often involves a tension between the desire to preserve a country's own culture and language and the desire to promote English proficiency (Olshtain, 1989). While English is a language to be mastered for social, economic, and political success, it may also threaten the local culture, local languages, and local educational systems (Phillipson, 1992). The tension around the formation of language policy for English teaching is particularly evident in an elementary English program, because these years are the formative period for establishing a student's first language proficiency and identity.

This chapter presents the findings of an investigation of issues in the planning and implementation process of Korea's new elementary English program. Through interviews with policymakers, case studies of three local elementary schools, and documentary analysis, we investigated how the government's language education policy is perceived and implemented by teachers, and what impact the policy has on the culture of elementary education in Korea.

INTRODUCTION TO THE NEW ELEMENTARY ENGLISH PROGRAM

In Korea, English as a major foreign language has been taught as a regular subject in middle school (from Grade 7 to 9) and High school (Grade 10 to 12) since 1945 (Kim, 1997). There has been constant criticism of this curriculum, however, focusing as it did on the teaching of grammar and reading for higher education (Ministry of Education, 1993). In 1994, a year after its inauguration, the seventh Korean government began a nationwide campaign aimed at globalization of the country, with a view to enhancing Korea's rapid economic growth and internationalization (Ministry of Education, 1997). To achieve this goal, the Presidential Committee for Globalization Policy decided to first reform foreign language education in schools, particularly English education (Ministry of Education, 1997). When implementing its globalization policy, the government acknowledged that the existing English program did not contribute to developing the students' oral English proficiency, a language skill considered necessary to cope with extensive international communication with other countries (Ministry of Education, 1997).

Against this background, the Korean government decided to create a new elementary English program with a view to shifting the existing middle and secondary English programs to a more oral communication-based English program and to encourage the development of students' oral

English ability from an earlier age (Ministry of Education, 1997). In March, 1997, the Korean government thus launched the new elementary English class as a compulsory subject in every public elementary school. Although English has been taught as an extracurricular subject in elementary schools since 1982 (Chun, 1995), the government initiative marked the first mandatory implementation in the public elementary schools of a regular English class with a national English curriculum and textbooks. Prior to its inauguration, the Korean government spent two years developing a national curriculum, providing English teacher training for elementary teachers, organizing multimedia facilities for the schools, and publishing textbooks in readiness for the program's implementation (Ministry of Education, 1997).

According to the national curriculum, students are to learn English from Grade 3 to Grade 6 for two periods (90 minutes in total) per week. The aim of the elementary English program is "to motivate a student's interest in English and to develop basic communicative competence" (Ministry of Education, 1996): "When teaching English, the emphasis should be laid not on accuracy but on successful communication and fluency, not on rote memory but on the acquisition of the language through actual use of it" (Lee, 1995). The new curriculum particularly emphasizes the development of oral English ability to avoid repeating the problems with grammar- and reading-based English teaching in the established middle and secondary English program. Thus, according to the curriculum, during the first year of the English program (Grade 3), students learn English exclusively through listening and speaking activities. The alphabet is not introduced until Grade 4 and written English constitutes only 10% of the Grade 4 curriculum. In Grades 5 and 6, students learn reading and writing, but written English is introduced only as a supplement to spoken English (*Ministry of Education, 1997*). The government further imposes strict restrictions on the number of the words and length of sentences to be mastered in each grade, so that students can enjoy the English class without the burden of "studying" English. The specific schedule for implementation of the program was as follows (Ministry of Education, 1996):

March.1, 1997: Grade 3—listening and speaking (100 words; 7 words in a sentence).

March 1, 1998: Grades 3 and 4—listening, speaking, and reading (add 100 words; 7 words in a sentence).

March 1, 1999: Grades 3, 4 and 5—listening, speaking, and reading (add 150 words; 9 words in a sentence).

March 1, 2000: Grades 3, 4, 5, and 6—listening, speaking, reading, and writing (add 150 words; 9 words in a sentence).

RESEARCH METHODOLOGY

The implementation of the new English elementary program provides fertile ground for research. We were interested in investigating the relationship between government policy on the one hand, and its implementation by teachers and administrators on the other. We were also interested in the sociocultural impact of the program on the educational system more broadly. For this purpose, we chose three schools in the greater Seoul area for case study analysis, and arranged to interview key policymakers who have been involved in planning and implementing the program. To conduct the research, Jung made two visits to Korea from May to June 1998 and September 1998 to January 1999. During this period, the new elementary English program was being implemented in Grades 3 and 4.

Prior to research in the schools, Jung examined government documents related to educational policy for the elementary English program, and then interviewed four people in the Ministry of Education, three university professors involved in policy development and teacher training, and the principals of three schools, referred to as School A, School B, and School C. Jung then administered a preliminary questionnaire to teachers teaching English in Grades 3 and 4 in these three schools. This laid the groundwork for a subsequent interview with the teachers, 17 of whom participated in the interview (see Table 12.1). Data have been translated into English.

In her second visit, Jung then conducted 20 hours of classroom observation of the teachers who participated in the interview. After each observation, Jung conducted a short informal interview with the teachers. In the final stage of the research, Jung administered a second questionnaire to all English teachers in each school to verify the results of preliminary questionnaires and to identify common issues among the teachers. Table 12.2 shows the number of questionnaires collected from English teachers in the final stage of the research.

Data from these questionnaires is the basis for analysis in the "Discussion" section below. Note that the two questionnaires from School A were completed by the English special teachers, but the number of teachers interviewed in School A included the two English special teachers as well as two regular classroom teachers. Pseudonyms are used throughout this chapter.

TABLE 12.1
Grade 3 and 4 Teachers Interviewed

	School A	School B	School C	Total
Number of teachers	4	6	7	17

TABLE 12.2
Second Questionnaires Completed by Grade 3 and 4 Teachers

	School A	School B	School C	Total
Number of Qs	2	7	20	29

ISSUES IN GOVERNMENTAL LANGUAGE PLANNING

In interviews with policymakers, we found that there were three questions of central concern. First, who would teach English to the elementary students? Second, how could an oral-based curriculum be implemented? Third, what sociocultural impact would the new elementary English program have on students? We will discuss each of these issues in turn.

The Training of English Teachers

When the new elementary English program was initiated, there was much concern about the English qualifications of elementary school teachers (*The Chosunilbo*, 1996). The government's position was that elementary teachers should teach elementary English, because such teachers are familiar with the characteristics of elementary students (Ministry of Education, 1997). However, given the Korean context, where even certified secondary English teachers have had difficulty teaching oral English in their classrooms (Ministry of Education, 1993), there was concern that elementary teachers who did not major in English would have even greater difficulty teaching conversational English to their students. In response to this concern, the government planned to provide extensive English teacher training for every elementary teacher by 2000. This training would comprise 120 hours of general teacher training in English and an additional 120 hours of intensive training for those who excelled in the general program. It was hoped that some of those teachers who received the intensive training might become English special teachers in the future. The training included English conversation classes with English native speakers, teaching methods, materials development, and presentation of teaching (Ministry of Education, 1996). Tables 12.3 and 12.4 show the number of teachers the government planned for both stages of English teacher training.

In addition, since 1997, the government has increased the number of students who specialize in English at the nine national teacher universities (by February 1998, 890 students; by February 2000, 933 students) and has also increased the hours of English instruction in the curriculum. Every student in the university program for elementary teachers is required to take 12 credits of English classes (previously six credits) and students who

TABLE 12.3

Teachers Planned for General English Teacher Training

	1996	1997	1998	1999	Total
Number of teachers	18,886	18,654	18,390	12,046	67,976

(Source: Ministry of education, 1998a)

TABLE 12.4

Teachers Planned for Intensive Teacher Training

	1996	1997	1998	1999	Total
Number of teachers	7,386	10,706	16,279	16,279	50,650

(Source: Ministry of education, 1998a)

specialize in English have to take 21 English credits (Ministry of Education, 1998a). Further, as of 1998, elementary teachers must pass an English conversation test in order to be considered eligible for employment at elementary schools (Ministry of Education, 1998b).

The government's plan for the new program was to allow two different English teacher systems: the classroom English teacher system and the English special teacher system. In the classroom English system, the regular classroom teacher is responsible for teaching English 90 minutes per week; in the English special teacher system, a single teacher is responsible for teaching English to a number of different classes each week. For English classes in Grades 3 and 4, the government recommended the classroom English teacher system in which each classroom teacher teaches English to his or her students, while for English classes in Grades 5 and 6, the government recommended the English special teacher system (Ministry of Education, 1998a). However, the government permitted principals to choose the system deemed best for their own particular needs and circumstances. Table 12.5 shows the distribution of English teacher systems across Grades 3 and 4 in 1998.

Teaching Methodology

Policymakers were concerned that the large elementary classes (approximately 40–48 students) would make communicative language teaching difficult. To compensate for the large number of students and to promote the oral English program, the government encourages the use of multimedia systems (VCR, large TV monitor, CD-ROMs) and has funded the installation of these systems in each class from Grade 3 (Ministry of Education, 1997). The government has also included diverse communicative language

TABLE 12.5

The English Teacher System in Grades 3 and 4 in 1998

	Grade 3 Number of Schools	Grade 4 Number of Schools
English special teacher	859	882
Classroom teacher	4,235	4,257
Other system (e.g. exchange teaching)	483	448
Total	5,577	5,587

(*Source*: Ministry of education, 1998b)

teaching methods in the teacher training and encouraged teachers to use a variety of hands-on activities, such as games, songs, chants, and arts. The government has developed a series of multimedia textbooks, accompanied by audio tapes, videotapes, and a teachers' guide. To improve the quality of English textbooks, the government introduced an open competition among publishers and has listed textbooks from 12 companies on an approved list from which local schools may choose (Ministry of Education, 1997).

The Sociocultural Impact of the Elementary English Program

Policymakers' third concern about the elementary English program was whether it could affect students' development of the Korean language and their Korean identity. Lee's (1992) research suggests that many people believe if a foreign language is introduced in Grade 3, the development of literacy in Korean may suffer. Lee also found concern that an early English program could promote a preference for English or American culture among students. In response to these concerns, the government, through its marketing materials, emphasized the particular importance of English as an international language, rather than just one of many foreign languages. The government has taken the position that early foreign language learning can promote a deeper appreciation of Korean culture alongside an understanding of other cultures: "By exposure to foreign language education at an earlier age, students can easily differentiate between the Korean and foreign language and it gives students a greater sensitivity about the Korean language" (Ministry of Education, 1996).

ISSUES IN IMPLEMENTATION: THREE CASE STUDIES

Having examined the central issues identified by policymakers of the new elementary English program, we now turn to our case studies of the three schools in the greater Seoul area. In each of the case studies, we provide details of the school site, its population, institutional support for the English program, and teacher perceptions of the English program.

School A. School A, with approximately 1800 students, is situated in a middle-class neighborhood in a suburban city near Seoul. The school, opened in 1992 as the new suburban residential areas emerged, now has 52 teachers (22 male and 30 female) with an average age of 43. During the research period, there were seven classes in each of Grades 3 and 4, with an average of approximately 42 students in each class. This school has opted for the English special teacher system; thus two English special teachers teach Grades 3 and 4 respectively. It was these two teachers, Yang Kyung and Soo Jin, that Jung interviewed. According to one of the regular classroom teachers interviewed, the principal deferred to the teachers in Grades 3 and 4 in making this decision:

> Our principal is quite democratic in administering the school policy. He asked us to decide the English teachers' system in our teachers meeting. We were talking about different options like combining the classroom teacher system and English special teacher system in the same grade if many teachers want to teach, but then classroom teachers became concerned they could be compared to English special teachers by the parents and students, so we decided to stick to the English special system (Min Hee, 1998).

Both English special teachers were female and both said they volunteered as English special teachers. One of the English special teachers, Yang Kyung (48 years old), who was teaching Grade 4, had been teaching English as an extracurricular subject since 1982 and during the research period was the president of the district elementary English teachers association. In contrast to Yang Kyung, the other teacher, Soo Jin, was a very young teacher (24 years old) undertaking elementary English teaching for the first time in 1998. Because of their differences in age and teaching experience, Soo Jin tended to follow Yang Kyung's direction for English teaching and they cooperated through active participation in the district elementary teachers association meetings. Yang Kyung completed the general and the intensive teacher training, while Soo Jin completed 120 hours of general teacher training. Compared to other teachers' classroom hours (30 per week), English special teachers in this school had fewer hours (20), allowing them to devote more time to lesson preparation. Soo Jin seemed to be happy with her working conditions: "I was interested in English so I volunteered as English teacher this year to have more time to study English. I enjoy my working conditions right now because compared to classroom teachers I have more time to prepare the class and to focus on materials development" (Soo Jin, 1998).

In 1997, the district school board allotted approximately $25,000 to every school to install a multimedia system in a special English room. Thus each class in Grades 3 and 4 was equipped with a multimedia system (large TV monitor, VCR, and recorder) and the school also had a special English room equipped with 30 monitors connected through the local area network (LAN), a 40-inch monitor, overhead projector, and multimedia projectors. Students could watch videotapes and CD-ROMS on each monitor right at their desks.

The principal's attitude towards the English program is generally supportive, but he does not want to treat English as a special subject: "I think the English subject should be considered as one of the subjects in the elementary school curriculum, but nothing more. I believe the current enthusiasm about English will be diminished after English becomes routine (principal, School A, 1998). Three of the four teachers interviewed in School A said that their colleagues generally expressed two distinct attitudes towards the English program. While they did not welcome the new English program because of the possibility of an increased workload, they still wanted to receive the English teacher training, if available, because they saw it as directly related to their career development. These contrasting views are expressed by Soo Jin and the principal, respectively:

> Having another subject always bugs teachers in terms of workload as well as their ability to teach. We have to acknowledge that not every teacher is positive about the introduction of the English program (Soo Jin, 1998).

> In the current situation, teachers feel that they should invest their time in learning English and computer skills, because without knowledge of English and the computer, they know they cannot survive in the educational field (principal in School A, 1998).

In terms of the classroom implementation of the program, both English special teachers made it clear that the purpose of their teaching was "to promote students' interest in learning English and confidence in English." To achieve their goals, they tried to introduce different kinds of activities, such as role-plays, games, songs, chants, and story telling in their classes:

> In our textbook, each unit consists of four hours. In the first hour, I usually start with greetings and asking about the weather; at other times I introduce songs and chants to capture the students' attention. Then we watch the videotape as a topic presentation. In the second hour, we do the role-play with the sentences we learned from the videotape and practice them with songs and chants. In the third hour, I introduce a game and other activities to reinforce what was learned. In the fourth hour, I check students' listening ability through worksheets (Soo Jin, 1998).

I introduce many story-telling activities in my class. Because we have 30 monitors in the English room, students listen to the story while watching it on the monitors (Yang Kyung, 1998).

Both teachers said that students enjoyed the English class. Since there is no evaluation of English as a subject and most of the English classes consist of hands-on activities, students were free from the sense of "studying" English. The teachers reported that about 70–80% of their students achieved the daily objectives of the English class. The most popular activity among the students was the "game" activity, which introduced a strong motivation for participation and fostered a sense of achievement. While students enjoyed these activities, Soo Jin said students are sometimes too excited to remember the purpose of the games: "Students just try to have fun, not considering the words they have to practice" (Soo Jin, 1998). Both teachers said they normally followed the sequence of the textbooks, but sometimes they changed the sequence of activities according to the students' interests. They relied on many other resources to vary the activities and also gathered ideas from local elementary teachers association meetings.

School B.   School B, with 1027 students, is located in a new middle- and upper-middle class apartment complex in a new city about 40 minutes from Seoul. The school first opened in 1994 and currently has 34 teachers (24 female and 10 male). Compared to School A, most teachers are relatively young (an average age of 35); 13 of the 34 teachers were new college graduates at the time of this research. The average class size in School B (48 students) is larger than School A (42 students), because this area has had rapid population growth. School B opted for the classroom English teacher system, because no one volunteered as an English special teacher. More than half of the teachers (four of seven) said that they were assigned to Grade 3 and 4 by the principal because they had completed teacher training. They did not volunteer for these positions.

With four classes each in Grades 3 and 4, and two Grade 3 English classes taught by the same classroom teacher, (because one teacher did not want to teach an English class), the total of seven classroom English teachers had an average age of only 26 years, except for one teacher who was 48 years old. The addition of English as a subject resulted in the Grade 3 and 4 teachers teaching two hours more than other teachers. Due to this increased workload, most of these positions were assigned to younger teachers. There was also a common perception among the teachers that the younger teachers were more proficient in English than the older teachers because they had better pronunciation skills. Jung found that this phenomenon was quite common across the schools; she observed that younger teachers were better represented than older teachers at workshops and seminars related to English teaching.

Among the seven classroom English teachers, five teachers received the general English teacher training, one teacher received both general and intensive training, and one senior teacher expected to receive the training in the coming winter vacation. Several teachers complained that there were not many opportunities for English teacher training even though they wanted it. As Hyun Jin said: "I have been waiting for the chance for intensive English teacher training since last summer, but I still haven't had the chance" (Hyun Jin, 1998).

This school has one teacher (Jung Ah) who majored in English and who generally prepared class presentations for parents and distributed the teaching materials to other teachers. In School B, she was the only teacher who participated in the local elementary teachers association. She was teaching Grade 3 as a classroom teacher in 1998, but she had worked as the English special teacher for Grade 3 in 1997. However, because of job conditions she did not apply for the English special teacher position in 1998. As she explained below:

> In this school, there is no space for special teachers. We have to stay in the teachers' office and I have to help with school administration work, because my teaching hours are fewer than other classroom teachers. Except for 20 hours teaching, I have to type documents all day. There is no place to put my teaching materials and I really want to have my own classroom. If the government wants to promote English special teachers, I think they should provide the appropriate working conditions for special teachers (Jung Ah, 1998).

Because of the shift from the English special teacher system in 1997 to the classroom teacher system in 1998, most of the teachers in Grade 4 had to teach English without the prior experience of teaching Grade 3 English. This created a greater burden for these Grade 4 teachers. As Hyun Jin and Young Mai said:

> In my case, I was assigned to Grade 4 at the end of February, and had to begin teaching English from the first week of March. Because I didn't teach English last year and there were no materials at all, I had to make everything. And I didn't have that much time (Hyun Jin, 1998).

> I couldn't guess how much students already knew and what they had already learned (Young Mi, 1998).

Three classrooms in Grade 3 were equipped with multimedia systems. The Grade 4 classrooms were to be ready in 1999. Like School A, School B also has a special English room, funded by the school board, with computers, English books, audio listening, and a role-playing area. Jung found, however, that because this school does not have an English special teacher, the English room was not managed very efficiently. Jung Ah was responsible for the special English room, but as a classroom teacher, she said she did not have much time to manage this additional room: "Right now, nobody is really in charge of this room and I am not the person. I am just a person to keep the key" (Jung Ah, 1998). Most of the teachers taught English in the room at least once per week, but some teachers did not want to use the space because they thought that students did not concentrate well there: "I normally go when I want to try different CDs related to the textbook, and students always think that room is a place for playing, not for studying" (Hwa Sun, 1998).

The principal was generally supportive of the English program. Five of the seven teachers said that the principal funded the development of materials if requested. The principal said, however, that he would prefer to have English special teachers because of the many individual differences in English ability among the classroom teachers. In terms of teachers' cooperation, unlike School A, teachers in School B did not have much communication with other English teachers because of their heavy workload as classroom teachers and the lack of a head teacher. The only time they did meet teachers in the same grade was on a Friday afternoon, but there were always issues other than English to deal with at that time.

> It would be much better if we can have more chance to exchange teaching ideas and materials. But our life here is so busy, because this school has a short history and fewer teachers than other schools (Jin Sook, 1998).

> Perhaps there is no teacher confident in English teaching. We have communication for other subjects, not for English (Dong Hee, grade 4 teacher, 1998).

Among class activities, Jung found that the CD-ROM activity was the most popular in School B. Teachers said that most of the students were very accustomed to handling CD-ROMs because of their high socioeconomic status. Regarding use of the textbook, while four of seven teachers said that they restructured the textbook according to students' interest, three teachers said they simply followed the sequence of the textbook.

School C.   Opened in 1937, School C is an old inner city school of 2,335 students located in the northern downtown area of Seoul. Because of its location, the socioeconomic status of most parents is low; most families depend on the school exclusively for their children's education. In other words, unlike schools A and B, students in School C do not have access to extracurricular schooling and academic support. Most of the 72 teachers in the school are very experienced. With an average age of 39 years, about

80% of the teachers have more than 10 years teaching experience, thus contrasting with the relatively inexperienced staff in School B.

This school opted for the classroom English teacher system; there were 20 classroom English teachers in Grades 3 and 4 (10 in each grade). The class size was relatively small (35 students) compared to other schools because there is a smaller population of children in the city than in the suburbs. The principal of this school was very enthusiastic about English education and had been actively involved in the Seoul Elementary English Teachers Association. The classroom teacher system was chosen by the principal, because, in contrast to the principal in School B, the principal in School C believed that through sustained opportunities for interaction, the classroom teacher could provide more language input to students in their school day. About 50% of the classroom teachers said that they were assigned to Grades 3 and 4 by the principal, rather than volunteering for this assignment. Due to the principal's enthusiasm for English education, this school also offered an English class to Grades 5 and 6 once a week, taught by an English special teacher.

In this school, Jung found that teachers expressed two contrasting views on the elementary English program. Most of the Grade 4 teachers were active and seemed very confident in English teaching, because most of them had taught Grade 3 English in 1997 with the same students. (In this school, the teachers retain their students for two years). Five of the 10 teachers in Grade 4 were involved in the district's elementary English teachers association and four teachers had been teaching English as an extracurricular subject since 1982. They also had a positive collegial relationship with other teachers. Seven out of 10 teachers said they had an active exchange of teaching ideas with other teachers, and there were regular workshops in the school for teaching methods and materials development. In Grade 4 there was a head teacher, Sun Mi, who had been teaching English for seven years in elementary schools. As an experienced senior teacher, Sun Mi generally helped other teachers by providing direction and weekly lesson plans for every class in Grade 4. She had also been working at the teacher-training center as an instructor. Due to the principal's enthusiasm for English and several other equally enthusiastic teachers, the situation for English teaching in the school was highly supportive.

In contrast to the situation in Grade 4, most of the teachers in Grade 3 were new to teaching English. They also did not have a head teacher to support their teaching and communication among teachers about English teaching was rare. Furthermore, since half of the teachers said rather than volunteering they were assigned by the principal to be classroom English teachers, many felt resistant and frustrated. As two teachers wrote in their questionnaires:

> I am not good at English at all, and I have to teach English. I really feel sorry for my students who have to learn English from me (classroom teacher, Grade 3, 1998).

> People think elementary teachers can teach English because the level is very low and easy, but "being able to teach" is different from "how to teach." There must be much difference in teaching done by somebody who likes English and who wants to teach, and who is good at English, and somebody who has to teach out of obligation. There must be something wrong in the concept that all elementary teachers should be involved in English teaching (classroom teacher, Grade 3, 1998).

Some teachers felt that this school overemphasized English at the expense of other subjects and the resulting tension created more stress in their teaching. As Kyung Mi, a Grade 3 teacher, said: "Our school has a diverse age range of teachers. To some old teachers or some that are not interested in teaching English, the atmosphere of this school is quite stressful. We sometimes feel excluded" (Kyung Mi, Grade 3 teacher 1998).

This school also offered an after-school English program run by a local private company. Since the parents at this school could not afford private English education outside school, students' participation in this program was very high. About 10 students in each class in Grades 3 and 4 attended this program. These students normally acted as group leaders in the regular English class.

Unlike schools A and B, School C did not have a special English room and the multimedia system had been installed in only five classrooms in Grades 3 and 4. Accordingly, unlike school A and B, where CD-ROMs were very popular, CD-ROM activities were very rare in School C. Teachers said that the most popular activity in School C was the "game activity": "I normally started with a review using a guessing game and then introduced different kinds of games in a group activity to reinforce what students learned" (Sun Mi, 1998). There was a wide range in textbook usage among the teachers. More than half of the teachers in this school said they restructured the textbook according to students' interests. While 72% of the teachers occasionally depended on the textbook in their class, about 20% depended totally on the textbook.

DISCUSSION: GOVERNMENT POLICY AND SCHOOL IMPLEMENTATION

In reflecting on government policy, on the one hand, and its implementation within schools, on the other, we have identified four issues for further discussion. These issues address teachers' perceptions of the English program; concerns about the English teacher system and teacher training; challenges in classroom implementation; and the sociocultural impact of the program on students and teachers. We address each of these issues in turn.

Teachers' Perceptions of The English Program

Drawing on the interviews, classroom observations, and the results of the second questionnaire, comprehensively completed by 29 teachers in schools A, B, and C, we found that 90% of the English teachers in the study agreed that it was necessary to teach English as a compulsory subject in elementary school. In contrast to the government's position that English should be promoted as an international language, however, about 60% of the teachers viewed English as only one of the foreign languages, rather than as a special international language. Thus they believed that English should not be unduly emphasized as a major subject in the elementary curriculum. While 9% believed that English should not be taught at elementary level at all, the remaining 31%, who did perceive English as an international language, also agreed that English should be a major subject in elementary schools. This suggests that if teachers perceive English to be an international language, they tend to promote it more vigorously in the elementary English program.

As to the timing of the program, 36% of the teachers thought that 1997 was an appropriate year for starting the elementary English program, but about 44% thought the timing premature, given the lack of preparation time for training the English teachers and developing teaching materials. As two teachers said:

> It was nonsense to ask elementary teachers to teach spoken English with only 120 hours of teacher training (classroom teacher, School C).

> Even with the materials, it is so hard to teach English. There are totally new methods, it is difficult to lead the class in English, it is difficult to talk to students in English, and it is difficult to prepare the materials (classroom teacher, School B).

In contrast, 20% of the teachers thought that Korea should have started elementary English education earlier. Teachers who were most enthusiastic towards English teaching frequently responded in this way.

The English Teacher System and Teacher Training

Most classroom teachers in schools A and C (15 out of 22) strongly favored the English special teacher system on the grounds that classroom teachers do not have enough time to prepare English teaching materials. As two of them said:

> We have to teach 10 subjects in Grade 3. How can we spend time preparing only for English class? (classroom teacher, School C).

> English class cannot be taught without materials. Most classes focus on games and plays. You can listen to the tapes and watch the videotapes. But if you don't have materials, you really cannot make the class interesting. But as a classroom teacher, we don't have that much time (classroom teacher in School B).

In addition, some teachers claimed that English teaching methods call on teachers to be outgoing and energetic, which causes discomfort among some Korean teachers. As one noted:

> The current goal of English teaching as much as possible is to encourage fun when learning English. Teachers should use lots of physical activities, songs, and games. If the teacher has an outgoing and cheerful personality, she or he will be a suitable person for this kind of teaching. I am not that kind of person. English teaching always makes me feel awkward and it's not me (Jung Min, Grade 3 teacher).

Some English special teachers, however, complained about the English special teacher system because they encountered difficulties with classroom management and discipline:

> It is so hard to manage 42 students as a special teacher. They don't listen to us if we are not their classroom teachers (English special teacher, School A).

> The main problem of English special teachers is that we don't have much rapport with students. Sometimes it is harder to check students' individual achievement (English special teacher, School A).

Furthermore, each school seemed to have a different policy about managing the English special teacher system. For example, while School A respected the English special teachers' need for preparation time, School B added additional duties to their workload. As noted earlier, another problem with the English special teacher system concerns its incompatibility with the current administrative structure. As the principal in School A pointed out: "In elementary schools, all teachers transfer to other schools every four years. Then how we can manage the English special teacher system?"

In sum, we found that despite the problems with the English special system, the majority of the teachers (60%) preferred the English special system over the classroom teacher system. The main concern of classroom teachers was that they did not have the time to prepare for English classes, nor did they have the time to become sufficiently proficient in English. We found, however, that if the classroom teachers were enthusiastic about English and if they made strong connections with other teachers to share ideas and resources, classroom teachers preferred the classroom teacher system. As the principal in School C believed, classroom teachers are in a position to give more language input to students throughout the day. Jung found that several classroom teachers used English during the lunch hour and at recess to remind students of what they had learned. In contrast, some English special teachers complained that students easily forgot what they had learned, because students did not receive any reinforcement during the week. In addition, the classroom teachers had a sound knowledge of individual student's achievement levels, an important factor in managing the large class size. Indeed, despite the challenges of the classroom English teacher, the head teachers in school B and C did not reject the classroom teacher system. The Grade 4 teachers in School C and the head teacher in School B led the English class successfully as classroom teachers, supported by strong connections with other teachers through the local teachers' meetings.

Notwithstanding the advantages of the classroom teacher system, when considering the day-to-day demands of the current classroom teacher situation in Korea—where teachers have to take care of over 40 students and teach 10 subjects—retaining the classroom teacher system will increase teachers' teaching load and possibly lower the quality of English teaching. An important point to note is that after the economic crisis of the late 1990s, the Korean government decided to continue the classroom teacher system rather than shift fully toward the special teacher system. Retaining the quality of the elementary English program under the classroom teacher system will likely be an ongoing challenge in the elementary English education program in Korea.

In terms of teacher training, we found that the government's extensive English teacher training program was effective in helping teachers understand clearly the purpose and direction of the program.

> The English teacher training helped me understand the direction of the program. If I didn't take the training, I would start to teach the alphabet (Grade 3 teacher).

Most of the teachers stated that teacher training was helpful for their lessons. Nevertheless, most active English teachers stated that English teacher training should be given to a restricted number of teachers who are interested in English and who want to develop their careers as English special teachers.

Issues in Classroom Implementation

Three issues emerged as the most difficult challenges facing elementary teachers in the classroom implementation of the new program: materials development, large class size, and teachers' English proficiency.

Almost 80% of the teachers pointed to materials development as the most difficult component in teaching English in the classroom. Most of the teachers said that they lacked the knowledge to develop the materials themselves: "Currently we have to make all flash cards, game boards, and picture cards. The textbook publishing company should provide the basic materials" (classroom teacher, School B).

Almost 70% of the English teachers highlighted large class size as another barrier preventing the implementation of the oral English program; this issue is directly related to the teachers' lack of time for materials development. In this regard, many teachers wanted to have workbook-style textbooks in which students can work individually. Otherwise, most teachers said it was very difficult to prepare a copy of the materials for each individual student. According to some classroom teachers, another way of overcoming problems of materials development was to make the materials with the students in the English or art class. By making the materials together, students could have a greater sense of participation and, at the same time, save time for teachers. To overcome the problem of large class size, many teachers also frequently used group activities in their classes. Jung found groupings of four to six students a common practice across the schools. In addition, the composition of groups contributed to addressing differences in English ability among the students, since most teachers usually mixed advanced students with weaker students and used the advanced students as group leaders.

Finally, about half of the teachers regarded their limited English proficiency as the most obvious challenge to successful classroom teaching, and in this regard, about 80% of the English teachers worked on developing their oral English skills. One senior teacher said he always listened to classroom English tapes during the commute to school. Several teachers said they attended a private language institute to improve their conversational English. Some teachers said they attended regular weekly English meetings with other colleagues. About 60% said they use English more than half of the time when they teach English, while 30% said they use English more than 70% of the time. In the classroom, most teachers reverted to Korean when giving instructions for games or explanations of situations. About 90% felt that it was much better for the class if teachers spoke more English, but because of their lack of proficiency, they felt disappointed with their performance in the class. To improve the elementary teachers' English ability, several teachers hoped that the government would provide a more continuous English class with English native speakers as a part of teacher training: "We need more constant support to improve our language skills through conversational classes with English native speakers" (Kyung Mi, 1998).

The Sociocultural Impact of The Elementary English Program

The sociocultural impact of the elementary English program can be seen as both positive and negative. From a positive point of view, the program has had an enormous impact on English education in Korea in terms of teacher education, teaching methodology, and materials development. By successfully setting up an oral English program in the elementary school, the government has sought to improve on the earlier curriculum, which focused primarily on reading and grammar. As well, through activity- and experience-based teaching, Korean teachers can modify traditional teaching methods and explore a variety of innovative teaching methods in English education. As indicated in the comments below, activity-based English teaching might also affect teaching in other subjects in a positive way.

> Our students are so used to writing . . . Because of the restrictions on the written words in the English program, however, students can learn that they don't need to write and they can learn something through the activity. I think the new English program would break down the students' and parents' preconceptions about learning (Yang Kyung, School A).
>
> I wish sometimes how nice it would be if I applied this method to teach Korean (classroom teacher, School C).
>
> I wish that my students could derive a sense of fun from learning in other subjects (classroom teacher, School C).

On a negative note, however, some teachers expressed concern that the elementary English program accelerates the dominance of English in Korean education, resulting in the neglect of other subjects:

> We had to eliminate one of our science labs to make a new English room (English special teacher, School A).
>
> The English textbook is much better and much more interesting than the Korean (classroom teacher, School B).
>
> Many teachers are questioning why so much money should be invested in English, while ignoring other subjects (classroom teacher, School B).
>
> If you look at the current educational situation, it seems like computer skills and English ability are the most important factors in judging who is a competent elementary teacher. There are a lot more important qualifications than these, and senior teachers would be frustrated with this situation (classroom teacher, School C).

Furthermore many teachers have expressed concern about students' preference for English class, fearing that it undermines their commitment to the Korean language and cultural practices. Students tend to be more attracted to English, not only because of its status as an international language, but also because of the appealing English teaching methods.

> I think students really like English. Unlike other subjects, English is more fun and teachers don't require discipline. That's why they like it (classroom teacher, School C).

> Students like English class much more than Korean class because of the different teaching methods. Korean class requires lots of thinking and practice, but English is a class of fun (classroom teacher, School B).

> Today, more children aspire to the Western culture. I am sometimes worried if we ignore our own culture too much (classroom teacher, School B).

> When we host English speech contests in our school, the parents are so excited and try to support their children as much as possible. In any Korean public speech contest, we wouldn't find such enthusiasm (classroom teacher, School B).

> Nobody appreciates if students are good at Korean, but if they are good at English, everyone appreciates that (classroom teacher, School C).

CONCLUSION

The new elementary English program has had a powerful impact on the Korean educational system in that it is bringing about revolutionary change, not only in the teaching of English, but also in terms of pedagogy and teacher training, more broadly. The implementation of the program shows the importance of support by principals and head teachers, as well as the crucial role of teacher training. In schools with adequate support, and where teachers themselves believe that English instruction is important, the conditions for effective language instruction seem to exist. For some, however, this success comes at a heavy price, if the Korean language and Korean educational practices are compromised. It remains to be seen whether the new elementary English program can indeed achieve the hope, expressed by policymakers, that "early foreign language learning [will] promote students' appreciation of Korean culture and understanding of other cultures." If this hope is not realized, policymakers may have to surrender their ideal of peaceful coexistence of the English language and educational practices alongside their Korean counterparts.

ACKNOWLEDGMENT

"This research was supported in part by funding from the Social Sciences and Humanities Research Council of Canada, grant # 410-2000-1141. This support is gratefully acknowledged."

REFERENCES

Chun, C. G. (1995). *Chodeung Yeong-eo Gyoyuk-ui Munjejeom-gwa Gaeseon Bang-an* [The problems in primary English education and suggestions]. M. A. thesis. Seoul: Kyung Hee University.

Kim, H. M. (1997). *Chodeung Yeong-eo Gyoyuk-ui Chongchejeok Jeopgeun-e Gwanhan Yeongu* [A general study of the elementary English program]. Doctoral dissertation. Seoul: Yeonse University.

Ko, K. S. (1993). *Gukmin Hakgyo Yeong-eo Gyoyuk-ui Segyejeok Donghyang-gwa Geu Gwaje* [The trend of primary English education in the world and the issues]. *English Teaching, 46,* 165–187.

Lee, H. B. (and the Sogang Elementary Curriculum Development Committee). (1995). *Gukmin Hakgyo Yeong-eo Gyoyuk Gwajeong Si-an* (The draft of the elementary English currriculum). Seoul: Sogang University.

Lee, J. H. (1992). *Gukmin Hakgyo Yeong-eo Gyoyuk-ui Hyogwa* [The effect of primary English education]. *English Teaching, 44,* 3–21.

Ministry of Education (1993). *Jung · Godeung Hakgyo Yeong-eo Gyoyuk Bogoseo* [Educational reports on English education in middle school and high school]. Seoul: Ministry of Education of Korea.

Ministry of Education (1996). *Chodeung Hakgyo Yeong-eo Gyoyuk I-reok-ke I-rwo-jimnida* [This is the way of elementary English education, public report]. Seoul: Ministry of Education.

Ministry of Education (1997). *Chodeung Hakgyo Yeong-eo Gyoyuk Jeongchaek Jaryojip* [The English education policies in elementary schools]. Seoul: Ministry of Education.

Ministry of Education (1998a). *98 nyeondo Chondeung Yeong-eo Damdang Gyosa Gyeongbi Jiwon Gyehoek* [The plan for teacher training for elementary school]. Seoul: Ministry of Education, Department of Teacher Training and Education.

Ministry of Education (1998b). *Chondeung Yeong-eo Damdang Gyosa Hwakbo Bang-an* [The plan for recruiting elementary English teachers]. Seoul: Ministry of Education, Department of Education Policy.

Olshtain, E. (1989). The fact-finding phase in the policy-making process: The case of a language of wider communication. In C. Kennedy (Ed.). *Language planning and English language teaching* (pp. 45–57). Cambridge: Cambridge University Press.

Pennycook, A. (1994). *The cultural politics of English as an international language.* New York: Longman.

Phillipson, R. (1992). *Linguistic Imperialism.* Oxford: Oxford University Press.

The Chosunilbo. Hyeonjang-ui Sori [The voices from the field]. Oct 10, 1996.

Tollefson, J. W. (1989). The role of language planning in second language acquisition. In C. Kennedy (Ed.), *Language planning and English language teaching* (pp. 23–41). Cambridge: Cambridge University Press.

Tollefson, J. W. (1995). *Power and Inequality in language education.* New York: Cambridge University Press.

13

The English Language in African Education: Dependency and Decolonization

Alamin M. Mazrui
Ohio State University

One prominent trajectory in the British colonial discourse on language in African education was the dichotomy between universalism and relativism. Colonial pioneers like Bishop A. Mackay seemed certain that cultural development in Africa would be served best by languages of wider communication like English or Kiswahili (Mackay, 1908, p. 215). On the other hand, there were the influential educational views of Westermann, who argued that:

> Mental life has evolved in each people in an individual shape and proper mode of expression; in this sense we speak of the soul of a people and the most immediate, the most adequate exponent of the soul of a people is its language. By taking away a people's language, we cripple or destroy its soul and kill its mental individuality . . . Any educational work which does not take into consideration the inseparable unity between African language and African thinking is based on false principle and must lead to the alienation of the individual from his own self, his past, his traditions, and his people (quoted by Gorman, 1974, p. 449).

When it came to colonial educational policies, this debate became, quite often, an issue between church and state, and between the imperatives of mental training and spiritual conversion.

267

POSTCOLONIAL AFRICA: UNIVERSALISM VERSUS RELATIVISM

The educational concerns of this debate were later to spill over into the post-colonial period, with the added consideration of linguistic strategies for decolonization. According to one nationalist school of thought, there is maximum convergence between language and thought and, for Africans, only African languages can genuinely connect them to an African world view. In the words of Peter Mwaura:

> Language influences the way in which we perceive reality, evaluate it and conduct ourselves with respect to it. Speakers of different languages and cultures see the universe differently, evaluate it differently, and behave towards its reality differently. Language controls thought and action and speakers of different languages do not have the same world view or perceive the same reality unless they have the same culture or background (1980, p. 27).

As a result of these lingo-cultural differences, "they cannot be said to be African cultural representatives who write in another language because, in spirit at least, they speak from the perspective provided for them by the effective apparatus of mental control exercised by the former colonial power" (Kunene, 1992, p. 32). For these nationalists, therefore, effective decolonization in Africa, in the realm of knowledge and discourse, can only be attained through the recentering of African languages in the academy and other institutions of knowledge and cultural production.

On the opposite side of the scale have been Esk'ia Mphahlele (1963, p. 8), Chinua Achebe (1976, p. 67) and Nuruddin Farah (1992, pp. 45–48) who, given the "reality" of the African linguistic condition, see no alternative to the continued reliance on the English language. Equally concerned about the cultural and epistemological decolonization of Africa, they have argued that English can be transformed to carry the weight of the African experience and to play the role of a counter-hegemonic medium. Their sentiments are in line with the call by Pennycook to all applied linguists and English teachers around the world to "become political actors engaged in a critical pedagogical project to use English to oppose the dominant discourses of the West, and to help the articulation of counter-discourses in English" (1995, p. 55).

The two contesting positions draw directly, of course, from the relativism of Benjamin Lee Whorf and Edward Sapir, on the one hand, and the universalism of Noam Chomsky, on the other. According to Sapir:

> Human beings are very much at the mercy of a particular language which has become the medium of expression for their society... The fact of the matter is that the "real world" is to a large extent built on the language habits of the group. No two languages are ever sufficiently similar to be considered as representing the same social reality (1929, p. 208).

Whorf (1959), of course, was an even more enthusiastic proponent of linguistic relativism, with a persuasion that often bordered on determinism. Chomsky, on the other hand, views language as a genetically predetermined, organized property of the human mind and not an acquired ability that is obtained from outside the individual by means of social, psychological, or cultural conditioning (1968, pp. ix–x). Chomsky thus came to support one of the Enlightenment's most cherished ideals—universal human identity, providing, in his linguistic account, what amounts to a general theory of human beings as uniquely defined by their linguistic capacity. This linguistic attribute, in turn, endows all humans in equal measure with the capacity for rational thought and for "free, causally undetermined creative activity which is nevertheless intelligible to others because all human beings share innate propensities which, under suitable circumstances, induce the development in each individual of standards of intelligibility which are similar to those which develop in other human individuals" (D'Agostino, 1986, p. 207).

In the final analysis, however, it is the forces in favor of retaining and promoting English in African education which have triumphed. In virtually every former colony of the British, English has continued to serve as the medium of instruction and to enjoy tremendous support in terms of human and material resources. English is sometimes introduced in schools as early as kindergarten. Even Tanzania, which made major strides to phase out English from its educational system, is now showing signs of back-peddling and a reluctance to proceed any further with its Swahilization program. Behind this consolidation of English has been the additional assistance provided by the British Overseas Development Administration, the British Council and the United States Agency for International Development.

In spite of South Africa's new language policy, intended to demote both English and Afrikaans and give greater prominence to several African languages, English has also gained new ground in that country. As McLean and McCormick have indicated:

> The recent restructuring of state and society which has enfranchised African language speakers achieved the recognition of all major languages as official, thereby effectively demoting Afrikaans and English to an equal status with nine others. The evidence from various domains, however, is that this policy thrust towards multilingualism is often intended and perceived as a symbolic statement, and that for instrumental purposes English remains the dominant language in South Africa (1996, p. 329).

Before the 1990s, English was officially co-equal with Afrikaans, but sometimes received fewer resources from the government. By the end of apartheid, the struggle had begun for the redistribution of resources towards a new linguistic hierarchy.

It might be remembered that, under apartheid, South Africa adopted a quasi-Whorfian language policy designed to keep Africans "African" and European power unchallenged. This was part of the legacy of the so-called Bantu Education. As a 1967 UNESCO document argued:

> In South Africa . . . the policy of apartheid has had recourse to the choice of the mother tongue as the main medium of instruction at the primary level (beyond which, it has shown, the vast majority of African children do not pursue their studies) in order to reinforce the linguistic, social and cultural isolation of the African population within the country as well as from the world at large (UNESCO, 1967, p. 67).

Justifying this policy as an exercise in *separate but equal* development, Afrikaners attempted to preempt the cultural westernization of Africans by restricting them to "African tongues," with English being accorded a subsidiary role in education. Afrikaans was introduced only at a later stage in education. However, partly in response to the racist and coercive manner in which "Bantu Education" was administered, Africans rebelled during the 1976 Soweto protest against Afrikaans and in favor, not of an indigenous African language, but of English, the language that was more widely used in the rest of Africa. English became not just the language of oppression but also, by a strange twist of destiny, the language of liberation, with enhanced status among Africans.

In post-apartheid South Africa, English has acquired additional value as the language of educational desegregation at the tertiary level. Institutions that had hitherto used Afrikaans as the language of instruction have tended to exclude a large majority of potential Black students whose additional language is English rather than Afrikaans. Some of these institutions are now experimenting with a bilingual instructional program, having added English to Afrikaans, with the resultant effect of widening their pool of potential Black students. Predominantly white and Afrikaner universities, then, are becoming increasingly integrated partly through the instrumentality of the English language.

But it is not only in British ex-colonies that English is conquering new frontiers. It has begun to penetrate regions of Africa that were once known to be the exclusive preserve of French and Portuguese. Educational institutions in Francophone countries, such as Zaire and Senegal, and Lusophone[1] countries from Mozambique to Angola are increasingly viewing the English language as a serious subject of study. While it is unlikely that English will phase out French and Portuguese altogether in the foreseeable future, it

---

[1]The terms "Francophone," "Lusophone," and "Anglophone" are employed here not to describe the proportion of people in those countries who speak these languages, but the degree and perhaps nature of the lingo-cultural dependence in the societies concerned.

may in time succeed in establishing itself as a co-equal of its sister European languages in a stable bilingual instructional program in many African universities.

ENGLISH PROFICIENCY AND AFRICAN EDUCATION

In spite of this extensive spread of English to the earliest levels of education and the tremendous resources invested in its promotion, there have been numerous claims of "falling standards" of English in educational institutions as well as in the society at large. Mukiibi notes that in Uganda there has been "an outcry from different corners, the media for one, and even from the Uganda National Examination Board (UNEB), at the gradually falling standards of English generally" (1991, p. 40). Mukiibi attributes this trend to the growing number of students in individual classrooms, lack of teaching materials, and supposedly insufficient time allocated to English in school timetables. In addition to being the only medium of instruction, then, it is now deemed necessary to accord English more time as a subject.

In Kenya, the fear of falling standards of English has been a recurrent issue in government reports and the media. A 1993 report of the Kenya National Examination Council, for example, notes that "the standard of English has been falling while that of Kiswahili has shown improvement since it was made a compulsory subject in the 8-4-4 system of education." The report goes on to state that students cannot follow basic instructions in English and end up giving irrelevant answers in examinations (*Daily Nation*, 14 August 1993).

But perhaps the most alarming statement on the falling standards of English in Kenya came from Professor J. Kiptoon, the vice-chancellor of Egerton University. Kiptoon claimed that many undergraduate students in Kenya's public universities are functionally illiterate in the language and could not even write a simple application for a job in English. Kiptoon went on to report that "a good number of employers have complained that many graduates cannot communicate effectively in English which is the official medium of instruction right from the primary to university level" (*Daily Nation*, 5 June 1993). Kiptoon's "revelation" triggered a long newspaper debate about the possible causes of this supposed decline in the standards of the English language.

A recurrent theme in this ongoing debate is that the decreasing quality of English as an instructional medium is leading to poor performance in other subjects. The impression is thus created that the whole of education in Kenya is virtually in a state of crisis, and that the only possible way to save the situation is to invest immensely more resources in raising students'

English proficiency. The Primary Education Strengthening Project and Secondary English Language Project, both sponsored by the British government, have in fact been launched partly to redress this academic problem (*Daily Nation*, 5 June 1993). Moreover, these concerns in Kenya and Uganda are shared by most other former British colonies in Africa.

Particularly noteworthy in this entire debate is the total absence of voices suggesting, even mildly, that perhaps the policy of English medium instruction from the earliest years of an African child's education deserves another look altogether. The question that preoccupied the British colonial administrators and missionaries—which language was most suited to learning in early childhood education—has virtually disappeared from current African debates on English as a medium of instruction and its implications for the acquisition of knowledge in other subjects in general. The situation affirms once again the triumph of the "English only" ideology and policy in education in many British ex-colonies in Africa.

But what have been the implications of this pro-English educational policy for Africa in relation to global configurations of power? And what alternative strategies are available to the continent to address some of these implications in the new millennium?

THE QUESTION OF DEPENDENCY

The triumph of English and the marginalization of African languages notwithstanding, the sociopolitical evidence from Africa's own historical experience does not unambiguously support the positions of either the universalists or the relativists. If English can be transmuted into a medium of counter-discourse, that potential is seriously constrained by the global imbalances in power relations, with America and the West having a controlling influence on both the medium and instruments of communication. Nor does the position address the problem of access to the knowledge imparted in English by the majority who have no proficiency in the language. As Ngugi wa Thiong'o puts it: "The peasant and the worker in Africa have done all they could to send their sons and daughters to schools and universities at home and abroad in order to scout for knowledge and skills which could relieve the community of these burdens but, lo and behold, each of them comes back speaking in tongues" (1998, p. 78).

The relativist position is perhaps equally problematic in its line of argumentation. There is really nothing inherent in African languages that prevents them from serving hegemonic agendas—as the experience of Bantu education in apartheid South Africa, for example, clearly demonstrates. In every language, in fact, we have the particular and the universal existing side by side, and every language is a potential instrument of both hegemony and counter-hegemony.

In spite of these limitations in the arguments of the relativist school, there are clear signs that the continued predominance of English in the African academy—culminating, in particular, with the African university—has deepened Africa's epistemological and intellectual dependency on the West. Modern science and technology are part of the Western package of "modernity."[2] But that package has also come to Africa with many cultural strings that seek to reproduce Africa in the image of the West. Such excessive dependency is, by definition, a denial of innovation. In this connection, it is worthwhile to contrast Africa with the Japanese experience.

Japan's original attempts at capacity-building involved considerable selectivity on the part of the Japanese themselves. A key aim of selective Japanese westernization was to protect Japan against the West, rather than merely to submit to western cultural attractions. The emphasis in Japanese education was, therefore, on the technical and technological techniques of the West, rather than on literary and verbal culture. The Japanese slogan of "western technique, Japanese spirit" at the time captured this ambition to borrow technology from the West while deliberately protecting a substantial part of Japanese culture. In a sense, Japan's westernization was designed to reduce the danger of other forms of dependency.

The nature of westernization in Africa has been very different. Far from emphasizing western productive technology and containing western lifestyles and verbal culture, Africa has reversed the Japanese order of emphasis. Among the factors which have facilitated this reversal has been the role of the African academy.

One primary function of culture is to provide a universe of perception and cognition—a societal paradigm or world view. Thomas Kuhn's work on the structure of scientific revolutions has provided insights about the process through which scientific paradigms shift, and new alternative systems of explaining phenomena that come to dominate scientific thought. But what about shifts in cultural paradigms? And how are these related to shifts in scientific ones?

Religion is often a cultural paradigm in its own right. Copernicus and Galileo between them, by helping to transform scientific thought on planetary movements, in time also helped to change the Christian paradigm of the universe. Charles Darwin, by helping to initiate a revolution in the biological sciences, also started the process of transforming the Christian

---

[2]The arguments in the rest of this section and in the following section are based on Mazrui and Mazrui (1999, pp. 177–188).

concept of creation. These are cases in which paradigmatic changes in the sciences have led to paradigmatic changes in religion.

Historically there have also been cases where religious revolutions have resulted in scientific shifts. The rise of Islam gave the Arabs for a while scientific leadership in the northern hemisphere. Puritanism and non-conformity in Britain in the 18th century were part of the background of both a scientific and an industrial revolution in that country.

But paradigmatic changes are caused not merely by great minds like those of Copernicus, Newton, Darwin, and Einstein, nor only by great social movements like Islam and the Protestant revolution, but also by acculturation and normative diffusion. It is in this sense that colonialism constituted a major shift in the cultural paradigm of one African society after another. Traditional ideas about how rain is caused, how crops are grown, how diseases are cured, and how babies are conceived have had to be reexamined in the face of a new epistemological culture of the West.

If the African academy had borrowed a leaf from the Japanese book, and initially concentrated on what is indisputably the West's real area of leadership and marginal advantage—science and technology—the resultant African dependency might have been of a different kind. But the initial problem lay precisely in the model of the academy itself, especially of the university, with its distrust of direct problem solving in the wider society. As Pyle explains with regard to what he calls Less Developed Countries (LDCs):

> There is much in our education system [in Britain] which makes it easier to define problems in terms of narrowly scientific objectives. The existing relationship between universities (with the unidirectional flow of "experts" and advisors, the flow of overseas students to this country, etc.) have tended to transfer the same standards and expectations to the LDCs ... Technologies for the satisfaction of basic needs and for rural development have received little attention... Curricula, textbooks, and teaching methods are too closely imitative of practice in industrialized countries. This has spilled over from teaching to research expectations. Universities have aimed to achieve international standards in defining the criteria for staff recognition and promotion: in practice this means using the international scientific and engineering literature as the touchstone (1978, pp. 2–3).

The one paradigmatic change which was necessary for the imported universities did not in fact occur. The missing factor was a change in the very conception of the academy itself and its purposes.

But the lack of change in the conception of the transplanted academy caused changes in the attitudes, values, and worldview of its products. Since the modern academy was so uncompromisingly foreign in the African context and the university was transplanted with few concessions to African cultures, its impact was more culturally alienating than it need have been. A whole generation of African graduates grew up despising their own ancestry and scrambling to imitate others.

Those African graduates who later became university teachers themselves have, on the whole, remained intellectual imitators and disciples of the West. African historians have indeed begun to innovate methodologically as they have attempted to grapple with the oral tradition and its implications for historical research. But most other disciplines are still condemned to paradigmatic dependency.

An important source of this intellectual dependency is the language in which African graduates and scholars are taught. For the time being, it is impossible for an African student or graduate to be even remotely familiar with the works of Marx or Ricardo without the help of a European language. *Das Kapital* is not yet available in major African lingua francas like Swahili and Hausa, let alone in smaller (in terms of number of speakers) and more ethnically confined languages such as Kidigo and Lutooro. In short, major intellectual paradigms of the West that abound in African university curricula are likely to remain unavailable in a single African language unless there is a genuine educational revolution involving widespread adoption of African languages as media of instruction.

As matters now stand, an African who has a good command of English has probably assimilated other aspects of western culture as well, because the process of acquiring the English language in Africa has tended to be overwhelmingly through a formal system of western style education. Thus the concept of an African Marxist who is not also westernized is at present time a sociolinguistic impossibility.

Similar statements need not apply to a Chinese or Japanese Marxist, where it is possible to undergo an ideological conversion at a sophisticated level without the explicit mediation of a foreign language. Japan especially has tamed its language to cope with a wide range of intellectual discourse. Of course, the Japanese range goes beyond ideological and political literature. But today, in Black Africa, a university trained surgeon who does not speak a European language is virtually a sociolinguistic impossibility. So are a modern physicist, a zoologist, and an economist.

Nor is it simply a case of a surgeon, or a physicist, or an economist acquiring an additional skill called a "European language" which (s)he is capable of discarding when (s)he discusses surgery or physics or economics with fellow professionals. Professional Japanese scientists or social scientists can organize a conference or convention and discuss professional matters almost entirely in Japanese. But a conference of African scientists devoted to scientific matters in an African language is not yet possible.

What is even more astonishing perhaps is that so many African intellectuals and scholars continue to regard their lack of knowledge in African
languages as perfectly justifiable. The situation at the beginning of the new
millennium continues to lend credibility to the claim by Mazrui and Tidy:
"Recommendations about paying more attention to African languages, systematically building up their vocabularies for certain new areas of national
life, and integrating them more fully into the educational system, have
often encountered either silent skepticism among black intellectuals and
scholars or outright derision" (1984, p. 314). Thus intellectual and scientific
dependency in Africa is virtually inseparable from linguistic dependency.
The choice of English as a medium of instruction in Anglophone African
academies has had profound cultural consequences for the societies which
are served by those educational institutions.

TOWARDS DECOLONIZATION

How, then, can Africa achieve that elusive goal of educational and intellectual capacity building without the chains of dependency? Ali A. Mazrui
(1995) has proposed that the process of decolonization in Africa must involve at least five processes: indigenization, domestication, diversification,
horizontal inter-penetration and vertical counter-penetration. Indigenization involves increasing the use of indigenous resources, ranging from
native personnel to aspects of traditional local technology. Domestication,
on the other hand, relates to western institutions existing in Africa. It is the
process by which such institutions are in part Africanized or traditional-
ized in local terms. Domestication involves making imported versions of
modernity more relevant to local needs, conditions, and society at large.
   The third strategy, diversification, means, at the broader level of society, diversifying the ways of perception, sources of expertise, techniques
of analysis, types of goods produced, markets for these products, general
trading partners, and aid-donors and other benefactors. The principle here
is to help an African country diversify those upon whom it is dependent,
with the understanding that excessive reliance on only one alien culture is
more dangerous for a weak state than reliance on half a dozen other cultures. Reliance on only the West is more risky than diversified dependency
on both East and West.
   The fourth strategy of decolonization is horizontal inter-penetration
among African countries themselves. In the field of technical assistance,
for example, it means that African countries with an apparent excess of
skilled human power in relation to their absorption capacity should not
only be prepared, but also encouraged to facilitate temporary or permanent

migration to other African countries. This process may be likened to a horizontal brain-drain—the transfer of skills from say, Egypt to the Sudan, or from Nigeria to Zambia.

Finally, there is the strategy of vertical counter-penetration. A case in point is, again, the brain-drain. On the whole African countries cannot afford to lose their skilled human resources. But, according to Ali Mazrui, it would be a mistake to assume that the northward brain drain is totally to the disadvantage of Africa. Intellectual penetration of Africa by the northern industrial states must one day be balanced with reverse intellectual penetration by Africa. Given the realities of an increasingly interdependent world, decolonization will never be complete unless penetration is reciprocal and more balanced.

Three of the strategies outlined above—namely, indigenization, domestication and diversification—have some direct relevance to our concern with the interplay between language and education in Africa. The promotion of Swahili as against English in Tanzania is a case of indigenization. By making the language a medium of instruction in its schools, Tanzania has been able to reduce its dependency on U.S. Peace Corps teachers relative to African countries that continue to rely on English in their educational institutions. More African countries need to experiment with their indigenous linguistic pool as part of a more general agenda to make the educational system more sensitive to local needs. The process of indigenization could also involve exposing African students to other indigenous forms of knowledge which continue to be articulated primarily in African languages.

Domestication will involve the transformation of English, as an alien medium, to make it respond to local imagery, figures of speech, sound patterns and the general cultural milieu of the region. It will also mean creating counter-hegemonic discourses with this same imperial language. English in Africa, then, needs to be Africanized in this broad sense that encompasses inscription of new meanings, while African languages need to be elaborated to make them more compatible with the present state of knowledge.

Clearly the two strategies of domestication and indigenization are closely related and sometimes impossible to disentangle, particularly when we apply these strategies of decolonization to educational institutions. The Western school in Africa is, of course, more linked with the English language than say, Swahili. The school is a piece of alien culture. Can it be domesticated?

The domestication of the school would first require increased indigenization of personnel. This would in turn require, first, greater commitment by African governments to promote relevant training at different levels for Africans; second, readiness on the part of both governments and employers to create a structure of incentives that would attract Africans of the right caliber; third, greater political pressure on education officials and school principals to develop Africa-related curricula; fourth, stricter domestication of the foreign component in the syllabus to make it more relevant to the local context; and fifth, a gradual introduction of African languages as media of instruction, moving upward slowly from lower to higher grades. All this will require a gradualist and planned approach.

With regard to diversification, African languages must be made to respond to the stimulus of a wider range of civilizations than merely to the West. Christian missionaries long ago translated the four gospels into African languages. Some of Shakespeare's plays also exist in Hausa, Swahili, and Zulu. Translations into Swahili have been completed for some of the works of Marx, Lenin, and Frantz Fanon. But when will the Indian poet Tagore or the Chinese philosopher Confucius be available in an African language? The *Qur'an* is available in Swahili and Hausa and so are the "Arabian Nights." But what about more recent classics of the cultures of Islam?

In short, a language cannot be developed merely by appointing a special commission with the task of coining new words. A language has to develop through facing new challenges and confronting new ideas that need to be expressed. The academy is a natural environment for such a challenge. If Swahili, for example, now abandons Arabic and borrows only from English, it may indeed become more "modernized," but also excessively westernized. And if it limits itself to European and Arab influences, it would deny itself the potential enrichment that can only come from more diverse stimulation.

Though less directly relevant, translation between different languages could also serve the objectives of both horizontal inter-penetration and vertical counter-penetration. Literature courses in East Africa, for example, currently may include the works of West African writers, but so far only those written in English. East African students are exposed to Chinua Achebe and Ama Ata Aidoo, but not writers and verbal artists in indigenous West African languages. Likewise, a course on African literature in Nigeria may include Ngugi wa Thiong'o, but is unlikely to include writers in Swahili like Muyaka or Kezilahabi. Governments and societies in Africa need to share with each other their cultural riches in local languages.

Likewise, more and more masterpieces in African languages need to be made available in translation in dominant world languages and taught in the academies of the West. This exercise can be part of the process of adding an African component to global civilization. The heritage of African languages has the potential for affecting the texture of world culture itself as Africa increases its contribution to the total heritage of humanity.

CONCLUSION: HOPE BORN OUT OF DESPAIR?

The implementation of these strategies of decolonization requires, of course, that the appropriate conditions are present to enhance the political climate for the recentering of African languages in African institutions. Is there evidence that such conditions are developing in Africa? In fact, there are two seemingly contradictory trends related to the structural adjustment prescriptions (SAPs) for Africa imposed by the International Monetary Fund (IMF) and the World Bank.

One of the standard demands of the IMF and the World Bank throughout Africa in the post-Cold War period has been the reduction of government subsidies in virtually every sphere of society, from health to education. Yet given the serious dearth of materials in local African languages, precipitated in part by colonial and in part by post-colonial policies, significant financial support from the government is indispensable in the promotion of local languages in African education. Do SAPs, therefore, pose the danger of reducing even further the potential support that African languages could receive from their governments?

SAPs in Africa may also be contributing to the consolidation of English in a demographic sense. SAPs are based on the assumption that state subsidies to African universities have been too high and parental responsibility for financing the education of their children too low. Both Western donors and international financial institutions have been less willing to subsidize African higher education with foreign aid. The World Bank has argued that the majority of African students can afford to pay for university education. Subsidies to public universities, in particular, are considered not only inefficient educational investment but also regressive social spending, because students enrolled in universities are alleged to be disproportionately from the upper end of the scale of income distribution (World Bank, 1994, p. 3).

Yet even World Bank data show unequivocally that the majority of students in African universities (an average of about 60%) come from the ranks of the peasantry, the working class, and petty traders who cannot be expected to meet the rising cost of university education. The natural outcome of reduced subsidies, therefore, is an increase in dropout rates among students from poorer family backgrounds. In Kenya's Moi and Egerton Universities, for example, with their combined population of about 6,000 students, over 2,000 were removed from registration rolls in early May 1996, over non-payment of tuition fees (*Daily Nation*, 4 May 1996, p. 18).

These tuition defaulters are more likely to have come from lower-class than upper-class families. One of the net effects of SAPs in education, therefore, may be to transform the African university into a "white-collar" institution in terms of the parental background of its student population.

The irony, in fact, is that enrollments are dropping in Kenya precisely at a time when demand for education is increasing. More than 200,000 of the children qualified for enrollment in high school in 1997 could not gain admission because schools were already filled to capacity. In 1995–1996, 75–80% of the students eligible for post-secondary education failed to gain places. The increase in university fees as recommended under SAP agreements provoked a direct decline in enrollments; and partly for reasons of the cost-sharing scheme, less than half of those who enrolled in elementary schools in the 1990s actually completed their course of study.

This shift in African universities may have important linguistic consequences. English in Africa has its strongest demographic base among children of white collar families. In some African cities, the English language is fast becoming the medium with which upper- and middle-class children feel most comfortable in virtually all conversational situations and domains. The exclusionary effect that SAPs seem to be having on the children of the poor, making university education accessible disproportionately only to the children of well-to-do parents, may give further impetus to the consolidation of English in education and, concomitantly, to the greater marginalization of African languages.

But, as indicated earlier, the university in Africa has been the ultimate instrument of cultural westernization. If SAPs are demoting tertiary education as a priority for the state, in the process making universities more elitist, are they also, inadvertently, arresting the pace of westernization in the society at large? Will western disengagement from African higher education also inadvertently help the task of de-westernizing African universities? If so, this should surely be counted among the gains. For too long, the human products of the African university were intended to be approximations of graduates of western institutions. In sub-Saharan Africa, the medium of instruction has remained the preserve almost entirely of European languages. Indeed, in only a minority of sub-Saharan universities are African languages taught at all.

If SAPs are demoting the African university, are they not *ipso facto* demoting the highest instrument of westernization in Africa? The bad news from SAPs is a possible shrinkage of the pool of educated human power and the aggravation of elitism in higher education. The good news may be the slowing of the processes of westernization and of de-Africanization in African societies. As the West continues to abandon Africa for Eastern

Europe, the continent may have no option but to find alternative strategies of development that are less dependent on the West.

REFERENCES

Achebe, C. (1976). *Morning yet on creation day. Garden City, NY: Anchor.*
Chomsky, N. (1968). *Language and mind.* New York: Harcourt.
D'Agostino, F. (1986). *Chomsky's system of ideas.* Oxford: Clarendon Press.
Farah, N. (1992). Nuruddin Farah. In F. Jussawalla & R. W. Dasenbrock (Eds.), *Interviews with writers of the post-colonial world* (pp. 43–62). Jackson: University of Mississipi.
Gorman, T. P. (1974). The development of language policy in Kenya with particular reference to the educational system. In W. H. Whiteley (Ed.), *Language in Kenya* (pp. 397–454). Nairobi, Kenya: Oxford University Press.
Kunene, M. (1992). Problems in African literature. *Research in African literatures, 23*(1), 27–44.
Mackay, A. (1908). *Eighteen years in Uganda and East Africa.* Volume 2. London: E. Arnold.
Mazrui, A. A. (1995). The "other" as the "self" under cultural dependency. In G. Brinker-Gabler (Ed.), *Encountering the other(s): studies in literature, history and culture* (pp. 333–362). Albany, NY: State University of New York.
Mazrui, A. A. & Mazrui, A. M. (1999). *Political culture of language: Swahili, society and the state* (2nd Edition). Binghamton: Institute of Global Cultural Studies, Binghamton University.
Mazrui, A. A. & Tidy, M. (1984). *Nationalism and new states in Africa.* Nairobi: Heinemann.
McLean, D. & McCormick, K. English in South Africa: 1940–1996. In J. A. Fishman, A. D. Conrad & A. Rubal-Lopez, *Post-imperial English: Status change in former British and American colonies, 1940–1990* (pp. 307–337). Berlin: Mouton de Gruyter.
Mphahlele, E. (1963). Polemics: the dead end of African literature. *Transition, 3* (11), 7–9.
Mukiibi, C. N. (1991). Is there a need for a communication skills course at Makerere University? *Proceedings of the conference on academic communication skills in African universities* (pp. 40–45). Nairobi: The British Council.
Mwaura, P. (1980). *Communication policies in Kenya.* Paris: UNESCO.
Ngugi wa Thiong'o. (1998). *Penpoints, gunpoints and dreams: Towards a critical theory of the arts and the state in Africa.* Oxford: Clarendon Press.
Pennycook, A. (1995). English in the world/the world in English. In J. W. Tollefson (Ed.), *Power and inequality in language education* (pp. 34–58). Cambridge: Cambridge University Press.
Pyle, L. (1978). Engineering in the universities and development. Paper presented at the conference on "The Future Relationships Between Universities in Britain and Developing Countries," held at the Institute of Developmental Studies, University of Sussex, England, March 17–20, 1978.
Sapir, E. (1929). The status of linguistics as a science. *Language, 5,* 207–214.
UNESCO. (1967). *Apartheid.* Paris: UNESCO.
Whorf, B. L. (1959). *Language, mind and reality: Selected writings of Benjamin Lee Whorf.* J. B. Carrol (Ed). Cambridge: MIT Press.
World Bank. (1994). *Higher education: the lessons of experience.* Washington, DC: World Bank.

VI

Critical Pedagogy and Social Change

This section explores the following critical issue: How can indigenous peoples and other language minorities develop educational policies and programs that serve their social and linguistic needs, in the face of significant pressures exerted by more powerful social and ethnolinguistic groups? The final chapter in the previous section, by Alamin M. Mazrui, proposed five strategies to "recenter" African languages in African higher education. Two chapters in this section examine programs in the United States and Solomon Islands that "recenter" indigenous languages and cultures in schools serving indigenous peoples. In Chapter 14, Teresa L. McCarty examines successful programs in the U.S. Southwest and Hawaii. She places these programs within a theoretical framework for indigenous educational language policy that includes historical and structural constraints as well as micro- and macro-level possibilities for status, corpus, and acquisition planning. Her framework emphasizes the rich possibilities for indigenous language education, including development of new pedagogies and teaching styles; elaboration and modernization of indigenous languages; creation of new literacies; identity formation; and development of new networks of language activists. Yet these possibilities are always actualized within historical and structural constraints, including federal and state language policies favoring English; ongoing language attrition; inadequate funding; and conflicts about authenticity and representation within indigenous communities.

In Chapter 15, David Welchman Gegeo and Karen Ann Watson-Gegeo report on similarly successful educational programs in the Solomon Islands. Like those described by McCarty, the Solomon Islands programs are characterized by local control and the valorization of indigenous knowledge and practices. Gegeo and Watson-Gegeo's descriptions of dehegemonic and counter-hegemonic teaching practices closely reflect some of the decolonization strategies described by Mazrui, particularly indigenization, domestication, and diversification. Taken together, the chapters by Mazrui, McCarty, and Gegeo/Watson-Gegeo present a powerful framework for rethinking indigenous and minority language education policy and practice. As these chapters demonstrate, and as McCarty eloquently argues, despite the constraints facing minority language communities, "the language choices children and their families make need not be either-or ones; 'indigenous' and 'modern' need not be oppositional terms. School . . . *can* be constructed as a place where children are free to be indigenous in the indigenous language—in all of its multiple and ever-changing meanings and forms."

In Chapter 16, James W. Tollefson offers an integrative summary of seven key themes of this book: the importance of school-community relations for successful language policies in educational contexts; the value of outside resources for language maintenance, revitalization, and reclamation programs; the variable relationship between language and sociopolitical conflict; the value of language rights in reducing the potential for language conflict; the role of language policy in governance; the impact of global processes upon language policies in education; and the importance of local concerns for implementing successful language programs. Finally, the chapter explores the central importance of educational language policies in solving the problems of multilingual and multiethnic states. Looking broadly at the growing tension in many contexts between state mandated centralist policies and demands for language rights by multilingual and multiethnic populations, the chapter argues that efforts to extend pluralist language policies are an important component in democratic systems of governance.

14

Between Possibility and Constraint: Indigenous Language Education, Planning, and Policy in the United States

Teresa L. McCarty
The University of Arizona

> In the difference of language to-day lies two-thirds of our trouble ... The object of greatest solicitude should be to break down the prejudices of tribe among the Indians; to ... fuse them into one homogeneous mass. Uniformity of language will do this—nothing else will. (1868 Peace Commission Report, cited in Atkins, 1887/1992)

> If a child learns only English, you have lost your child. (Navajo elder in oral testimony, Rough Rock, Navajo Nation, Arizona, 1995)

These two statements, made more than a century apart, embody the struggle for indigenous self-determination in the United States. They also place language squarely within the heart of that struggle. By 1887, when Commissioner of Indian Affairs J.D.C. Atkins wrote the report in which the euphemistically named Peace Commission's pronouncement appeared, the U.S. government had turned from the military to the schools in its attempts to coerce the assimilation of indigenous peoples. "There is not an Indian pupil... who is permitted to study any other language than our own," Commissioner Atkins continued, calling English "the language of the greatest, most powerful, and enterprising nationalities beneath the sun" (1887/1992, p. 49).

English-only policies took their toll, as did the invasion of Native lands, containment on reservations, enslavement, and genocide. Language statistics are one index of the legacy of those policies. Of the 300 or more languages once spoken in what is now the United States, 175 remain. Of these, only 20 are still being passed on to the young (Krauss, 1996, 1998). Thus, nearly 90% of all indigenous languages in the United States are in danger of falling silent within the next 20 to 40 years. Moreover, it is by no means certain that even those languages with significant numbers of child speakers will survive the 21st century.

But statistics tend to sanitize and objectify the conditions they purport to represent. Languages do not exist as abstract, alienable products; they live and breathe within communities of users (Dauenhauer & Dauenhauer, 1998; Warner, 1999). The Navajo elder whose testimony introduces this chapter suggests the human costs of language loss: the concrete "destruction of intimacy, family, and community" by more powerful, homogenizing forces (Fishman, 1991, p. 4). This crisis has engulfed virtually all Native North American communities. It is a crisis of values, morality, and ways of knowing—of identity and whether children will, indeed, be "lost," disconnected from the words and worlds of their forebears.

Schools and education policies are heavily implicated in the crisis. Schools have been both sites of coercive assimilation, and, more recently, of indigenous resistance. In this chapter, I examine indigenous language planning and policies emanating within and around schools, drawing upon critical theories of language and education (see, e.g., Bourdieu, 1991; Fine, 1996; Forester, 1985; Freire, 1970, 1993, 1998; Levinson, Foley, & Holland, 1996; Pennycook, 1999; Tollefson, 1991), and upon 20 years of ethnographic and collaborative work with indigenous educators. The latter experiences have involved me in grass roots language planning and policy development at the local and national levels (see, e.g., McCarty & Watahomigie, 1999). Hence, this is not a disinterested or dispassionate account. It reflects my position as an invested outsider, and is guided by a commitment to social justice. I begin with some demographic and historical background.

THE SOCIAL-HISTORICAL CONTEXT OF INDIGENOUS SCHOOLING

At the dawn of the 21st century, over two million people identify as American Indian, Alaska Native, or Native Hawaiian. More specifically, individuals identify as members of one of approximately 550 indigenous nations. A substantial proportion of the indigenous population resides within reservation lands held in trust by the federal government for indigenous use (see Fig. 14.1). The Navajo Nation is geographically the largest, with a land base equivalent to the state of West Virginia or the country of Austria, and a population of over 225,000. The Cherokee Nation is the most populous, with approximately 370,000 members (U.S. Census Bureau, 1990).

Nearly a quarter of the indigenous population are school-age children who attend federal schools operated by the Bureau of Indian Affairs (BIA), tribal or community-controlled schools funded through grants and contracts with the federal government, public schools, private schools, and mission or parochial schools (National Center for Education Statistics, 1995). According to the U.S. Census Bureau, these children are more likely to live in poverty than any other group in the United States (Paisano, 1999). They also are heavily overrepresented in compensatory and special education programs, and they experience the highest school dropout rates in the country (Swisher & Tippeconnic, 1999; U.S. Department of Education, 1991)

All indigenous peoples in the United States share the experience of being colonized, and, concomitantly, of having certain collective rights embodied in federal law. From its first encounters with Native peoples, the U.S. Congress has recognized a special, government-to-government relationship with tribes, which entails broad federal trust obligations, including federal guarantees of education, health, and other social services. The federal-tribal trust relationship distinguishes indigenous peoples from other ethnic and linguistic minorities in the United States in a real and permanent way. It is at once the cornerstone and the crucible of indigenous self-determination.

For example, under government campaigns lasting well into the 20th century, Indian education was synonymous with forced assimilation. In her discussion of the "unnatural history of American Indian education," Lomawaima (1999) defines colonial education as "the reculturing and reeducation of American Indians by secular and religious institutions" (p. 3). Perhaps most telling of this is the title of the legislation by which the federal government empowered itself to transform indigenous lives. The 1819 Civilization Act gave the U.S. government primary authority for the formal education of indigenous children and youth. For decades, that authority was exercised in federal support for missionary activities aimed at converting indigenous souls. By the latter part of the 19th century, however, federal residential schools had become the battleground in the "great march for civilization" (Sherman, cited in Prucha, 1984, p. 179).

Stories abound of young children being kidnapped from their homes and taken on horseback by Indian agents to distant boarding schools, often

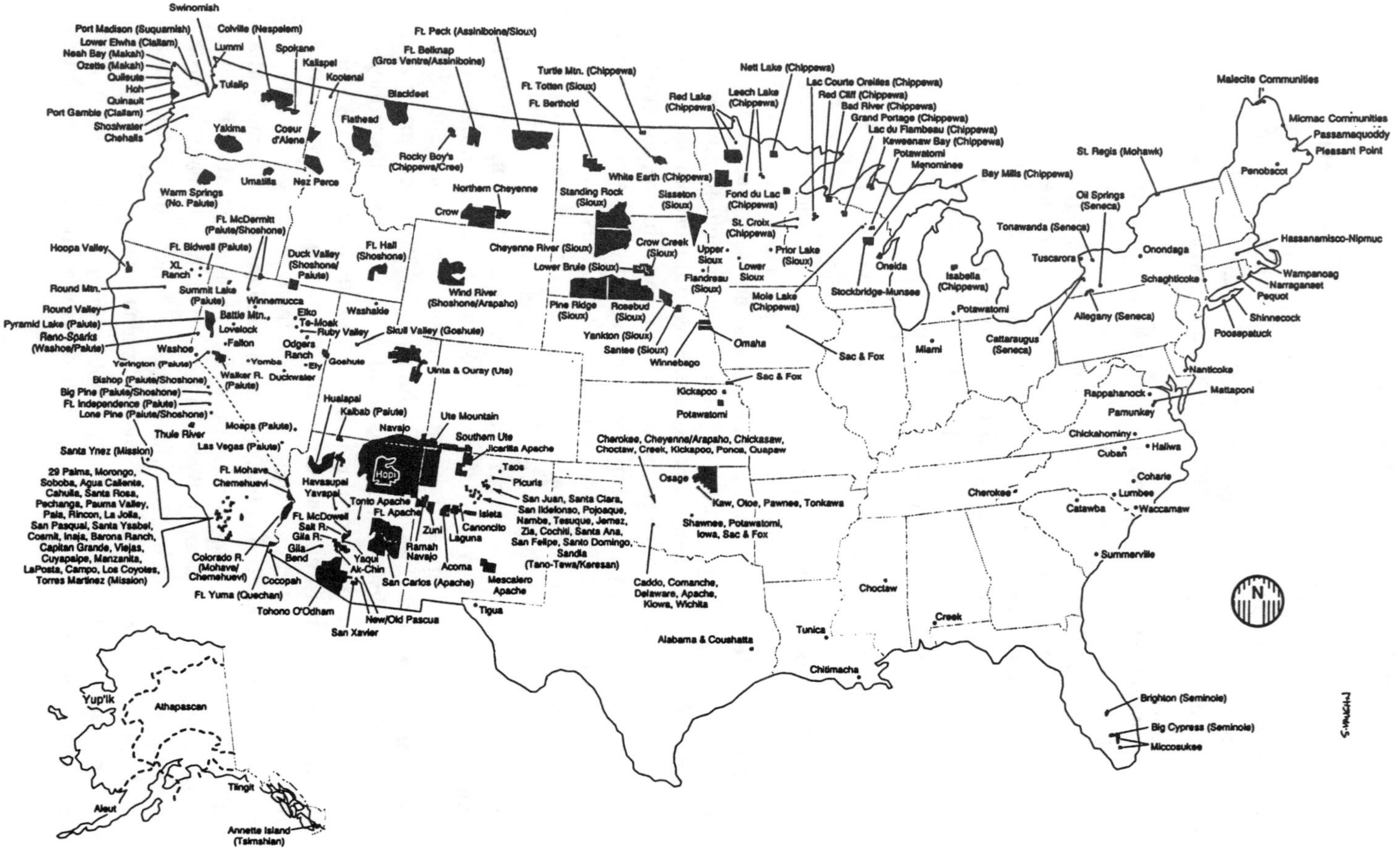

FIG. 14.1. American Indian and Native Alaskan lands in the contemporary United States.

converted military forts that had served as government staging areas against the tribes just a few years before. There, children faced militaristic discipline, forced manual labor, and physical and psychological abuse for "reverting" to the mother tongue (Medicine, 1982). This account by a Hualapai elder from Peach Springs, Arizona, is typical of the experience of many people:

> One thing that was hard for me when I was a young adult on the reservation, was to be thrown into the government boarding school, where I found that they were trying to knock out the Hualapai part of me. . . . A number of us have gone through that. We found when we spoke in our language, they used belts and hoses to really knock it out of us. But it stayed with us (Watahomigie & McCarty, 1996, p. 101).

For this elderly man and others of his generation, the Native language and identity "stayed with us." For others, especially younger adults, the boarding school experience and racist messages received from the dominant society induced shame and ambivalence about the Native language and culture. "What the boarding schools taught us," one Navajo teacher remarked to me, "was that our language was second best." The residue has been internalized ambivalence about the language, and often, the conscious socialization of children in English.

The legacy of the past also has generated resistance to linguistic oppression. In the context of the 1960s Civil Rights movement and indigenous activism manifested most visibly in protests by the American Indian Movement (see, e.g., Johnson, Champagne, & Nagel, 1999), some schools emerged as sites for furthering indigenous interests. Yet co-opting schools for indigenous purposes has been fraught with difficulty. Schools are contradictory resources. Even when they are under indigenous community control, they lead out of and away from the community they serve (Fishman, 1984; Levinson et al., 1996). The school's "real thrust, at any time," Joshua Fishman (1984) writes, "depends on the contextual circumstances surrounding and controlling it" (p. 55).

In the following sections, I present a portrait of those circumstances as they are manifested in three key cases: the Rough Rock Navajo and Peach Springs Hualapai Bilingual/Bicultural Education Programs in the U.S. Southwest, and the Hawaiian Immersion Schools. The data for these cases derive from my long-term ethnographic research at Rough Rock and Peach Springs, collaborative work with the cofounders of the Hawaiian Immersion Schools, and the written accounts of others. Each case represents a distinct set of sociohistorical experiences. Each shows the ways in which indigenous communities work to assert their linguistic and educational rights within contexts of constraint and possibility—what Lois Weis (1996) calls "that space *between* structure and agency" (p. xi; see also

McCarty, Watahomigie, & Yamamoto, 1999). Together, the cases illustrate the tensions and contradictions inherent in this struggle, even as they suggest the "seeds of transformation" (Tollefson, 1991, p. 32) through which positive change has occurred. I begin this discussion with the case of Rough Rock.

WHEN THE UNTHINKABLE BECAME "DOABLE"

On July 7, 1966, five leaders from the Diné (Navajo) community of Rough Rock, Arizona, met to chart the direction of the new local school they had been elected to govern. The five had been chosen to inaugurate a different kind of school, one to be controlled by Navajo people, which would position parents and community members at the center of their children's schooling.

Rough Rock at the time was one of the most economically impoverished areas in the United States (McCarty, 1989, in press). A community of approximately 1,500 located in the center of the Navajo Nation (see Fig. 1), Rough Rock families were still recovering from government policies implemented decades before which had forcibly reduced their livestock holdings and attenuated their rights to land. As one measure of the effects of these and other federal policies of containment, annual per capita cash income at Rough Rock in 1966 was an astonishing $85.00 (McCarty, in press).

The school entered this socioeconomic situation not as a autochthonous, grass roots development, but as part of the apparatus of a then beneficent state. An offshoot of federal War on Poverty programs, the demonstration school (as it was called), was underwritten by a contract between the local Navajo governing board, a tribal board of trustees, the Bureau of Indian Affairs, and the Office of Economic Opportunity. That contract provided the legal authority and financial means for the board to operate the school. (For more on the school's founding, see Johnson, 1968; McCarty, 1989, in press; Roessel, 1977.) This unique contract established Rough Rock as the first indigenous community-controlled school, and the first to teach in the Native language since the famed 19th century Cherokee and Choctaw schools (see, e.g., Noley, 1979; Tippeconnic, 1999). The privileging of Navajo in the school curriculum was intended not simply to aid children in learning English, but was constructed as a "terrain of knowledge and a field of possibilities for community action" (Rivera, 1999, p. 485; see also Roessel, 1977).

To understand Rough Rock's significance, readers are asked to suspend conventional notions of what "doing school" is about. Imagine, for example, a school whose goal was education in the broadest sense: cultivating the talents and resources of the community, fostering a sense of shared purpose and hope, *creating* a community around the school. "This is a community-oriented school, rather than child-oriented," the school's first director, Robert A. Roessel, Jr., told a reporter in 1967. "In the past Indian schools have taken little interest in their communities, but here we want to involve adults and teenagers, dropouts, and people who have never been to school" (Roessel, quoted in Conklin, 1967, p. 8). That involvement included school-sponsored economic and cultural development projects—a poultry farm, a student-run greenhouse, a toy and furniture factory, a Native arts and crafts program, and a program to train ritual specialists—and, most importantly, the employment of local people, many of whom had never held paying jobs. Reflecting on these school initiatives, a bilingual teacher at Rough Rock recalled: "A lot of these people who worked at the school really didn't have that formal education, but they had jobs. I think that broadened a lot of community interest in the school."

Now, imagine a school organized around principles of kinship and reciprocity. This was most evident in a dormitory parent program in which community members were hired as surrogate parents, providing moral support and counseling to resident students, and sharing their knowledge of oral traditions during evening storytelling sessions (McCarty, in press; Roessel, 1977). In this and other ways, the school functioned as an arm of the extended family, purchasing lamb starter milk for families hard-hit by drought, airlifting supplies to families stranded by a winter storm, and distributing stock and domestic water to community residents—in general, supporting community members and interceding in times of need.

Finally, imagine a school in the mid-20th century United States, in which virtually every communication need could be satisfied in Navajo. With the exception of ESL (English-as-a-second language) lessons and interactions with non-Navajo outsiders, this was the setting of the early Rough Rock Demonstration School. Bilingual/bicultural education was a natural extension of the community and the school's community development mission.

But what of materials for teaching the Native language? With over 100,000 speakers, Navajo has a written tradition dating back to the 19th century. When the Rough Rock Demonstration School was founded, extant Navajo language materials included a few dictionaries, primers developed by the BIA, and biblical tracts (Holm, 1996; Spolsky, 1972). None was very useful for Rough Rock teachers, prompting one to write that "the need for adequate instructional materials was constant" (Platero, 1968, p. 81). At the same time, the number of certified Navajo teachers could be counted on a few hands. In response to these needs, the school board sought and received federal funds to found the first Native American curriculum development center. Through a variety of federal programs, the board also supported community members in obtaining their teaching degrees.

These developments came about as a result of intense lobbying by school leaders and other indigenous educators for national educational reforms, and under the gaze of enormous public attention. Hundreds of visitors passed through Rough Rock classrooms and the board room each month, many of whom were, or would become powerful political allies of the school. Senator Edward (Ted) Kennedy delivered the first graduation address. His brother Robert, then Chairman of the Senate Select Subcommittee on Indian Education, also visited Rough Rock, as did his niece, President John F. Kennedy's daughter, Caroline. Rough Rock leaders testified frequently before Congress on Indian education matters. Following one set of hearings before his subcommittee, Robert Kennedy proclaimed that "Rough Rock has proven its point," and should serve as a model for a comprehensive "new national Indian policy" (U.S. Congress, 1969, p. 1055).

That policy came to fruition in two pieces of legislation that inaugurated a federal policy of tribal self-determination (Swisher & Tippeconnic, 1999; Szasz, 1974). In 1972, Congress passed the Indian Education Act, the first federal program to support the preparation of indigenous teachers and the development of Native language teaching materials. Three years later, the Indian Self-Determination and Educational Assistance Act was passed, formalizing the procedures through which tribes and indigenous communities could contract with the federal government for the operation of social and educational services. In conjunction with the 1968 Bilingual Education Act, this legislation laid the legal and financial framework for reconstituting indigenous schooling as bilingual/bicultural education.

From its inception, the school at Rough Rock has been controversial (see, e.g., a November 1970 issue of *School Review* entitled "Skirmish at Rough Rock;" McCarty, in press). It has suffered a host of set backs, including financial insolvency, chronic teacher turnover, and curricular instability, especially in the bilingual/bicultural program (McCarty, 1989). These circumstances are directly linked to the community's economic and political marginalization, and to institutional arrangements that make reservation schools dependent for their survival on fluctuating federal programs, policies, and funds. These issues and their implications are elaborated in the final sections of this chapter.

Despite these difficulties, the school at Rough Rock is widely recognized as opening a window of opportunity for indigenous self-determination. "Before Rough Rock," the director of the Navajo Nation's current Language Program states, "the notion that you have to have some form of community-responsive curriculum, or that you had to have some forms of empowerment in the community . . . it was just literally unthinkable" (Wayne Holm, interview, 1996). Within a decade of the demonstration school's founding, a dozen other indigenous schools had contracted with the Bureau of Indian Affairs to operate their own schools, and the majority of non-contract BIA schools had local advisory boards (Tippeconnic, 1999). Legislation enabling the creation of tribally controlled colleges had been passed, and the first such college had been established by Rough Rock's cofounders in the town of Many Farms, about 15 miles away. (There are now 31 tribal colleges in the United States and Canada.) Schools across the United States had Native language education programs (Bernard Spolsky counted 84 in 1974), and indigenous materials development and teacher preparation projects proliferated (Spolsky, 1974; McCarty, in press).

These developments "did not happen because of the goodwill of Congress or presidential administrations," John Tippeconnic III, the former director of the U.S. Office of Indian Education, notes (1999, p. 37). Rather, "it was because of the political wisdom and persistence of Indian educators, Indian institutions, Indian organizations, tribes, and other driving forces behind legislative and executive branch decisions" (Tippeconnic, 1999, p. 37). In the words of a prominent Navajo educator involved in these changes, a fundamental "paradigm shift" was under way: What had been unthinkable only a few years before had become "doable" (Pfeiffer, 1993).

In the light of these reforms, the seeds of transformation began to grow in many indigenous communities. I turn now to one remarkable example, the Hualapai Bilingual/Bicultural Program at Peach Springs School.

"WE SAW AN OPENING"

About 400 miles west of Rough Rock, on the edge of the Grand Canyon in northern Arizona, the town of Peach Springs straddles the main line of the Santa Fe Railroad and U.S. Highway 66. The tribal seat for the 1,800-member Hualapai Tribe, Peach Springs has a K-12 school, a small general store, a post office, two gas stations, and tribal government and U.S. Public Health Service offices. Clusters of homes built through the federal office of Housing and Urban Development line both sides of the railroad tracks. This is where the majority of the members of the Hualapai Tribe resides, although the reservation itself encompasses nearly a million acres of surrounding desert plateau and evergreen forest (see Fig. 14.1).

Hualapai is a Yuman language, related to the Hokan-Coahuiltecan language group whose speakers reside in what is now California, Arizona, the Baja Peninsula, and the Gulf of California in Mexico. Until a few decades ago, Hualapai lacked a practical writing system. Since that time, and under the auspices of a federally funded bilingual/bicultural education program, Hualapai educators have collaborated with academic linguists to develop an orthography, a grammar, and a corpus of children's literature, and they have made Hualapai the co-medium of instruction in the local public school.

In relating these developments, I am reminded of a question posed by Nancy Hornberger (1997) in her analysis of three telling language planning cases: "To what degree," she asks, "could such communities of support exist without the often heroic efforts of particular individuals?" (p. 100). In 1975, there was but one Hualapai certified teacher. Her name is Lucille Watahomigie. Returning to Peach Springs after completing her university degree, she began teaching at the local school. At the time, Watahomigie was told by the non-Indian principal that state law prohibited use of the Native language in public schools. Ninety percent of the fifth grade class at Peach Springs had been referred to special education because they spoke Hualapai as their primary language. Watahomigie (1998) recalls: "Finally, one brave little boy asked me in Hualapai, 'Like this, teacher?' I began teaching the students in Hualapai even though the principal had forbidden it" (p. 6).

Recruiting academic linguists to assist in the development of a writing system and its elaboration for classroom use, Watahomigie and other community members began the cultural and linguistic work to make Peach Springs a bilingual/bicultural school. In the summer of 1976, the bilingual program staff attended the Summer Institute of Linguistics for Native Americans (SILNA), a program founded by the Wycliffe Bible Translators. The current bilingual program coordinator reports: "We decided we were going to learn linguistics—we were going to be our own linguists" (Watahomigie & McCarty, 1996, p. 103). Co-opting knowledge gained from their time at SILNA, Hualapai educators worked with academic linguists to refine the orthography, develop a grammar, and, over several years, produce what would become a nationally recognized bilingual/bicultural curriculum.

The present curriculum includes a series of teaching units on Hualapai cultural-environmental studies, literacy, mathematics, and science, as well as dozens of attractively illustrated children's books in Hualapai. The bilingual program also includes an interactive technology component in which students undertake community-based research—studying the geology and petroglyphs of the Grand Canyon region, for instance—and act as videographers in documenting their findings. Students' bilingual video products, as well as their desk-top publications, are used as teaching resources for younger children at the school.

As at Rough Rock, none of these developments occurred in a linear, lock-step fashion, or within a social space free of conflict. Rather, the work at Peach Springs can be characterized as a long-term process of committed social action, carried out within a context of possibility and constraint. Initially, the Hualapai staff faced opposition from non-Indian teachers, who viewed the Hualapai materials as irrelevant, harmful to children's academic progress, and a threat to the "regular" curriculum (Watahomigie & McCarty, 1994, 1996). Children's positive responses to the Hualapai materials (and their improved academic achievement) gradually wore down those objections, as did the certification of more Hualapai teachers and thus the penetration of the school infrastructure by local people. But conflict also resided within the community, a situation that must be understood in terms of the power relations that have shaped it. "When I was in grade school," one community member recalled, "I was punished because I spoke my language." Her subsequent words speak volumes about the destructive and lingering effects of colonial education: "I turned against my language," she said (Watahomigie & McCarty, 1996, p. 106).

Helping community members "turn toward" their language required a public discourse Watahomigie (1995) describes as "reverse brainwashing." "We have had to re-educate our parents on the importance and priority of the values and knowledge embodied in our culture," she writes (1995, p. 191). In public meetings held to discuss the bilingual/bicultural program, the ongoing question community members struggled with was, "Why have the schools failed to educate our people?" (Watahomigie & McCarty, 1996, p. 105). In much the way that Freire (1970, 1993, 1998) describes, a dialogic process triggered by this question made clear the problem the bilingual/bicultural program and its participants faced: How could the school, historically an agent of Anglo-American oppression, become an instrument of community empowerment?

"Critical reflection is a social act of knowing undertaken in a public arena as a form of social and collective empowerment," McLaren and Tadeu da Silva state (1993, p. 55). At Peach Springs, critical reflection and public dialogue, as well as parents' observations of their children's academic growth with bilingual/bicultural schooling, gradually transformed community resistance into support. "We saw an opening," the present program coordinator stated in a 1993 interview. "The thing is perseverance... something Native people have been told they can't do" (Watahomigie & McCarty, 1996, p. 106).

This account would be incomplete without acknowledging one of the most far-reaching offshoots of the work at Peach Springs. In 1978, Lucille Watahomigie and a group of academic linguists organized the Yuman Language Institute, a university-accredited summer program that brought together a small group of parents, elders, educators, and linguists to develop indigenous writing systems and teaching materials. As the number of American Indian bilingual education programs grew, additional communities became involved, and the Yuman Language Institute evolved into the American Indian Language Development Institute (AILDI), now an international teacher preparation program housed at The University of Arizona.

Since its beginnings in 1978, the Institute has prepared over 1,000 parents and school-based educators to work as researchers, curriculum developers, bilingual teachers, and advocates for the cultivation of indigenous languages (McCarty, Watahomigie, Yamamoto, & Zepeda, 1997, in press). AILDI also has created a forum for language education policy development and activism. In 1988, AILDI faculty and participants drafted the resolution that became the Native American Languages Act (NALA). Passed by Congress in 1990 and authorized for funding in 1992, NALA is the only federal legislation that explicitly vows to protect and promote indigenous linguistic rights. Though funding for NALA has been meager, it has sponsored some of the boldest efforts in language revitalization to date (see Cantoni, 1996; Hinton, 1994; Reyhner, 1997).

The passage of NALA was helped by alliances between AILDI faculty members and other indigenous educators, who mustered the necessary Congressional support. Senator Daniel Inouye, Democrat of Hawai'i and then Vice-Chairman of the Senate Committee on Indian Affairs, introduced and helped steer the Native American Languages Act through Congress. Inouye's involvement was neither fortuitous nor surprising, as Watahomigie and her AILDI colleagues had been consulting with Hawaiian language educators for some time. Both the substance of NALA and its passage grew out of this collaborative work (Wilson, 1999). And so we now move from Peach Springs to the Hawaiian Immersion Programs, the final case to be considered here.

"A LONG AND DIFFICULT PROCESS"

Geographically the most isolated Aboriginally inhabited island chain in the world, Hawai'i developed free of external influence for "countless generations" (Wilson, 1998a, p. 126). Even after the invasion by Captain James Cook and his ships in 1778, the Hawaiian language, under an indigenous monarchy, remained the language of government, commerce, religion, the media, and education. Missionaries introduced an orthography, and, in 1834, the first Hawaiian newspaper was printed. According to William Wilson, cofounder of the contemporary Hawaiian Immersion Schools, by the late 19th century, over 100 Hawaiian newspapers were in print. In addition to conveying local and world news, these periodicals "served as vehicles for the discussion and preservation of Hawaiian traditions" (Wilson, 1998a, p. 127).

Cook's arrival also brought devastating disease and political and economic upheaval. From a population of 300,000 in 1778, Native Hawaiians were reduced to less than 50,000 just a century later (Warner, 1999; Wilson, 1998a). In 1893, the United States military, backing American business interests on the islands, overthrew the Hawaiian monarchy. Five years later, Hawai'i was annexed as a U.S. territory, and, in 1959, it became the 50th state (Warner, 1999; Wilson, 1998a, 1998b).

The years following the U.S. takeover saw the rapid decline of Hawaiian as a mother tongue. With the establishment of English-language schools, "pressure was placed on the general population... to adopt English as its daily language and teachers were sent into the community to coerce the adoption of English in the home" (Wilson, 1998a, p. 129). The effect was to disenfranchise schoolchildren from the language of their parents and elders, while promoting Hawaiian English Creole as the language of the young. "The ban on Hawaiian was extremely effective," Warner (1999) writes: "Hawaiian children educated after 1900 were the last generation to speak Hawaiian as a native language" (p. 71). The exception was a single, privately owned island, Ni'ihau, where Hawaiian continues to be transmitted as a mother tongue.

Against the backdrop of Civil Rights reforms, and in alliance with other Pacific Islanders (especially those in Aotearoa/New Zealand), a contemporary language revitalization movement took root. Known as the Hawaiian Renaissance, the movement began with university language classes, a weekly Hawaiian language talk show, a newsletter, student and teacher organizations, the promotion of Hawaiian street names, and Hawaiian-only camping trips to traditional areas. In 1978, during the first constitutional convention since statehood, Hawaiian was re-established as the state's co-official language. The new constitution also mandated that Hawaiian language, history, and culture be taught in public schools (Wilson, 1998b).

These developments, though important and promising, were unlikely to reverse the decline of Hawaiian as a mother tongue. "Those of us most involved in Hawaiian language study were sure that short lessons in colors, body parts and greetings... would not revitalize the language," Wilson (1998b, p. 331) states. "What we saw as essential was re-establishment of the public Hawaiian-medium schools" (1998b, p. 331).

With a group of like-minded parents, Wilson and his wife, language educator Kauanoe Kamanā, founded 'Aha Pūnana Leo (Nest of Voices), a total immersion preschool, in 1983. Supported by parentally paid tuition and parental labor, the program enabled children to interact entirely in Hawaiian with fluent speakers such as Ni'ihauans, elders from other communities, and university Hawaiian language graduates (Wilson, 1998b). As their children graduated from the preschools, parents and other language activists lobbied the state for Hawaiian-immersion primary schools. By the late 1980s, Hawaiian-medium instruction was extended to Grade 6, and later, through secondary school.

In the spring of 1999, the first two classes of students who participated in Hawaiian immersion from preschool to Grade 12 graduated from high school. Their testimony suggests the critical literacy developed in the course of their schooling. "I understand who I am as a Hawaiian, and where Hawaiians stood, and where they want to go," one graduate affirms (Infante, 1999, p. E3). According to Sam No'eau Warner (1999), "there are roughly 1,800 children who have learned to speak Hawaiian through Hawaiian immersion programs" (p. 74). The opportunity for an education in Hawaiian now extends from preschool to graduate school (Warner, 1999; Wilson, 1998a).

Like the indigenous language initiatives begun at Rough Rock and Peach Springs, Hawaiian language revitalization has faced strong opposition. Lobbying by parents and language educators eventually succeeded in overturning still extant 19th century legal barriers to public and private education in Hawaiian (Warner, 1999; Wilson, 1998a). Even as the demand for schooling in Hawaiian and the number of programs increased, the state legislature failed to appropriate additional funds. As a consequence, Warner (1999) notes, funds have been spread among more school sites and classrooms, making Hawaiian language education "more and more difficult with each passing year" (p. 75).

It would be inaccurate and misleading, however, to portray the Hawaiian language movement, or any other, as simply a struggle between indigenous interests and the state. The situation is much more complex, for competing opinions and ideologies exist within the movement as well. For example, Warner (1999) raises questions of representation or *kuleana* (Native rights, responsibility, and authority), involving non-indigenous language educators and academics, who, he says, attempt to speak for Hawaiians, diminishing the voices of Hawaiians themselves. "Efforts to establish, strengthen, and expand the [immersion] program have been . . . a long and difficult process," Warner (1999) states, and "can be viewed as another example of the struggle against colonial oppression" (p. 75).

In her discussion of "Authenticity and the Revitalization of Hawaiian," Wong (1999) complicates these issues. Competing ideologies also are reflected in binary sources of corpus planning authority: that held by university instructors who are second language speakers of Hawaiian and "more than casually influenced by English worldviews," and by the *kūpuna* or elders, who, according to Wong, "have not been immune to the effects of colonization" (1999, pp. 99–100). These competing interests are expressed in dualistic standards that defy an easy interpretation of "authenticity." On the one hand there is the need to modernize the language, identifying parallels to English and children's lived social worlds; on the other, there is the desire of elders to safeguard the "purity" of the language (Wong, 1999, p. 111). Authenticity, Wong argues, is socially constructed and constantly changing. As Hawaiian grows in the domains of its use and the numbers of its speakers, what counts as "authentic" Hawaiian must be renegotiated. "In the negotiation of what authentic Hawaiian is and will be," Wong claims, "it is necessary to involve input from Hawaiian communities, whether they speak Hawaiian or not" (1999, p. 112).

A CRITICAL FRAMEWORK FOR INDIGENOUS LANGUAGE EDUCATION, PLANNING, AND POLICY

The three cases presented here provide a glimpse into the range of indigenous language education, planning, and policy activities currently under way. Much previous research has cast these processes as ideologically neutral; that is, as apolitical, ahistorical, and focused on the individual rather than the group. Tollefson (1991) refers to this as the neo-classical approach, juxtaposing it to a critical, historical-structural approach that "seeks the origins of constraints on planning... and the social, political, and economic factors which constrain or impel changes in language structure and language use" (p. 31). A critical analysis suggests the ways in which historically structured power relations percolate throughout the social-educational system, influencing both the nature of language-related problems and the ways in which individuals and communities respond to those problems.

Table 14.1 outlines a framework for such a critical analysis. Building upon typologies developed by Cooper (1989), Haugen (1983), Hornberger (1994, 1996), and Ruiz (1984), the framework unites language planning and education under three rubrics: status planning, or how and where the indigenous language will be used, particularly with respect to schools; acquisition/cultivation planning, or who will use the language and for what purposes; and corpus planning, or the development of the language in written form for instructional purposes. Micro-pedagogical and macro-social possibilities are charted for each rubric, and shown as mediated by a number of historical-structural constraints. The overriding orientation is of "language as resource" (Ruiz, 1984); that is, my assumption is that

TABLE 14.1

Possibilities and Constraints in Indigenous Language Education, Planning, and Policy Development

Language Planning & Education Processes	Micro-Level Possibilities	HISTORICAL/ STRUCTURAL <—CONSTRAINTS—>	Macro-Level Possibilities
Status planning	Indigenous language as the language of the school, community, and indigenous nation	English imperialism Boarding school legacy Assimilative role of schools Political-economic marginalization Restrictive national policies Federal paternalism	Ideological clarification/commitment Public valorization for Native languages Schools as community centers Development of local leadership Employment/economic development Tribal and national policy development Local and tribal self-determination
Acquisition/ cultivation planning	Development of new pedagogies and teaching styles (e.g., immersion, critical literacy) Heritage language as a first or second language Enhanced educational achievement and cultural/linguistic pride	Language attrition Societal privileging of English Inadequate school/program funding	Language revitalization/maintenance Identity affirmation Preparation of indigenous teachers Development of professional classes/ heightening class consciousness National network of language educators and activists
Corpus planning	Codification Elaboration/modernization Curriculum planning and development	Conflicts surrounding authenticity and representation Pressures for educational "accountability" and standardization	Creation of new literacies and literatures Privileging indigenous voices/writers Strengthened bonds between speakers Affirmation of sovereignty and local education control

indigenous languages are sources of identity and self-determination for their speakers, and resources for society at large (see also Hornberger, 1996, p. 608).

It should be noted that the processes outlined in Table 14.1 are not discrete or easily separable, but are interdependent, co-occurring, and mutually constitutive. Moreover, they cannot be isolated from planning and education activities involving other languages, which may compete with, overlap, or reinforce those highlighted here. Finally, all of this activity takes place within politically charged and contested social environments such as those described for Rough Rock, Peach Springs, and Hawai'i. Table 14.1 distills critical lessons from these three cases. In the remainder of this section, I elaborate some of those lessons.

Status Planning. Prescribing the indigenous language as the language of the school, community, and indigenous nation creates a host of macro-social possibilities, including the initiation of community dialogue for the purposes of ideological clarification and commitment to action. These possibilities are illustrated by the case of Peach Springs. Privileging the local language also encourages the development of local leadership, while positioning the school as the community center and promoting larger policy reforms. Rough Rock, Peach Springs, and the Hawaiian Immersion Schools all demonstrate the ways in which such transformations may occur. The work entailed by these transformations, however, must confront dominant-group interests: the hegemony of English; colonial education and its residue of internalized ambivalence about Native languages and identities; and compensatory and paternalistic national policies. Moreover, this work must be carried out within a context of political and economic marginalization, and thus, against the dominant race, class, and power structure.

Acquisition/Cultivation Planning. Language planning and education oriented toward (re)acquisition of the heritage language provide opportunities to promote bilingualism, enhanced educational achievement, and cultural pride. These micro-level changes not only help revitalize the heritage language, they set into motion more diffuse sociopolitical and economic transformations. Bilingual schooling requires bilingual teachers. Thus, one effect of bilingual schooling is to cultivate a professional class of indigenous educators. As evidenced by the case of Peach Springs and AILDI, as a group these educators constitute a powerful force for asserting indigenous linguistic and educational rights. The very fact of language loss, however, imperils the work of indigenous educators and bilingual programs. Moreover, indigenous educators must struggle against the power of English and its pervasiveness in virtually all aspects of modern social life. They also must contend with inadequate and inconsistent bilingual program funding. The latter is endemic in reservation schools, which depend for their livelihood on BIA and other discretionary federal contracts and grants. When cutbacks in federal funding become government policy, as they did during the Reagan and Bush administrations of the 1980s and early 1990s, indigenous schools and their bilingual/bicultural programs are seriously weakened (McCarty, 1989, in press; see also Fishman, 1991, p. 208).

Corpus Planning. Corpus planning has been defined as "those aspects of language planning which are primarily linguistic and hence internal to language" (Kaplan & Baldauf, 1997, p. 38). Corpus planning is that, but it is much more. The codification and elaboration of indigenous languages opens the possibility of anchoring the school curriculum in the local language and culture. It creates new literacies and literatures, giving voice to indigenous writers and challenging colonizing texts. These are social and political acts, and they are central to local education control. They also are acts bathed in the tensions surrounding representation and authenticity, which must contend with relentless pressures for homogenization and "accountability"—pressures that may force compliance with the very hegemonic practices (e.g., English standardized tests) that debilitate indigenous students and stigmatize their languages and cultures in school.

SCHOOLS AND LANGUAGE RECLAMATION

It is evident that language education, planning, and policy development by and for indigenous communities, while potential sources of local empowerment, confront a multitude of constraints. For those concerned with the crisis of language loss, the question becomes: To what extent can the crisis be ameliorated by processes and possibilities such as those outlined in Table 14.1 and illustrated by the three cases presented here?

A study of language shift in two Navajo communities by Evangeline Parsons-Yazzie (1996/97) sheds some light on this question. Parsons-Yazzie found that even in Navajo-speaking homes, young children tended to respond to their parents' and grandparents' Navajo *in English*. At the age of four and five (in some cases *before* they had entered school), children had internalized the covert and overt silencing messages of an English-dominant society. Holm (in press) elaborates: "We see situations in which the adult initiates in Navajo and the child responds in English. . . . We see situations where the adult initiates in Navajo and the child responds—but non-verbally. . . . We see situations where . . . the child hears the adult as so much 'static'." In these and other ways, Holm asserts, "young children set the language policy of the home; they 'train' the adults around them to talk only English" (in press).

Yet the adults in Parsons-Yazzie's study, like those in the communities described here, said they *want* their children and grandchildren to acquire the heritage language, "so we and our kids can talk the same language, and so we won't be mainstreamed with people of other races.... So [the children] won't lose their native language and culture" (Parsons-Yazzie, 1996/97, p. 64). These desires make clear that language loss and reclamation are about cultural survival; they are fundamental issues of tribal sovereignty and self-determination. What role can schools play in this struggle?

Fishman (1991, 1996), Krauss (1998), and others argue that schools are secondary or tertiary institutions in language revitalization; schools "should be on tap and not on top of a language," Fishman says, insisting that the bastion of mother tongue maintenance is the family and the home (1996, p. 194, 1991). The problem, as Parsons-Yazzie's study makes clear, is that the pressures on families to abandon the heritage language are so intense— the social injustices and dislocations so extreme—that if left to individuals and families alone, the crisis of language loss will go unabated. "When more children gain access to formal education, much of the ... language learning, which earlier took place in the community, must now take place in schools," Skutnaab-Kangas points out (1999, p. 10). "Parents need all the help they can get," Holm (in press) states; schools must become the allies of parents who want their children to acquire the indigenous language.

Schools such as those at Rough Rock, Peach Springs, and in Hawai'i are critical, if contentious, resources in the struggle. If their possibilities for local empowerment are to be realized, however, the tensions and risks schools harbor must be acknowledged and strategically addressed. Doing this requires informed resistance to dominant class interests. The cases here attest to the possible ways in which such resistance may be instantiated, even as these cases demonstrate the constancy of the struggle. Hornberger (1996) refers to this as language planning from the "bottom up" (see also Kaplan & Baldauf, 1997).

The politics, language, and culture of the school *can* be assets for heightening collective consciousness, promoting community dialogue, and mobilizing action. By their presence and their positions, bilingual educators demonstrate the instrumental value of the Native language. As we have seen in the cases here, bilingual educators can be opinion leaders; they can act politically on behalf of the language and its users. Indigenous educators can assert the primacy of the Native language in the public domain of the school; they also can enlist the support of and assist community stakeholders in reinforcing the Native language at home.

It is undeniable that indigenous schools and educators engage in such dialogue and interaction against a backdrop of oppression, and within school and community environments that are contradictory and full of conflict. For better or worse, schools continue to be a prime arena in which these conflicts are confronted and negotiated. Schools are not the only place for language reclamation and the social transformations that must accompany it, but they are a necessary place for this work. If school-based resources for linguistic, cultural, and educational self-determination are not used, the remaining, largely negative forces at work will only accelerate the rate of language loss. Further, schools and their participants will be complicit in the loss.

CODA

"Critical pedagogy must serve as a form of critique and also a referent of hope," McLaren and Tadeu da Silva write (1993, p. 69). I end this discussion on a note of possibility and hope.

There is no question that indigenous peoples can survive and are surviving without their heritage languages (see, e.g, Warner, 1999, p. 77). But, as González (1999) points out, "It is through and by language... that selfhoods are constructed, identities are forged, and social processes are enacted" (p. 433). Being indigenous in the indigenous language is qualitatively different from constructing and enacting an indigenous identity in English. To paraphrase Navajo language educator Clay Slate (1993), a society that enables one to be indigenous in the heritage language is a society worth maintaining.

Schools have the potential to silence or give voice to identities rooted in the heritage language. The language choices children and their families make need not be either-or ones; "indigenous" and "modern" need not be oppositional terms. School, especially, *can* be constructed as a place where children are free to be indigenous in the indigenous language—in all of its multiple and ever-changing meanings and forms.

REFERENCES

Atkins, J. D. C. (1887/1992). Barbarous dialects should be blotted out ... In J. Crawford (Ed.), *Language loyalties* (pp. 47–51). Chicago: University of Chicago Press.

Bourdieu, P. (Ed.) (1991). *Language and symbolic power.* Cambridge, MA: Harvard University Press.

Cantoni, G. (Ed.) (1996). *Stabilizing indigenous languages.* Flagstaff: Northern Arizona University Center for Excellence in Education.

Conklin, P. (1967). Good day at Rough Rock. *American Education, 3,* 4–9.

Cooper, R. L. (1989). *Language planning and social change*. Cambridge: Cambridge University Press.

Dauenhauer, N. M., & Dauenhauer, R. (1998). Technical, emotional, and ideological issues in reversing language shift: Examples from Southeast Alaska. In L. A. Grenoble & L. J. Whaley (Eds.), *Endangered languages: Language loss and community response* (pp. 57–98). Cambridge, UK: Cambridge University Press.

Fine, M. (1996). Working the hyphens: Reinventing self and other in qualitative research. In N. K. Denzin & Y. S. Lincoln (Eds.), *Handbook of qualitative research* (pp. 70–82). London: Sage.

Fishman, J. A. (1984). Minority mother tongues in education. *Prospects, 14*, 51–56.

Fishman, J. A. (1991). *Reversing language shift*. Clevedon: Multilingual Matters.

Fishman, J. A. (1996). Maintaining languages—What works? What doesn't? In G. Cantoni (Ed.), *Stabilizing indigenous languages* (pp. 186–198). Flagstaff: Northern Arizona University Center for Excellence in Education.

Forester, J. (1985). *Critical theory and public life*. Cambridge, MA: MIT Press.

Freire, P. (1970). *Pedagogy of the oppressed*. New York: Seabury Press.

Freire, P. (1993). *Pedagogy of the City*. New York: Continuum.

Freire, P. (1998). *Pedagogy of Freedom*. Oxford: Rowman & Littlefield.

González, N. (1999). What will we do when culture does not exist anymore? *Anthropology & Education Quarterly, 30*, 431–435.

Haugen, E. (1983). The implementation of corpus planning: Theory and practice. In J. Cobarrubias & J. A. Fishman (Eds.), *Progress in language planning: International perspectives* (pp. 269–290). Berlin: Mouton.

Hinton, L. (1994). *Flutes of Fire*. Berkeley, CA: Heyday Books.

Holm, W. (1996). On the role of "YounganMorgan" in the development of Navjao literacy. *Journal of Navajo Education, 13*, 4–11.

Holm, W. (in press). The goodness of bilingual education for Native American children. In T. L. McCarty & O. Zepeda (Eds.), *One voice, many voices: Recreating indigenous language communities*. Tucson, AZ: American Indian Language Development Institute.

Hornberger, N. H. (1994). Literacy and language planning. *Language in Education, 8*, 75–86.

Hornberger, N. H. (Ed.)(1996). *Indigenous literacies in the Americas: Language planning from the bottom up*. Berlin and New York: Mouton de Gruyter.

Hornberger, N. H. (1997). Literacy, language maintenance, and linguistic human rights: Three telling cases. *International Journal of the Sociology of Language, 127*, 87–103.

Infante, E. M. Living the language: Growing up in immersion school taught its own lessons. *The Honolulu Advertiser*, May 30, 1999, pp. E1, E3.

Johnson, B. H. (1968). *Navaho education at Rough Rock*. Rough Rock, AZ: Rough Rock Demonstration School.

Johnson, T. R., Champagne, D., & Nagel, J. (1999). American Indian activism and transformation: Lessons from Alcatraz. In T. R. Johnson (Ed.), *Contemporary Native American political issues* (pp. 283–314). Walnut Creek, CA: AltaMira Press.

Kaplan, R. B., & Baldauf, R. B. (1997). *Language planning: From practice to theory*. Clevedon: Multilingual Matters.

Krauss, M. (1996). Status of Native American language endangerment. In J. Reyhner (Ed.), *Stabilizing indigenous languages* (pp. 16–21). Flagstaff: Northern Arizona University Center for Excellence in Education.

Krauss, M. (1998). The condition of Native North American languages: The need for realistic assessment and action. *International Journal of the Sociology of Language, 132*, 9–21.

Levinson, B. A., Foley, D. E., & Holland, D. C. (1996). *The cultural production of the educated person: Critical ethnographies of schooling and local practice*. Albany: State University of New York Press.

Lomawaima, K. T. (1999). The unnatural history of American Indian education. In K. G. Swisher & J. W. Tippeconnic III (Eds.), *Next steps: Research and practice to advance Indian education* (pp. 1–31). Charleston, WV: Clearinghouse on Rural Education and Small Schools.

McCarty, T. L. (1989). School as community: The Rough Rock demonstration. *Harvard Educational Review, 59,* 484–303.

McCarty, T. L. (in press). *A place to be Navajo: Rough Rock and the struggle for self-determination in indigenous schooling.* Mahwah, NJ: Lawrence Erlbaum.

McCarty, T. L., & Watahomigie, L. J. (1999). Indigenous education and grassroots language planning in the USA. *Practicing Anthropology, 21,* 5–11.

McCarty, T. L., Watahomigie, L. J., & Yamamoto, A. Y. (Eds.) (1999). *Reversing language shift in indigenous America: Collaborations and views from the field.* Special issue, *Practicing Anthropology, 21.*

McCarty, T. L., Watahomigie, L. J., Yamamoto, A. Y., & Zepeda, O. (1997). School- community-university collaborations: The American Indian Language Development Institute. In J. Reyhner (Ed.), *Teaching indigenous languages* (pp. 85–104). Flagstaff: Northern Arizona Center for Excellence in Education.

McCarty, T. L., Watahomigie, L. J., Yamamoto, A. Y., & Zepeda, O. (in press). Indigenous teachers as change agents: Case studies of two language insititutes. In L. Hinton & K. Hale (Eds.), *The green book of language revitalization in practice.* San Diego, CA: Academic Press.

McLaren, P., & Tadeu da Silva, T. (1993). Decentering pedagogy: Critical literacy, resistance and the politics of memory. In. P. McLaren & P. Leonard (Eds.), *Paulo Freire: A critical encounter* (pp. 47–89). London: Routledge.

Medicine, B. (1982). Bilingual education and public policy: The cases of the American Indian. In R. V. Padilla (Ed.), *Ethnoperspectives in bilingual education research: Bilingual education and public policy in the United States* (pp. 295–407). Ypsilanti: Eastern Michigan University.

National Center for Education Statistics (1995). *Characteristics of American Indian and Alaska Native Education.* Washington, DC: U.S. Department of Education, Office of Educational Research and Improvement.

Noley, G. (1979). Choctaw bilingual and bicultural education in the nineteenth century. In *Multicultural education and the American Indian* (pp. 25–39). Los Angeles: American Indian Studies Center, University of California.

Paisano, E. L. (1999). *The American Indian, Eskimo, and Aleut population.* <http://www.census.gov/population/www/pop-profile/amerind.html>.

Parsons-Yazzie, E. (1996/97). Niha'átchíní dayistł'ǫ́ nahalin. *Journal of Navajo Education, 14,* 60–67.

Pennycook, A. (1999). Introduction: Critical approaches to TESOL. *TESOL Quarterly, 33,* 329–348.

Pfeiffer, A. (1993). American Indian educational issues. Panel presentation at the Quarterly Regional Meeting of the Bilingual/Multicultural Personnel Training Alliance. BUENO Center for Multicultural Education, University of Colorado, Boulder (August).

Platero, P. (1968). Phase II—Navaho language. In R. A. Roessel, Jr. (Compiler). *The twenty-third monthly report of Rough Rock Demonstration School month of May, 1968* (p. 81). Rough Rock, AZ: Rough Rock Demonstration School.

Prucha, F. P. (1984). *The great father: The United States government and the American Indians.* Lincoln: University of Nebraska Press.

Reyhner, J. (1997). *Teaching indigenous languages.* Flagstaff: Northern Arizona University Center for Excellence in Education.

Rivera, K. (1999). Popular research and social transformation: A community-based approach to critical pedagogy. *TESOL Quarterly, 33,* 485–500.

Roessel, R. A., Jr. (1977). *Navajo education in action: The Rough Rock Demonstration School.* Chinle, AZ: Navajo Curriculum Center Press.

Ruiz, R. (1984). Orientations in language planning. *NABE Journal, 8,* 15–34.

Skutnaab-Kangas, T. (1999). Linguistic human rights—Are you naive, or what? *TESOL Journal, 8,* 6–12.

Slate, C. (1993). Finding a place for Navajo. *Tribal College, 4,* 10–14.

Spolsky, B. (1972). *The situation of Navajo literacy projects. Navajo Reading Study Progress Report No. 17.* Albuquerque: The University of New Mexico.

Spolsky, B. (1974). *American Indian bilingual education. Navajo Reading Study Progress Report No. 24.* Albuquerque: The University of New Mexico.

Swisher, K. G., & Tippeconnic III, J. W. (Eds.). (1999). *Next steps: Research and practice to advance Indian education.* Charleston, WV: Clearinghouse on Rural Education and Small Schools.

Szasz, M. (1974). *Education and the American Indian: The road to self-determination.* Albuquerque: University of New Mexico Press.

Tippeconnic III, J. W. (1999). Tribal control of American Indian education: Observations since the 1960s with implications for the future. In K. G. Swisher & J. W. Tippeconnic III (Eds.), *Next steps: Research and practice to advance Indian education* (pp. 33–52). Charleston, WV: Clearinghouse on Rural Education and Small Schools.

Tollefson, J. W. (1991). *Planning language, planning inequality: Language policy in the community.* London: Longman.

U.S. Census Bureau (1990). *1990 Census of population, social and economic characteristics, American Indian and Alaska Native areas.* Washington, DC: U.S. Census Bureau.

U.S. Congress, Senate Committee on Labor and Public Welfare, Special Subcommittee on Indian Education (1969). *The study of the education of Indian children, Part 3.* Washington, DC: U.S. Government Printing Office.

U.S. Department of Education (1991). *Indian nations at risk: An educational strategy for action. Final report of the Indian Nations at Risk Task Force.* Washington, DC: U.S. Department of Education.

Warner, S. L. N. (1999). *Kuleana:* The right, responsibility, and authority of indigenous peoples to speak and make decisions for themselves in language and culture revitalization. *Anthropology & Education Quarterly, 30,* 68–93.

Watahomigie, L. J. (1995). The power of American Indian parents and communities. *The Bilingual Research Journal, 19,* 189–194.

Watahomigie, L. J. (1998). The native language is a gift: A Hualapai language autobiography. *International Journal of the Sociology of Language, 132,* 5–7.

Watahomigie, L. J., & McCarty, T. L. (1994). Bilingual/bicultural education at Peach Springs: A Hualapai way of schooling. *Peabody Journal of Education, 69,* 26–42.

Watahomigie, L. J., & McCarty, T. L. (1996). Literacy for what? Hualapai literacy and language maintenance. In N. H. Hornberger (Ed.), *Indigenous literacies in the Americas: Language planning from the bottom up* (pp. 95–113). Berlin: Mouton de Gruyter.

Weis, L. (1996). Foreword. In B. A. Levinson, D. E. Foley, & D. C. Holland (Eds.), *The cultural production of the educated person* (pp. ix–xiv). Albany: State University of New York Press.

Wilson, W. H. (1998a). I ka 'ōlelo Hawai'i ke ola, "Life is found in the Hawaiian language." *International Journal of the Sociology of Language, 132,* 123–137.

Wilson, W. H. (1998b). The sociopolitical context of establishing Hawaiian-medium education. *Language, Culture, and Curriculum, 11,* 325–338.

Wilson, W. H. (1999). Return of a language. *Common Ground,* Fall, 40–41.

Wong, L. (1999). Authenticity and the revitalization of Hawaiian. *Anthropology & Education Quarterly, 30,* 94–115.

15

The Critical Villager: Transforming Language and Education in Solomon Islands

David Welchman Gegeo
and Karen Ann Watson-Gegeo
University of California, Davis, Davis, California

> I have been observing [rural development] more closely for these past few years, and today I realize that we the village people just didn't know. We were being forced to do things in a different way, and that is why we did all kinds of things. But nowadays our eyes are open. (Codrington Irotalau, rural Solomon Islander, 1993)

> People's power doesn't mean we are finally going to take over. But it does mean that people, especially the chiefs and local leaders, will want greater participation, more involvement. Like falling out of a small one-man canoe, the first time we usually get a wetting. But surely the time is coming, I think it's already here, that we will paddle the canoe without fear of getting wet. (John Roughan, urban Solomon Islander, 1998[1])

Solomon Islands (SI) achieved independence from Great Britain in 1978, and for a decade thereafter rural villagers waited for the postcolonial

---

[1]Codrington Irotalau is a traditional land owner, head of a large extended family, and village leader in rural West Kwara'ae. He has been involved in a variety of large- and small-scale development projects over the past 30 years. John Roughan is the founder of Solomon Islands Development Trust (SIDT), one of the most successful indigenously managed non-governmental organizations in the Pacific islands.

government to take leadership in rural development. They also continued to believe schools to be the primary (perhaps only) source of knowledge and gateway to economic success for their children (Watson-Gegeo & Gegeo, 1995). In the past 10 years, however, the inability of national and provincial institutions to support meaningful rural development has begun to be answered by an emerging critical perspective among a small but growing number of local villagers.

This chapter focuses on Malaita island/province where members of SI's largest linguistic and ethnic minority (no ethnic group is in the majority) are beginning to rethink language, education, and development, and to pursue intellectual and practical projects that (re)construct knowledge towards rural empowerment. We examine two directions villagers are taking this critical perspective with regard to practice: 1) counter-hegemonic teaching in rural classrooms; and 2) dehegemonic village-based projects that make effective and creative use of people's literacy skills, indigenous knowledge, and previous off-island experiences toward adult education. We use examples from both to explore the possibilities of a new paradigm for rural education in the Solomons based on indigenous epistemology (Gegeo, 1994) and indigenous critical praxis, and incorporating both an expanded conception of literacy (Street, 1995) and attention to issues of situated cognition (Lave & Wenger, 1991).

POLICY, PEDAGOGY, PRAXIS, AND EPISTEMOLOGY

Language policy issues and pedagogical assumptions and practices are linked together in schools. Much has been written over the past 30 years about the need to de-couple schooling in Third World[2] societies from Anglo-European educational models originally imported through colonialism, which have persisted due to lack of funding, poorly trained teachers, and local, national, and international assumptions about what constitutes schooling (see Luke, 1988; Meyer, Kamens & Benavot, 1992; Lockheed & Levin, 1993). Current pressures to upgrade educational systems to fit a high-tech, free trade-oriented globalized market have had little impact on poor rural schools in the Third World. If anything, the gap in schooling experiences between rural villages and urban centers has widened (parallel to the problem for inner-city urban and outlying rural schools in the "developed" nations).

---

[2]We use the term "Third World" and "developing nation(s)" interchangeably, and also "Anglo-European" and "West/Western" interchangeably, for want of better terms. We are fully aware of the problems with these phrasings.

Many curricular and pedagogical interventions have been tried in Third World schools over the past several decades in an attempt to bring the latest innovations out to the periphery, or simply improve rural children's academic skills. Yet for a variety of reasons, these innovations typically fail to improve the rates with which children pass school, the quality of education children receive, and the skill levels they attain. Innovations have failed partly because they, like the older colonial model of schooling, are based on assumptions about values and behavior indigenous to Western but not local societies, or equally problematic, on assumptions that foreigners have about what Third World (in the SI case, Pacific islands) children are like. The latter assumptions are based, in turn, on outsiders' studies of Pacific cultures that often distort cultural characteristics and misinterpret behavior. In short, for most children in countries like SI, the Anglo-European educational models are simply not working.

We believe that what needs to be attended to as Third World societies rethink education is what rural villagers themselves do: their systems of knowledge, learning, and pedagogy in the rich and nuanced lives they live everyday. Doing so takes us toward understanding indigenous knowledge systems and indigenous pedagogical practices.

With regard to indigenous knowledge systems, "language policy" in relation to schooling usually refers to a concern primarily with the highly complex and difficult issues of models of language instruction, medium of instruction, and issues of standard and non-standard language varieties. Corpus planning and historical-structural approaches do consider *indigenous cultural knowledge* in a general sense (see Tollefson, 1991). Yet they, too (Davis, 1999 is an exception), typically neglect the most important issue lying at the intersection of language, culture, education, and development: indigenous epistemology and its relation to epistemological assumptions in imposed educational models. *Indigenous epistemology* refers to a cultural group's ways of thinking and of creating and reformulating knowledge using traditional discourses and media of communication, and anchoring the truth of the discourse in culture (Gegeo, 1998; Gegeo & Watson-Gegeo, 1999; Watson-Gegeo & Gegeo, 1999). At the heart of indigenous epistemology are cultural models (Holland & Quinn, 1987; D'Andrade & Strauss, 1992; Shore, 1996) for thinking and acting, and cultural ways of conceptualizing and creating knowledge about the human and natural worlds. Whereas the anthropological notion "worldview"—defined as a "way of looking at reality" consisting of culturally-grounded "basic assumptions and images" (Kearney, 1984, p. 41)—tended to be idealist and divorced from sociopolitical context (Bowlin & Stromberg, 1997), indigenous epistemology focuses on the process through which knowledge is constructed and validated by a cultural group, and the role of that process in shaping thinking and behavior. It assumes that all epistemological systems are socially constructed and informed (formed by and of) through sociopolitical, economic, and historical context and processes.[3]

With regard to indigenous pedagogical practices, the educational literature has tended to represent indigenous education systems as "informal" or "non-formal," although the definitions of "formal" and "in/non-formal" are usually vague and contradictory, often resting on the degree to which outsiders perceive the learning moment to involve a high degree of verbalization and, especially, decontextualized language. Yet in most societies some type of formal educational event occurs, with implications for pedagogical practices in schools.

Beyond recognizing indigenous formal educational contexts, however, Western scholars have been slow to recognize that indigenous epistemology also involves *indigenous critical praxis*—i.e., people's own critical reflection on culture, history, knowledge, politics, economics, and the sociopolitical contexts in which they are living their lives; *and then* their taking the next step to act on these critical reflections (Gegeo & Watson-Gegeo, in press). Indigenous critical praxis flows from and is deeply rooted in indigenous ways of knowing and doing things, that is, in indigenous epistemology. When indigenous critical praxis is applied to teaching and learning situations within a people's own sociocultural settings, the result is a critical pedagogy—not one that despite its good intentions is introduced from the outside (Livingstone, 1987; Giroux & McLaren, 1989; Kanpol, 1999), but one that is created indigenously. In rediscovering everyday life, *indigenous critical pedagogy* also transforms it.

Echoing Freire (1970, 1994), Lefebvre (1990, p. 202) links this transformation to language: "everyday life translated into language becomes a different everyday life by becoming clear; and the transfiguration of everyday life is the creation of something new, something that requires new words." This formulation raises the possibility of a different way of thinking about "language" in "language policy." Language is the medium for transformation, and in being so, itself is transformed. But this latter

---

[3]Jaimes (1995) has described "Indigenism" as being grounded in non-Western (and therefore alternative) worldview and value systems. In the past two decades there has been a growing interest in the social sciences, education, applied linguistics, and community and rural development in *indigenous knowledge* from both cultural insider and outsider perspectives (e.g., Brokensha, Warren & Werner, 1980; Rosaldo, 1980; Lambek, 1983; Pieterse & Parekh, 1995; Brush & Stabinsky, 1996; Nader, 1996; Scott, 1996; Keck, 1998). However, these studies do not examine epistemology. The few studies that do examine *indigenous epistemology* are either outsider accounts (e.g., Salmond, 1985) or if by insiders, have been deeply influenced by particular Anglo-European perspectives (e.g., Smith, 1999—in this case, radical feminist theory). In the Pacific, Maori (New Zealand) and Hawaiian scholars are currently at work on projects that focus on indigenous epistemology.

transformation must be based on and guided by indigenous epistemology and indigenous critical praxis, processes which are themselves encoded in a people's indigenous language. For it is only when people think in a language—i.e., a symbol system—which they fully understand that this transformation can occur.

EDUCATION FOR WHAT?—INTERROGATING THE PURPOSE OF SCHOOLING

Francis Bugotu, former SI Education Officer, first posed the above question in his master's thesis in the 1960s, because the colonial model of schooling in SI looked outward: geared towards Western values and an urban lifestyle. When Bugotu et al. (1973) posed the question again, the context was a rising tide of decolonization in the Third World and Pacific islands. Buguto et al. aimed to reform education towards making the country politically independent—a counter-hegemonic rather than a dehegemonic concern.[4] This aim persisted despite the talk of "indigenizing" education in the 1980s following national independence in 1978. "Indigenization" turned out to mean, as some local observers joked, replacing "white" faces with "brown" faces in the ranks of teachers and administrators.

In re-posing the question at the beginning of the new century, we extend the decolonization paradigm first to take education more broadly to include not just schools, but also village learning experiences for adults; and secondly, to rescue the concept of "indigenization" from its prior misuse and employ it instead in a manner that resonates with its central meaning of knowledge construction, processes, and activities anchored in local indigenous culture. In Kwara'ae, this means going back to a grounding in the philosophy of *gwaumauri'anga* (literally, "state of being at the head of life," i.e., living the complete [*ali'afu*] life), with being and praxis grounded in culture.

---

[4]*Counter-hegemonic* refers to any activity the objective of which is to block or undermine the spread of Western (in this case) hegemony (e.g., institutions). *Dehegemonic* refers to attempting to undo the already established hegemony—which is much more difficult than blocking hegemonic forces. In the literature these two terms are frequently used interchangeably, although they should be kept distinct. *Hegemony* in the Gramscian sense is "the legitimation of the cultural authority of the dominant group, an authority that plays a significant role in social reproduction" (Woolard, 1985, p. 739). With Woolard, we take the problem of hegemony to be "the problem of authority and collaboration or consent, in contrast to domination and coercion, in the maintenance of a particular social formation." Hegemony begins with coercion and domination (colonialism), then becomes internalized, essentially self-perpetuating, and largely unquestioned. Foucault (1980, 1984) refers to it as "normalization." An example is Third World countries buying into Western schooling and modernization, "imitating Western ideas, consumption patterns, and social relationships" (Nyerere et al., 1990, p. 46), so that even the imitation is accepted as the normal and preferable pattern of behavior.

Under the modernization paradigm, SI has experienced negative social-ization to many Anglo-European values and practices (see Gegeo, 1994). Recently there has been a concerted movement by many SI-ers to reaf-firm and reconstruct traditional culture and society. We have described islanders' working through the contradictions between these two philo-sophical and cultural poles as a dialectic between the discourse of mod-ernization and the discourse of development (Watson-Gegeo & Gegeo, 1994). Solomon Islands is a dual society, one in which a large, economi-cally poor, rural subsistence society (85% of the population) co-exists with an Anglo-European-oriented society in urban and peri-urban centers. For employment, visiting relatives, taking a break from urban jobs, purchasing goods unavailable to villages, and connecting with their village roots, in-dividuals move back and forth, both metaphorically and literally, between these two societies (called "circular migration;" see Chapman, 1987, 1992). Up to now, education has been viewed as job preparation and being suc-cessful in the modern world, which ultimately means leaving the village for urban areas or even metropolitan countries—despite the fact that most students who finish secondary school cannot find jobs. The few counter-vailing voices argue that children should instead be educated to return to the village, where most will ultimately end up anyway.

Yet because SI is a dual society and people do move back and forth between both worlds, children need to be educated to succeed in either world. This requires a new model of education that would provide the skills to make it possible for children to make choices. Moreover, education must be viewed holistically across the life-span. And for both adults and children, education must be indigenized.

Finally, indigenization means an expanded notion of literacy and learn-ing. Central here is the work of Street (1993, 1995) and others on lit-eracy/ies as ideological and social practices that vary situationally and cross-culturally and are constantly being invented (the "new literacies"). The processes of knowledge/literacy/ies creation, learning, and reformu-lation occur in social contexts of situation. As Lave & Wenger (1991) effec-tively argue, learners develop knowledge and skills through "legitimate peripheral participation" in a community of practice: i.e., learners begin as recognized participants on the periphery of an activity and gradually move to full participation in the center, as their skills develop. Learning is more than just situated in practice: "learning is an integral part of gener-ative social practice in the lived-in world" (Lave & Wenger, 1991, p. 35). Thus learners have considerable agency in how and what they learn, and they themselves create new knowledge.

We turn now to an examination of counter-hegemonic classroom teach-ing and adult villagers' dehegemonic creation and use of knowledge in local projects in SI.

COUNTER-HEGEMONIC TEACHING IN RURAL CLASSROOMS

We have previously discussed and documented the abysmal educational conditions in the Solomons generally, and on Malaita specifically (Watson-Gegeo & Gegeo, 1992, 1994). Our sociolinguistic study of two rural Malaita schools has involved audiotaping language arts lessons of seven teachers at varying primary grade levels, in 1981, 1990, 1992, and 1994, and in-depth teacher interviews (Watson-Gegeo & Gegeo, 1992, 1994, 1995). Here we discuss teaching practices of two teachers: Lindsay (recorded in 1990, 1992, and 1994), and Rebekah (recorded in 1994).

Lindsay and Rebekah are both recognized locally as excellent rural primary school teachers. We consider Lindsay to be an exemplary teacher despite having only a Standard 7 (primary) education and one year of teacher training (in SI Ministry of Education classification, a "partially trained" teacher). Rebekah is a "trained" teacher, having graduated from the Solomon Islands College of Higher Education's teacher training program. Both are experienced rural teachers: Lindsay at several grade levels, and Rebekah at "prep" (pre-school) and kindergarten levels.

We call Lindsay's teaching "counter-hegemonic" because his practices are grounded in indigenous epistemology, they model for students indigenous critical praxis, and they prepare students for further schooling or returning to the village. In kindergarten, where the Ministry policy allows some use of children's first language, Lindsay alternates lessons in Kwara'ae and English (the official school medium of instruction); at higher grade levels, he uses English and SI Pijin. In a discourse analytic study of Lindsay's kindergarten language arts lessons (Watson-Gegeo & Gegeo, 1994), we found that Lindsay uses village conversational discourse patterns and pieces of caregiver-child interactional routines known to his students, during literacy tasks. His interactive lessons contrast sharply with those of typical SI rural classroom teachers' recitation format inherited from colonial days. Most striking is Lindsay's use of a traditional Kwara'ae argument technique found in planning, debate, and oratory: *'ini te'ete'e suli ru'anga* (literally, "inching with the fingers along it"). The metaphor (from gardening) refers to careful, step-by-step systematic reasoning well-supported with evidence, and involves a set of clearly marked discourse routines. Kwara'ae children are familiar with those routines not only from attending village events with their parents, but also from their use to teach children linguistic, social, and intellectual skills at home. We believe that Lindsay's use of this strategy is one factor in his students' success in learning English.

Rebekah, who grew up in Honiara, was trained for urban schools where she had her first teaching experience. She is skilled in questioning patterns, reformulation of student answers, and preparation of materials.

Recognizing the needs of her rural students, Rebekah has begun to incorporate local interactional features into her teaching, and also what we might identify as a local feminist style. As the only female teacher in her school at present, she models for her female students the possibility of a career that is compatible with changing rural cultural expectations for women, yet is a break from expectations of a generation ago. Her interactional style in the classroom has shifted to intonational contours used in adult-child interactions in the village, and she teaches in English and SI Pijin, code-switching to Kwara'ae to connect emotionally with the children. She has begun to move in the direction of Lindsay's strategy of using *'ini te'ete'e suli ru'anga* in language arts lessons. The students in her class, as in Lindsay's classes, are highly engaged and interactive with her during lessons.

These two teachers' valuing of indigenous culture is particularly revealed in their incorporating *fa'amanata'anga*, the traditional Kwara'ae equivalent of schooling, into their classrooms. *Fa'amanata'anga* is a general Kwara'ae term for "teaching," and literally means "shaping the mind." In its specialized meaning, it refers to a formal, serious-to-sacred event in which direct teaching and interpersonal counseling are undertaken in high rhetoric, the formal discourse register in Kwara'ae (Watson-Gegeo & Gegeo, 1990). In the family, *fa'amanata'anga* begins in early childhood (often at 18 months) and continues throughout life. Its presence and frequency is a marker for the degree to which a family is committed to traditional Kwara'ae culture and values.

Rebekah uses strategies from *fa'amanata'anga* in some kinds of lessons related to village life, health, and related topics. In doing so, she is legitimizing for the children the worth of the most central interactional event in their culture, the one through which Kwara'ae values, reasoning strategies, philosophy, esoteric technical knowledge, and cultural meanings are learned, taught, and (re)created from generation to generation.

Lindsay, however, goes further to employ *fa'amanata'anga* in an even more counter-hegemonic way. An example is the lesson we recorded in 1990, when Lindsay's classroom was visited by a young local villager (Robinson) who at that time was undertaking graduate education in a foreign university, and had come to visit the school he attended as a child. In talking about Robinson's accomplishment, Lindsay emphasized that Robinson would now turn the tables and "teach white people"—an inversion of the status relationship which Lindsay's students had already been socialized to expect. Despite Robinson's advanced schooling, Lindsay argued that he is "still one of us," because he always returns to his home village, lives with his family, associates with everyone, and continues to speak fluent Kwara'ae. Lindsay went on to argue that knowledge is knowledge (i.e., to be equally privileged), whether it is from school or village;

and that one can succeed in school without abandoning one's own culture and community, and succeed in the village using traditional and school knowledge.

Lindsay draws on indigenous critical praxis to question the assumptions in his own practice and those in teacher training:

> In teacher training they told us that [village] children are disobedient and difficult to teach. But if you observe [the children] closely [you see that] they are really kind, and this moves them towards learning (From a 1987 interview).

"Kindness" also means "cooperation" in Kwara'ae. That kindness is essential to learning is a deeply held Kwara'ae cultural belief. Here Lindsay expresses his faith in all village children's ability and willingness to learn. The success of Lindsay's students has led to his becoming headmaster of his school, despite his limited educational background; and under his leadership, we expect more counter-hegemonic moves to be made.

DEHEGEMONIC VILLAGE-BASED PROJECTS

Since the 1960s, rural development agencies have emphasized people-oriented development, grassroots projects, and high levels of local participation (summarized in Gegeo, 1994). Such projects are typically based on Anglo-European epistemology. Increasingly, however, villagers in rural SI are implementing small-scale projects of their own design. Moreover, on Malaita several villager-led projects to revitalize *kastom* (SI Pijin, "culture") have been undertaken since the 1970s. Of these, we discuss one in Kwara'ae that began as the recording of culture and has become concerned with empowerment, development, and adult education.

The Kwara'ae Genealogy Project began in 1994 when members of a Liana clan village decided to conduct their own research, interviewing a range of traditional elders and cultural experts across several clans on culture, language, and history. They planned to discuss and record cultural and linguistic information passed via oral tradition, using the literacy skills and tape-recording technology they had among them. In this way the knowledge of the older generation could be preserved in print, and the debates and discussions to revitalize and reform these traditions could also become part of the Kwara'ae historical record. They also were concerned that as knowledge was passed down orally in the rapidly changing contemporary situation, older information on land ownership, kinship, and other village concerns was being lost and becoming less reliable. Social change was affecting people's memory across their own lifetime, and leading them to embellish historical information with modern customs.

Although the project was to be about Kwara'ae language and culture as practiced by the Liana, it was deliberately given the title Genealogy Project. In Kwara'ae, genealogy is the foundation (*fuli*) or basis of society, and the starting point for all investigation of cultural knowledge. Initially, therefore, members of the project reconstructed genealogy for the clan, its sub-clans, and extended families.

To collect information, they used a set of strategies that have always been part of Kwara'ae *talingisilana ala'anga*, "enlightened dialogue" or critique, which involves simultaneous deconstruction and reconstruction of ideas. First, the overarching approach is dialogic: a topic is posed in the form of a question, which may be set up through someone's retelling of a remembered event that involves an ambiguity or a point that continues to be questioned as knowledge is passed down. Or an issue is posed, and sternly challenged by the poser—e.g., a land claim or someone's account of his/her genealogy. Key points of possible conflict are selected out of the larger ongoing cultural "oral text" and then discussed dialogically.

Second, in pursuing a resolution or new version to any of these claims, the participants necessarily engage in critical discussions of cultural concepts that are entailed in a given debate, following out the lines or branches that lead from a specific issue to definitions of terms or discussions of processes and events involved in traditional institutions. In Kwara'ae this form of discussion is called *abira'anga*, "branching out." As a result, over the several years of the project, the complexities involved in major cultural institutions such as marriage, language, land, kinship and descent, traditional religion, the position of women, tribal warfare, migration, compensation and retribution, and traditional law have been discussed and analyzed.

Third, in following the branches outward, participants necessarily get into the semantics of terms, creating and recreating knowledge via analyzing the grammatical classes and morphology of words, and their semantic boundaries. Indeed, in Kwara'ae, culture is seen as anchored in language: "culture is impossible without language, language is impossible without culture;" they are inseparable (*teo fiku*). The Kwara'ae view language not just as a tool for communication, but as social action. In engaging in discourse, people use language to transform knowledge, ideas, and understanding, and in the process, language itself is also transformed. New meanings are given to existing words, words may take on new grammatical classes, and sets of terminologies may also be expanded. Some older words may begin to lose their meanings and are eventually dropped, or pairs of words can become interchangeable.

Fourth, evidence given through oral accounts is very carefully interrogated in a variety of ways, including verification through landmarks or other physical evidence, other historical accounts, and from lived experience (does something sound logical, given the experience of everyday life?).

Among Kwara'ae terms for forms of reasoning used in enlightened dialogue is 'ini te'ete'e suli ru'anga, mentioned earlier. Another is manata kali ru'anga, putting a given piece of evidence in the center and interrogating its context in concentric circles via question/answer, supporting evidence, and other rhetorical techniques. The Kwara'ae dialogic approach is not like Anglo-European interview strategies that fire one question after another to a respondent. Rather, questions evolve through dialogue/multilogue that typically begins with a narration or sometimes an explication. Direct questions are used primarily to challenge. To ask most questions of information, participating speakers build mini-narratives or descriptions out of which a question is then posed. This strategy is meant to incorporate rather than distance interactants.[5]

To guide the process effectively, the project group evolved to a format in which interviews or meetings are held on certain days in a village meeting house. Most of the participants are non-schooled and have no or few literacy skills. Diagrams, terms, and issues that come up are written on a blackboard by someone with basic literacy; and all discourse is tape recorded and transcribed by three men (mid-40s; all literate but virtually unschooled) who worked briefly as transcribers in a research project some years ago. The hand-written transcripts are then typed by a young woman who learned typing in school. Eventually the results will be edited to be published as a book.

From the beginning of the project, members have been sending us letter-tapes describing their involvement. We noticed over the course of the first year that members' knowledge was being deepened, and their analytical abilities were dramatically increasing. In the initial tapes they described what they had done so far, and said they didn't know what to do next. By the second set of tapes, they were describing what they had noticed in analyzing the first set of data, and what they were planning to do next to follow up those findings. By the third set of tapes, they were no longer seeking advice about what to do, but were merely asking for reassurance that they had made the best choices. Moreover, by this point their

---

[5]Kwara'ae villagers regard most anthropological interviews as the interviewer asking questions "all over the place," jumping from one part of a topic to another, each discussion being truncated.

discourse style treated us as colleagues rather than as experts. Because we were interested in the indigenous nature of this project, our feedback was deliberately vague. We were sure from the beginning that they could do this project themselves.

By the second year, from the letter-tapes and other materials we saw that three unintended outcomes had evolved for participants: empowerment, development, and adult education.

The Kwara'ae concept of empowerment (*fa'a ngasi ngasi'anga*) embraces several dimensions, including self-reliance (*talau'anga*), self-sufficiency (*talasasiru'anga*), intellectual enlightenment (*mā'ifi'anga*), foresight (*liatau'anga*), and thinking in depth (*manatalalo'anga*). Project members report that they have been empowered through their work in several ways. For example, Irosulia (late 40s, 2nd-grade education) and Malau (mid-20s, 10th-grade education) both talked of "having my eyes opened" by the project, and that now even new ideas coming from outside seem familiar and non-threatening to them. They were also awed by the analytical depth they had achieved in their analyses. Their new "intellectual audacity" also translated into physically being unafraid to challenge people representing power positions (government, church) who came to the village for various purposes, they said. Namokalitau, an elected village chief in his early 50s (non-literate), reported that other chiefs who serve as judges in customary courts, many of them far more experienced and school-educated, were impressed at his level of analysis of evidence in court hearings, his ability to see subtleties that they missed, and his facility in arguing for reasonable verdicts in complicated cases. Sometimes chiefs had directly asked him where he attended school. Project members also joked that members of surrounding villages now tease them by saying that the project villagers are "a bunch of watchdogs" with regard to their analytical abilities in debate and their audacity in challenging government, church, and *kastom* officials. The view of empowerment through the project that participants report is congruent with African development scholar Dei's (1995, p. 148) definition of empowerment:

> . . . empowerment means local peoples having the voice to articulate locally defined legitimate concerns. It also means local peoples having autonomy over their own resources and dictating their own path to meeting basic livelihoods and group survival. After all, no one can empower anyone.

Dei's connection between empowerment and transformative development is congruent with project members' own making of this connection. Leading up to the founding of the Kwara'ae Genealogy Project, like other people in West Kwara'ae, participants in the project were rethinking the notion of rural development and beginning to incorporate indigenous epistemology into projects they designed themselves (Gegeo, 1994). Iro-talau's opening quotation in this chapter reflects the trend. Central to the Kwara'ae notion of "development" is that development that lasts is not concerned only with meeting physical and economic needs. Rather, it is concerned with personal growth and social well-being, which are involved in the philosophy of *gwaumauri'anga* (mentioned above; see Gegeo, 1998 for a comprehensive discussion). When asked why they are spending time do-ing the genealogy project, participants respond that "we have tried devel-opment through an economic perspective, and it has failed for us." Rather, they argue that to be successful in the small-scale family economic projects they are already pursuing, they must also attend to human well-being. Theirs is a holistic view of development. They argue that the transforma-tion they have achieved through the genealogy project is what has been lacking up to now in their attempts to pursue economic development. As Gwalona (late 30s, minimal schooling) commented:

> I feel that I achieve *'inoto'a'anga* [dignity, empowerment] when I pursue my own ideas rather than being dictated to pursue [outsider introduced] ideas, even if those ideas bring me money. . . Money is not something you start with to improve yourself, it comes after.

His implication is that human qualities must be developed first.

The connection between development and adult education was already being made by participants before they began the genealogy project. In earlier interviews, several said that they regarded designing and carrying out their own small-scale development projects, based on indigenous epis-temology, as a form of adult education. To them, "school" is for children. Adult education has always been part of their traditional culture, through critical praxis and *fa'amanata'anga*. The message given to villagers since early colonialism, however, has been that critical thinking skills can only be learned in school and from Western pedagogy. Nevertheless, through projects like the genealogy project, people are discovering what they al-ways knew: that indigenous ways of knowing and critiquing are equally effective in solving modern as well as traditional problems and issues, and equally valid as an alternative way of reasoning towards valid con-clusions. This realization is one reason participants say that through the project "our eyes have been opened." It is also why participation in the project has grown and spread since 1994. Moreover, participants are ap-plying their new skills to contemporary issues, such as questioning na-tional government policies. One source of humor in West Kwara'ae is that candidates for elected provincial and national offices dread coming to the project village to give political speeches, because project participants are able to deconstruct their conclusions about national policies. Ironically, non-project members with considerable local schooling are unable to do this kind of critical thinking—even though many Anglo-European scholars have argued that literacy in itself should result in the development of critical thinking skills. Project participants are living examples of empowerment and critical thinking without literacy. We are not, of course, arguing that villagers need not be literate. Project members recognize the power of combining traditional critical skills with literacy skills, and documenting their knowledge and work on paper.

A CRITICAL SYNTHESIS: TOWARDS A NEW PARADIGM

What, then, are implications of the foregoing examples for reforming and indigenizing schooling and adult education in "developing" countries such as Solomon Islands? We are arguing for schools that Western and indigenous epistemology, praxis, pedagogy, and knowledge be integrated and given equal weight in the classroom. If this becomes the case, children will be prepared for whatever the outcome of their schooling may be, and even if they go further in Western education, will not experience the feeling of alienation, loss of identity, and ignorance of their traditional culture and village life that happens now to so many who succeed in the "modern" world. Conversely, for those children who are unable to go further in school, they will be prepared to return to village life and still be able to deal with the challenges of modernity—via critical praxis—that reach into every village today. At the same time, they will return to the village with respect for their culture and village life, and without the overwhelming sense of defeat and failure that is currently the case when children fail the national exam into secondary school. The goals we are setting here for schools admittedly require a radical revision of school curricula, and especially, a radical revision of teacher training. The latter can be done, we believe, at the school site by identifying teachers like Lindsay and Rebekah who could engage in critical pedagogical discussions with their colleagues around real classroom activities and issues. The village context is in fact the perfect milieu for the kind of transformative critical praxis that we are calling for here.

With the majority of adults having never been to school in SI, the need for adult education is great. The Kwara'ae Genealogy Project is a good model for the kind of paradigm shift effective adult education would require. Many people function expertly in the village context without the "advantages" of schooling or literacy skills. They can do so because traditionally, village activities involved each person contributing according to his/her own skills, and by sharing knowledge and skills, everyone played a part recognized as important. This is the way the genealogy project has functioned, and the transformation of knowledge and the empowerment experienced by project members illustrate well how learning can be a "generative social practice in the lived-in world" (Lave & Wenger, 1991, p. 35). An important implication is that acquisition of literacy skills should not be the yardstick for measuring adult education. A paradigm for adult education based on indigenous epistemology, critical praxis, and critical pedagogy would not have as its target everyone ending up necessarily learning the same skills and making identical contributions to each other's learning. Instead, participants contribute their strengths to the group effort, and the growth that each person experiences (in whatever knowledge or skills he/she develops) contributes to the growth of everyone else. Transformation comes through interaction and is a relationship to others and to a skill. For some, it may come through new ideas, for others through deepening knowledge, and for some through acquiring literacy. Large discursive village meetings, which still play an important role in many SI communities, are another context for adult education, although they are less focused and more periodic than the genealogy project. Small amounts of development monies set aside for these kinds of projects and activities could go a long way in promoting indigenously organized adult education in rural areas. As such projects and activities are initiated and carried out by villagers themselves, they are extremely cost effective compared to massive adult education efforts sponsored by external and internal development agencies.

Finally, the argument we have made here requires a rethinking of "language" in the concept of "language policy." As mentioned earlier, for the Kwara'ae and other rural SI-ers, language is inseparable from culture, which is inseparable from indigenous epistemology. Unless all of these complexities are incorporated into a model of language planning and education, then language planning will serve its own professional interests rather than the needs and concerns of villagers. And the results will be destructive.

We strongly believe that with the resurgent interest in the revitalization of *kastom* (traditional culture) in SI and elsewhere, now is the time to invest effort into realizing a transformative paradigm for language policy and for education.

REFERENCES

Bowlin, J. R., & Stromberg, P. G. (1997). Representation and reality in the study of culture. *American Anthropologist, 99*, 123–134.
Brokensha, D. W., Warren, D. M., & Werner, O. (Eds.). (1980). *Indigenous knowledge systems and development*. Washington, D.C.: University Press of America.

Brush, S. B., & Stabinsky, D. (Eds.). (1996). *Valuing local knowledge: Indigenous people and intellectual property rights*. Covelo, CA: Island Press.

Bugotu, F., & Members of the EPR Committee. (1973). *Educational for what? A report on the findings of the British Solomon Islands Protectorate Educational Policy Review Committee*. Honiara, Solomon Islands: Secretariat of the Governing Council.

Chapman, M. (1987). Population movement studied at microscale: Experience and extrapolation. *GeoJournal, 15*, 347–65.

Chapman, M. (1992). Population movement: Free or constrained? In R. Crocombe & E. Tuza (Eds.), *Independence, dependence, interdependence: The first ten years of Solomon Islands independence* (pp. 75–97). Honiara: Solomon Islands College of Higher Education, Institute of Pacific Studies and Solomon Islands Centre, University of the South Pacific.

D'Andrade, R. G., & Strauss, C. (Eds.). (1992). *Human motives and cultural models*. Cambridge: Cambridge University Press.

Davis, K. A. (1999). The sociopolitical dynamics of indigenous language maintenance and loss: A framework for language policy and planning. In T. Huebner & K. A. Davis (Eds.), *Sociopolitical perspectives on language policy and planning in the USA* (pp. 67–98). Amsterdam: John Benjamins.

Dei, G. J. S. (1995). Indigenous knowledge as an empowerment tool for sustainable development. In N. Singh & V. Titi (Eds.), *Empowerment: Towards sustainable development* (pp. 147–161). Atlantic Highlands, NJ: Zed.

Foucault, M. (1980). *Power/knowledge: Selected interviews and other writings 1972–1977*. New York: Pantheon Books.

Foucault, M. (1984). *The Foucault reader*. Paul Rabinow (Ed.). New York: Pantheon Books.

Freire, P. (1970). *Pedagogy of the oppressed*. New York: Continuum.

Freire, P. (1994). *Pedagogy of hope: Reliving the pedagogy of the oppressed*. New York: Continuum.

Gegeo, D. W. (1994). Kastom *and* bisnis: *Toward integrating cultural knowledge into rural development in the Solomon Islands*. Unpublished Ph.D. dissertation, Dept. of Political Science, University of Hawai'i, Mānoa.

Gegeo, D. W. (1998). Indigenous knowledge and empowerment: Rural development examined from within. *The Contemporary Pacific, 10*, 289–315.

Gegeo, D. W., & Watson-Gegeo, K. A. (1999). Adult education, language change, and issues of identity and authenticity in Kwara'ae (Solomon Islands). *Anthropology and Education Quarterly, 30*, 22–36.

Gegeo, D. W., & Watson-Gegeo, K. A. (in press). "How we know:" Kwara'ae rural villagers doing indigenous epistemology. *The Contemporary Pacific, 13*, 1, Spring, 2001.

Giroux, H. A., & McLaren, P. L. (Eds.). (1989). *Critical pedagogy, the state, and cultural struggle*. Albany: State University of New York.

Holland, D., & Quinn, N. (Eds.). (1987). *Cultural models in language and thought*. New York: Cambridge University Press.

Jaimes, M. A. (1995). Native American identity and survival: Indigenism and environmental ethics. In M. K. Green (Ed.), *Issues in Native American cultural identity* (pp. 273–296). New York: Peter Lang.

Kanpol, B. (1999). *Critical pedagogy: An introduction*. 2nd edition. Westport, CT: Bergin and Garvey.

Kearney, M. (1984). *World view*. Novato, CA: Chandler and Sharp.

Keck, V. (Ed.). (1998). *Common worlds and single lives: Constituting knowledge in Pacific societies*. New York: Berg.

Lambek, M. (1983). *Knowledge and practice in Mayotte: Local discourses of Islam, sorcery and spirit possession*. Toronto: University of Toronto Press.

Lave, J., & Wenger, E. (1991). *Situated learning: Legitimate peripheral participation*. Cambridge: Cambridge University Press.

15. LANGUAGE AND EDUCATION IN SOLOMON ISLANDS   325

Lefebvre, H. (1990). *Everyday life in the modern world*. Trans. Sacha Rabinovitch. London: Transaction.

Livingstone, D. W. (Ed.). (1987). *Critical pedagogy and cultural power*. South Hadley, MA: Bergin and Garvey.

Lockheed, M. E., & Levin, H. M. (1993). *Effective schools in developing countries*. London: Falmer.

Luke, A. (1988). *Literacy, textbooks and ideology: Postwar literacy instruction and the mythology of Dick and Jane*. London: Falmer.

Meyer, J. W., Kamens, D. H., & Benavot, A. (Eds.). (1992). *School knowledge for the masses: World models and national primary curricular categories in the twentieth century*. Washington, D.C.: Falmer.

Nader, L. (Ed.). (1996). *Naked science: Anthropological inquiry into boundaries, power, and knowledge*. New York: Routledge.

Nyerere, J. K., & Members of The South Commission. (1990). *The challenge to the South: The report of the South Commission*. Oxford, England: Oxford University Press.

Pieterse, J. N., & Parekh, B. (Eds.). (1995). *The colonization of imagination: Culture, knowledge and power*. London: Zed.

Rosaldo, M. (1980). *Knowledge and passion: Ilongot notions of self and social life*. New York: Cambridge University Press.

Salmond, A. (1985). Maori epistemologies. In J. Overing (Ed.), *Reason and morality* (pp. 40–70). London: Tavistock.

Scott, C. (1996). Science for the West, myth for the rest? The case of James Bay Cree knowledge construction. In L. Nader (Ed.), *Naked science: Anthropological inquiry into boundaries, power, and knowledge* (pp. 69–87). New York: Routledge.

Shore, B. (1996). *Culture in mind: Cognition, culture, and the problem of meaning*. New York: Oxford University Press.

Smith, L. T. (1999). *Decolonizing methodologies: Research and indigenous peoples*. London: Zed.

Street, B. V. (Ed.). (1993). *Cross-cultural approaches to literacy*. Cambridge: Cambridge University Press.

Street, B. V. (1995). *Social literacies: Critical approaches to literacy in development, ethnography and education*. London: Longman.

Tollefson, J. W. (1991). *Planning language, planning inequality: Language policy in the community*. London: Longman.

Watson-Gegeo, K. A., & Gegeo, D. W. (1990). Shaping the mind and straightening out conflicts: The discourse of Kwara'ae family counseling. In K. A. Watson-Gegeo & G. M. White (Eds.), *Disentangling: Conflict discourse in Pacific societies* (pp. 161–213). Stanford: Stanford Univerisity Press.

Watson-Gegeo, K. A., & Gegeo, D. W. (1992). Schooling, knowledge and power: Social transformation in the Solomon Islands. *Anthropology and Education Quarterly, 23*, 10–29.

Watson-Gegeo, K. A., & Gegeo, D. W. (1994). Keeping culture out of the classroom in rural Solomon Islands schools: A critical analysis. *Educational Foundations, 8*, 27–55.

Watson-Gegeo, K. A., & Gegeo, D. W. (1995). Understanding language and power in the Solomon Islands: Methodological lessons for educational intervention. In J. W. Tollefson (Ed.), *Power and inequality in language education* (pp. 59–72). Cambridge: Cambridge University Press.

Watson-Gegeo, K. A., & Gegeo, D. W. (1999). Culture, discourse, and indigenous epistemology: Transcending the current models in language policy and planning. In T. Huebner & K. A. Davis (Eds.), *Sociopolitical perspectives on language policy and planning in the USA* (pp. 99–116). Amsterdam: John Benjamins.

Woolard, K. A. (1985). Language variation and cultural hegemony: Toward an integration of sociolinguistic and social theory. *American Ethnologist, 12*, 738–48.

16

Conclusion: Looking Outward

James W. Tollefson
University of Washington

Language policies in education are not formed in isolation, but rather emerge in response to important social forces: political conflicts, changes in government, migration, changes in the structure of local economies, globalization, and elite competition, to name a few. A major purpose of this collection has been to look outward from the classroom in order to explore the important connections between language policies in education and these broader sociopolitical issues. Although the authors of these articles examine widely diverging situations, in which language policies are shaped by radically different global and local forces, a number of common issues appear. I will summarize those issues as a way of emphasizing the connections that exist across the chapters.

1. *The importance of school-community relations.*
   The widely held belief that schools alone can counter the powerful forces shaping language behavior and language acquisition often leads to unrealistic programs and policies that almost inevitably end in disappointment. In his important study of efforts to reverse language shift and maintain threatened minority languages, Fishman argues that the school alone cannot be expected to foster the "cumulative, intergenerational transmissibility of any language which is still all too seldom a mother tongue" (1991, p. 369). Despite popular faith in the power of schools for social transformation—faith

327

held by many teachers, program administrators, sociolinguists, and parents—language programs in schools are fundamentally constrained by a range of powerful social and other important forces: ideologies of language, political ideologies, funding, local and national politics, and patterns of employment that affect enrollment patterns. Although language policies in schools often play a necessary role in shaping language behavior and language acquisition, these policies alone are rarely sufficient for achieving many language goals without "extensive and recurring pre-school, out-of-school and post-school societal reinforcement" (Fishman, 1991, p. 372). Thus the link between the school, the family, and the community is critical for understanding language policies in education and for developing effective language teaching and language maintenance programs.

The articles in this collection particularly draw attention to the importance of the community. Individual families, especially linguistic minorities, are often under enormous social and economic pressures, with adults affected by unemployment and under-employment, and subject to the social forces driving language shift to dominant varieties. Moreover, as children are left in daycare and after-school care for longer periods of the day, parents have less control over language socialization, with a variety of community institutions playing a greater role. The research reported here about critical pedagogy for social change shows that school-community connections are often essential to the success of educational language policies. For example, the Cree program in Canada succeeded only after the community became intimately involved, while in the United States, school-community connections are crucial in indigenous language revival programs. Indeed, indigenous language programs in North America are most successful when they are linked with broad programs of community development; these programs may include road building (so children can get to school), employment programs (so school graduates can obtain work), emergency aid (so families in crisis can recover enough for education to be feasible), and health and nutrition (so poor health of children and their families does not interfere with schooling). Moreover, while professional linguists, teachers, and other language specialists can contribute in many ways to the success of language programs, the broad involvement of parents and other community members is critical. In the Solomon Islands, some communities have been able to develop effective educational programs outside the core educational institutions. Community-based schools are particularly likely to establish links between school and community development, thereby avoiding the isolation from community that too often affects traditional schools. Indeed, community-based programs in some settings may offer powerful alternatives to schools that are controlled by dominant language groups.

2. *The value of outside resources.*
While some language minority communities build successful programs, many around the world lack the financial resources to develop and support ongoing educational programs. Thus, outside sources of funding and other support are often essential. For instance, in the United States, federal aid is crucial to language reclamation and revitalization efforts. In the United states, Canada, and elsewhere, outside experts often play an important role in providing teacher training, technical linguistic analysis, and other forms of professional expertise. In Africa, international assistance for higher education has a direct and dramatic impact on enrollment; reductions in external funding not only reduce the number of students able to pursue higher education, but also change the composition of the student population, with students from lower- and middle-class families most likely to drop out of school. In Africa, such changes may inadvertently help languages other than English, since high enrollment in English-medium tertiary institutions is a major factor in the ongoing process of language shift to English. Yet in North American minority language maintenance programs such as those examined in this book, as well as in most traditional school-based educational programs in English-dominant states, funding cuts are most likely to hurt minority languages while furthering the shift to English monolingualism in education.

Yet outside support rarely comes with no strings attached. Thus, communities that rely on outside funding usually find that they must yield major areas of control to institutions from outside the community. The village-based programs in the Solomon Islands avoid outside control: these indigenous, village-based educational projects not only offer an alternative to dominant educational institutions, they also seek to counter the hegemonic forces of those institutions. This paradigm for rural education—based upon indigenous epistemology, indigenous critical praxis, local conceptions of literacy, and locally situated conceptions of cognition—has direct relevance for schools elsewhere, including Africa, Asia, Latin America, and rural areas of the U.S. Southwest and Canada.

3. *The variable relationship between language and sociopolitical conflict.*
The chapters on India and Yugoslavia examine two countries in which political movements were organized around language-related demands. Despite remarkable similarities in the ethnolinguistic

configurations of India and Yugoslavia, people have used their language demands to push in different directions: toward integration in the case of India, and toward disintegration in the case of Yugoslavia. The chapters in this collection remind us that in a world in which multilingualism is the norm rather than the exception, and all large states are multilingual, it is essential that state authorities, opinion leaders, and sociolinguists exercise caution in making generalizations about the relationship between language diversity and sociopolitical conflict. The potential link between linguistic diversity and sociopolitical conflict is highly variable, depending not on the degree of diversity, but instead on the particular "local" connections between language and various forms of social and economic inequality. For instance, in North America, mother tongue promotion policies are usually progressive efforts to improve the cultural, educational, and economic conditions of linguistic minorities. In contrast, in Yugoslavia, Serbian mother tongue promotion policies were essentially efforts to restrict the rights of linguistic minorities.

The cases of Hong Kong and Anglophone Africa also highlight the importance of local politics. Together, they provide examples of superficially similar proposals emerging from diametrically opposed motives and concerns, as both some colonial governors and some Africans who are now working for decolonization have promoted indigenous language education and criticized Western education as disabling. Clearly, the historical context is crucial if we are to adequately understand these calls for indigenous language education. Particularly important is the link between language and inequality. Both Yugoslavia and the Official English movement in the United States demonstrate that long-standing economic disparities create fertile ground for demagogues or other elites to exploit mother tongue promotion and official-language policies in order to create political conflict and mobilize masses of citizens who can be manipulated for selfish and destructive political purposes.

4. *The effect of language rights in reducing the potential for language conflict.* Several chapters in this collection illustrate the power of the symbolic politics of language. In India and Yugoslavia, pedagogical considerations, such as the value of particular languages for teaching subject-area content, were lost in the intense discussion of language as symbol of nation, nationality, belonging, identity, and inequality. The cases of India, Yugoslavia, and the United States show that a broad system of language rights in education and in other institutions can offer significant protections for linguistic minorities, with a direct impact on reducing the potential for political conflict and social disorder.

In India, language rights are an arena for the struggle by linguistic minorities for acceptance within the dominant political system, with this struggle taking different forms in different states. In Yugoslavia before the 1980s, a broad system of language rights was the key to mitigating social conflict; language rights, particularly in education, were a central component in the sociopolitical system that successfully maintained a peaceful and united Yugoslavia for four decades. Accordingly, efforts to rescind the system of language rights were widely seen as a direct attempt to break up the country; and calls for Serbian language rights were central components in a set of proposals with hegemonic aims. Thus India and Yugoslavia in the 1990s had fundamentally different fates, with India maintaining its political/administrative unity, while Yugoslavia disintegrated in a series of brutal wars. Indeed, because language is a potent force for mobilizing public opinion to affect not only language policies, but broad issues of state formation, politics, and administration, a system of language rights can protect all citizens from leaders who wish to use language for destructive and unscrupulous aims.

India, Yugoslavia and the United States also illustrate McGroarty's point that the conception of language rights and the sociopolitical function of language rights vary significantly from one locale to another. Indeed, debates about language policy often involve competing visions of the nature and extent of language rights. In particular, what should be the basis for language rights? In many states, two alternatives are offered: rights based upon territory and rights based upon ethnolinguistic identity. In Yugoslavia, Slobodan Milošević argued that Serbs deserved both types of rights: the borders of Serbia should be the basis for a Serbian state, despite the presence of Albanians, Hungarians, and other minorities; and ethnic Serbs outside Serbia should have the right to self-determination, even when they constituted a minority. A third basis for rights—citizenship—may have offered an alternative to dissolution and civil war, but this alternative was not an option in Yugoslavia in the late 1980s. Many other countries struggle with the question of what should be the basis for rights in general, and for rights to an education in specific languages in particular (Phillipson, 2000). In a multilingual world, where multilingualism is commonplace, Yugoslavia illustrates the most extreme result of centralist policies that seek to suppress the language rights and language demands of linguistic minorities. In the light of the experience of Yugoslavia, Wiley's call for stronger federal support for minority-language rights and language maintenance programs in the United States takes on added urgency.

5. *The role of language policy in governance.*

   Language policies in education should be examined within the context of processes of governance. In this collection, we have seen two analyses of current political processes shaping language policies: the policymaking process within governmental institutions in Australia (Moore), and the electoral and judicial processes in the United States (Donahue). These analyses show that recent language policies in education in both countries are linked with conservative attempts to roll back progressive policies and programs beneficial to immigrants and other linguistic minorities, and to reassert the dominance of English speakers. Both analyses draw on political theories about the relations between individuals, groups, and the state. Indeed, Moore's term "factions" is reasonably applicable to the Official English movement in the United States, and Donahue's plea for a principled approach to language policymaking applies also to Australia.

   The chapters on Hong Kong and Anglophone Africa examine the close link between colonial governance and language policies in education. Some colonial authorities in Hong Kong favored indigenous language education as a mechanism for colonial control (although most supported English), while in much of Anglophone Africa, colonial authorities favored English—a position that continues to receive support from many African intellectuals educated in the system. This language debate continues in the post-colonial period, with supporters of African decolonization differing about the potential of English to serve as a language of intellectual and cultural liberation from the West. Since Hong Kong returned to mainland Chinese authority in 1997, the shift away from English and toward Chinese medium schools has accelerated, though not without protest from many parents who continue to view English as the language of economic opportunity (Tsui et al., in press). In order to understand this ongoing controversy, it is crucial to view language not only as a symbol of various forms of indigenous, Western, and other identities, but also to understand the practical and everyday role that language plays in processes of governance, in both colonial and postcolonial states.

6. *The impact of global processes.*

   As a central historical process ending in the middle of the 20th century, colonization continues to influence language policy. In the postcolonial period, other global forces have also begun to have direct and immediate impact on language policies in education. Although most educational policies continue to be national or local decisions, language policymaking is also internationalized. Most striking of all is the direct impact of such global economic institutions as the International Monetary Fund and the World Bank on higher education in Africa. In Japan, Korea, and Vietnam—East Asian countries with very different histories but strikingly common experiences (Chinese influence and Western military intervention)—the foreign presence was both resisted and accommodated in ways that shaped language policies. Currently, the governments of capitalist Korea and socialist Vietnam are taking serious steps to increase and improve language education as part of broad economic development programs. Despite deeply felt and persistent concerns about the future of the Korean and Vietnamese languages, English promotion policies have begun to dominate educational language policies in Korea and Vietnam, as they have in many countries around the world. The emphasis on English comes with an implicit promise—that dedicating vast resources to the spread of English will yield concrete economic benefits. Should those benefits not be forthcoming, then either an alternative rationale for English promotion policies must be developed, or the policies changed.

Japan, with its high level of economic development, continues its long history of maintaining a fundamental link between the Japanese language and identity. Yet globalization is highly complex, involving structural changes in finance and government that have important demographic consequences. Thus even in Japan, the movement of labor and resulting migration of speakers of other languages to Japan increase pressure for changes in language policies in education, and ultimately may make untenable the ideological link between language and nation that continues in Japanese discourse about language. Indeed, the rapid and dramatic worldwide increase in migration since the 1970s—involving political refugees, economic migrants seeking employment, and learners seeking new skills—is forcing policymakers to rethink fundamental issues in educational language policy, including not only ideologies of language and nation and medium of instruction, but also teaching methods, materials, and other everyday details in the lives of teachers and learners.

7. *The importance of local concerns.*
The sharp reduction in international funding for higher education in Africa demonstrates that global forces gain meaning and significance as they have impact upon local programs. Mazrui's call for the decolonization of African education closely parallels Gegeo and Watson-Gegeo's call for dehegemonic and counter-hegemonic indigenous education. How can language groups, in Mazrui's words, "break the

chains" of dependency? Mazrui outlines five processes for decolonization: indigenization, domestication, and diversification of education, as well as greater interchange of technical assistance among African countries (horizontal interpenetration) and efforts to bring African cultural and intellectual capital to developed countries (vertical counter-penetration). Gegeo and Watson-Gegeo's paradigm for rural education based upon indigenous ways of knowing, indigenous critical praxis, and critical pedagogy, including expanded conceptions of literacy, also is aimed at reforming structural relations between minority and dominant groups. A framework for a decolonizing, dehegemonic, and counter-hegemonic education that undermines historical processes of domination must be further elaborated by minority language communities and educators working for language and cultural maintenance.

Effective language policies in education also require careful attention to the "local" concerns of everyday life in classrooms: materials, class size, daily and weekly schedules for the study of language and other subjects, and teachers' time for course planning, problem solving, and professional development. Jung and Norton's discussion of the implementation of the new national English program in Korea is especially important in this regard. Their study of teacher training, methods and materials, and program design found that teachers' experience and their working conditions are crucial to program success. Enthusiastic teachers are more likely to volunteer to work in innovative programs and to be more effective as well. Interestingly, technology and other forms of special support may play a less important role in program success than working conditions such as teaching load, leadership from experienced head teachers, and regular meeting times for the purpose of exchanging ideas about teaching. Lack of materials in particular can have overwhelming impact on teachers' time and ultimately their support for a program. Whether we consider English language education in Korea, Vietnam's efforts to improve language instruction, English programs for immigrants in Canada, indigenous language programs in Canada and the United States, rural education in the Solomon Islands, or the difficulties in decolonizing African higher education, it is clear that innovative language programs require ongoing support by school principals and other local administrators in the form of concrete measures that directly improve conditions for teachers in classrooms. Policies are not likely to be successful if they fail to consider the specific challenges that teachers confront in their daily working lives.

THE IMPORTANCE OF LANGUAGE POLICIES IN EDUCATION

A critical approach to language policies in education is increasingly important in solving the problems of multilingual and multiethnic states. Indeed, due to migration and other global forces, ethnically and linguistically homogenous states may largely have become a thing of the past (Denitch, 1996). Under such conditions, state authorities have at their disposal two broad alternative approaches for managing ethnolinguistic diversity: they can repress ethnolinguistic differences or they can extend democratic pluralism. Successfully repressing ethnolinguistic differences requires that state power be directed toward establishing and maintaining two categories of citizens: those who enjoy full rights and privileges of membership in the state, and those who do not (cf. Benhabib, 1999; Jacobson, 1996; Kymlicka, 1995). The recent history of multilingual and multiethnic states that have managed ethnolinguistic diversity through repression suggests that this approach, while it can be temporarily successful, nevertheless entails significant costs and often eventually leads to greater social conflict (e.g., apartheid South Africa, Yugoslavia, Turkey, Rwanda, Indonesia).

Extending democratic pluralism entails abolishing discrimination based upon ascribed social categories such as ethnicity and language, as well as reducing the social and political distance between ethnolinguistic groups created by excessive inequalities in the distribution of economic resources (Denitch, 1996). The key challenge in adopting this approach is to find ways to structure democratic forms of governance in multiethnic and multilingual states. Though this question is especially applicable to the new states of Eastern Europe, Central Asia, and sub-Saharan Africa, it applies also to the United States, Canada, Australia, and elsewhere. Language policies in education are critical to this endeavor. Both new and old multilingual states that attempt democratic forms of governance require progressive language policies to ensure that language minority communities gain the language competencies necessary for economic opportunity and simultaneously that they retain the languages and cultures essential to identity and belonging. Failure to develop effective policies to achieve these goals will in many contexts exacerbate the problem of unequal distribution of economic resources and increase the probability of ethnic and linguistic conflict.

A second problem for democratic pluralism is: How can democratic forms of governance be developed at a time of increasing domination by supranational structures of decision making? As nation states become less able to respond to local demands and ever less relevant to the lives of their citizens, ethnolinguistic groups may seek to protect themselves by demanding autonomy based upon the principle of territoriality. Facing repression by more powerful groups and loss of faith in the ability of state authorities and international agencies such as the United Nations to offer protection, ethnolinguistic groups in many contexts may turn to ethnolinguistic nationalism. Ethnolinguistic nationalism also offers an appealing alternative to globalization—a kind of "jihad against McWorld" (Denitch, 1996, p. 197). The list of multiethnic states already facing such movements is a long one, including Romania, Bulgaria, Spain, the United Kingdom, Slovakia, Turkey, Iran, Iraq, Nigeria, Sudan, Kenya, Uganda, Ethiopia, Pakistan, India, Indonesia, the Philippines, Mexico, and Guatemala. Thus far, the response of many state authorities has been to impose some form of centralism, such as educational policies favoring the dominant language (e.g., Australia, the United Kingdom); official language laws (e.g., the United States); immigration restrictions (e.g., those inspired by the ultranationalist movements in France, Germany, and Italy); martial law (e.g., as imposed in Kosovo in the 1980s and 1990s); and military repression (e.g., Turkey). Yet, by responding with measures that restrict minority language rights, many states are pushing minorities further toward ethnolinguistic nationalism. Pluralism offers a peaceful alternative to repression, if pluralist policies can be developed that are workable within differing political, economic, social, and historical contexts. In this effort, language rights will be increasingly important, not only for maintaining linguistic and cultural diversity, but also for countering the forces of hegemony and neo-fascism.

Developing democratic systems of decision making that meaningfully include ethnolinguistic minorities presents a third major challenge: a conception of "citizenship" must be developed that acknowledges the important social function of ethnolinguistic identity but does not lead to the creation of classes of citizens with unequal rights and privileges. Unfortunately, leaders in many new states insist on "authentic national roots" and the mythic history of a people as the foundation for states (Denitch, 1996, p. 141; also see Anderson, 1983). Such arguments are also favored by ultranationalists in the old states of France, Germany, Italy, and the United States. McGroarty's plea for closer ties between theoretical work on language policy and citizenship is especially important in light of the need for rethinking the bases for exclusion and inclusion of individuals in state decision making (also see Riggins, 1997).

A final challenge is that democratic pluralism must gain some degree of acceptance by dominant groups. Why should dominant groups give up their advantage by accepting pluralist systems and policies, particularly when the changes may lead to redistribution of wealth and realignments in political power? This question is especially difficult in light of the opportunities for manipulation that Donahue describes, whereby dominant groups have a variety of strategies available to maintain their advantages, even in democratic electoral systems in which minorities are gaining in numerical strength.

For critical linguists and advocates of progressive policies, it is important to remember that ethnolinguistic conflict is often *created*, as part of broad strategies to gain or retain political power, and thus it is neither "natural" nor inevitable. Alternative progressive policies and ideologies must be developed that will respond to the demands of individual citizens facing their own fears and concerns about the future. Indeed, without the mitigating power of ethnic and linguistic belonging, individuals in conditions of anomie and feeling increasingly powerless in the face of globalization often turn to various repressive forms of nationalism. Progressive policies that ensure ethnolinguistic rights must offer an alternative to such forms of nationalism, based upon a vision of a realistic and workable democratic pluralism. Donahue argues that critical linguists have a particularly important role to play in this effort by aggressively analyzing policies, and identifying and fully characterizing their underlying ideologies. In doing so, the field of educational language policy will not only develop a better understanding of the links between language policies and broader social and political processes, but it may also contribute to an informed and (in Donahue's words) cerebral and skeptical citizenry—the foundation for democratic pluralism.

REFERENCES

Anderson, B. (1983). *Imagined communities: Reflections on the origin and spread of nationalism.* London: Verso.

Benhabib, S. (1999). Citizens, residents, and aliens in a changing world: Political membership in the global era. *Social Research, 66,* 709–744.

Denitch, B. (1996). *Ethnic nationalism: The tragic death of Yugoslavia.* Minneapolis: University of Minnesota Press.

Fishman, J. A. (1991). *Reversing language shift.* Clevedon: Multilingual Matters.

Jacobson, D. (1996). *Rights across borders: Immigration and the decline of citizenship.* Baltimore: Johns Hopkins Press.

Kymlicka, W. (1995). *Multicultural citizenship.* Oxford: Oxford University Press.

Phillipson, R. (Ed.) (2000). *Rights to language: Equity, power, and education.* Mahwah, NJ: Lawrence Erlbaum.

Riggins, S. H. (Ed.) (1997). *The language and politics of exclusion: Others in discourse.* Thousand Oaks, CA: Sage Publications.

Tsui, A. B. M., Shum, M. S. K., Wong, C. K., Tse, S. K., & Ki, W. W. (in press). Which agenda?—the medium of instruction policy in post-1997 Hong Kong. *Language, Culture and Curriculum.*

Author Index

Subject Index